CONSUMER

1992 EDITION

CONSUMER BUYING GUIDE

Contents

Introduction

If you have ever gone shopping for a car, a major appliance, a television set, or stereo components, you know that buying wisely is more than a matter of luck. It takes experience and expert knowledge. This is especially true today when rapid advances in technology and shifts in the world's economy can quickly change the price, availability, and long-term usefulness of a product.

No one can ever know everything about every available product; there is simply too much to know. CONSUMER GUIDE® recognizes that it's a challenge to pick a "best buy," which meets your requirements for quality, performance, and value. Our experts in the major product fields have done the research, testing, and comparison shopping for you. We have taken the guesswork out of making major purchases. CONSUMER GUIDE® has no ties to manufacturers or retailers, we accept no advertising, and we are not interested in selling products. Our sole purpose is to provide you with the information you need to make intelligent purchases.

We have tried to review a wide variety of products in this publication, ranging from small personal items, such as travel irons and small-capacity automatic drip coffee makers, to major purchases, such as refrigerators and stereo systems. We have not limited ourselves to lower-priced products or top-of-the-line products. A product is a Best Buy only if it meets your needs, so we have selected products in a variety of sizes and prices to match the requirements of different shoppers.

Beyond simple supply and demand, many factors influence the prices of products. This year's prices reflect two opposing economic trends. Some products cost less because they incorporate microchips or other modular electronic devices, while other products have higher prices because of the decline in the value of the U.S. dollar and increased production costs. Many products such as CD players, personal cassette players, computers, and food processors are much less expensive today than they were when they first came on the market. But some products, including stereo equipment, major appliances, and camcorders, may have become more expensive over the last year.

To make the best use of this book, first review the introductory material at the beginning of each chapter. This introduction contains important information about the product, describes its features, and explains the terminology you need to know when you shop. Once you are acquainted with the criteria we use to select products, go on to our Best Buy selections. These products were chosen for their usefulness, high quality, and overall value. A Best Buy isn't necessarily the least expensive model; it's the highest-quality product available at a reasonable price. Recommended selections are also good products, but for one reason or another, they do not measure up to our Best Buy standards. Such a product may carry a high price tag, it may have limited appeal, or it could be so new on the market that we don't yet know how it will perform over time.

When you shop, compare prices and models. If a dealer quotes a price close to the Approximate Low Price in this publication, then you know that you are getting first-rate value for your money. All the prices listed were accurate at the time of printing, but due to currency fluctuations and manufacturers' price adjustments both retail and low prices may change. In some cases prices were not available. All products were checked to make sure that they would be available to consumers in 1992, but product manufacture and distribution is beyond our control, and manufacturers may discontinue models in the future without notice.

Cars, Minivans, and 4-Wheel Drive Vehicles

The auto editors of CONSUMER GUIDE® have selected Best Buys and Recommended vehicles in ten categories of passenger cars, minivans, and 4-wheel drive vehicles. Vehicles are assigned to one of these categories based on their size, price, and market position. This way, a $10,000 subcompact competes against other low-priced small cars, not against $40,000 luxury cars.

At least one Best Buy has been selected in each category. Some categories include models labeled Recommended that are also worthy of attention. Road-test results play a major role in the selections. Some new models, such as the Honda Civic, were not available for road testing in time to be considered for this issue. Other factors used to select Best Buys among cars include price, cost of ownership, warranties, reputation for reliability and durability, and safety features. Profiles of the cars are first, followed by the price charts.

SUBCOMPACT CARS

NISSAN SENTRA

The Nissan Sentra offers an attractive combination of good fuel economy and high quality. The front-drive Sentra comes in 2- and 4-door sedan styling. Most Sentras sold in the U.S. are built in Tennessee, but some are still imported from Japan. All models except the sporty SE-R have an economical 1.6-liter 4-cylinder engine. The SE-R has a spunky 2.0-liter 4-cylinder engine that is also used in the more expensive Infiniti G20, which is marketed as a "near-luxury" sedan. Anti-lock brakes are optional on the most-expensive Sentra, the GXE, and the SE-R, giving Nissan a safety advantage over most subcompact rivals. The Sentra E 2-door, which starts at less than $9,000 with manual transmission, is the least-expensive model. However, it isn't available with power steering, a feature most buyers want. The XE versions, which start at about $10,000, come with power steering and are available with discounts on option packages that include air conditioning.

MAZDA 323/PROTEGE, FORD ESCORT, AND MERCURY TRACER

RECOMMENDED

Ford Motor Company owns an equity interest in Mazda Motor Corporation, and the two companies collaborated on the design of the Mazda 323 and Protege, which are built in Japan, and the Ford Escort and Mercury Tracer, which are built in the U.S. and Mexico. The 323 is a 3-door hatchback and Protege—a 4-door sedan. The Escort comes in four body styles: 3- and 5-door hatchbacks, a 5-door station wagon, and a 4-door sedan that is new for 1992. The Tracer comes as a 4-door sedan and 5-door wagon. All of these cars have front-wheel drive. Though most Escort and Tracer parts are built in North America, all their transmissions and some of their engines are supplied by Mazda. All models have good fuel economy and commendable assembly quality. In addition, dealers should be discounting prices, no matter which brand you choose.

Prices are accurate at time of printing; subject to manufacturer's change.

TOYOTA COROLLA AND
GEO PRIZM

RECOMMENDED

The Toyota Corolla and Geo Prizm are known for their commendable reliability, low maintenance costs, and high fuel economy. Prizm is built from the same design as Corolla, but has different exterior styling and is sold through Chevrolet dealers with Geo franchises. Prizm comes only as a 4-door sedan, while Corolla comes as a 4-door sedan and a 5-door station wagon. All versions have 1.6-liter 4-cylinder engines and front-wheel drive except the Corolla All-Trac wagon, which has permanently engaged 4-wheel drive. All Prizms and some Corolla 4-door sedans are built at a General Motors-Toyota plant in California. Some Corollas sold in the U.S. are built in Canada and Japan. There are no apparent differences in quality between North American-built Corollas and those imported from Japan. Since Corolla and Prizm share mechanical components, they should be equally reliable.

COMPACT CARS

DODGE SPIRIT AND
PLYMOUTH ACCLAIM

✓ **BEST BUY**

The Dodge Spirit and Plymouth Acclaim are nearly identical front-drive 4-door sedans that have a standard driver-side air bag, ample passenger and cargo space, and reasonable prices. Spirit comes in four price levels: base, LE, ES, and R/T (a limited-production, high-performance version). Acclaim's lineup has been trimmed to one model for 1992. Three Chrysler 4-cylinder engines and a Mitsubishi 3.0-liter V-6 are available on Spirit. A 100-horsepower Chrysler 4-cylinder is standard on Acclaim and the V-6 is optional. The V-6 is the quietest and smoothest engine offered, but the 100-horsepower 4-cylinder is the most economical. Anti-lock brakes are optional on Spirit and Acclaim, which are assembled in the U.S. Since rebates and option-package discounts are usually available on both models, a well-equipped Spirit or Acclaim with automatic transmission, air conditioning, and anti-lock brakes should sell for less than $15,000.

Prices are accurate at time of printing; subject to manufacturer's change.

TOYOTA CAMRY

The Toyota Camry has been redesigned for 1992 and has a roomier interior, more powerful engines, and a standard driver-side air bag. Toyota advertises the new Camry as a mid-size car based on interior volume. However, the 103.1-inch wheelbase (distance between the front and rear wheels) makes it a compact by our reckoning. Regardless, the new Camry sedan has ample room for five adults and a spacious trunk that can be expanded by folding down the rear seatback. Initially, only a 4-door sedan is available. In spring 1992, a 5-door wagon is scheduled to be added. Some Camry sedans are imported from Japan, but most sedans and all wagons sold in the U.S. are built in Kentucky at a Toyota factory, which recently was rated the highest-quality auto manufacturing plant in North America. All models have front-wheel drive. Base engine is a 135-horsepower 2.2-liter 4-cylinder. A 185-horsepower 3.0-liter V-6 is optional. Anti-lock brakes are optional on all models. The previous Camry set high standards for a compact family car. The new one sets higher standards.

SUBARU LEGACY
RECOMMENDED

The Subaru Legacy offers buyers a broad range of models and features at attractive prices. Legacy comes in 4-door sedan and 5-door wagon styling with front-wheel drive or a permanently engaged 4-wheel drive system that provides outstanding traction without any input from the driver. Most models have a 130-horsepower 4-cylinder engine, but the Sport Sedan model has a 160-horsepower turbocharged engine that delivers impressive acceleration. A driver-side air bag is standard on the LS and LSi models and optional on the base L. It is scheduled to become optional on the Sport Sedan later in the year. Anti-lock brakes are standard on all models except the L, on which they are optional. Some Legacys are imported from Japan; most sold in the U.S. are built in Indiana at a plant Subaru shares with Isuzu, another Japanese auto manufacturer. Subaru was giving its dealers large incentives to discount their prices on 1991 Legacys. That should continue through the 1992 model year, making it a buyer's market for this car.

MID-SIZE CARS

FORD TAURUS AND
MERCURY SABLE

✔ **BEST BUY**

Nearly all the exterior body panels on the Ford Taurus and Mercury Sable are new for 1992, though they retain the basic look of the 1986-91 models, which introduced aerodynamic styling to the mid-size family car market. Besides their appearance, the biggest change this year is the addition of a front passenger-side air bag as an option. A driver-side air bag has been standard since 1990. Anti-lock brakes are optional on all models. Base engine is a 140-horsepower 3.0-liter V-6. An optional 3.8-liter V-6 has the same horsepower rating, but produces more torque (215 pounds/feet versus 160), making it better suited to hauling heavy loads and trailer towing. The front-drive Taurus and Sable, which are built in the U.S., are functionally the same and similarly priced, from a minimum of $15,000 to more than $20,000, depending on the model and how lavishly it is equipped. All versions have roomy, ergonomically sound interiors and ample cargo space. The best values are Taurus GL and Sable GS models with one of the "preferred equipment" packages that offer popular options at a discount.

HONDA ACCORD

✔ **BEST BUY**

The front-drive Honda Accord now comes in three body styles—4-door sedan, 2-door coupe, and 5-door wagon—and all models have a standard driver-side air bag for 1992. The wagon was added to the line last year and was the only Accord with an air bag. Anti-lock brakes are standard on the Accord EX models, but are not offered on the base DX or mid-level LX. About 25 percent of Accords sold in the U.S. are imported from Japan. Most sedans and all coupes and wagons are built in Ohio. All Accords are powered by peppy, economical, 2.2-liter 4-cylinder engines; have ample room for five people and their luggage; and impressive assembly quality. In addition, Accord has traditionally had commendable reliability and high resale value. Though Accord is one of the best-selling cars in the U.S., intense competition among car companies has forced Honda dealers to discount their prices the past few years. You no longer have to pay full retail price or higher for an Accord. On the contrary, discounts of more than $1,000 are common.

FULL-SIZE CARS

BUICK LE SABRE, OLDSMOBILE EIGHTY EIGHT, AND PONTIAC BONNEVILLE

 ✔BEST BUY

The Buick LeSabre, Oldsmobile Eighty Eight, and Pontiac Bonneville have been redesigned for 1992 and, though they're built from the same design, each has distinctive exterior styling. All three cars come only as 4-door sedans and are built in North America. Under the skin, they share their front-drive chassis, 3.8-liter V-6 engine, and 4-speed automatic transmission. The engine and transmission are the same ones used in the more expensive Buick Park Avenue and Oldsmobile Ninety Eight. New features this year include a standard driver-side air bag on all models. A front passenger-side air bag is standard on the Bonneville SSEi model and optional on the SSE. Antilock brakes are standard or optional on all models. Though these cars differ in exterior styling and interior features, they have several things in common. All three have strong acceleration and better fuel economy than V-8-powered, full-size cars, and their front-wheel drive design gives them better traction in snow than rear-drive rivals. They also have more passenger and cargo space this year and they're built with corrosion-resistant galvanized steel, eliminating the need for extra-cost rustproofing. These are competent full-size cars that have modern styling, good assembly quality, and proven powertrains.

FORD CROWN VICTORIA AND MERCURY GRAND MARQUIS

RECOMMENDED

The rear-drive Ford Crown Victoria and Mercury Grand Marquis have new styling for 1992 and several new features that make them attractive alternatives to front-drive, full-size cars. Among the new features are a standard driver-side air bag and an

Prices are accurate at time of printing; subject to manufacturer's change.

optional front-passenger-side air bag (scheduled to become available later in the model year). Anti-lock brakes are also a new option for 1992. Both cars are built in Ontario, Canada, and come only as 4-door sedans. They share a new 4.6-liter engine that is unique among American V-8s for having overhead camshafts, a design feature that improves fuel economy and horsepower compared to overhead-valve engines of similar size. This new engine is also much quieter and smoother than Ford's previous V-8s. Both cars have modern interior designs, space for up to six people, and roomy trunks. In addition, the rear-drive Crown Victoria and Grand Marquis can tow trailers as heavy as 5,000 pounds, considerably more than their front-drive rivals. Their styling and interior features are different, but their prices are similar and their major mechanical components are the same.

PREMIUM COUPES

CADILLAC ELDORADO

The Cadillac Eldorado has new styling for 1992 and several functional improvements that make it a good choice among premium coupes. Among the improvements are a stiffer body and frame to reduce noise and vibration; a more sophisticated Computer Command Ride suspension system; platinum-tipped spark plugs that are supposed to last 100,000 miles; and larger brakes with new linings that Cadillac says should last at least 50,000 miles. Computer Command Ride automatically changes suspension firmness based on vehicle speed to control ride quality and how the vehicle handles in turns, acceleration, and braking. The front-drive Eldorado has a 200-horsepower 4.9-liter V-8 engine and a smooth-shifting automatic transmission. An anti-lock brake system and a driver-side air bag are standard features. The Eldorado accelerates briskly, stops quickly and safely, rides comfortably, and seats four adults in comfort and style. Cadillac's quality has improved greatly in recent years and the U.S.-built Eldorado has the fit and finish expected on a car in the $35,000 price range. Cadillac's warranty covers major powertrain components and mechanical systems for 4 years/50,000 miles.

Prices are accurate at time of printing; subject to manufacturer's change.

ACURA LEGEND   RECOMMENDED

A new Acura Legend bowed last year with larger dimensions, more power, and more standard features. The Legend 2-door coupe comes in two price levels, L and LS, and both have as standard equipment dual front air bags and anti-lock brakes. No other car in this class has air bags for both the driver and front passenger. The front-drive Legend, built in Japan, is powered by a smooth, refined 3.2-liter V-6 engine that delivers brisk acceleration and returns reasonable fuel economy. Acura's reputation for quality and durability and the Legend's history of high resale value are additional reasons to consider this car. The L model is a few thousand dollars cheaper than the LS, yet it sacrifices only a few convenience features such as automatic climate control and heated front seats.

LEXUS SC 300/400   RECOMMENDED

The Lexus SC is a 2-door luxury/sports coupe that's mechanically related to the highly successful LS 400 sedan, the flagship of Toyota's Lexus division. Two versions of the coupe are available, the SC 300 and the SC 400. The major difference between them is that the SC 300 has a 225-horsepower 3.0-liter inline 6-cylinder engine, and the SC 400 has the same 250-horsepower 4.0-liter V-8 engine as the LS 400. These coupes are built in Japan, but were designed at Toyota's California styling center. One of their unique features is a 4-link door hinge that swings the doors out and forward for easier entry/exit. Except for a deeper exhaust note, crisper handling, and a slightly firmer ride, the SC 400 coupe feels much like the LS 400 sedan, which is high praise because the sedan is our highest-rated car. The SC 300 isn't quite as fast, but offers nearly as much as the SC 400 for a more reasonable price.

PREMIUM SEDANS

LEXUS LS 400   BEST BUY

The Lexus LS 400 carries a base price of $42,200 for 1992, making it the most expensive Best Buy the editors have chosen. The LS 400 is a rear-drive sedan with a 250-horsepower

---

Prices are accurate at time of printing; subject to manufacturer's change.

4.0-liter V-8, anti-lock brakes, and a driver-side air bag among its standard features. Traction control is one of the few options offered. The Japanese-built LS 400 is one of the quietest cars we've driven, and its V-8 engine is powerful and incredibly smooth. The ride is stable at high speed, yet absorbent on bumpy roads. The interior is elegant, comfortable, and as quiet as a library. Assembly quality is exceptional. Lexus shared the top spot in the most recent J.D. Power customer-satisfaction survey, a testament to the quality of this car and the service provided by Lexus dealers. The LS 400 is a reliable, durable car that will have excellent resale value.

NISSAN MAXIMA
✔ BEST BUY

The Japanese-made Nissan Maxima, a front-drive 4-door, earns a Best Buy because it is competent, well-built, and a bargain. Maxima's base prices are $19,695 for the GXE and $20,815 for the sportier SE, undercutting most rivals by thousands of dollars. The GXE uses a 160-horsepower V-6 engine that provides smooth, brisk acceleration. The SE has a new 190-horsepower 3.0-liter V-6 that gives it stronger acceleration. The SE also has a firmer suspension and a viscous limited-slip differential that gives it better traction. A driver-side air bag and anti-lock brakes are optional on both models. Maxima has a modern design, more than adequate room for four adults, and quality workmanship. It isn't in the same league as the Lexus LS 400, but it costs half as much. No other premium sedan in the same price range matches the Maxima in performance or features.

ACURA LEGEND
RECOMMENDED

The Acura Legend was redesigned for 1991 and the new version is longer on the outside, roomier inside, and has a more powerful engine—a 200-horsepower 3.2-liter V-6. Anti-lock brakes and a driver-side air bag are standard on all Legends, and the L and LS models also have a passenger-side air bag. The Japanese-built Legend performs on a par with more expensive sedans and comes with nearly all the features expected on a luxury sedan in the $30,000-35,000 range. And, it also boasts outstanding assembly quality. The 1986-90 Legend earned a reputation for low maintenance costs and

Prices are accurate at time of printing; subject to manufacturer's change.

high resale value. The current model should maintain those high standards.

CADILLAC DE VILLE AND FLEETWOOD

Cadillac's De Ville and Fleetwood are American-made, front-drive sedans that differ only in that the Fleetwood has more standard features and higher prices. Both have a potent 200-horsepower V-8 engine, a smooth-shifting electronic 4-speed automatic transmission, and Computer Command Ride, which varies shock-absorber firmness based on vehicle speed. Anti-lock brakes and a driver-side air bag are standard on all models. These full-size sedans have room for six adults to sit comfortably, plus a spacious trunk that can hold lots of luggage. Cadillac has improved the assembly quality, reliability, and durability of these cars in recent years, making them well worth considering. Because there is so much competition in the premium sedan market, Cadillac dealers should be offering big discounts.

SPORTS COUPES

ACURA INTEGRA

The Japanese-built, front-drive Acura Integra comes in two body styles—a 3-door hatchback coupe and a 4-door sedan with a longer wheelbase and roomier interior. The sportier hatchback is the more popular. Both have a 140-horsepower 1.8-liter 4-cylinder engine that delivers spirited acceleration and high fuel economy. This engine is livelier and more economical with the 5-speed manual transmission than the optional 4-speed automatic. Since most buyers prefer automatic, the best deals are on manual-shift Integras. Anti-lock brakes are standard on the top-line GS models, but are not available on others.

MITSUBISHI ECLIPSE, EAGLE TALON, AND PLYMOUTH LASER

The Mitsubishi Eclipse, Eagle Talon, and Plymouth Laser are nearly identical versions of the same car sold under three different brand names. Since there are only minor differences among them, all are Best Buys. All are built in Illinois by Diamond-Star Motors, a partnership between Mitsubishi and Chrysler. All three brands are available with front-wheel drive or permanently engaged all-wheel drive, which gives these sporty cars outstanding traction. Anti-lock brakes are available in each line. Like most sporty cars, these three put form far ahead of function, so they have cramped interiors with tiny back seats.

SPORTS AND GT CARS

MAZDA MIATA

The Mazda Miata was heralded as the revival of the classic sports car when it debuted as an early 1990 model. It's a 2-seat convertible with racy styling, spirited performance, rear-wheel drive, and road-hugging handling. However, unlike the European sports cars of 25 years ago, the Japanese-made Miata is well-built and reliable. The Miata is also reasonably priced, starting at less than $15,000. Among the standard features are a driver-side air bag and a manual folding top that can be raised or lowered by one person from inside the car in less than a minute. For those who live in the Snow Belt, a detachable hardtop with a rear window defogger is available for the winter months. Anti-lock brakes are optional. When this car first went on sale, there was so much demand that buyers were paying thousands of dollars over suggested retail. These days you should be able to buy a Miata for less than suggested retail.

TOYOTA MR2   RECOMMENDED

The Japanese-made Toyota MR2 is a 2-seat sports car with a unique design. The engine is mounted transversely behind the seats and drives the rear wheels. This mid-engine layout, usually found only on expensive, exotic sports cars and racing cars, gives the MR2 an ideal weight distribution that improves its handling and roadholding ability. Two engines are available, a base 130-horsepower 2.2-liter 4-cylinder and a turbocharged 200-horsepower 2.0-liter four. A 4-speed automatic is optional only with the base engine. With either engine, buyers can

---

Prices are accurate at time of printing; subject to manufacturer's change.

choose a fixed roof or a T-bar roof with removable panels that allow nearly topless motoring. A driver-side air bag is standard and anti-lock brakes are optional. With either engine, this is a terrific little sports car. The least-expensive model starts at nearly $16,000, while a Turbo with the T-bar roof and all the options zooms to the $25,000 range.

MINIVANS

DODGE CARAVAN AND PLYMOUTH VOYAGER

The Dodge Caravan and Plymouth Voyager, Chrysler's nearly identical minivans, were substantially revised for 1991, when they became the first minivans to offer a driver-side air bag. The air bag was a no-cost option during the last half of the 1991 model year; this year it's standard. Caravan and Voyager claim another first this year: They're the first vehicles to offer integrated child seats. An optional bench seat can be used as a regular seat or converted for use by two toddlers by folding down sections of the backrest. Anti-lock brakes are optional on the Caravan and Voyager, which are available with either front-wheel drive or permanently engaged all-wheel drive. In addition to safety features, the Chrysler minivans have other advantages. They have ample room for up to seven people and their luggage; they're almost as easy to get in or out of as cars; and they are the most carlike of the minivans to drive. The similar Chrysler Town & Country is a more expensive version of these minivans with no substantive advantages, so we don't include it as a Best Buy. Chrysler's minivans are built in Windsor, Ontario, and St. Louis, Missouri.

TOYOTA PREVIA ✓BEST BUY

The Toyota Previa is the first minivan to meet all passenger-car safety requirements. For 1992 Previa gains a driver-side air bag and a center high-mounted stop lamp as standard equipment. The Previa, which was introduced last year, already met passenger-car safety standards for roof crush resistance and side-door impact protection. None of those features are required on vans. Previa comes in Deluxe and LE price levels, and both are available with rear-wheel drive or permanently engaged 4-wheel drive. Anti-lock brakes are optional on all models. Previa has a 138-horsepower 2.4-liter 4-cylinder engine mounted behind the front axle and below the front seats, tilted to one side to reduce intrusion into the interior. Previa, which is built in Japan but styled in the U.S., is a modern and versatile minivan that has more passenger and cargo room than most rivals. While Previa lacks the V-6 power and front-drive traction of the Chrysler minivans, it boasts superior assembly quality.

MAZDA MPV   RECOMMENDED

The Mazda MPV (Multi-Purpose Vehicle) is a good choice in a minivan. Unlike most other rear-drive compact vans, the MPV is carlike to drive and similar to the Caravan/Voyager in most respects. A 4-wheel drive model with a convenient on-demand 4WD system is also available. A 121-horsepower 2.6-liter 4-cylinder engine is standard on rear-drive MPVs, but we recommend the optional 150-horsepower 3.0-liter V-6. The V-6 is standard on the 4WD model, which weighs nearly 500 pounds more than the rear-drive version. That extra weight slows acceleration and hurts fuel economy, so opt for 4WD only if you really need it. The MPV, built in Japan, offers seating arrangements for five to eight people. The Mazda MPV also offers good assembly quality, a comfortable ride, and easy access to all seating positions.

4WD VEHICLES

FORD EXPLORER

Ford Explorer comes in 3- and 5-door body styles and though we rate both highly, we give our heartiest endorsement to the 5-door version. It's a roomy family wagon that combines carlike ride and handling with trucklike hauling ability. Entry/exit is almost as easy as in a car, and the interior has a convenient dashboard and control layout. A 160-horsepower 4.0-liter V-6 provides ample acceleration and passing power. Standard on

4WD Explorers is Touch-Drive, which engages or disengages 4WD by pushing a dashboard button whether the vehicle is moving or stationary. Anti-lock rear brakes are standard on all Explorers. The 5-door Explorer is at the head of this class with its spacious, well-designed interior, convenient 4WD system, and strong engine. Mazda sells a similar 3-door wagon as the Navajo. The Explorer and Navajo are built in Louisville, Kentucky.

JEEP CHEROKEE

The Jeep Cherokee isn't as roomy as the Explorer, but it earns a Best Buy because it does so many things so well. Cherokee, built in Toledo, Ohio, has come in 3- and 5-door body styles since 1984, while Ford just added a 5-door model for 1991. Cherokee still has more horsepower than most rivals—190 with the 4.0-liter 6-cylinder engine—and is available with two 4WD systems, both of which allow changing in and out of 4WD at any road speed (some Japanese rivals still don't offer this feature). The optional Selec-Trac 4WD system can be left permanently engaged. Anti-lock brakes are optional, and Jeep's system works on all four wheels in both 2WD and 4WD. Despite its modest exterior dimensions, Cherokee has enough interior room to easily hold four adults and a considerable amount of luggage. Because there is so much competition, Jeep dealers should be offering big discounts.

PRICES FOR CARS, MINIVANS, AND 4-WHEEL DRIVE VEHICLES

Acura Integra	Retail Price	Dealer Invoice	Low Price
RS 3-door hatchback, 5-speed	$12100	$10164	$11225
RS 3-door hatchback, automatic	12825	10773	11950
LS 3-door hatchback, 5-speed	13975	11739	13100
LS 3-door hatchback, automatic	14700	12348	13825
LS Special 3-door, 5-speed	14675	12327	13800
GS 3-door hatchback, 5-speed	16105	13528	15230
GS 3-door hatchback, automatic	16830	14137	15955
GS 3-door, 5-speed, leather interior	16605	13948	15730
GS 3-door, automatic, leather interior	17330	14557	16455
RS 4-door notchback, 5-speed	13025	10941	12025
RS 4-door notchback, automatic	13750	11550	12750
LS 4-door notchback, 5-speed	14725	12639	13725
LS 4-door notchback, automatic	15450	12978	14450
GS 4-door notchback, 5-speed	16645	13982	15645
GS 4-door notchback, automatic	17370	14591	16370
GS 4-door, 5-speed, leather interior	17145	14402	16145
GS 4-door, automatic, leather interior	17870	15011	16870
Destination charge	325	325	325

Standard equipment:

RS: 1.8-liter DOHC 16-valve PFI 4-cylinder engine, 5-speed manual or 4-speed automatic transmission, 4-wheel disc brakes, power steering, motorized front shoulder belts, cloth reclining front bucket seats, split folding rear seat, tinted glass, remote fuel door and decklid/hatch releases, dual outside mirrors, fog lights, rear defogger, rear wiper/washer (hatchback), tachometer, coolant temperature gauge, tilt steering column, intermittent wipers, door pockets, cargo cover (hatchback), 195/60R14 85H tires. **LS** adds: power mirrors, power windows, power locks (4-door), power sunroof (hatchback), AM/FM cassette with power antenna, driver-seat lumbar-support adjustment, cruise control, map lights (hatchback). **LS Special** adds: color-keyed spoiler and dual power mirrors, leather-wrapped steering wheel, alloy wheels. **GS** adds to LS: anti-lock brakes, map lights, adjustable side bolsters on driver's seat, power sunroof, alloy wheels.

OPTIONS are available as dealer-installed accessories.

Acura Legend	Retail Price	Dealer Invoice	Low Price
L 2-door coupe, 5-speed	$30900	$25338	—
L 2-door coupe, automatic	31700	25994	—
L 2-door w/leather trim, 5-speed	32400	26568	—
L 2-door w/leather trim, automatic	33200	27224	—
LS 2-door coupe, 5-speed	35500	29110	—
LS 2-door coupe, automatic	36300	29766	—
4-door notchback, 5-speed	27250	22345	—

Prices are accurate at time of printing; subject to manufacturer's change.

CONSUMER GUIDE®

	Retail Price	Dealer Invoice	Low Price
4-door notchback, automatic	28050	23001	—
L 4-door notchback, 5-speed	29250	23985	—
L 4-door notchback, automatic	30050	24641	—
L 4-door w/leather trim, 5-speed	30750	25215	—
L 4-door w/leather trim, automatic	31550	25871	—
LS 4-door notchback, 5-speed	34050	27921	—
LS 4-door notchback, automatic	34850	28577	—
Destination charge	325	325	325

Low price not available at time of publication.

Standard equipment:

3.2-liter SOHC 24-valve PFI V-6, 5-speed manual or 4-speed automatic transmission, anti-lock 4-wheel disc brakes, power steering, driver-side air bag, air conditioning, fabric reclining front bucket seats, driver-seat lumbar support and power height adjustments, power windows and locks, cruise control, telescopic steering column, tinted glass, power mirrors, AM/FM cassette with power diversity antenna, security system, intermittent wipers, bodyside moldings, rear defogger, remote fuel door and decklid releases, lighted visor mirrors, front door pockets, center console with armrest and covered storage, folding rear armrest, digital clock, 205/60R15 90V tires on alloy wheels. **L** adds: power sunroof, power driver's seat, upgraded audio system with EQ and steering-wheel-mounted auxiliary controls, heated mirrors, cellular phone pre-wire, map lights. **LS** adds: passenger air bag, leather trim, automatic climate control, Acura/Bose audio system, illuminated entry, walnut interior trim, power passenger seat.

OPTIONS are available as dealer-installed accessories.

Buick LeSabre	Retail Price	Dealer Invoice	Low Price
Custom 4-door notchback	$18695	$16227	$16852
Limited 4-door notchback	20775	18033	18658
Destination charge	555	555	555

Standard equipment:

Custom: 3.8-liter PFI V-6, 4-speed automatic transmission, power steering, air conditioning, driver-side air bag, cloth 55/45 seat with recliners and armrest, tinted glass, power windows, AM/FM radio, tilt steering column, intermittent wipers, trip odometer, Pass-Key theft deterrent system, 205/75R15 tires. **Limited** adds: anti-lock brakes, front storage armrest with cupholders, rear defogger, misc. lights, upgraded exterior moldings.

Optional equipment:

Anti-lock brakes, base	764	649	688
Traction control system, Ltd.	175	149	158
Premium Pkg. SC, Custom	801	681	721
Cruise control, rear defogger, white-stripe tires, front seat storage armrest, trunk net.			
Luxury Pkg. SD, Custom	1271	1080	1144

Prices are accurate at time of printing; subject to manufacturer's change.

CAR PRICES

Pkg. SC plus cassette player, wire wheel covers, striping, floormats.
Prestige Pkg. SE, Custom 2254 1916 2029
Pkg. SD plus anti-lock brakes, power driver's seat, power antenna, lighted visor mirror, door edge guards, remote trunk release.
Premium Pkg. SC, Ltd. 1201 1021 1081
Power driver's seat, power locks, cruise control, cassette player, power antenna, floormats, trunk net, whitewall tires.
Luxury Pkg. SD, Ltd. 1706 1450 1535
Pkg. SC plus wire wheel covers, power mirrors, remote trunk release, lighted visor mirror, front door courtesy lights, door edge guards.
Prestige Pkg. SE, Ltd. 2611 2219 2350
Pkg. SD plus UX1 audio system, power passenger seat, dual control air conditioning, remote keyless entry, cornering lamps.
Gran Touring Pkg., w/Pkg. SC 724 615 652
w/SD/SE 484 411 436
Gran Touring suspension, 215/60R15 tires on alloy wheels, 3.06 axle ratio, leather-wrapped steering wheel, automatic level control.
3.06 axle ratio . . . . NC NC NC
Trailer Towing Pkg. w/o Gran Touring Pkg. 325 276 293
w/Gran Touring Pkg. 150 128 135
Engine and transmission oil coolers, automatic level control suspension.
Gauges & tachometer, Ltd. 138 117 124
Electri-Clear windshield 250 213 225
Cassette player, Custom w/SC & Ltd. 140 119 126
UX1 audio system, Custom w/SC 360 306 324
Custom w/SD/SE & Ltd. w/SC/SD 220 187 198
Includes tape search/repeat, EQ, and Concert Sound speakers.
U1A audio system, Custom w/SC 624 530 562
Custom w/SD/SE & Ltd. w/SC/SD 484 411 436
Ltd. w/SE 264 224 238
Power antenna 85 72 77
Bodyside stripes 45 38 41
Full vinyl top 200 170 180
Power driver's seat, Custom 305 259 275
Leather/vinyl 55/45 seat, Ltd. 500 425 450
Alloy wheels, w/SC 325 276 293
w/SD/SE 85 72 77
Wire wheel covers, w/SC 240 204 216
205/70R15 whitewall tires 76 65 68
Warranty enhancements for New York 25 21 23
California emissions pkg. 100 85 90

Cadillac De Ville/Fleetwood	Retail Price	Dealer Invoice	Low Price
Coupe de Ville 2-door notchback	$31740	$27233	$28148
Sedan de Ville 4-door notchback	31740	27233	28148
De Ville Touring Sedan	35190	30193	—
Fleetwood 2-door notchback	36360	31197	32112
Fleetwood 4-door notchback	36360	31197	32112

Prices are accurate at time of printing; subject to manufacturer's change.

Fleetwood Sixty Special 4-door notchback	39860	34200	35115
Destination charge	600	600	600

De Ville Touring Sedan low price not available at time of publication.

Standard equipment:

De Ville: 4.9-liter PFI V-8, 4-speed automatic transmission, anti-lock brakes, power steering, driver-side air bag, power 45/55 cloth reclining front seats with manual recliners, front storage armrest, automatic climate control, outside temperature readout, power windows, automatic power locks, heated power mirrors, cruise control, AM/FM cassette with EQ, power antenna, automatic level control, automatic parking brake release, Twilight Sentinel, solar-control glass, intermittent wipers, trip odometer, tilt steering column, remote decklid release, rear defogger, Fuel Data Center, Pass-Key theft-deterrent system, seatback pockets, door edge guards, litter receptacle, 205/70R15 whitewall tires on alloy wheels. **Touring Sedan** adds: Computer Command Ride System, larger front and rear stabilizer bars, sport suspension, 2.97:1 final drive ratio, walnut accents, leather seating area with power front seat recliners, leather-wrapped steering wheel, 215/60R16 Goodyear GA tires. **Fleetwood** adds: vinyl roof (4-door), cabriolet roof (2-door), fender skirts, remote fuel door release, automatic day/night mirror, front and rear lighted visor mirrors, floormats. **Sixty Special** adds: Ultrasoft leather upholstery, 22-way power heated front seats (includes 2-position memory, adjustable lumbar and side bolsters, and power head restraints).

Optional equipment:

Traction control, De Ville	175	147	156
Option Pkg. B, De Ville	356	299	317
Illuminated entry, lighted visor mirrors, power decklid pull-down, trunk mat.			
Option Pkg. C, De Ville	803	675	715
Pkg. B plus remote fuel door release, digital instruments, automatic day/night mirror, trumpet horn.			
Security Pkg.	295	248	263
Remote keyless entry, theft-deterrent system.			
Cold Weather Pkg.	369	310	328
Engine block heater, heated windshield.			
Custom Seating Pkg., Fleetwood	425	357	378
Memory seat, power front seat recliners.			
Touring Sedan Pkg. 1SC	NC	NC	NC
Power decklid pull-down, trunk mat, lighted visor mirrors, remote fuel door release, digital instruments, trumpet horn, remote keyless entry, theft deterrent system, Delco/ Bose cassette system or CD player (Pkg. 1SD).			
Astroroof	1550	1302	1380
Coachbuilder Pkg., Sedan De Ville	1000	840	890
Computer Command Ride System, De Ville	380	319	338
Gold Ornamentation Pkg.	395	332	352
HD Livery Pkg., Sedan De Ville	1000	840	890
Leather seating area (std. Sixty)	570	479	507
Delco/Bose audio system	576	484	513
w/CD player	872	732	776

Prices are accurate at time of printing; subject to manufacturer's change.

CAR PRICES

Formal cabriolet roof, Coupe De Ville	925	777	823
Padded vinyl roof, Sedan De Ville	925	777	823
Full cabriolet roof, Coupe De Ville	1095	920	975
Phaeton roof, Sedan De Ville	1095	920	975
Wire wheel discs, De Ville	235	197	209
Fleetwood	NC	NC	NC
Lace alloy wheels, De Ville	235	197	209

Cadillac Eldorado	Retail Price	Dealer Invoice	Low Price
2-door notchback	$32470	$27859	—
Destination charge	600	600	600

Low price not available at time of publication.

Standard equipment:

4.9-liter PFI V-8, 4-speed automatic transmission, anti-lock 4-wheel disc brakes, power steering, driver-side air bag, Computer Command Ride System, automatic level control, cloth power front seats with manual recliners, center console with armrest and storage bins, automatic climate control, power windows and locks, cruise control, heated power mirrors, rear defogger, AM/FM cassette with EQ, power antenna, remote fuel door and decklid releases, power decklid pulldown, illuminated entry, Driver Information Center, lighted visor mirror (passenger), intermittent wipers, floormats, Pass-Key theft-deterrent system, tinted glass, leather-wrapped steering wheel, tilt steering column, Twilight Sentinel, trip odometer, 225/60R16 tires on alloy wheels.

Optional equipment:

Option Pkg. B	181	152	—
Lighted visor mirrors, floormats, trunk mat, decklid liner, underhood lamp.			
Security Pkg.	480	403	—
Remote keyless entry, theft-deterrent system, automatic door locks, central door unlocking system.			
Seating Pkg.	340	286	—
Power front seat recliners, power lumbar supports, articulating front headrests; requires leather seats.			
Touring Coupe Pkg.	2100	1764	—
Uprated suspension, Eagle GA tires, leather seats with power recliners and lumbar support adjusters, Security Pkg.			
Astroroof	1550	1302	—
Heated windshield system	309	260	—
Leather seating area	650	546	—
Heated front seats	120	101	—
Sport interior	146	123	—
Automatic day/night mirror	110	92	—
Monotone Firemist paint	240	202	—
Gold/white diamond paint	240	202	—
Delco/Bose audio system, w/cassette & CD	972	816	—
225/60R16 tires	76	64	—

Prices are accurate at time of printing; subject to manufacturer's change.

CONSUMER GUIDE®

	Retail Price	Dealer Invoice	Low Price
Striping	75	63	—
California emissions pkg.	100	84	—

Dodge Caravan

	Retail Price	Dealer Invoice	Low Price
Base SWB w/Pkg. 21S (2.5-liter/5-speed)	$13678	$12287	$12983
w/Pkg. 22S (2.5-liter/automatic 3)	14254	12776	13515
w/Pkg. 24S (3.0-liter/automatic 3)	14948	13366	14157
Base standard equipment.			
w/Pkg. 21T (2.5-liter/5-speed)	13891	12468	13180
w/Pkg. 22T (2.5-liter/automatic 3)	14467	12957	13712
w/Pkg. 24T (3.0-liter/automatic 3)	15161	13547	14354
21-24T add: air conditioning, dual-note horn, remote liftgate release, map and cargo area lights, bodyside moldings, storage drawer under front passenger seat.			
Base Grand w/Pkg. 24E (3.0-liter/automatic 3)	17174	15362	16268
Base standard equipment plus: air conditioning, map and cargo area lights.			
SE SWB w/Pkg. 22A (2.5-liter/automatic 3)	15527	13914	14721
w/Pkg. 24A (3.0-liter/automatic 3)	16221	14504	15363
w/Pkg. 26A (3.0-liter/automatic 4)	16394	14651	15523
w/Pkg. 28A (3.3-liter/automatic 4)	16496	14737	15617
SE SWB AWD w/Pkg. 28A (3.3-liter/automatic 4)	18698	16704	NA
Grand SE w/Pkg. 28A (3.3-liter/automatic 4)	17359	15526	16443
Grand SE AWD w/Pkg. 28A (3.3-liter/automatic 4)	19455	17370	NA
SE standard equipment.			
w/Pkg. 22B (2.5-liter/automatic 3)	15740	14095	14918
w/Pkg. 24B (3.0-liter/automatic 3)	16434	14685	15560
w/Pkg. 26B (3.0-liter/automatic 4)	16607	14832	15720
w/Pkg. 28B (3.3-liter/automatic 4)	16709	14918	15814
SE SWB AWD w/Pkg. 28B (3.3-liter/automatic 4)	18911	16885	NA
Grand SE w/Pkg. 28B (3.3-liter/automatic 4)	17572	15707	16640
Grand SE AWD w/Pkg. 28B (3.3-liter/automatic 4)	19668	17551	NA
22-28B add: air conditioning, rear defogger, map and cargo area lights.			
w/Pkg. 22D (2.5-liter/automatic 3)	16928	15105	16017
w/Pkg. 24D (3.0-liter/automatic 3)	17622	15695	16659
w/Pkg. 26D (3.0-liter/automatic 4)	17795	15842	16819
w/Pkg. 28D (3.3-liter/automatic 4)	17897	15928	16913
SE SWB AWD w/Pkg. 28D (3.3-liter/automatic 4)	20099	17895	NA
Grand SE w/Pkg. 28D (3.3-liter/automatic 4)	18760	16717	17739
Grand SE AWD w/Pkg. 28D (3.3-liter/automatic 4)	20856	18561	NA
22-28D add to 22-28B: front console, cruise control, tilt steering column, added sound insulation, floormats, tachometer, oil pressure gauge, voltmeter, lighted visor mirrors, Light Group, power locks, styled steel wheels.			
LE SWB w/Pkg. 24J (3.0-liter/automatic 3)	19688	17581	18635
w/Pkg. 26J (3.0-liter/automatic 4)	19861	17728	18795
w/Pkg. 28J (3.3-liter/automatic 4)	19963	17814	18889
LE SWB AWD w/Pkg. 28J (3.3-liter/automatic 4)	22130	19724	NA
Grand LE w/Pkg. 28J (3.3-liter/automatic 4)	20670	18440	19555
Grand LE AWD w/Pkg. 28J (3.3-liter/automatic 4)	23270	19936	NA
LE standard equipment.			

Prices are accurate at time of printing; subject to manufacturer's change.

CAR PRICES

w/Pkg. 24K (3.0-liter/automatic 3)	20267	18073	19170
w/Pkg. 26K (3.0-liter/automatic 3)	20440	18220	19330
w/Pkg. 28K (3.3-liter/automatic 4)	20452	18307	19380
LE SWB AWD w/Pkg. 28K (3.3-liter/automatic 4)	22709	20217	NA
Grand LE w/Pkg. 28K (3.3-liter/automatic 4)	21249	18932	20091
Grand LE AWD w/Pkg. 28K (3.3-liter/automatic 4)	22949	20428	NA

24-28K add: power driver's seat, power windows, Infinity I audio system, sunscreen glass, two-tone paint.

w/Pkg. 24L (3.0-liter/automatic 3)	20899	18610	19755
w/Pkg. 26L (3.0-liter/automatic 4)	21072	18757	19915
w/Pkg. 28L (3.3-liter/automatic 4)	21174	18844	20009
LE SWB AWD w/Pkg. 28L (3.3-liter/automatic 4)	23267	20691	NA
Grand LE w/Pkg. 28L (3.3-liter/automatic 4)	21807	19406	20607
Grand LE AWD w/Pkg. 28L (3.3-liter/automatic 4)	23507	20902	NA

24-28L add to 24-28K: Woodgrain Decor Group (woodgrain appliques and moldings, luggage rack, 205/70R15 whitewall tires, wire wheel covers); deletes two-tone paint.

w/ES Pkg. 24M (3.0-liter/automatic 3)	20899	18629	19764
w/ES Pkg. 26M (3.0-liter/automatic 4)	21072	18776	19924
w/ES Pkg. 28M (3.3-liter/automatic 4)	21174	18863	20019
LE SWB AWD w/ES Pkg. 28M (3.3-liter/automatic 4) . .	23220	20666	NA
Grand LE w/ES Pkg. 28M (3.3-liter/automatic 4)	21760	19381	20571
Grand LE AWD w/ES Pkg. 28M (3.3-liter/automatic 4) .	23460	20877	NA

24-26M adds to 24-28K: ES Decor Group (body-color fascia and cladding, sport suspension, sunscreen glass, fog lights, 205/70R15 tires on alloy wheels), power driver's seat, power windows, Infinity I audio system; deletes two-tone paint.

Destination charge	540	540	540

SWB denotes short wheelbase; AWD denotes All Wheel Drive.

AWD low prices not available at time of publication.

Engines and transmissions: 2.5-liter TBI 4-cylinder with 5-speed manual or 3-speed automatic; 3.0-liter PFI V-6 with 3- or 4-speed automatic; 3.3-liter PFI V-6 with 4-speed automatic.

Standard equipment:

Base: driver-side air bag, power steering, 5-passenger seating (front bucket seats, 3-passenger middle bench seat), tinted glass, trip odometer, coolant temperature gauge, dual outside mirrors, visor mirrors, AM/FM radio, intermittent wipers, rear wiper/washer, 195/75R14 tires. **SE** adds: 7-passenger seating (2-passenger middle and 3-passenger rear seats), dual-note horn, power mirrors, remote liftgate release, rear trim panel storage and cup holders, striping, sport wheel covers. **LE** adds: front air conditioning, front storage console, overhead console with outside temperature readout and mini trip computer, rear defogger, power front windows, power quarter vent windows, power locks, remote fuel door release, tachometer, oil pressure gauge, voltmeter, illuminated entry, headlamp delay system, heated power mirrors, lighted visor mirrors, bodyside moldings, cruise control, tilt steering column, sport steering wheel, storage drawer under front passenger seat, floormats. **Grand** models have 3.3-liter PFI V-6, 4-speed automatic transmission (base has 3.0-liter PFI V-6, 3-speed automatic transmission), power mirrors, remote liftgate release, dual-note horn, storage

Prices are accurate at time of printing; subject to manufacturer's change.

drawer under front passenger seat, sport wheel covers, 205/70R15 tires. **All Wheel Drive** models have 3.3-liter PFI V-6, 4-speed automatic transmission, 7-passenger seating, power mirrors, 205/75R15 tires.

Optional equipment:

3.0-liter V-6, 2WD SWB	694	590	638
3.3-liter V-6, SE/LE 2WD SWB	796	677	732
3-speed automatic transmission, base 2WD	576	490	530
4-speed automatic transmission, SE/LE w/V-6	173	147	159
Anti-lock brakes, SWB SE w/3.3-liter V-6	687	584	632
SWB SE w/Trailer Towing Group, Sport Handling Group or 14″ whitewall tires, Grand SE	599	509	551
LE SWB w/J, K or L Pkgs.	687	584	632
LE SWB w/M Pkg. and 3.3-liter V-6	599	509	551
LE w/Trailer Tow Group, Sport Handling Group or 14″ whitewall tires	599	509	551
Grand SE & LE	599	509	551
Front air conditioning, base & SE	857	728	788
Air conditioning w/rear heater, base Grand	699	594	643
Grand SE 28A/28B	699	594	643
Requires rear defogger.			
Grand SE 28A/28B w/Trailer Towing Group	636	541	585
Grand SE 28D	466	396	429
Grand SE 28D w/Trailer Towing Group	404	343	372
Rear air conditioning, Grand LE	466	396	429
Grand LE w/Trailer Towing Group	571	485	525
Grand SE 2WD w/Trailer Towing Group	509	433	468
Rear bench seat, base SWB	397	337	365
Includes trim panel storage area and cup holders.			
Seven-passenger seating w/integrated child seat, base SWB	597	507	549
SE & LE SWB, Grand	200	170	184
Quad Command Seating, SE & LE	597	507	549
Two front and two middle bucket seats, 3-passenger rear bench seat.			
Converta-Bed 7-pass. seating, SE SWB, base/SE Grand	553	470	509
Leather trim, LE w/K, L or M Pkgs.	865	735	796
HD Trailer Towing Pkg., SE, LE w/J or K Pkgs.	557	473	512
LE w/L Pkg.	483	411	444
SE	443	377	408
Grand SE/LE	265	225	244
LE w/Pkgs. J or K and Sport Handling Group			
HD alternator, battery, flasher, radiator, and transmission oil cooler, trailer wiring harness; 2WD adds: HD suspension, sport wheel covers, 205/70R15 tires with conventional spare.			
Deluxe Convenience Pkg., base & SE	372	316	342
Cruise control, tilt steering column.			
Power Convenience group, SE SWB w/A or B Pkgs., Grand SE	530	451	488

Prices are accurate at time of printing; subject to manufacturer's change.

SE SWB w/D Pkg.	265	225	244
Power front windows, power locks.			
Sport Handling Group, SE SWB	207	176	190
Grand SE	93	79	86
LE SWB w/J, K or M Pkgs.	207	176	190
Grand LE w/J, K or M Pkgs.	93	79	86
HD brakes, rear sway bar, sport wheel covers, 205/70R15 tires.			
Rear defogger, base w/o Pkgs.	217	184	200
Base w/Pkgs. 22-28, SE	168	143	155
Base includes remote liftgate release w/Pkgs. 22-28.			
Power locks, base & SE	265	225	244
Sunscreen glass	414	352	381
Luggage rack	143	122	132
Cassette player	155	132	143
Infinity I audio system, SE/LE SWB, Grand SE/LE	461	392	424
Infinity II system, LE w/K, L or M Pkgs.	214	182	197

Dodge Spirit	Retail Price	Dealer Invoice	Low Price
4-door notchback w/Pkg. 21A	$11270	$10264	$10549
w/Pkg. 22A (2.5-liter/automatic 3)	11827	10561	10846
w/Pkg. 21C (2.5-liter/5-speed)	11700	10453	10738
w/Pkg. 22D (2.5-liter/automatic 3)	12257	10927	11212
w/Pkg. 26D (3.0-liter/automatic 3)	12982	11543	11828
w/Pkg. 22E (2.5-liter/automatic 3)	12994	11553	11838
w/Pkg. 26E (3.0-liter/automatic 3)	13719	12169	12454
w/Pkg. 28E (3.0-liter/automatic 3)	13802	12240	12525
LE 4-door notchback w/Pkg. 22P	13330	11900	12185
w/Pkg. 22U (2.5-liter/automatic 3)	13872	12361	12646
w/Pkg. 24U (Turbo/automatic 3)	14597	12977	13262
w/Pkg. 26U (3.0-liter/automatic 3)	14597	12977	13262
w/Pkg. 28U (3.0-liter/automatic 4)	14690	13056	13341
ES 4-door notchback w/Pkg. 23X	14241	12702	12987
w/Pkg. 23U (Turbo/5-speed)	14783	13163	13448
w/Pkg. 24U (Turbo/automatic 3)	15340	13636	13921
w/Pkg. 28U (3.0-liter/automatic 4)	15423	13707	13992
R/T 4-door notchback	18474	16427	—
Destination charge	485	485	485

R/T low price not available at time of publication.

Standard equipment:

2.5-liter TBI 4-cylinder engine, 5-speed manual transmission, power steering, driver-side air bag, cloth reclining front bucket seats, tachometer, coolant temperature and oil pressure gauges, voltmeter, trip odometer, center console, tinted backlight, remote mirrors, visor mirrors, narrow bodyside moldings, AM/FM radio with two speakers, intermittent wipers, 185/70R14 tires. **LE** adds: 3-speed automatic transmission, rear defogger, tinted glass, Message Center, front armrest, remote trunk release, four

Prices are accurate at time of printing; subject to manufacturer's change.

speakers, cruise control, tilt steering column, wide bodyside moldings, floormats, added sound insulation, full wheel covers. **ES** adds: 2.5-liter turbocharged PFI engine, 5-speed manual transmission, 4-wheel disc brakes, performance suspension, leather-wrapped steering wheel, cassette player, trip computer, 205/60R15 tires on alloy wheels. **R/T** adds: 2.2-liter DOHC 16-valve turbocharged engine, rear spoiler, heated power mirrors, 205/60VR15 tires. **Base Pkgs. 21C/22D/26D:** air conditioning, rear defogger, tinted glass, floormats, four speaker radio, cruise control, tilt steering column. **Base Pkgs. 22E/26E/28E:** Pkgs. 21C/22D/26D plus power windows and locks, power mirrors, remote trunk release. **LE Pkgs. 22U/24U/26U/28U:** air conditioning, power windows and locks, power mirrors. **ES Pkgs. 23U/24U/28U:** air conditioning, power windows and locks, power mirrors.

Optional equipment:

2.5-liter turbo engine, LE	725	616	638
3.0-liter V-6, base & LE	725	616	638
ES	NC	NC	NC
3-speed automatic transmission, base & ES	557	473	490
4-speed automatic transmission, base & ES	640	544	563
LE	93	79	82
Available only with V-6.			
Anti-lock 4-wheel disc brakes	899	764	791
Power Equipment Pkg., R/T	543	462	478
Power windows and locks.			
Interior Illumination Group, base	293	249	258
others	195	166	172
Illuminated entry, lighted visor mirrors, misc. lights, message center.			
Interior Convenience Group (NA base)	400	340	352
Overhead console, reading lamps, compass, Interior Illumination Group.			
Center armrest, base w/5-speed	81	69	71
Console w/armrest, base	155	132	136
Rear defogger, base	173	147	152
Cassette player & 4 speakers, base	155	132	136
w/seek/scan, LE	155	132	136
w/seek/scan, ES & R/T	275	234	242
Cassette player w/Infinity speakers, LE	430	366	378
ES & R/T	275	234	242
w/EQ, ES & RT	490	417	431
Power driver's seat (NA base)	296	252	260
50/50 split front seat, base	102	87	90
w/split folding rear seat, base	250	213	220
w/split folding rear seat, LE	61	52	54
Front bucket seats, base	148	126	130
Includes split folding rear seat.			
195/70R14 whitewall tires, base w/22D or 22E	104	88	92
base w/26- or 28E	73	62	64
205/60R15 tires, LE w/22U	177	150	156
LE w/24U, 26U or 28U	146	124	128
Requires alloy wheels.			
Alloy wheels, LE	328	279	289

Prices are accurate at time of printing; subject to manufacturer's change.

Conventional spare tire, base & LE	95	81	84
Extra-cost paint	77	65	68
California emissions pkg.	102	87	90

Eagle Talon	Retail Price	Dealer Invoice	Low Price
3-door hatchback (5-speed)	$13631	$12498	$12903
w/Pkg. 23B (5-speed)	14458	13201	13659
w/Pkg. 24B (automatic)	15159	13797	14299
B Pkgs. add: air conditioning.			
w/Pkg. 23C (5-speed)	15255	13878	14387
w/Pkg. 24C (automatic)	15956	14474	15027
C Pkgs. add to B: cruise control, rear wiper/washer, power windows and locks.			
w/Pkg. 23D (5-speed)	15751	14300	14840
w/Pkg. 24D (automatic)	16452	14896	15480
D Pkgs. add to C: premium audio system with EQ, alloy wheels.			
TSi 3-door hatchback (5-speed)	14963	13697	14153
TSi 3-door hatchback (automatic)	15803	14411	14920
w/Pkg. 25F (5-speed)	16587	15077	15637
w/Pkg. 26F (automatic)	17427	15791	16404
F Pkgs. add: air conditioning, cruise control, rear wiper/washer, power windows and locks.			
w/Pkg. 25G (5-speed)	17083	15499	16090
w/Pkg. 26G (automatic)	17923	16213	16857
G Pkgs. add to F: premium audio system with EQ, alloy wheels.			
TSi AWD 3-door hatchback (5-speed)	16905	15445	15975
TSi AWD 3-door hatchback (automatic)	17745	16159	16743
w/Pkg. 25J (5-speed)	18529	16825	17459
w/Pkg. 26J (automatic)	19369	17539	18226
J Pkgs. add: air conditioning, cruise control, rear wiper/washer, power windows and locks.			
Destination charge	343	343	343

Standard equipment:

2.0-liter DOHC 16-valve PFI 4-cylinder engine, 5-speed manual or 4-speed automatic transmission, 4-wheel disc brakes, power steering, motorized front shoulder belts, cloth reclining front bucket seats, driver-seat lumbar support adjustment, folding rear seat, console (with armrest, storage, and cup holders), rear defogger, tinted glass, tachometer, coolant temperature and oil pressure gauges, trip odometer, map lights, power mirrors, visor mirrors, AM/FM cassette, remote fuel door and hatch releases, tilt steering column, tonneau cover, intermittent wipers, floormats, 205/55HR16 tires. **TSi** adds: turbocharged engine, sill extensions and specific fascias, driving lamps, performance seats, turbo boost gauge, leather-wrapped steering wheel and shift handle, 205/55VR16 tires. **TSI AWD** adds: permanent 4-wheel drive, limited-slip differential, uprated suspension, alloy wheels.

Optional equipment:

Anti-lock brakes (base and TSi)	943	802	830

Prices are accurate at time of printing; subject to manufacturer's change.

w/TSi AWD	681	579	599

Requires security alarm on TSi & AWD; deletes limited-slip differential from AWD.

Security alarm, TSi & AWD	163	139	143

Requires anti-lock brakes.

Premium audio system, AWD	212	180	187
AM/FM cassette w/CD player (TSi)	506	430	436
w/TSi AWD	718	610	620
Pop-up sunroof	373	317	328
Leather upholstery, TSi & AWD	435	370	383
Alloy wheels, base & TSi	234	241	206

Ford Crown Victoria	Retail Price	Dealer Invoice	Low Price
4-door notchback	$18728	$16154	$16504
LX 4-door notchback	19543	16846	17196
Touring Sedan 4-door notchback	23349	20081	20431
Destination charge	535	535	535

Standard equipment:

4.6-liter PFI V-8, 4-speed automatic transmission, 4-wheel disc brakes, power steering, driver-side air bag, air conditioning, cloth reclining split bench seat, map pockets, digital clock, power windows, coolant temperature gauge, trip odometer, tilt steering column, tinted glass, automatic parking brake release, intermittent wipers, AM/FM radio, 215/70R15 all-season tires. **LX** adds: trunk cargo net, upgraded interior trim, Light/Decor Group, remote fuel door release, carpeted spare tire cover. **Touring Sedan** adds: leather-wrapped steering wheel, cruise control, power front seats with armrest and cup holders, floormats, Handling and Performance Package.

Optional equipment:

Passenger-side air bag	488	415	439
Anti-lock brakes w/electronic traction assist	1035	880	932
Preferred Pkg. 111A, base	1547	1315	1392

Rear defogger, floormats, illuminated entry system, Light/Decor Group, Power Lock Group, cassette player, remote fuel door release, power driver's seat, leather-wrapped steering wheel, cruise control, spare tire cover, trunk cargo net, wheel covers.

Preferred Pkg. 113A, LX	1018	865	916

Rear defogger, floormats, illuminated entry system, Power Lock Group, cassette player, power driver's seat, leather-wrapped steering, cruise control, cornering lamps, power antenna, alloy wheels.

Pkg. 114A, LX	3666	3116	3299

Preferred Pkg. 113A plus anti-lock brakes, electronic traction control, high-level audio system, electronic climate control, trip computer, electronic instrumentation, keyless entry system, rear air suspension, power front seats.

Pkg. 115A, Touring Sedan	905	769	815

Rear defogger, illuminated entry, Power Lock Group, cornering lamps, power antenna, high-level audio system, keyless entry system.

Leather seating surfaces, LX	555	472	500
Touring Sedan	339	288	305

Prices are accurate at time of printing; subject to manufacturer's change.

CAR PRICES

White sidewall tires	82	69	74
Full-size spare tire	85	72	77
Heavy-duty battery	27	23	24
Front cornering lamps	68	58	61
Rear window defroster	160	136	144
Floor mats, front	26	22	23
Floor mats, rear	17	14	15
Engine block heater	26	22	23
Illuminated entry system	82	70	74
Keyless entry system (NA base)	137	116	123
Rear air suspension	285	243	257
Remote fuel door release (std. LX)	41	35	37
Power driver's seat	290	247	261
Power driver/passenger seats, LX	779	662	701
w/Pkgs. 111A or 113A	489	416	440
Spare tire cover	18	16	16
Cruise control	273	232	246

Includes leather-wrapped steering wheel.

Trailer Towing Pkg.	490	417	441
w/Pkg. 121A	463	394	417
w/Pkg. 114A	205	174	185

Includes rear air spring suspension, heavy-duty battery, flasher system and U-joint, extra cooling, dual exhaust, wiring harness, power steering and transmission oil coolers, full-size spare tire, Traction-Lok axle (except w/anti-lock brakes). Not available with Handling and Performance Package.

Alloy wheels	440	374	396
w/Pkg. 111A	129	110	116

Not available with Handling and Performance package.

Spoke wheel covers	311	264	280
Insta-Clear windshield (NA base)	305	259	275
Light/Decor Group, base	222	189	200

Includes illuminated visor mirrors, misc. lights, striping.

Power Lock Group	276	235	248

Includes power door locks, remote decklid release.

Electronic Group	516	439	464

Automatic climate control, electronic instrumentation, trip computer. Requires rear defogger. Not available with Handling and Performance Pkg.

w/Pkg. 113A	1512	1286	1361
w/Pkg. 114A	191	163	172

Includes performance springs, shocks and stabilizer bars, alloy wheels, anti-lock brakes w/electronic traction control, dual exhaust w/210 bhp engine rating, 3.27 axle ratio, 225/70R15 tires. Not available with Trailer Towing Pkg., Electronic Group, other wheel, wheel cover, and tire options, or with conventional spare tire w/JBL audio system.

Cassette player	155	132	140
High Level audio system	490	417	441
w/Pkg. 111A or 113A	335	285	302

60-watt AM/FM stereo cassette w/electronic volume control, scan and search feature, upgraded amplifier and speakers.

Prices are accurate at time of printing; subject to manufacturer's change.

     CONSUMER GUIDE®

JBL audio system	488	415	440
Power antenna	82	70	74
Radio delete (credit)	(206)	(175)	(185)
California emissions pkg.	100	85	90

Ford Escort	Retail Price	Dealer Invoice	Low Price
Pony 3-door hatchback	$8355	$7723	$8023
LX 3-door hatchback	9055	8197	8497
GT 3-door hatchback	11871	10685	10985
LX 4-door notchback	9795	8838	—
LX-E 4-door notchback	11933	10740	—
LX 5-door hatchback	9483	8559	8859
LX 5-door wagon	10067	9080	9380
Destination charge	375	375	375

4-door low prices not available at time of publication.

Standard equipment:

Pony: 1.9-liter PFI 4-cylinder engine, 5-speed manual transmission, motorized front shoulder belts, cloth and vinyl reclining bucket seats, one-piece folding rear seatback, tinted glass, coolant temperature gauge, trip odometer, intermittent wipers, cargo cover, door pockets, right visor mirror, 175/70R13 tires. **LX** adds: upgraded upholstery, 60/40 split rear seatback, console storage bin and cupholders, AM/FM radio, bodyside molding, full wheel covers. **Sedan** adds: tachometer, intermittent wipers, 175/65R14 tires. **GT/LX-E** adds: 1.8-liter DOHC 16-valve engine, power steering, 4-wheel disc brakes, sport suspension, tachometer, cloth sport seats, AM/FM cassette, Light Group, lighted visor mirrors, removable cupholder tray, remote fuel door and hatch releases, power mirrors, variable intermittent wipers, fog lights (except sedan), rear spoiler, rocker panel cladding, 185/60HR15 tires on alloy wheels. **Sedan** has 185/60R × 14 tires.

Optional equipment:

4-speed automatic transmission	732	645	641
Air conditioning, LX & GT	759	645	664
Power steering, LX	261	222	228
Pony Comfort Group	841	715	736
Air conditioning, power steering.			
Preferred Pkg. 320A, LX	248	211	217
Power steering, Light/Convenience Group, rear defogger.			
Preferred Pkg. 325A, LX-E	554	471	485
Rear defogger, air conditioning, tilt steering column, cruise control.			
Preferred Pkg. 330A, GT	554	471	485
Air conditioning, rear defogger, Luxury Convenience Group.			
Cayman Decor Group, GT	274	233	240
Clearcoat paint, specific alloy wheels, leather-wrapped steering wheel, Cayman-colored accents on seats, doors, and floormats.			
Rear defogger	170	145	149
Light/Convenience Group, LX	317	269	277

Prices are accurate at time of printing; subject to manufacturer's change.

CAR PRICES

Light Group, power mirrors, remote fuel door and hatch releases, removable tray with cup holders.

Light Group/Removable Cupholder Tray	118	100	103

Removable cupholder tray, dual map, cargo area, underhood and ignition key lights, headlights-on warning chime, illuminated visor mirrors.

Luxury Convenience Group, LX 3- and 5-door wagon . .	428	364	375
LX/LX-E 4-door, GT	369	314	323

Tilt steering column, cruise control, tachometer, power locks.

Power Equipment Group, LX/LX-E 4-door wagon

w/Luxury Convenience Group	296	252	259
wagon w/o Luxury Convenience Group	355	302	311

Power windows and locks, tachometer.

Power mirrors	98	83	86
Power moonroof, LX, LX-E, GT	549	467	480
Remote duel door/liftgate releases	101	86	88
AM/FM radio, Pony	312	265	273
AM/FM cassette, Pony	467	397	409
LX	155	132	136
Premium sound system	138	117	121
Radio delete (credit), LX	(312)	(265)	(265)
LX-E & GT (credit)	(467)	(397)	(397)
Wagon Group	250	213	219

Luggage rack, rear wiper/washer.

Clearcoat paint	91	77	80
Engine block heater	20	17	18
California emissions pkg.	72	61	63

Ford Explorer	Retail Price	Dealer Invoice	Low Price
XL 3-door wagon, 2WD	$15609	$13976	$14326
XL 3-door wagon, 4WD	17399	15551	15901
Sport 3-door wagon, 2WD	16991	15192	15542
Sport 3-door wagon, 4WD	18721	16715	17065
Eddie Bauer 3-door wagon, 2WD	20187	18005	18355
Eddie Bauer 3-door wagon, 4WD	21918	19528	19878
XL 5-door wagon, 2WD	16515	14817	15567
XL 5-door wagon, 4WD	18378	16412	17162
XLT 5-door wagon, 2WD	18749	16739	17489
XLT 5-door wagon, 4WD	20504	18283	19033
Eddie Bauer 5-door wagon, 2WD	21694	19331	20081
Eddie Bauer 5-door wagon, 4WD	23449	20875	21625
Destination charge	485	485	485

Standard equipment:

XL: 4.0-liter PFI V-6, 5-speed manual transmission, anti-lock rear brakes, power steering, Touch Drive electronic shift (4WD), knitted vinyl front bucket seats, split folding rear seat, tinted glass, flip-open opera windows (3-door), intermittent wipers, dual outside mirrors, carpet, load floor tiedown hooks, rear seat heat duct, tachometer,

Prices are accurate at time of printing; subject to manufacturer's change.

coolant temperature gauge, trip odometer, AM/FM radio, 225/70R15 tires with full-size spare. **Sport** adds: rear quarter privacy glass, rear wiper/washer, rear defogger, Light Group, map light, load floor tiedown net, cargo area cover, leather-wrapped steering wheel, lighted visor mirrors, alloy wheels. **XLT** adds: cloth captain's chairs, floor console, power mirrors, upgraded door panels with pockets, power windows and locks, cruise control, tilt steering column, full privacy glass (5-door; 3-door has rear window privacy glass), floormats. **Eddie Bauer** adds to Sport: premium captain's chairs, floor console, power mirrors, power windows and locks, cruise control, tilt steering column, roof rack, upgraded door panels with pockets, floormats, garment bag, duffle bag, Ford Care maintenance and warranty program.

Optional equipment:

4-speed automatic transmission	890	757	788
Limited-slip rear axle	252	215	223
Air conditioning	780	663	690
w/manual transmission	NC	NC	NC
Preferred Pkg. 931A, Sport	602	512	533
Air conditioning, power windows and locks, power mirrors, cloth captain's chairs, outlined white letter tires.			
Preferred Pkg. 932A, Eddie Bauer 3-door	—	—	—
Air conditioning, premium cassette player.			
Preferred Pkg. 941A, XLT w/automatic	435	370	385
XLT w/5-speed	NC	NC	NC
Air conditioning, striping, premium cassette player.			
Preferred Pkg. 942A, Eddie Bauer	480	408	425
Air conditioning, premium cassette player.			
Cloth captain's chairs, XL, Sport	274	233	242
Cloth 60/40 split bench seat, XL 5-door	232	197	205
XLT (credit)	(43)	(36)	(36)
Cloth sport bucket seats, Sport	956	813	846
XLT, Sport w/captain's chairs	540	459	478
Leather sport seats, XLT	1434	1219	1269
XLT, Sport w/captain's chairs	1368	1163	1211
Eddie Bauer w/automatic transmission	412	350	365
Eddie Bauer w/manual transmission	NC	NC	NC
Super engine cooling	56	48	50
Privacy glass	226	192	200
Manual locking hubs, 4WD (credit)	(104)	(88)	(88)
Light Group	29	25	26
Bodyside molding	121	103	107
Power Equipment Group, Sport	620	527	549
Luggage rack	126	107	112
w/manual transmission	NC	NC	NC
Tilt-up air roof	250	213	221
Cruise control & tilt steering column	383	325	339
w/manual transmission	NC	NC	NC
Alloy wheels, XL 2WD	326	277	289
XL 4WD	265	225	235
Deluxe wheels w/trim rings, 2WD	61	52	54

Prices are accurate at time of printing; subject to manufacturer's change.

CAR PRICES

Trailer Towing Pkg.	106	90	94
Rear defogger & wiper/washer	279	237	247
AM/FM cassette	122	104	108
Premium AM/FM cassette	200	170	177
w/manual transmission	NC	NC	NC
Ford JBL Audio System	688	585	609
Upgrade from premium cassette	488	415	432
Ford JBL Audio System w/CD player	983	835	870
Upgrade from premium cassette	783	665	693
Cargo area cover	80	68	71
Engine block heater	33	28	29
Deluxe tape stripe, 5-door	55	47	49
Deluxe two-tone paint	122	104	108
All-terrain tires	228	194	202
Floormats	50	43	44
California emissions pkg.	100	85	89

Ford Taurus	Retail Price	Dealer Invoice	Low Price
L 4-door notchback	$14913	$12851	$13226
GL 4-door notchback	15213	13106	13481
LX 4-door notchback	17434	14994	15369
SHO 4-door notchback	23772	20381	20756
L 5-door wagon	15824	13626	14001
GL 5-door wagon	16101	13861	14236
LX 5-door wagon	19024	16346	16721
Destination charge	490	490	490

Standard equipment:

L: 3.0-liter PFI V-6, 4-speed automatic transmission, power steering, driver-side air bag, cloth reclining split bench seat with dual center armrests, tilt steering column, power mirrors, tinted glass, intermittent wipers, cup/coin holder, door pockets, AM/FM radio, 205/70R14 tires. **GL** adds: visor mirrors, striping. **LX** adds: (3.8-liter V-6 on wagon), air conditioning, power windows and locks, power driver's seat, power front lumbar supports, variable-assist power steering, remote fuel door and decklid releases, tachometer, diagnostic alert lights, automatic parking brake release, automatic on/off headlamps, cornering lamps, bodyside cladding, Convenience Kit (vinyl pouch with fluorescent lantern, tire pressure gauge, gloves, poncho, shop towel, distress flag, headlamp bulb), Light Group, cargo tiedown net, 205/65R15 tires on alloy wheels. **SHO** deletes automatic parking brake release and remote fuel door and decklid releases and adds: 3.0-liter DOHC 24-valve V-6 with dual exhaust, anti-lock 4-wheel disc brakes, foglamps, front bucket seats with console, high-level audio system, power antenna, leather-wrapped steering wheel, rear defogger, cruise control, floormats, 215/60VR16 tires on alloy wheels.

Optional equipment:

3.8-liter V-6 (std. LX wgn, NA on L)	555	472	488

Prices are accurate at time of printing; subject to manufacturer's change.

Anti-lock brakes (std. SHO)	985	838	867
Passenger-side airbag	488	415	429
Manual air conditioning, L & GL	841	715	740
Automatic air conditioning, LX & SHO	183	156	161
Preferred Pkg. 203A (L Plus), L	711	604	626
Air conditioning, rear defogger.			
Preferred Pkg. 204A, GL 4-door	2023	1720	1780
GL wagon	1754	1491	1544
Air conditioning, rear defogger, power windows and locks, power driver's seat, remote fuel door release, remote decklid release (4-door), Light Group, cassette player, cruise control, deluxe wheel covers, cargo tiedown net.			
Preferred Pkg. 208A, LX 4-door	768	654	676
LX wagon	1059	902	932
Rear defogger, cruise control, high-level audio system, power antenna, keyless entry, leather-wrapped steering wheel, floormats. Wagon adds: cargo area cover, picnic table load floor extension, rear wiper/washer.			
Preferred Pkg. 211A, SHO	229	195	202
Keyless entry, automatic climate control.			
Luxury Convenience Group, LX	1407	1196	1238
Power front seats, power moonroof, Ford JBL audio system.			
Bucket seats w/console, GL	NC	NC	NC
Leather bucket seats w/console, GL	618	525	544
LX & SHO	515	438	453
Leather split bench seat, LX	515	438	453
Vinyl seat trim, L	37	31	33
AM/FM cassette (std. SHO)	171	145	150
Premium sound, L Plus, GL, & LX	168	143	148
Power antenna, LX	85	73	75
High-level audio system, GL & LX	502	427	442
GL w/204A	332	282	292
LX w/Pkg. 207A	167	142	147
CD player, (NA L)	491	418	432
Ford JBL audio system, L Plus, GL, LX & SHO	526	447	463
Autolamp system, LX & SHO	73	62	64
Cargo area cover, wagons	66	56	58
Cargo tie-down net (NA L)	44	37	39
Convenience Group, GL	830	706	730
L	540	459	475
L w/Pkg. 203A	315	267	277
Power windows and locks, power driver's seat.			
Cornering lamps, L Plus & GL	68	58	60
Rear defogger	170	145	150
Extended-range fuel tank (std. SHO)	46	39	40
Remote fuel door & decklid release, 4-doors	101	86	89
Remote fuel door release, wagons	41	35	36
Illuminated entry (NA L)	82	69	72
Keyless entry, LX & SHO	146	124	128
Electronic instruments, GL	351	288	309
LX	239	196	210

Prices are accurate at time of printing; subject to manufacturer's change.

Light Group	59	50	52
Picnic table load floor extension, GL & LX wagons . . .	90	77	79
Power locks	257	218	226
Requires power windows.			
Power windows	256	218	225
Lighted visor mirrors, L Plus & GL	100	85	88
Rocker panel moldings, L Plus & GL	55	47	48
Power moonroof, LX, & SHO	776	659	683
Automatic parking brake release, L, L Plus, & GL	12	10	11
Rear-facing third seat, wagons	155	132	136
Power seats, each	305	259	268
Cruise control	224	191	197
Speed-sensitive power steering (NA SHO)	104	88	92
Leather-wrapped steering wheel, LX & SHO	96	82	84
HD suspension (NA SHO)	26	22	23
Rear wiper/washer, wagons	135	115	119
Styled road wheels, L Plus & GL	193	164	170
LX	128	109	113
Finned wheel covers	65	55	57
Alloy wheels, GL	389	331	342
w/Pkg. 204A	239	203	210
205/65R15 tires w/wheelcovers, GL	150	128	132
Conventional spare tire (NA SHO)	73	62	64
HD battery (NA SHO)	27	23	24
HD suspension (NA SHO)	26	22	23
Clearcoat paint	188	160	165
Paint stripe	61	52	54
California emissions pkg.	100	85	88

Geo Prizm	Retail Price	Dealer Invoice	Low Price
4-door notchback	$10125	$9366	$9566
GSi 4-door notchback	13770	12737	12937
Destination charge	345	345	345

Standard equipment:

1.6-liter DOHC PFI 4-cylinder engine, 5-speed manual transmission, door-mounted automatic front shoulder belts, cloth reclining front bucket seats, tinted glass, door pockets, cup holders, left remote mirror, remote fuel door release, bodyside molding, 155/80R13 tires. **GSi** adds: higher-output engine, 4-wheel disc brakes, power steering, uprated suspension, air conditioning, tilt steering column, driver's-seat height adjustment, split folding rear seat, tachometer and oil pressure gauge, rear spoiler, left remote and right manual mirrors, remote decklid release, rear defogger, AM/FM radio, visor mirrors, floormats, 185/60HR14 tires on alloy wheels.

Optional equipment:

3-speed automatic transmission, base & LSi	495	421	433

Prices are accurate at time of printing; subject to manufacturer's change.

4-speed automatic transmission, GSi	775	659	678
Air conditioning (std. GSi)	745	633	652
Preferred Group 2, base	760	646	665

AM/FM radio, power steering, left remote and right manual mirrors, full wheel covers, 175/70SR13 tires.

Preferred Group 3, base	1785	1517	1562

Group 2 air conditioning, power locks, remote decklid release.

LSi Group 1, base	2628	2234	2300

Air conditioning, AM/FM radio, power steering, tachometer, power locks, tilt steering column, remote decklid release, rear defogger, cargo area lamp, full wheel covers, body-colored bumpers, custom interior, map pockets, dual outside mirrors (left remote), dual visor mirrors, split folding rear seat, 175/705RB tires.

LSi Preferred Group 2, base	3143	2672	2750

Group 1 items plus power windows, cruise control, intermittent wipers.

Preferred Group 2, GSi	735	625	643

Power windows and locks, cruise control, intermittent wipers.

Rear defogger	105	89	92
Power sunroof	530	451	464
AM/FM cassette	140	119	123
Floormats	40	34	35
California emissions pkg.	70	60	61

Honda Accord	Retail Price	Dealer Invoice	Low Price
DX 2-door notchback, 5-speed	$13025	—	—
DX 2-door notchback, automatic	13775	—	—
LX 2-door notchback, 5-speed	15625	—	—
LX 2-door notchback, automatic	16375	—	—
EX 2-door notchback, 5-speed	18045	—	—
EX 2-door notchback, automatic	18795	—	—
DX 4-door notchback, 5-speed	13225	—	—
DX 4-door notchback, automatic	13975	—	—
LX 4-door notchback, 5-speed	15825	—	—
LX 4-door notchback, automatic	16575	—	—
EX 4-door notchback, 5-speed	18245	—	—
EX 4-door notchback, automatic	18995	—	—
LX 5-door wagon, 5-speed	17450	—	—
LX 5-door wagon, automatic	18200	—	—
EX 5-door wagon, 5-speed	19900	—	—
EX 5-door wagon, automatic	20650	—	—
Destination charge	290	290	290

Dealer invoice and low price not available at time of publication.

Standard equipment:

DX: 2.2-liter SOHC 16-valve PFI 4-cylinder engine, 5-speed manual or 4-speed automatic transmission, power steering, driver-side air bag, cloth reclining front bucket seats, folding rear seatback, tachometer, coolant temperature gauge, trip odometer, tinted

Prices are accurate at time of printing; subject to manufacturer's change.

CAR PRICES

glass, tilt steering column, intermittent wipers, rear defogger, remote fuel door and decklid releases, door pockets, maintenance interval indicator, 185/70R14 87S tires. **LX** adds: air conditioning, cruise control, power windows and locks, power mirrors, AM/FM cassette, power antenna, rear armrest, beverage holder; **wagon** has cargo cover, 195/60R15 87H tires. **EX** adds: 130-horsepower engine, anti-lock brakes, driver-seat lumbar support adjuster, front spoiler, power sunroof, sport suspension, upgraded audio system, 195/60R15 Michelin MXV3 tires on alloy wheels; wagon has 140-horse-power engine, remote keyless entry, alloy wheels.

OPTIONS are available as dealer-installed accessories.

1991 Jeep Cherokee	Retail Price	Dealer Invoice	Low Price
3-door 2WD, Pkg. 23A (2.5/5-speed)	$13187	$11890	$12140
3-door 2WD, 25A (4.0/5-speed)	14346	12919	13169
3-door 2WD, 26A (4.0/automatic)	14001	12581	12831
3-door 2WD, 25B (4.0/5-speed)	15024	13451	13701
3-door 2WD, 26B (4.0/automatic)	15901	14196	14446
3-door 4WD, 23A (2.5/5-speed)	15832	14227	14477
3-door 4WD, 25A (4.0/5-speed)	14744	13256	13506
3-door 4WD, 26A (4.0/automatic)	15621	14002	14252
3-door 4WD, 25B (4.0/5-speed)	16644	14871	15121
3-door 4WD, 26B (4.0/automatic)	17521	15617	15867
5-door 2WD, 23A (2.5/5-speed)	15357	13809	14259
5-door 2WD, 25A (4.0/5-speed)	14107	12701	13151
5-door 2WD, 26A (4.0/automatic)	14984	13447	13897
5-door 2WD, 25B (4.0/5-speed)	16007	14316	14766
5-door 2WD, 26B (4.0/automatic)	16884	15062	15512
5-door 4WD, 23A (2.5/5-speed)	16842	15116	15566
5-door 4WD, 25A (4.0/5-speed)	15727	14121	14571
5-door 4WD, 26A (4.0/automatic)	16604	14867	15317
5-door 4WD, 25B (4.0/5-speed)	17627	15736	16186
5-door 4WD, 26B (4.0/automatic)	18504	16482	16932

Pkg. 25B/26B: air conditioning, carpet, console with armrest, rear wiper/washer, roof rack, spare tire cover, tilt steering column, dual remote mirrors, intermittent wipers, wheel trim rings, 205/75R15 tires.

	Retail Price	Dealer Invoice	Low Price
Sport 3-door 2WD, 25C (5-speed)	13470	12130	12380
Sport 3-door 2WD, 26C (automatic)	14347	12876	13126
Sport 3-door 2WD, 25D (5-speed)	15123	13535	13785
Sport 3-door 2WD, 26D (automatic)	16000	14281	14531
Sport 3-door 4WD, 25C (5-speed)	15090	13550	13800
Sport 3-door 4WD, 26C (automatic)	15967	14296	14546
Sport 3-door 4WD, 25D (5-speed)	16743	14956	15206
Sport 3-door 4WD, 26D (automatic)	17620	15701	15951
Sport 5-door 2WD, 25C (5-speed)	14453	12995	13445
Sport 5-door 2WD, 26C (automatic)	15330	13741	14191
Sport 5-door 2WD, 25D (5-speed)	16106	14400	14850
Sport 5-door 2WD, 26D (automatic)	16983	15146	15596
Sport 5-door 4WD, 25C (5-speed)	16073	14451	14901

Prices are accurate at time of printing; subject to manufacturer's change.

CONSUMER GUIDE®

Sport 5-door 4WD, 26C (automatic)	16950	15161	15611
Sport 5-door 4WD, 25D (5-speed)	17726	15821	16271
Sport 5-door 4WD, 26D (automatic)	18603	16566	17016

Pkg. 25D/26D: air conditioning, cassette player, console with armrest, tachometer and gauges, spare tire cover, tilt steering column, dual remote mirrors, intermittent wipers.

Laredo 5-door 2WD, 25J (5-speed)	15937	14257	14707
Laredo 5-door 2WD, 26J (automatic)	16814	15002	15452
Laredo 5-door 2WD, 25K (5-speed)	18092	16088	16538
Laredo 5-door 2WD, 26K (automatic)	18969	16834	17284
Laredo 3-door 4WD, 25J (5-speed)	17174	15322	15572
Laredo 3-door 4WD, 25K (5-speed)	19184	17030	17280
Laredo 3-door 4WD, 26J (automatic)	18051	16067	16317
Laredo 3-door 4WD, 26K (automatic)	20061	17776	18026
Laredo 5-door 4WD, 25J (5-speed)	17557	15677	16127
Laredo 5-door 4WD, 26J (automatic)	18434	16422	16872
Laredo 5-door 4WD, 25K (5-speed)	19712	17509	17959
Laredo 5-door 4WD, 26K (automatic)	20589	18254	18704

Pkg. 25K/26K: air conditioning, power windows, power locks with keyless entry, cassette player with premium speakers, cruise control, tilt steering column.

Limited 5-door 4WD	24876	22176	22626
Briarwood 5-door 4WD	24799	22118	22568
Destination charge	485	485	485

Standard equipment:

2.5-liter PFI 4-cylinder or 4.0-liter PFI 6-cylinder engine, 5-speed manual or 4-speed automatic transmission, power steering, vinyl front bucket seats, folding rear seat, mini console, AM/FM radio, vinyl floor covering, tinted glass, 195/75R15 tires; **4WD** system is Command-Trac part-time. **Sport** adds: 4.0-liter 6-cylinder engine, carpet, hockey-stick-style armrests, cargo tiedown hooks, 225/75R15 outlined white letter all-terrain tires on alloy wheels. **Laredo** adds: reclining front bucket seats, fabric upholstery, cargo cover, skid strips, console with armrest and storage, rear defogger, upgraded sound insulation, tachometer, coolant temperature and oil pressure gauges, voltmeter, trip odometer, deep-tinted rear quarter windows (3-door), swing-out rear quarter windows (3-door), dual-note horn, headlamp delay system, misc. lights, dual outside mirrors, roof rack, spare tire cover, leather-wrapped steering wheel, intermittent wipers, rear wiper/washer, 215/75R15 outlined white letter tires. **Limited** adds: 4-speed automatic transmission, Selec-Trac transfer case, air conditioning, leather upholstery, power front seats, power windows, power locks with keyless entry, overhead console (with outside temperature readout, compass, bins, map lights), cruise control, fog lamps, deep-tinted glass, illuminated entry, power mirrors, cassette player, power antenna, tilt steering column, 225/70R15 Eagle GT+4 tires. **Briarwood** adds: bright trim, woodgrain exterior applique, 215/75R15 tires.

Optional equipment:

Anti-lock brakes	799	679	699
Available only on 4WD models with 4.0-liter engine and Selec-Trac.			
Air conditioning, base, Sport, & Laredo	836	711	732

Prices are accurate at time of printing; subject to manufacturer's change.

CAR PRICES

Selec-Trac, base, Sport, & Laredo 4WD	394	335	345
Carpet, base	209	178	183
Fabric seats, base & Sport	137	116	120
Console w/armrest, base & Sport	142	121	124
Rear defogger, base & Sport	161	137	141
Cassette player, base, Sport, & Laredo	201	171	176
Premium speakers, Laredo	174	148	152
Roof rack, base & Sport	139	118	122
Tilt steering column, base, Sport, & Laredo	132	112	116
Base & Sport require Visibility Group.			
Spare tire cover, Sport	46	39	40
Visibility Group, base & Sport	138	117	121
Dual outside mirrors, intermittent wipers.			
Rear wiper/washer, base & Sport	147	125	129
Deep-tinted glass, base & Sport 3-door	333	283	291
Tachometer & gauges, Sport	158	134	138
Front vent windows	91	77	80
Rear quarter vent windows, 3-doors	161	137	141
HD Alternator & Battery Group, base, Sport, & Laredo .	135	115	118
Base, Sport, & Laredo w/A/C	72	61	63
Fog lamps, Laredo	110	94	96
Overhead console, Laredo	203	173	178
Illuminated entry, Laredo	78	66	68
Requires Power Window & Lock Group.			
Power Window & Lock Group, Sport, & Laredo 3-door .	437	371	382
Sport & Laredo 5-door	582	495	509
Power windows, power locks with keyless entry.			
Power mirrors, Laredo	100	85	88
Power front seats, Laredo	416	354	364
Security alarm, Laredo	226	192	198
Includes illuminated entry; requires Power Window & Lock Group.			
Skid Plate Group, 4WD models	144	122	126
Cruise control, base, Sport, & Laredo	230	196	201
Tilt steering column, Laredo	132	112	116
Trailer Tow Pkg. B	358	304	313
4WD models w/Off-Road Pkg.	242	206	212
Off-Road Pkg. (4WD only), base	982	835	859
Sport	552	469	483
Laredo	579	492	507
Manual sunroof, Laredo	357	303	312
Limited & Briarwood	154	131	135
Protection Group, base & Sport	164	139	144
Front bumper guards, cargo skid strips, floormats, bodyside moldings.			
205/75R15 tires, base 2WD	46	39	40
215/75R15 OWL tires, base	359	305	314
Base 4WD w/Pkg. 25B/26B	313	266	274
Laredo	46	39	40
225/75R15 tires, base 4WD	405	344	354
Base 4WD w/Pkg. 25B/26B	359	305	314

Prices are accurate at time of printing; subject to manufacturer's change.

Spare tire cover, base	46	39	40
Outside spare tire carrier, base & Sport	173	147	151
Laredo	101	86	88
4 styled steel wheels, base	103	88	90
5 styled steel wheels, base	129	110	113
4 alloy wheels, base	348	296	305
Base w/Pkg. 25B/26B	283	241	248
5 alloy wheels, base	432	367	378
Base w/Pkg. 25B/26B	367	312	321
Leather-wrapped steering wheel, Sport	48	41	42
Metallic paint	173	147	151
California emissions pkg.	124	105	109

Lexus LS 400	Retail Price	Dealer Invoice	Low Price
4-door notchback	$42200	$33760	—
Destination charge	350	350	350

Low price not available at time of publication.

Standard equipment:

4.0-liter DOHC 32-valve PFI V-8, 4-speed automatic transmission, anti-lock braking system, 4-wheel disc brakes, power steering, driver-side air bag, automatic climate control, leather upholstery, reclining front bucket seats, power windows and locks, remote entry, cruise control, power mirrors, tachometer, trip odometer, coolant temperature gauge, tilt/telescopic steering column, AM/FM cassette, intermittent wipers, tool kit, first aid kit, 205/65VR15 tires on alloy wheels.

Optional equipment:

Moonroof	1000	800	923
Traction control & heated front seats	1700	1360	1569
Electronic air suspension	1500	1200	1385
Requires all-season tires and moonroof.			
Memory system	800	640	738
Lexus/Nakamichi audio system	1000	750	897
Requires CD changer.			
Remote 6-CD auto-changer	900	675	808
All-season tires	NC	NC	NC

Lexus SC 300/400	Retail Price	Dealer Invoice	Low Price
300 2-door notchback, 5-speed	$31100	—	—
300 2-door notchback, automatic	32000	—	—
400 2-door notchback	37500	30000	—
Destination charge	350	350	350

Low prices and 300 invoice prices not available at time of publication.

Prices are accurate at time of printing; subject to manufacturer's change.

CAR PRICES

Standard equipment:

300: 3.0-liter DOHC PFI V-6 engine, 5-speed manual or 4-speed automatic transmission, 4-wheel anti-lock disc brakes, variable-assist power steering, driver-side air bag, automatic climate control, tinted glass, power front seats, power tilt/telescoping steering wheel, rear defogger, heated power mirrors, power windows and door locks, remote keyless entry system, cruise control, tachometer, 7-speaker AM/FM cassette, power antenna, full size spare, 215/60VR15 Eagle GSD tires on alloy wheels. **400** adds: 4.0-liter DOHC PFI V-8 engine, 4-speed automatic transmission, leather upholstery, power front seats with driver-side memory system, 225/55VR16 Eagle GSD tires.

Optional equipment:

Traction control system	1600	1280	—
Includes heated front seats.			
Remote CD player w/auto changer	900	675	—
Lexus/Nakamichi premium sound system	1000	750	—
Requires CD player.			
Leather seats, 300	1700	NA	—
Includes memory system.			

Mazda 323/Protege	Retail Price	Dealer Invoice	Low Price
323 3-door hatchback	$6999	—	—
323 SE 3-door hatchback	8299	—	—
Protege DX 4-door notchback	9999	—	—
Protege LX 4-door notchback	11699	—	—
Destination charge	350	350	350

Dealer invoice and low price not available at time of publication.

Standard equipment:

323: 1.6-liter PFI 4-cylinder engine, 5-speed manual transmission, motorized front shoulder belts, vinyl reclining front bucket seats, one-piece folding rear seat, left remote mirror, coolant temperature gauge, trip odometer, cargo cover, console with storage, rear defogger, 155SR13 tires. **SE** adds: cloth upholstery, 60/40 split rear seat, dual remote mirrors, tinted glass, door pockets, bodyside moldings, wheel covers. **Protege DX**: 1.8-liter SOHC 16-valve 4-cylinder engine, 5-speed manual transmission, motorized front shoulder belts, cloth reclining front bucket seats, 60/40 folding rear seat, remote mirrors, coolant temperature gauge, trip odometer, console with storage, tinted glass, bodyside moldings, door pockets, remote fuel door and decklid releases, right visor mirror, digital clock, rear defogger, 175/70R13 tires. **LX** adds to DX: DOHC 16-valve engine, 4-wheel disc brakes, power steering, velour upholstery, power windows and locks, cruise control, AM/FM cassette, power mirrors, intermittent wipers, tachometer, cupholder, left visor mirror, 185/60R14 tires.

Optional equipment:

4-speed automatic transmission	700	630	649

Prices are accurate at time of printing; subject to manufacturer's change.

	Retail Price	Dealer Invoice	Low Price
Protege 4WD	750	675	695
Power steering, 323	250	213	226
Air conditioning	795	636	698
Convenience Pkg., 323 SE	—	—	—
Convenience Pkg., Protege DX	—	—	—
Value Pkg., Protege DX	270	238	248
Power steering, AM/FM cassette, tilt steering column, intermittent wipers.			
Value Pkg., Protege LX	1160	1009	1058
Air conditioning, power sunroof, alloy wheels.			
AM/FM cassette, 323 SE, Protege DX & 4WD	450	342	386
Power sunroof, Protege LX	555	444	487
Alloy wheels, Protege	NA	NA	NA
Floormats	59	43	50

Mazda Miata	Retail Price	Dealer Invoice	Low Price
2-door convertible	$14800	—	—
Destination charge	350	350	350

Dealer invoice and low price not available at time of publication.

Standard equipment:

1.6-liter DOHC 16-valve PFI 4-cylinder engine, 5-speed manual transmission, 4-wheel disc brakes, driver-side air bag, cloth reclining bucket seats, tachometer, coolant temperature gauge, trip odometer, intermittent wipers, remote decklid release, 185/60R14 tires.

Optional equipment:

4-speed automatic transmission	720	634	720
Anti-lock brakes	900	765	900
Requires Pkg. B; not available with CD player.			
Air conditioning	805	644	805
Detachable hardtop	1400	1134	1400
Includes rear defogger; requires Option Pkg. A or B.			
Option Pkg. A	1370	1151	1370
Power steering, alloy wheels, leather-wrapped steering wheel, AM/FM cassette.			
Option Pkg. B	1965	1651	1965
Pkg. A plus power windows, cruise control, headrest speakers, power antenna.			
Limited-slip differential	250	200	250
CD player	600	480	600
Requires Option Pkg. A or B.			
Floormats	59	43	59

Mazda MPV	Retail Price	Dealer Invoice	Low Price
Wagon, 5-pass., 2.6	$15165	—	—
Wagon, 7-pass., 2.6	16585	—	—
Wagon, 7-pass., 3.0	17365	—	—

Prices are accurate at time of printing; subject to manufacturer's change.

CAR PRICES

4WD wagon, 7-pass., 3.0   20135   —   —

Destination charge   400   400   400

Dealer invoice and low price not available at time of publication.

Standard equipment:

5-passenger: 2.6-liter PFI 4-cylinder engine, 4-speed automatic transmission, anti-lock rear brakes, power steering, reclining front bucket seats, 3-passenger middle bench seat, remote mirrors, tachometer, coolant temperature gauge, trip odometer, intermittent wipers, rear defogger and wiper/washer, tinted glass, door pockets, remote fuel door release, tilt steering column, AM/FM cassette, 205/70R14 tires. **7-passenger:** 2.6-liter 4-cylinder or 3.0-liter PFI V-6, two-passenger middle and 3-passenger rear bench seats, power mirrors. **4WD** has selectable 4WD, 215/65R15 tires on alloy wheels.

Optional equipment:

Single air conditioning	859	704	791
Dual air conditioning (3.0 req.)	1497	1228	1380
Eight-passenger seating	NA	NA	NA
Cold Pkg.	298	256	281
HD battery, larger windshield washer solvent reservoir, rear heater.			
Value Pkg. A, 2WD w/7-pass. seating	495	426	466
Power windows and locks, cruise control, privacy glass.			
Value Pkg. B, 2WD w/7-pass. seating	895	770	843
Pkg. A plus 215/65R15 tires on alloy wheels, color-keyed exterior treatment, pushbutton heater controls.			
Value Pkg. C, 4WD	695	598	655
Pkg. A plus color-keyed exterior treatment, pushbutton heater controls.			
Luxury Pkg. (Option Pkg. D), 2WD	3883	3223	3598
4WD	3423	2841	3172
Value Pkg. B (2WD), Value Pkg. C (4WD), leather seating, leather-wrapped steering wheel, color-keyed bodyside moldings, two-tone paint, lace alloy wheels.			
CD player	699	559	637
Requires Value Pkg. B or C, or Luxury Pkg.			
Power moonroof	NA	NA	NA
Two-tone paint	251	206	231
Towing Pkg., 2WD w/3.0	498	428	469
4WD automatic	398	342	375
Transmission oil cooler, HD radiator and fan, conventional spare, automatic load leveling (2WD).			
Floormats, w/5-pass. seating	59	42	51
w/7-pass. seating	84	59	72

Mercury Grand Marquis	Retail Price	Dealer Invoice	Low Price
GS 4-door notchback	$19361	$16697	$17497
LS 4-door notchback	19789	17061	17861
Destination charge	535	535	535

Prices are accurate at time of printing; subject to manufacturer's change.

Standard equipment:

GS: 4.6-liter PFI V-8, 4-speed automatic transmission, 4-wheel disc brakes, power steering, driver-side air bag, cloth split bench seat with recliners and dual armrests, air conditioning, power windows and mirrors, tinted glass, AM/FM radio, right visor mirror, intermittent wipers, tilt steering column, trip odometer, Autolamp system, remote fuel door release, automatic parking brake release, 215/70R15 tires. **LS** adds: upgraded upholstery, rear head restraints.

Optional equipment:

Anti-lock brakes w/Traction Assist	1035	880	932
Passenger-side air bag	488	415	439
Preferred Pkg. 156A, GS	1082	920	974
Power driver's seat, illuminated entry, cruise control, rear defogger, Power Lock Group, Luxury Light Group, bodyside paint stripe, floor mats, WSW tires.			
Preferred Pkg. 157A, GS	1348	1146	1213
Pkg. 156A plus cassette player, locking radial-spoked wheel covers.			
Preferred Pkg. 172A, LS	1549	1317	1394
Pkg. 157A plus front cornering lamps, leather-wrapped steering wheel, cassette player, aluminum wheels, power antenna.			
Rear defogger	160	136	144
Insta-Clear windshield	305	259	275
Power Lock Group	276	235	248
Includes remote decklid release.			
Illuminated entry system	82	70	74
Keyless entry system	137	116	123
Handling and Performace Pkg.	1952	1659	1757
w/Pkg. 172A	1430	1216	1287
w/Pkgs. 156A or 157A	1870	1590	1683
Includes performance springs, shocks and stabilizer bars, alloy wheels, anti-lock brakes w/electronic traction control, dual exhaust w/ 210 bhp engine rating, 3.27 axle ratio, 225/70R15 tires. Not available with Trailer Towing Pkg., Electronic Group, other wheel, wheel cover, tire options, or conventional spare tire w/JBL audio system.			
Rear air-spring suspension	285	242	257
Trailer Towing Pkg.	490	417	441
Power driver's seat	290	247	261
Power front seats w/power lumbar	779	662	701
With Pkg. 156A, 157A, or 172A	489	416	440
Leather seat trim, LS	555	472	500
Requires power front seats.			
Cruise control	210	179	189
AM/FM cassette	155	132	140
Radio delete option (credit)	(206)	(175)	(175)
High-level audio system	490	417	441
With Pkg. 157A or 172A	335	285	302
Ford JBL audio system	488	415	439
Power antenna	82	70	74
Electronic Group	516	439	464

Prices are accurate at time of printing; subject to manufacturer's change.

Automatic climate control, digital instrumentation, trip computer. Requires rear window defogger.

215/70R15 WSW all-season tires	82	70	74
Conventional spare tire	85	72	77
Cast aluminum wheels	440	374	396
With Pkg. 157A	129	110	116
Locking radial-spoked wheel covers	311	264	280
Front cornering lamps	68	58	61
Luxury Light Group	179	152	161
Leather-wrapped steering wheel	63	54	57
Requires cruise control.			
Heavy duty battery	27	23	24
Front floor mats	26	22	23
Rear floor mats	17	14	15
Engine block heater	26	22	23
Bodyside paint stripe	61	52	55
California emissions pkg.	100	85	90

Mercury Sable	Retail Price	Dealer Invoice	Low Price
GS 4-door notchback	$16351	$14089	$14464
LS 4-door notchback	17031	14896	15271
GS 5-door wagon	17329	14920	15295
LS 5-door wagon	18328	15769	16144
Destination charge	490	490	490

Standard equipment:

3.0-liter PFI V-6, 4-speed automatic transmission, power steering, driver-side air bag, air conditioning, cloth reclining 50/50 front seat with armrests, tinted glass, intermittent wipers, tachometer, coolant temperature gauge, trip odometer, power mirrors, tilt steering column, AM/FM radio, slide-out cupholders and coin holder, front door pockets, rear armrest (4-door), covered package tray storage bin (4-door), visor mirrors, cargo net, 205/70R14 tires; **wagon** has 60/40 folding rear seat, tiedown hooks, luggage rack. **LS** adds: power windows, automatic parking brake release, remote fuel door and decklid releases, Light Group, bodyside cladding, power lumbar supports, seatback pockets, lighted visor mirrors.

Optional equipment:

3.8-liter V-6	555	472	488
3.0-liter V-6, wagons (credit)	(555)	(472)	(472)
Passenger-side air bag	488	415	429
Anti-lock 4-wheel disc brakes	985	838	867
Automatic climate control, LS	183	155	161
Preferred Pkg. 450A, GS	909	773	800
Power windows and locks, cruise control, rear defogger.			
Preferred Pkg. 451A, GS	1259	1069	1108
Pkg. 450A plus power driver's seat, cassette player, Light Group, floormats, alloy wheels.			

Prices are accurate at time of printing; subject to manufacturer's change.

Preferred Pkg. 461A, LS	1546	1315	1360

3.8-liter V-6, power driver's seat, leather-wrapped steering wheel, cruise control, rear defogger, cassette player with premium sound, power antenna, power locks, floormats, alloy wheels.

Preferred Pkg. 462A, LS	2344	1994	2063

Pkg. 461A plus keyless entry, electronic instruments, Autolamp system, automatic climate control, High Level Audio System.

Autolamp system, LS	73	62	64
Cargo area cover, wagons	66	56	58
Rear defogger	170	144	150
Extended-range fuel tank	46	39	40
Electronic instruments, LS	351	299	309
Includes extended-range fuel tank.			
Keyless entry, LS	228	194	201
Includes illuminated entry; requires Power Lock Group.			
Light Group, GS	59	50	52
Power Lock Group, GS	358	305	315
LS	257	219	226
Power locks, remote fuel door and decklid releases.			
Power moonroof, LS	776	659	683
Cassette player	171	145	150
High Level Audio System, GS (450A), LS (462A)	502	427	442
GS w/Pkg. 451A	332	282	292
LS w/Pkg. 461A	163	139	143
CD player	491	418	432
Requires High Level Audio System.			
Ford JBL sound system, 4-doors	526	447	463
High Level Audio System or CD player.			
Premium sound system	168	143	148
Power antenna	85	73	75
AM/FM radio delete (credit)	(206)	(175)	(175)
Rear-facing third seat, wagons	155	132	136
Power front seats, each	305	259	268
Bucket seats w/console, GS	NC	NC	NC
Leather seat trim, LS	515	437	453
Vinyl seat trim, GS wagon	37	31	33
Cruise control	224	191	197
Leather-wrapped steering wheel	96	82	84
Requires cruise control.			
HD suspension	26	22	23
Rear wiper/washer, wagons	135	115	119
Requires rear defogger.			
Power windows, GS	356	303	313
Requires rear defogger.			
Picnic tray, wagons	90	77	79
Conventional spare tire	73	62	64
Alloy wheels	270	229	238
Engine block heater	20	17	18
Floormats	45	38	40

Prices are accurate at time of printing; subject to manufacturer's change.

CAR PRICES

HD battery	27	23	24
California emissions pkg.	100	85	88

Mercury Tracer	Retail Price	Dealer Invoice	Low Price
4-door notchback	$9773	$8828	$9128
5-door wagon	10794	9737	10037
LTS 4-door notchback	12023	10831	11131
Destination charge	375	375	375

Standard equipment:

1.9-liter PFI 4-cylinder engine, 5-speed manual transmission, motorized front shoulder belts, cloth reclining front bucket seats, 60/40 split rear seatback, AM/FM radio, tachometer, coolant temperature gauge, right seatback pocket, tinted glass, 175/70R13 tires. **Wagon** adds: power steering, variable intermittent wipers, remote fuel door release, power mirrors, rear defogger, cargo cover, rear wiper/washer, 175/65R14 tires, full wheel covers. **LTS** adds: 1.8-liter DOHC 16-valve engine, 4-wheel disc brakes, sport suspension, tilt steering column, AM/FM cassette, remote decklid release, Light Group, driver-seat tilt adjustment, cruise control, center console with removable tray, leather-wrapped steering wheel, 185/60R14 82H tires on alloy wheels.

Optional equipment:

4-speed automatic transmission	732	622	641
Requires power steering.			
Power steering, base 4-door	261	200	228
Air conditioning	759	632	664
Requires power steering.			
Preferred Pkg. 572A, base 4-door	543	460	475
Wagon	116	98	102
Power steering, intermittent wipers, remote fuel door and decklid releases, power mirrors, rear defogger, Light Group, full wheel covers.			
Preferred Pkg. 573B, base 4-door	1234	1046	1080
Wagon	657	557	575
Pkg. 572A plus air conditioning, driver-seat tilt adjustment, tilt steering column.			
Preferred Pkg. 575A, base 4-door	1584	1346	1386
Rear defogger, base	170	144	149
Remote fuel door release, base	41	35	36
Remote decklid release, base	60	51	53
Driver-seat tilt adjustment, base	37	31	32
Light Group, base	116	98	102
Tilt steering column, base	145	123	127
Cruise control, base	224	191	196
Power windows	330	281	289
Power mirrors, base 4-door	98	83	86
Power locks	205	174	179
Intermittent wipers, base 4-door	65	55	57
Luggage rack, wagon	115	97	101

Prices are accurate at time of printing; subject to manufacturer's change.

Cassette player, base	155	132	136
Premium sound system	138	117	121
Requires cassette player.			
Power moonroof (NA wagon)	549	466	480
AM/FM delete, base (credit)	(245)	(208)	(208)
AM/FM cassette delete, LTS (credit)	(400)	(340)	(340)
175/65R14 tires, base 4-door	132	112	116
Engine block heater	20	17	18
California emissions pkg	72	61	63

Mitsubishi Eclipse

	Retail Price	Dealer Invoice	Low Price
3-door hatchback, 5-speed	$11259	$9852	$10556
3-door hatchback, automatic	11919	10427	11173
GS 1.8 3-door hatchback, 5-speed	12529	10900	11715
GS 1.8 3-door hatchback, automatic	13189	11475	12332
GS DOHC 3-door hatchback, 5-speed	13469	11719	12594
GS DOHC 3-door hatchback, automatic	14129	12294	13212
GS Turbo 3-door hatchback, 5-speed	17109	14886	15998
GS Turbo 3-door hatchback, automatic	17899	15575	16737
GSX 3-door hatchback, 5-speed	18849	16402	17626
GSX 3-door hatchback, automatic	19649	17091	18370
Destination charge	368	368	368

Standard equipment:

1.8-liter PFI 4-cylinder engine, 5-speed manual or 4-speed automatic transmission, 4-wheel disc brakes, motorized front shoulder belts, cloth reclining front bucket seats, split folding rear seat, tilt steering column, map lights, remote fuel door and hatch releases, visor mirrors, tachometer, coolant temperature gauge, dual trip odometers, intermittent wipers, automatic-off headlamp feature, AM/FM radio, tinted glass, remote mirrors, 185/70R14 tires. **GS** adds: power steering, 3-way driver's seat, upgraded door panels, power mirrors, rear defogger, cargo cover, center console with coin and cup holders, AM/FM cassette, full wheel covers. **GS DOHC** adds: 2.0-liter DOHC 16-valve engine, sport suspension, power antenna, 205/55HR16 tires. **GS DOHC Turbo** adds: turbocharged engine, air conditioning, rear wiper/washer, air dam and rear spoiler, sill extensions, 6-way front sport seats, cruise control, power windows and door locks, leather-wrapped steering wheel, V-rated tires on alloy wheels. **GSX** adds: permanent 4-wheel drive, limited-slip differential, dual exhausts.

Optional equipment:

Anti-lock brakes, GS Turbo, GSX	943	773	858
Power steering, base	267	219	243
Air conditioning	827	678	753
AM/FM cassette, base	173	142	158
AM/FM cassette w/EQ, GS DOHC & GSX	212	174	193
AM/FM cassette w/CD player, Turbo & GSX	718	589	654
Power Pkg., exc. base	459	376	418

Prices are accurate at time of printing; subject to manufacturer's change.

Power windows and locks.

	Retail Price	Dealer Invoice	Low Price
Alloy wheels, GS DOHC	321	263	292
Rear wiper/washer (std. Turbo)	132	108	120
Cruise control (std. Turbo)	213	175	194
Sunroof (NA base)	373	306	340
Rear defogger, base	121	103	112
Wheel covers, base	102	84	93
Rear spoiler, GS DOHC	339	278	309
Wheel locks, Turbo & GSX	29	19	24
Floormats	56	37	47

Nissan Maxima	Retail Price	Dealer Invoice	Low Price
GXE 4-door notchback, automatic	$19695	—	—
SE 4-door notchback, 5-speed	20815	—	—
SE 4-door notchback, automatic	21750	—	—
Destination charge	300	300	—

Dealer invoice and low price not available at time of publication.

Standard equipment:

3.0-liter PFI V-6, 4-speed automatic transmission, power steering, motorized front shoulder belts, air conditioning, power windows and locks, keyless entry system, velour reclining front bucket seats, driver-seat height and lumbar adjustments, power mirrors, cruise control, tinted glass, AM/FM cassette with diversity antenna, motorized front shoulder belts with manual lap belts, theft deterrent system, tilt steering column, variable intermittent wipers, rear defogger, remote fuel door and decklid releases, illuminated entry, tachometer, trip odometer, coolant temperature gauge, digital clock, 205/65R15 tires on alloy wheels. **SE** deletes keyless entry and adds: 3.0-liter DOHC PFI V-6 engine, 5-speed manual or 4-speed automatic transmission, 4-wheel disc brakes, limited slip differential, Nissan-Bose audio system, rear spoiler, leather-wrapped steering wheel and shifter.

Optional equipment:

Anti-lock brakes	995	—	—
Driver-side air bag	500	—	—
Luxury Pkg., GXE	2225	—	—
Power sunroof, 4-way power front seats, Nissan-Bose audio system, automatic climate control, leather-wrapped steering wheel and shifter.			
Leather Trim Pkg., GXE	1000	847	—
SE	1400	—	—
SE includes 4-way power front seats; requires Luxury Pkg. on GXE.			
Pearlglow paint	350	297	—
Power sunroof	825	—	—

Nissan Sentra	Retail Price	Dealer Invoice	Low Price
E 2-door notchback, 4-speed	$8495	—	—

Prices are accurate at time of printing; subject to manufacturer's change.

E 2-door notchback, automatic	9565	—	—
XE 2-door notchback, 5-speed	9880	—	—
XE 2-door notchback, automatic	10605	—	—
SE 2-door notchback, 5-speed	10560	—	—
SE 2-door notchback, automatic	11285	—	—
SE-R 2-door notchback	11850	—	—
E 4-door notchback, 5-speed	9550	—	—
E 4-door notchback, automatic	10525	—	—
XE 4-door notchback, 5-speed	10565	—	—
XE 4-door notchback, automatic	11290	—	—
GXE 4-door notchback, 5-speed	12950	—	—
GXE 4-door notchback, automatic	13675	—	—
Destination charge	300	300	300

Dealer invoice and low price not available at time of publication.

Standard equipment:

E 2-door: 1.6-liter DOHC 16-valve PFI 4-cylinder engine, 4-speed manual or 3-speed automatic transmission, door-mounted automatic front shoulder belts, cloth reclining front bucket seats, rear defogger, coolant temperature gauge, trip odometer, 155/80R13 tires (models with automatic transmission have 175/70R13 tires, power steering, and tilt steering column); **4-door** has motorized front shoulder belts, 5-speed manual or 3-speed automatic transmission, right visor mirror. **XE** adds: 5-speed manual or 4-door automatic transmission, power steering, tilt steering column, power mirrors, bodyside molding, intermittent wipers, right visor mirror, digital clock, 175/70R13 tires. **GXE** adds: air conditioning, power windows and locks, AM/FM cassette with diversity antenna, cruise control, velour upholstery, tachometer, storage bin under passenger seat, alloy wheels. **SE** adds to XE: multi-adjustable seats with upgraded upholstery, rear spoiler; deletes bodyside molding. **SE-R** adds: 2.0-liter engine, 4-wheel disc brakes, limited-slip differential, sport suspension, bodyside molding, fog lights, 185/60R14 tires on alloy wheels.

Optional equipment:

Anti-lock brakes, GXE & SE-R	700	593	—
Air conditioning (std. GXE)	850	720	—
Power sunroof, GXE & SE-R	825	NA	NA
Not available with anti-lock brakes on GXE.			
Value Option Pkg., E & XE	995	843	—
SE & SE-R	1295	NA	NA
Air conditioning, AM/FM cassette, cruise control.			
Cruise control (NA E)	220	NA	NA
AM/FM cassette (NA E)	450	NA	NA
Metallic paint, E	100	85	93
California emissions pkg.	70	NA	NA

	Retail Price	Dealer Invoice	Low Price
Oldsmobile Eighty Eight Royale			
4-door notchback	$18495	$16054	—

Prices are accurate at time of printing; subject to manufacturer's change.

CAR PRICES

LS 4-door notchback 21395   18571   —

Destination charge   555   555   555

Low price not available at time of publication.

Standard equipment:

3.8-liter PFI V-6, 4-speed automatic transmission, power steering, driver-side air bag, air conditioning, 55/45 cloth front seat with armrest, power windows, left remote and right manual mirrors, tinted glass, AM/FM radio, intermittent wipers, tilt steering column, Pass-Key theft-deterrent system, trip odometer, glove box and courtesy lights, 205/70R15 all-season whitewall tires. **LS** adds: anti-lock brakes, cruise control, power locks, power mirrors, front seat recliners, AM/FM cassette, power antenna, floormats, front armrest with storage.

Optional equipment:

Option Pkg. 1SB, base 1212   1030   —
Front seat recliners, front storage armrest, cruise control, power mirrors, power locks, power driver's seat, rear defogger, floormats.
Option Pkg. 1SC 2173   1847   —
Pkg. 1SB plus anti-lock brakes, remote keyless entry system, power antenna, front and rear reading lamps, reminder package, cargo net.
Option Pkg. 1SC, LS 1152   979   —
Automatic climate control, power driver-seat, remote keyless entry system, rear defogger, cornering lamps, reminder package.
Option Pkg. 1SD 1713   1456   —
Pkg. 1SC plus power front passenger's seat, rear seat storage armrest, lighted visor mirrors, automatic day/night mirror.
LSS Pkg., LS 1995   1696   —
Rear defogger   170   145   —
Electriclear heated windshield, LS   250   213   —
Touring Suspension Pkg.   718   610   —
LS w/leather seats   664   564   —
Special suspension and steering, leather-wrapped steering wheel, automatic load-leveling suspension, 225/60R16 tires on alloy wheels. Requires Option Pkg. 1SB, 1SC, or 1SD. Not available with wire wheel covers or 15" alloy wheels.
Towing Pkg.   325   276   —
w/Touring Suspension Pkg   150   128   —
HD and automatic load-leveling suspension, 3.06 axle ratio, oil cooler, high-capacity battery and cooling system. Requires Option Pkg. 1SB, 1SC, or 1SD.
Traction control system, LS   175   149   —
Engine block heater   18   15   —
Leather seats w/rear storage armrest, LS   565   480   —
w/1SD   515   438   —
Striping   45   38   —
Wire wheel covers   240   204   —
Locking 15" alloy wheels w/blackwall tires   274   233   —
w/whitewall tires   330   281   —
Electronic instrumentation, LS   449   382   —

Prices are accurate at time of printing; subject to manufacturer's change.

Requires Pkg. 1SC or 1SD.

AM/FM cassette, base	240	204	—
AM/FM cassette w/EQ, LS	120	102	—
AM/FM cassette and CD, LS	396	337	—
AM/FM cassette and CD w/EQ, LS	516	439	—
Warranty enhancements for New York state	25	21	—
California emissions pkg.	100	85	—

Plymouth Acclaim	Retail Price	Dealer Invoice	Low Price
4-door notchback w/Pkg. 21A (2.5-liter/5-speed)	$11470	$10264	$10549
w/Pkg. 22A (automatic 3)	12027	10737	11022
Standard equipment.			
w/Pkg. 21C (5-speed)	11900	10629	10914
w/Pkg. 22D (2.5-liter/automatic 3)	12457	11103	11388
w/Pkg. 26D (3.0-liter/automatic 3)	13182	11719	12004
Pkg. 21A plus air conditioning, rear defogger, tilt steering column, cruise control, 4 speakers, tinted glass, floormats.			
w/Pkg. 22E (2.5-liter/automatic 3)	13194	11729	12014
w/Pkg. 26E (3.0-liter/automatic 3)	13919	12345	12630
w/Pkg. 28E (3.0-liter/automatic 4)	14002	12416	12701
Pkg. 21C/22D/26D plus power windows and locks, power mirrors, remote decklid release.			
Destination charge	485	485	485

Standard equipment:

2.5-liter TBI 4-cylinder engine, 5-speed manual transmission, power steering, driver-side air bag, cloth reclining front bucket seats, coolant temperature gauge, voltmeter, trip odometer, dual remote mirrors, AM/FM radio with two speakers, remote decklid release, intermittent wipers, misc. lights, visor mirrors, bodyside moldings, 185/70R14 tires.

Engines and transmissions: 2.5-liter TBI 4-cylinder with 5-speed manual or 3-speed automatic transmission, 3.0-liter PFI V-6 with 3- or 4-speed automatic transmission.

Optional equipment:

Anti-lock brakes	899	764	791
Console & Armrest Group, w/21C	81	69	71
Front armrest; requires bucket seats.			
w/Pkg. D or E	155	132	136
Full floor console with armrest; requires bucket seats.			
Interior Illumination Group	293	249	258
Illuminated entry system, lighted visor mirrors, message center, map and underhood lights, cigarette lighter; requires Pkg. E.			
Rear defogger, base	173	147	152
50/50 split front seat	102	87	90
Requires automatic transmission.			
w/split folding rear seat	250	213	220
Requires Pkg. D or E.			

Prices are accurate at time of printing; subject to manufacturer's change.

CAR PRICES

Front bucket seats	148	126	130
Includes split folding rear seat.			
Cassette player w/4 speakers	155	132	136
Cassette player w/Infinity speakers	430	366	378
Power driver's seat	296	252	260
195/70R14 whitewall tires, w/22D & 22E	104	88	92
w/26 or 28E	73	62	64
Conventional spare tire	95	81	84
w/195/70R14	95	81	84
Extra-cost paint	77	65	68
California emissions pkg.	102	87	90

Plymouth Laser	Retail Price	Dealer Invoice	Low Price
3-door hatchback (5-speed)	$11206	$10331	$10731
w/Pkg. 21B (5-speed)	11814	10848	11248
w/Pkg. 22B (automatic)	12515	11444	11844
B Pkgs. add: power steering, rear defogger, tonneau cover, console cupholder, wheel covers, floormats.			
w/Pkg. 21C (5-speed)	12641	11551	11951
w/Pkg. 22C (automatic)	13342	12147	12547
C Pkg. adds to B: air conditioning.			
w/Pkg. 21D (5-speed)	13052	11901	12301
w/Pkg. 22D (automatic)	13753	12496	12896
D Pkg. adds to C: cassette player, cruise control.			
RS 3-door hatchback (5-speed)	13101	11981	12381
w/Pkg. 23F (5-speed)	13928	12683	13083
w/Pkg. 24F (automatic)	14629	13280	13680
F Pkg. adds: air conditioning.			
w/Pkg. 23G (5-speed)	14311	13009	13409
w/Pkg. 24G (automatic)	15012	13605	14005
G Pkg. adds to F: cassette player w/EQ, console cupholder, rear wiper/washer, floormats.			
w/Pkg. 23H (5-speed)	15032	13622	14022
w/Pkg. 24H (automatic)	15733	14218	14618
H Pkg. adds to G: power windows and locks, cruise control, fog lights.			
RS Turbo 3-door hatchback (5-speed)	14392	13143	13543
w/Pkg. 25G (5-speed)	15602	14171	14571
w/Pkg. 26G (automatic)	16442	14885	15285
G Pkg. adds to F: air conditioning, cassette player with EQ, console cupholder, rear wiper/washer, floormats.			
w/Pkg. 25H (5-speed)	16323	14784	15184
w/Pkg. 26H (automatic)	17163	15498	15898
K Pkg. adds to G: power windows and locks, cruise control, fog lights.			
RS Turbo 4WD 3-door hatchback (5-speed)	16368	14921	15321
w/Pkg. 25N (5-speed)	17195	15624	16024
N Pkg. adds: air conditioning.			
w/Pkg. 25P (5-speed)	17578	15950	16350
P Pkg. adds to N: console with cupholder, floormats, cassette player with EQ, rear			

Prices are accurate at time of printing; subject to manufacturer's change.

wiper/washer.
w/Pkg. 25Q (5-speed) 18299   16563   16963
Q Pkg. adds to P: power windows and locks, cruise control, fog lights.

Destination charge 368   368   368

Standard equipment:

1.8-liter PFI 4-cylinder engine, 5-speed manual or 4-speed automatic transmission, motorized front shoulder belts, cloth reclining front bucket seats, split folding rear seatback, center console, tachometer, coolant temperature and oil pressure gauges, trip odometer, tinted glass, remote fuel door and hatch releases, dual remote mirrors, visor mirrors, AM/FM radio, tilt steering column, intermittent wipers, 185/70R14 tires. **RS** adds: 2.0-liter DOHC PFI 4-cylinder engine, power steering, driver-seat lumbar-support adjustment, rear defogger, center armrest, power mirrors, cassette player, tonneau cover, 205/55HR16 tires. **RS Turbo** adds: turbocharged, intercooled engine, 205/55VR16 tires. **RS Turbo 4WD** adds: sport suspension, alloy wheels.

Optional equipment:

4-speed automatic transmission, Base & RS 701   596   631
   RS Turbo 2WD 840   714   756
Anti-lock brakes, RS & RS Turbo 943   802   849
   RS requires Pkg. H; RS Turbo 2WD requires Pkg. H; RS Turbo 4WD requires Pkg. Q.
Cassette player, base w/Pkg. B or C 198   168   178
CD player, RS & RS Turbo 2WD w/Pkg. H; RS Turbo 4WD
   w/Pkg. Q 506   430   455
Rear defogger, base 127   108   114
Sunroof 373   317   336
Alloy wheels, RS & RS Turbo 2WD 321   273   289
   RS requires Pkg. G or H.

Plymouth Voyager	Retail Price	Dealer Invoice	Low Price
Base SWB w/Pkg. 21S (2.5-liter/5-speed)	$13678	$12287	$12983
w/Pkg. 22S (2.5-liter/automatic 3)	14254	12776	13515
w/Pkg. 24S (3.0-liter/automatic 3)	14948	12366	13657
Base standard equipment.			
w/Pkg. 21T (2.5-liter/5-speed)	13891	12468	13180
w/Pkg. 22T (2.5-liter/automatic 3)	14467	12957	13712
w/Pkg. 24T (3.0-liter/automatic 3)	15161	13547	14354
21-24T add: air conditioning, dual-note horn, remote liftgate release, map and cargo area lights, bodyside moldings, storage drawer under front passenger seat.			
Base Grand w/Pkg. 24E (3.0-liter/automatic 3)	17174	15362	16268
Base standard equipment plus: air conditioning, map and cargo area lights.			
SE SWB w/Pkg. 22A (2.5-liter/automatic 3)	15527	13914	14721
w/Pkg. 24A (3.0-liter/automatic 3)	16221	14504	15363
w/Pkg. 26A (3.0-liter/automatic 4)	16394	14651	15523
w/Pkg. 28A (3.3-liter/automatic 4)	16496	14737	15617
SE SWB AWD w/Pkg. 28A (3.3-liter/automatic 4)	18698	16704	—

Prices are accurate at time of printing; subject to manufacturer's change.
CONSUMER GUIDE®

CAR PRICES

Grand SE w/Pkg. 28A (3.3-liter/automatic 4)	17359	15526	16443
Grand SE AWD w/Pkg. 28A (3.3-liter/automatic 4)	19455	17370	—
SE standard equipment.			
w/Pkg. 22B (2.5-liter/automatic 3)	15740	14095	14918
w/Pkg. 24B (3.0-liter/automatic 3)	16434	14685	15560
w/Pkg. 26B (3.0-liter/automatic 4)	16607	14832	15720
w/Pkg. 28A (3.3-liter/automatic 4)	16709	14918	15814
SE SWB AWD w/Pkg. 28B (3.3-liter/automatic 4)	18911	16885	
Grand SE w/Pkg. 28B (3.3-liter/automatic 4)	17572	15707	16640
Grand SE AWD w/Pkg. 28B (3.3-liter/automatic 4)	19668	17551	—
22-28B add: air conditioning, rear defogger, map and cargo area lights.			
w/Pkg. 22D (2.5-liter/automatic 3)	16879	15063	15971
w/Pkg. 24D (3.0-liter/automatic 3)	17573	15653	16613
w/Pkg. 26D (3.0-liter/automatic 4)	15800	17746	16773
w/Pkg. 28D (3.3-liter/automatic 4)	17848	15887	16868
SE SWB AWD w/Pkg. 28D (3.3-liter/automatic 4)	20050	17853	—
Grand SE w/Pkg. 28D (3.3-liter/automatic 4)	18711	16675	17693
Grand SE AWD w/Pkg. 28D (3.3-liter/automatic 4)	20807	18520	—
22-28D add to 22-28B: front console, cruise control, tilt steering column, added sound insulation, floormats, tachometer, oil pressure gauge, voltmeter, lighted visor mirrors, Light Group, power locks.			
LE SWB w/Pkg. 24J (3.0-liter/automatic 3)	19639	17538	18589
w/Pkg. 26J (3.0-liter/automatic 4)	19812	17685	18749
w/Pkg. 28J (3.3-liter/automatic 4)	19914	17771	18843
LE SWB AWD w/Pkg. 28J (3.3-liter/automatic 4)	22081	19681	
Grand LE w/Pkg. 28J (3.3-liter/automatic 4)	20621	18396	19509
Grand LE AWD w/Pkg. 28J (3.3-liter/automatic 4)	22321	19892	—
LE standard equipment.			
w/Pkg. 24K (3.0-liter/automatic 3)	20218	18030	19124
w/Pkg. 26K (3.0-liter/automatic 4)	20391	18172	19282
w/Pkg. 28K (3.3-liter/automatic 4)	20493	18263	19378
LE SWB AWD w/Pkg. 28K (3.3-liter/automatic 4)	22660	20173	
Grand LE w/Pkg. 28K (3.3-liter/automatic 4)	21200	18889	20045
Grand LE AWD w/Pkg. 28K (3.3-liter/automatic 4)	22900	20385	—
24-28K add: power driver's seat, power windows, Infinity I audio system, sunscreen glass, two-tone paint.			
w/Pkg. 24L (3.0-liter/automatic 3)	20899	18609	19754
w/Pkg. 26L (3.0-liter/automatic 4)	21072	18756	19914
w/Pkg. 28L (3.3-liter/automatic 4)	21174	18842	20008
LE SWB AWD w/Pkg. 28L (3.3-liter/automatic 4)	23267	20689	
Grand LE w/Pkg. 28L (3.3-liter/automatic 4)	21807	19405	20606
Grand LE AWD w/Pkg. 28L (3.3-liter/automatic 4)	23507	20901	—
24-28L add to 24-28K: Woodgrain Decor Group (woodgrain appliques and moldings, luggage rack, 205/70R15 whitewall tires; wire wheel covers); deletes two-tone paint.			
LE SWB w/LX Pkg. 24M (3.0-liter/automatic 3)	20899	18629	19764
w/LX Pkg. 26M (3.0-liter/automatic 4)	21072	18776	19924
w/LX Pkg. 28M (3.3-liter/automatic 4)	21174	18863	20019
LE SWB AWD w/LX Pkg. 28M (3.3-liter/automatic 4) . .	23220	20666	
24-28M adds to 24-28K: LX Decor Group (body-color fascia and cladding, rear sway			

Prices are accurate at time of printing; subject to manufacturer's change.

bar, fog lights, 205/70R15 tires on alloy wheels); deletes two-tone paint.

Destination charge   540   540   540

SWB denotes short wheelbase; AWD denotes All Wheel Drive.

AWD low prices not available at time of publication.

Engines and transmissions: 2.5-liter TBI 4-cylinder with 5-speed manual or 3-speed automatic tranmission; 3.0-liter PFI V-6 with 3- or 4-speed automatic transmission; 3.3-liter PFI V-6 with 4-speed automatic transmission.

Standard equipment:

Base: driver-side air bag, power steering, 5-passenger seating (front bucket seats, 3-passenger middle bench seat), tinted glass, trip odometer, coolant temperature gauge, dual outside mirrors, visor mirrors, AM/FM radio, intermittent wipers, rear wiper/ washer, 195/75R14 tires. **SE** adds: 7-passenger seating (2-passenger middle and 3-passenger rear bench seats), dual-note horn, power mirrors, remote liftgate release, rear trim panel storage and cup holders, striping, sport wheel covers. **LE** adds: front air conditioning, front storage console, overhead console with outside temperature readout and mini trip computer, rear defogger, power front windows, power quarter vent windows, power locks, remote fuel door release, tachometer, oil pressure gauge, voltmeter, illuminated entry, headlamp delay system, heated power mirrors, lighted visor mirrors, bodyside moldings, cruise control, tilt steering column, sport steering wheel, storage drawer under front passenger seat, floormats. **Grand** models have 3.3-liter PFI V-6, 4-speed automatic transmission (base has 3.0-liter PFI V-6, 3-speed automatic transmission), power mirrors, remote liftgate release, storage drawer under front passenger seat, sport wheel covers, 205/70R15 tires. **All Wheel Drive** models have 3.3-liter V-6, 4-speed automatic transmission, 7-passenger seating, power mirrors, 205/75R15 tires.

Optional equipment:

Anti-lock brakes, SWB SE w/3.3-liter V-6	687	584	632
SWB SE w/Trailer Towing Group, Sport Handling			
Group or 14″ whitewall tires, Grand SE	599	509	551
LE SWB w/J, K, or L Pkgs.	687	584	632
LE SWB w/M Pkg. and 3.3-liter V-6	599	509	551
LE w/Trailer Towing Group, Sport Handling			
Group or 14″ whitewall tires	599	509	551
Grand SE & LE	599	509	551
Front air conditioning, base & SE	857	728	788
Air conditioning w/rear heater, base Grand	699	594	643
Grand SE 28A/28B	699	594	643
Requires rear defogger.			
Grand SE 28A/28B w/Trailer Towing Group	636	541	585
Grand SE 28D	466	396	429
Grand SE 28D w/Trailer Towing Group.	404	343	372
Rear air conditioning, Grand LE	466	396	429
Grand LE w/Trailer Towing Group	571	485	525

Prices are accurate at time of printing; subject to manufacturer's change.

CAR PRICES

Grand SE 2WD w/Trailer Towing Group	509	433	468
Rear bench seat, base SWB	397	337	365
Includes rear trim panel storage area and cup holders.			
Seven-passenger seating w/integrated child seat,			
base SWB	597	507	549
SE & LE Grand	200	170	184
Quad Command Seating, SE & LE	597	507	549
Two front and two middle bucket seats, 3-passenger rear bench seat.			
Converta-Bed 7-pass. seating, SE SWB, base/SE Grand .	553	470	509
Leather trim, LE w/K, L, or M Pkgs	865	735	796
HD Trailer Tow Pkg., SE SWB	557	473	512
SE & LE w/L Pkg.	483	411	444
SE SWB w/Sport Handling Group	443	377	408
LE w/J or K Pkg. & Sport Handling Group	443	377	408
Grand SE/LE	443	377	408
HD alternator, battery, flasher, radiator, and transmission oil cooler, trailer wiring harness, HD suspension (2WD), sport wheel covers, 205/70R15 tires with conventional spare.			
Deluxe Convenience Pkg., base & SE	372	316	342
Cruise control, tilt steering column.			
Power Convenience Pkg., SE SWB w/A or B Pkgs.,			
Grand SE	530	451	488
SE w/D Pkg.	265	225	244
Power front windows, power locks.			
Sport Handling Pkg., SE SWB	207	176	190
Grand SE, Grand LE w/J, K, or M Pkgs.	93	79	86
LE SWB w/J, K, or M Pkgs.	207	176	190
HD brakes, rear sway bar, sport wheel covers, 205/70R15 tires.			
Rear defogger, base w/o Pkgs.	217	184	200
Base w/Pkgs. 22-28, SE	168	143	155
Base includes remote liftgate release w/Pkgs. 22-28.			
Power locks, base & SE	265	225	244
Sunscreen glass	414	352	381
Cassette player	155	132	143
Infinity I audio system, SE/LE	461	392	424
Infinity II system, SE/LE w/K, L, or M Pkgs.	214	182	197

Pontiac Bonneville	Retail Price	Dealer Invoice	Low Price
SE 4-door notchback sedan	$18599	$16144	—
SSE 4-door notchback sedan	23999	20831	—
SSEi 4-door notchback sedan	28045	24343	—
Destination charge	555	555	555

Low price not available at time of publication.

Standard equipment:

SE: 3.8-liter PFI V-6, 4-speed automatic transmission, power steering, driver-side air

Prices are accurate at time of printing; subject to manufacturer's change.

CONSUMER GUIDE®

bag, air conditioning, cloth 45/55 reclining front seats with armrest, rear armrest with cupholders, power windows, power locks, AM/FM radio, fog lamps, Pass-Key theft deterrent system, 215/65R15 tires on alloy wheels. **SSE** adds: anti-lock brakes, variable-assist power steering, electronic leveling, 45/45 bucket seats with console, rear defogger, cassette player with EQ, Driver Information Center, 225/60R16 touring tires on alloy wheels. **SSEi** adds: supercharged 3.8-liter PFI V-6, passenger-side air bag, traction control, automatic climate control, 12-way power front seats, illuminated remote keyless entry system, Head up Display, theft-deterrent system, 225/60ZR16 tires.

Optional equipment:

Anti-lock brakes, SE	450	383	—
Option Pkg. 1SB, SE	383	326	—
Cruise control, rally gauges, tachometer, Lamp Group.			
Option Pkg. 1SC, SE	901	766	—
Pkg. 1SB plus power driver's seat, power mirrors, illuminated entry system, remote decklid release.			
Option Pkg. 1SD, SE	1242	1056	—
Pkg. 1SC plus remote keyless entry system, lighted visor mirrors, Twilight Sentinel, leather-wrapped steering wheel.			
Option Pkg. 1SB, SSE	845	718	—
Passenger-side air bag, Head-up display, automatic climate control, remote keyless entry system, illuminated entry system, automatic day/night mirror, 8-speaker sound system.			
Option Pkg. R6A, SE	261	222	—
Monotone appearance pkg., 15-inch alloy wheels.			
Option Pkg. R6B, SE	424	360	—
Monotone appearance pkg., custom trim group, 225/60R16 BW touring tires on alloy wheels.			
Option Pkg. R6C, SE	200	170	—
Monotone appearance pkg., cassette player.			
Option Pkg. R6A, SSE	1835	1560	—
45/45 split front seat with leather trim, power sunroof.			
SSEi	1195	1016	—
Premium Equipment Pkg., SSE w/o Pkg. 1SB	1345	1143	—
Identical to SSE Option Pkg. 1SB.			
Convenience Group, SE w/Pkg. 1SB	213	181	—
Remote decklid release, illuminated entry system, power mirrors.			
Enhancement Group, SE w/Pkg. 1SC	206	175	—
Lighted visor mirrors, leather-wrapped steering wheel, Twilight Sentinel.			
Trailer Towing Pkg., SE	614	522	—
Engine and transmission oil coolers, sport suspension, 225/60R16 BW touring tires on alloy wheels.			
SE Sport Pkg., w/o Pkg. R6A, R6B, or R6C	1145	973	—
w/Pkg. R6A	659	560	—
w/Pkg. R6B	551	468	—
Pkg. R6C	965	820	—
Includes monotone appearance pkg., sport suspension, anti-lock brakes, dual exhausts, 225/60R16 BW touring tires on alloy wheels.			

Prices are accurate at time of printing; subject to manufacturer's change.

CAR PRICES

	Retail Price	Dealer Invoice	Low Price
Rear decklick spoiler, SE & SSE	95	81	—
Rear decklid spoiler delete, SSE (credit)	(95)	(81)	(81)
Traction control	175	149	—
Rear window defogger, SE & SSE	170	145	—
Heated windshield, SSE & SSEi	250	213	—
Power sunroof, SE w/o Pkg. 1SD, Enhancement group, & 45/45 bucket seats	1326	1127	—
SE w/Pkg. 1SD, Enhancement group, or 45/45 bucket seats	1230	1046	—
SSE & SSEi	1216	1034	—
45/45 bucket seats, SE w/Pkg. 1SB or 1SC	315	268	—
w/Pkg. 1SD	220	187	—
Includes floor and overhead consoles, lighted visor mirrors.			
45/45 articulating leather bucket seats, SSE	1419	1206	—
Custom interior trim, SE w/1SB, 1SC, or 1SD & w/o R6B	130	111	—
w/Option pkg. R6B	NC	NC	NC
Includes trunk security net.			
45/45 articulating leather seats, SSEi	779	662	—
Includes floor and overhead consoles with storage, power outlets.			
Power driver's seat, SE	305	259	—
Remote keyless entry system, SE & SSE	135	115	—
Theft-deterrent system, SSE	190	162	—
Cassette player, SE	140	119	—
Cassette w/EQ, SE w/o Pkg. R6C	650	553	—
SE w/Pkg. R6C	510	434	—
AM/FM w/EQ and CD player, SE w/o Pkg. R6C	876	745	—
SE w/Pkg. R6C	736	626	—
SSE & SSEi	226	192	—
Power antenna, SE	85	72	—
Monotone appearance pkg., SE w/o Sport pkg. & R6A, R6B, or R6C	180	153	—
w/Sport pkg. & R6A, R6B, or R6C	NC	NC	NC
16-inch cross-lace alloy wheels, SE w/o R6A & R6B	340	289	—
SE w/R6A	34	29	—
16-inch five-blade alloy wheels, SE w/o R6A	340	289	—
SE w/R6A	34	29	—
16-inch six-spoke alloy wheels, SE w/o R6A	306	260	—
215/65R15 BW touring tires, SE	NC	NC	NC
215/65R15 WW touring tires, SE	76	65	—
225/60R16 BW touring tires, SE w/o Sport pkg. & R6B	74	63	—
Engine block heater	18	15	—
Warranty enhancements for New York	25	21	—
California emissions pkg.	100	85	—

Subaru Legacy	Retail Price	Dealer Invoice	Low Price
L 4-door notchback	$11999	—	—
L 5-door wagon	12999	—	—
L 4WD 5-door wagon	14099	—	—

Prices are accurate at time of printing; subject to manufacturer's change.

L Plus 4-door notchback	12999	—	—
L Plus AWD 4-door notchback	14599	—	—
L Plus 5-door wagon	14499	—	—
L Plus AWD 5-door wagon	15099	—	—
LS 4-door notchback	18299	—	—
LS 4WD 4-door notchback	19799	—	—
LS 5-door wagon	18799	—	—
LS 4WD 5-door wagon	20299	—	—
LSi 4-door notchback	19699	—	—
LSi 4WD 4-door notchback	21199	—	—
Sport Sedan 4WD 4-door	18799	—	—
Destination charge	445	445	445

Dealer invoice and low price not available at time of publication.

Standard equipment:

L: 2.2-liter 16-valve PFI 4-cylinder engine, 5-speed manual transmission, 4-wheel disc brakes, power steering, motorized front shoulder belts, cloth reclining front bucket seats, split folding rear seat, driver's-seat lumbar support adjustment, power mirrors, bodyside moldings, rear defogger, tinted glass, tachometer and gauges, remote fuel door and decklid releases, cupholder, tilt steering column, intermittent wipers, 175/70HR14 tires. **L Plus** adds: air conditioning, power windows and locks, AM/FM cassette with equalizer, power antenna. **LS** adds: 4-speed automatic transmission, anti-lock brakes, driver-side air bag, cruise control, driver's-seat height adjustment, variable intermittent wipers, power antenna, power moonroof, rear armrest and trunk-through (4-door), lighted visor mirrors, leather-wrapped steering wheel and shift knob, air suspension (4WD wagon with automatic), 185/70HR14 tires on alloy wheels. **LSi** adds: leather upholstery and trim. **Sport Sedan** adds: turbocharged engine, 5-speed manual transmission, 4-wheel drive, sport seats, front air dam and rear spoiler, split folding rear seat, coin tray, full console, map lights, 195/60HR15 tires.

Optional equipment:

4-speed automatic transmission & air conditioning, L	1000	NA	NA
Anti-lock brakes & cruise control, L Plus wagon	1000	NA	NA
All other L Plus	1500	—	—
Driver-side air bag, L & L Plus	800	—	—

Toyota Camry	Retail Price	Dealer Invoice	Low Price
DLX 4-door notchback, 5-speed	$14368	—	—
DLX 4-door notchback, automatic	15168	—	—
LE 4-door notchback, automatic	16998	—	—
XLE 4-door notchback, automatic	18848	—	—
DLX V6 4-door notchback, automatic	16808	—	—
LE V6 4-door notchback, automatic	18638	—	—
XLE V6 4-door notchback, automatic	20508	—	—

Dealer invoice and low price not available at time of publication.

Prices are accurate at time of printing; subject to manufacturer's change.

CAR PRICES

Dealer invoice and destination charge may vary by region.

Standard equipment:

DLX: 2.2-liter DOHC 16-valve PFI 4-cylinder engine, 5-speed manual or 4-speed automatic transmission, driver-side air bag, power steering, tachometer, coolant temperature gauge, trip odometer, cloth reclining front bucket seats, split folding rear seat with armrest, remote fuel door and decklid releases, rear defogger, dual outside mirrors, front door pockets, tilt steering column, intermittent wipers, AM/FM radio, tinted glass, 195/70HR14 tires. **LE** adds: power mirrors, 5-way adjustable driver's seat, cruise control, power windows and locks, air conditioning, cassette player. **XLE** adds: power moonroof, 7-way power driver's seat with lumbar-support adjuster, illuminated entry, map lights, lighted visor mirrors, variable intermittent wipers, alloy wheels.

Optional equipment:

Anti-lock brakes, 4-cyl.	1245	—	—
V6	1130	—	—
Air conditioning	870	—	—
Leather trim, XLE	950	—	—
Alloy wheels, LE.	400	—	—
LE V6	420	—	—
Moonroof, LE	900	—	—
Includes map lights.			
Cruise control, DLX	230	—	—
AM/FM cassette, DLX	150	—	—
Includes power antenna.			
Premium AM/FM cassette, LE & XLE	290	—	—
Includes power antenna.			
CD player, XLE	990	—	—
California emissions pkg.	100	—	—

Toyota Corolla	Retail Price	Dealer Invoice	Low Price
4-door notchback, 5-speed	$9418	—	—
4-door notchback, automatic	9918	—	—
Deluxe 4-door notchback, 5-speed	10408	—	—
Deluxe 4-door notchback, automatic	10908	—	—
LE 4-door notchback, automatic	12598	—	—
Deluxe 5-door wagon, 5-speed	11078	—	—
Deluxe 5-door wagon, automatic	11578	—	—
Deluxe All-Trac wagon, 5-speed	12688	—	—
Deluxe All-Trac wagon, automatic	13498	—	—

Dealer invoice and low price not available at time of publication.

Dealer invoice and destination charge may vary by region.

Standard equipment:

1.6-liter DOHC 16-valve PFI 4-cylinder engine, 5-speed manual or 3-speed automatic

Prices are accurate at time of printing; subject to manufacturer's change.

transmission, door-mounted automatic front shoulder belts, cloth reclining front bucket seats, console with storage, coolant temperature gauge, trip odometer, door pockets, 155SR13 tires. **Deluxe** adds: rear defogger, remote fuel door and decklid releases, intermittent wipers, split folding rear seat (wagon). **All-Trac wagon** has permanent 4-wheel drive, 5-speed manual or 4-speed automatic transmission, mud guards, rear wiper, 165SR13 tires. **LE** adds: 4-speed automatic transmission, power steering, dual remote mirrors, AM/FM radio, 6-way driver's seat with lumbar support adjustment, split folding rear seatback, tachometer, tilt steering column, full wheel covers, 175/70SR13 tires.

Optional equipment:

Air conditioning	820	NA	NA
Power steering (std. LE)	250	NA	NA
Alloy wheels, LE	410	NA	NA
Includes 175/70R13 tires, mud guards.			
Exterior Appearance Pkg., Deluxe 4-door & All-Trac	85	NA	NA
Tilt steering column, Deluxe & All-Trac	120	NA	NA
Sunroof, Deluxe, LE, & All-Trac	550	NA	NA
Includes map lights, visor mirrors.			
Fabric seats, wagons	70	NA	NA
Rear wiper, 2WD wagon	135	NA	NA
Audio Accommodation Pkg., All-Trac	115	NA	NA
AM/FM radio w/2 speakers, wagons	210	NA	NA
AM/FM radio w/4 speakers (std. LE; NA wagon)	340	NA	NA
AM/FM cassette w/2 speakers, 2WD wagon	390	NA	NA
All-Trac	490	NA	NA
w/4 speakers, base & Deluxe 4-doors	490	NA	NA
w/4 speakers, LE	150	NA	NA
Power Pkg., LE	560	NA	NA
Power windows and locks.			
Tachometer, Deluxe w/5-speed, All-Trac	60	NA	NA
Cruise control, Deluxe & LE	230	NA	NA
Includes variable intermittent wipers.			
Split folding rear seat, Deluxe 4-door	110	NA	NA
Value Pkg., Deluxe 4-door	514	NA	NA
2WD wagon	524	NA	NA
All-Trac	580	NA	NA
LE	719	NA	NA

Deluxe: power steering, AM/FM cassette with 4 speakers (4-door; 2 speakers on wagon), digital clock, split folding rear seat, floormats, fabric seats (wagon). LE adds: air conditioning, power windows and locks, cruise control, variable intermittent wipers, floormats.

Two-tone paint, All-Trac	235	NA	NA
All Weather Guard Pkg., base 4-door	160	NA	NA
2WD wagon	190	NA	NA
Deluxe & LE 4-doors	55	NA	NA
HD battery, rear defogger, HD heater and boost ventilator, rear wiper (2WD wagon).			
California emissions pkg.	75	NA	NA

Prices are accurate at time of printing; subject to manufacturer's change.

CAR PRICES

Toyota MR2

	Retail Price	Dealer Invoice	Low Price
2-door notchback, 5-speed	$16048	—	—
2-door notchback, automatic	16848	—	—
2-door notchback w/T-bar roof, 5-speed	16998	—	—
Turbo 2-door notchback, 5-speed	19378	—	—
Turbo w/T-bar roof, 5-speed	20278	—	—

Dealer invoice and low price not available at time of publication.

Dealer invoice and destination charge may vary by region.

Standard equipment:

2.2-liter DOHC 16-valve PFI 4-cylinder engine, 5-speed manual or 4-speed automatic transmission, 4-wheel disc brakes, driver-side air bag, cloth reclining bucket seats, tilt steering column, AM/FM radio, tachometer, coolant temperature gauge, trip odometer, 195/60HR14 front and 205/60HR14 rear tires on alloy wheels. **Turbo** adds: 2.0-liter turbocharged engine, AM/FM cassette, power mirrors, rear spoiler, V-rated tires.

Optional equipment:

Anti-lock brakes	1130	NA	—
Electro-hydraulic power steering	600	NA	—
Air conditioning	NA	NA	NA
Pop-up/removable sunroof	380	NA	—
Power Pkg., base	575	NA	—
Turbo	465	NA	—
Power windows and locks, power mirrors (std. Turbo).			
Cruise control & intermittent wipers	265	NA	—
Rear spoiler, base	225	NA	—
Theft deterrent system	165	NA	—
Alloy wheels, base	400	NA	—
Leather Trim Pkg., base	1750	NA	—
Turbo	1275	NA	—
Seven-way leather seats, leather interior trim, power windows and locks, power mirrors, center storage box.			
AM/FM cassette, base	260	NA	—
Premium AM/FM cassette, base	635	NA	—
Base w/T-bar roof	570	NA	—
Turbo	310	NA	—
Includes seven speakers, biamplified woofer, power antenna.			
Premium AM/FM cassette w/CD player, base	1335	NA	—
Base w/T-bar roof	1270	NA	—
Turbo	1010	NA	—
California emissions pkg.	100	NA	—

Toyota Previa

	Retail Price	Dealer Invoice	Low Price
Deluxe 2WD, 5-speed	$16518	—	—
Deluxe 2WD, automatic	17318	—	—

Prices are accurate at time of printing; subject to manufacturer's change.

CONSUMER GUIDE®

LE 2WD, automatic	21448	—	—
Deluxe All-Trac, 5-speed	19128	—	—
Deluxe All-Trac, automatic	20018	—	—
LE All-Trac, automatic	24058	—	—

Dealer invoice and low price not available at time of publication.

Dealer invoice and destination charge may vary by region.

Standard equipment:

Deluxe: 2.4-liter DOHC 16-valve PFI 4-cylinder engine, 5-speed manual or 4-speed automatic transmission, driver-side air bag, power steering, tilt steering column, cloth reclining front bucket seats, 3-passenger middle seat, tinted glass, digital clock, dual outside mirrors, bodyside moldings, full carpet, full wheel covers, P205/75R14 tires. **LE adds:** dual air conditioning, 4-wheel disc brakes, power windows and locks, power mirrors, fold-down third seat, cruise control, rear defogger, power locks, privacy glass, AM/FM radio, intermittent wipers, P215/65R15 tires with full-size spare.

Optional equipment:

Anti-lock brakes, Deluxe	1405	NA	—
LE	1130	NA	—
Dual air conditioning, Deluxe	1500	NA	—
Convenience Pkg., Deluxe	710	NA	—
Rear defogger, fold-down third seat.			
Power Pkg., Deluxe	655	NA	—
Power windows and locks, power mirrors.			
Rear wiper & cruise control, Deluxe w/5-speed	455	NA	—
Deluxe w/automatic	395	NA	—
Privacy glass, LE	365	NA	—
Cruise control, Deluxe w/5-speed	300	NA	—
Includes tachometer.			
Deluxe w/automatic	240	NA	—
AM/FM radio, Deluxe	340	NA	—
AM/FM cassette, Deluxe	530	NA	—
LE	190	NA	—
Premium AM/FM cassette, LE	500	NA	—
Premium AM/FM cassette w/CD, LE	1230	NA	—
Dual sunroofs, LE	1470	NA	—
Captain's chairs w/armrests, LE	750	NA	—
Fold-down third seat, Deluxe	600	NA	—
Theft deterrent system, Deluxe	165	NA	—
LE	410	NA	—
Alloy wheels, LE	420	NA	—
Full-size spare tire, Deluxe	65	NA	—
California emissions pkg.	100	NA	—

Prices are accurate at time of printing; subject to manufacturer's change.

Television Sets and TV/VCR Combinations

There are new wide-screen TVs on the horizon, but they will not take over the market in the foreseeable future. However, big rear-projection and direct-view sets with 30- to 35-inch tubes are coming down in price and being loaded with new features. Such big sets don't fit into every budget or viewing room. The 20- to 27-inch sets offer a great range of features and options at competitive prices.

Some TV sets over 20 inches have various electronic means for providing up to 800 lines of horizontal resolution (in contrast to the 200-odd lines provided by broadcast signals or 400 plus for laser discs). The results are quite arresting but must be weighed against the price and your viewing habits.

Color Picture-In-Picture (PIP) is available on many new models, and the PIP is far better and clearer than was the case just a few years ago. This is another result of digital TV. (The term is misused; most new TV sets are digital except for the picture tube, but no U.S. telecasts are digital yet.) One of the best benefits of digital TV is maintenance—the integrated chips

(ICs) do not wear out as rapidly as vacuum tubes and transistors. Most of the mosaic and other exotic digital effects have faded, but freeze frame and interlacing (which eliminates scan lines) are available and useful features.

All these features need to be carefully evaluated according to your tastes and budget. It takes a modest effort to do comparative shopping of the new crop of TVs. The quality is high, but minor differences and the range of possible adjustments can have an impact on your viewing enjoyment.

With stereo telecasts and videotapes, audio has become an important part of video again. Most monitor/receivers allow you to feed the stereo sound signal into an existing stereo system. Many of the new sets, however, have internal sound systems that can provide stunning audio for a true home theater experience. Listen just as carefully as you look.

Warranties that have been standard for years (1 year parts, 90 days labor, 2 years picture tube) seem to be getting competitive. Some firms are using longer warranties to attract customers while others have been shortening them and offering consumer insurance, which can be expensive. You as the buyer must be aware and alert.

Features and Terminology

Here are some of the terms you should know before you shop for a television:

Closed caption decoder displays captions (when available) on-screen for hearing impaired or language impaired viewers. This feature can also help some people with reading problems, as well as people learning English.

Comb filters provide better edges and definition of a picture.

Dynamic sound enhancement uses a computer chip (or chips) to expand the sound signal to increase dynamic range, which is the difference between the loudest and softest sounds in any musical selection. Some dynamic sound enhancers may expand the sense of stereo field as well.

Express tuning allows the viewer to scan channels quickly and easily.

Freezing allows the viewer to fix a video image digitally on the screen.

Fuzzy logic is a digital process that makes delicate adjustments on picture quality.

On-screen displays can be channel numbers, time of day, or guides to all the adjustments that can be made to improve the picture and sound.

Pay for view direct dialing enables you to order a pay-for-view event with your TV set rather than dialing your cable system by phone.

Picture enhancement may involve a special computer chip, which will sample the electronic signal and enhance it to provide better color or to overlap two pictures to eliminate scan lines. Remember that the TV image consists of 270 to 800 or more lines swept across the screen from top to bottom with space between each line. The next picture consists of another set of lines swept into the spaces between the previous lines. Even though our eyes compensate for these scan lines, computer chips do it better.

Picture-In-Picture (PIP) permits the user to view an alternate video image from a second video source in a box on the main screen.

Rotary tuning can be either mechanical or electronic. Mechanical rotary tuners are likely to wear badly and/or to get dirty. Avoid mechanical rotary tuners in favor of electronic tuners, which are standard on quality sets.

Stereo decoder chips extract stereo from the MTS (multichannel television sound) signal. Some of these chips provide matrix (electronically stimulated) stereo from monaural sources. Others can decode Dolby surround-sound signals and provide sound for rear speakers that fill a room with sound as clear as that heard at the movies.

S-VHS separates luminance (brightness portion of color TV signal) and chrominance (color portion of color TV signal) to significantly sharpen any picture when the S output is available.

Video noise-reduction chips clean out most of the white streaks and ghosts that can intrude from off-the-air or cable signals.

Stereo Sound

When you shop for a new television set be sure that you understand how stereo TV works. The MTS (multichannel television sound) decoder built into the TV set receives the stereo signal. Stereo-ready or stereo-capable televisions can receive stereo signals only with the addition of a separate adapter. While some adapters must be installed by a trained technician, CONSUMER GUIDE® recommends adapters that can be easily attached by the TV owner. With these adapters, installation is as easy as plugging the converter into a jack in the back of the TV set.

If you are satisfied with your monaural TV set but would like to enjoy stereo sound, consider purchasing a stand-alone stereo decoder. This is essentially a radio that is capable of receiving stereo TV broadcasts and is connected to an external pair of speakers to produce two-channel sound.

Satellite Television

Satellite broadcasts are no longer free for the taking. For years, satellite dish owners had their pick of hundreds of channels because program distributors, such as HBO and Showtime, did not scramble the signals they bounced off satellites in order to send them to local cable companies. Recently, distributors have begun scrambling the signals so the broadcast received by the dish is an unwatchable garble. But dish owners can still use their systems; distributors now rent converter boxes like those used to receive cable service. A satellite dish is still a good buy for consumers who live in areas where they cannot receive quality over-the-air broadcasts.

New Tube Shapes and Sizes

Most manufacturers have replaced their round-cornered screens with squarer, flatter tubes. Although they function in exactly the same way as tubes with rounded corners, the flat tubes eliminate much of the distortion of concave screens.

Projection TV offers viewers a much larger picture than a conventional television set. Rear-projection TVs have improved considerably this year. These sets have a brighter picture, a wider viewing angle, and enhanced pictures. They use picture processing, comb filters, and S-Video connections to refine and clarify the video signal. Although these sets compete directly with the 30-inch and larger direct-view TV sets, they are still very large and have fairly big price tags.

Evaluating a Television Set

Since differences in major-brand televisions are slight, manufacturers have added all sorts of special features to their sets in an attempt to differentiate them. Deciding which television to buy is a matter of matching a set's features with your needs. For example, some TVs offer a feature called **channel block** that allows parents to program the set so their small children cannot tune in certain stations, such as cable channels that offer adult programming. If you do not have children, you will have little use for a set with this feature.

TVs are becoming more automated. Many sets now have a sleep-timer function that lets you nod off to late-night television and sleep securely in the knowledge that the set will automatically turn itself off, usually at a preselected 30-, 60-, or 90-minute interval. Other sets can be programmed to turn themselves on and off at preselected times either as a security measure or as a way to make sure you do not miss your favorite program.

The most popular TV feature is remote control, which has now sprouted many new functions of its own. Today, more than half of all TVs come equipped with remotes. CONSUMER GUIDE® recommends a set with a digital remote because it is more versatile and less prone to interference than other types of remote control. You may also want to consider other convenience features, such as random access, channel memory, and sound mute. Many manufacturers have conveniently designed their sets with either a slot or a spring-loaded holder for the remote, reducing the chance of misplacing it.

If you have more than one remote-controlled piece of equipment, you may want to buy a programmable remote that can "learn" the infrared control codes of a number of different products, such as VCRs, disc players, and cable boxes, made by different manufacturers.

Cable Terminology

A major cause of confusion for television shoppers is the term **cable ready**. Many people incorrectly believe a cable-ready TV set will let them receive cable programming, such as HBO and Showtime, for free. A cable-ready set only eliminates the need for a converter box. You still have to pay the initial cable hookup costs and monthly fees. If you want any of the premium services for which the cable company charges extra, you will need the converter box to unscramble the signal.

Because the converter box may render a TV's remote control useless, some cable companies offer boxes that have their own remotes. CONSUMER GUIDE® suggests that you call your local cable company before buying a cable-ready set. If you are not buying a set with a remote, you will not mind using the converter box. If you subscribe to a premium service, you may not need a cable-ready set.

Best Buys '92

Our Best Buy and Recommended television sets and TV/VCR combinations follow. The unit we consider the best of the Best Buys is first, followed by our second choice, and so on. The picture quality of most of the major-brand televisions varies only slightly, and differences are highly subjective. Some of this year's choices are included because they offer a particularly good picture, but most sets were chosen because they offer packages of desirable features. While features and styling change from model to model, TV technology is often carried through a company's entire line. This means that many of the TVs from the same manufacturer offer the same quality picture, but the combination of features in addition to the price of the set is the basis for our choice of one TV over another as a Best Buy. For this reason, the Best Buy and Recommended designations apply only to the model listed and not necessarily to other models from the same manufacturer.

31-INCH AND ABOVE COLOR TV SETS

ZENITH ZB3294S   ✔BEST BUY

The Zenith ZB3294S is a 32-inch set that stands alone as a superior home-theater unit. It has an especially fine picture and admirable surround-sound from a Bose Acoustimass and Bose Twiddler speaker system. The nested on-screen display for the many adjustable options makes it easy to get the best sound and picture. The digital color Picture-In-Picture (PIP) offers an alternate channel view. With an S-VHS source, this set delivers up to 700 lines of resolution for a dazzling picture. When you add the remarkable Bose sound and 42-key remote control, this set clearly ranks as a Best Buy. The 42-key wireless remote

control gives you mastery over what could be an intimidating machine.
Specifications: height, 45¹¹⁄₁₆″; **width,** 30⁵⁄₁₆″; **depth,** 22⅛″; **weight,** 203 pounds. **Warranty: parts,** one year; **labor,** 90 days; **picture tube,** two years.

Approx. retail price	Approx. low price
$1,995	$1,474

MITSUBISHI CS-3535R   RECOMMENDED

The Mitsubishi CS-3535R has a 35-inch screen; the size and weight of this set make it almost awesome. Mitsubishi pioneered the 35-inch tube and has the longest track record with it. The CS-3535R offers up to 700 lines of resolution for a picture with snap and definition. There is a channel block feature to keep children from watching unsuitable channels, but a child's ability to use the pay-for-view dial-up system could turn some parents away from this set. S-VHS input is almost a must with such a large screen. The subwoofer output allows for big bass to accompany the big picture, and the range of monitor jacks makes this a flexible video center. The front jacks and swivelling panel are necessary in such a massive set.
Specifications: height, 28⅝″; **width,** 38⁷⁄₁₆″; **depth,** 23½″; **weight,** 186½ pounds. **Warranty: parts and labor,** one year; **picture tube,** two years (in-home service).

Approx. retail price	Approx. low price
$2,899	$2,106

SHARP 32A-S300   RECOMMENDED

The Sharp 32A-S300 is a 32-inch model that offers a sensible and comprehensive range of features, together with a big, beautiful picture. The 39-key wireless remote controls the full range of available video and audio options without taxing the user's patience or electronic skills. Channel block is available, together with a full range of on-screen displays. The MTS and SAP (second audio program) sound make this a set to see and hear.
Specifications: height, 28¹³⁄₃₂″; **width,** 32⅝″; **depth,** 22²⁷⁄₃₂″; **weight,** 143³⁄₁₀ pounds. **Warranty: parts and labor,** one year; **picture tube,** one year.

Prices are accurate at time of printing; subject to manufacturer's change.

Approx. retail price	Approx. low price
$1,250	$1,248

27-INCH COLOR TV SETS

TOSHIBA CX2786A

✓BEST BUY

The Toshiba CX2786A is a 27-inch TV set that fits the bill for most domestic purposes. It also makes clear that you need sacrifice nothing but expense and size when selecting a relatively modest unit. The features of the CX2786A are world class. The Cyclone ABX sound system found in this set provides sparkling audio with a self-enclosed bass reflex subwoofer and a digital sound processor that allows the 27 watts of total audio output to recreate the ambience of a theater, concert hall, stadium, or night club. This complements a picture with 650 lines of resolution. The full-color PIP (Picture-In-Picture) provides an impressive alternate image. The digital picture, sound, channel, volume, and timer displays are all available on-screen. There is a channel block and a sleep-timer feature as well. This set includes an S-video input, two audio/video inputs, two RF inputs, and one RF output, as well as external speaker terminals.

Specifications: height, 24$^{13}\!/_{32}$"; **width,** 32$^{41}\!/_{64}$"; **depth,** 21$^{17}\!/_{64}$"; **weight,** 92$^{3}\!/_{5}$ pounds. **Warranty: parts and labor,** one year; **picture tube,** two years.

Approx. retail price	Approx. low price
$1,099	$627

HITACHI CT 7897B

RECOMMENDED

The Hitachi CT 7897B has many features, but the most winning is the complete autodemonstration feature. This allows you to learn or to recall the many exceptional features the CT 7897B possesses—from color PIP and freeze to dynamic bass and an effective comb filter. The 650 lines of resolution possible with an S-VHS signal deliver a picture that is exceptionally detailed. Hitachi's picture tubes use special phosphors that bring out greens with particular delicacy and accuracy. The VideoBrain II wireless remote can learn the commands for your other remote-controlled hardware. There are enough stereo audio/video inputs to accommodate a VCR and a videodisc player. This is a flexible set that conceals many of its virtues in its restrained black cabinet.

Specifications: height, 22⅞″; **width,** 27¹⁄₁₆″; **depth,** 20⅜″; **weight,** 94 pounds. **Warranty: parts,** two years; **labor,** one year; **transistors,** ten years.

Approx. retail price	Approx. low price
$1,000	$850

FISHER PC-1627 [RECOMMENDED]

The Fisher PC-1627 is noteworthy for its active color equalizer, which keeps the picture consistent from channel to channel. A flesh-tone corrector monitors skin tone and automatically adjusts for the best picture. The combination of a color-noise reduction system and a color-noise limiter also helps insure a clear picture. While the three watts-per-channel audio output may seem modest to some, this is adequate for many viewing rooms. There are audio outputs should you wish additional amplification. The 178-channel tuning is more than enough for current cable systems. The preprogrammed wireless universal remote control makes this set easy to operate. This is a very solid performer.

Specifications: height, 24³⁄₁₀″; **width,** 26³⁄₁₀″; **depth,** 21¹⁄₁₀″; **weight,** 78³⁄₁₀ pounds. **Warranty: parts and labor,** one year; **picture tube,** two years.

Approx. retail price	Approx. low price
$700	$599

RCA F27203WN [RECOMMENDED]

The RCA F27203WN features side-firing speakers, which help keep the cabinet very compact. There is a surround-sound option for home theater effects from the MSS sound. Electronically expanded stereo gives a more spacious quality to the sound from the modest cabinet. The F27203WN has a channel block feature. The 38-key wireless remote controls the primary functions of 56 different brands of VCRs and 27 different remote cable boxes, as well as the complete range of adjustments and operating controls of the set itself. The sleep

Prices are accurate at time of printing; subject to manufacturer's change.

TELEVISION SETS AND TV/VCR COMBINATIONS

timer is a standard feature, and the alarm timer can awaken you to morning news on the channel of your choice. There is a full range of monitor inputs and outputs, which makes this a properly designated monitor/receiver.
Specifications: height, 23"; **width,** 27¼"; **depth,** 19½"; **weight,** 94 pounds. **Warranty: parts,** one year; **labor,** 90 days (in-home service); **picture tube,** two years.

Approx. retail price	Approx. low price
$669	$594

JVC AV-2771S RECOMMENDED

The JVC AV-2771S is a particularly good example of the full range of features that can be found in a 27-inch set at a reasonable price. Master Command Ai analyzes your daily viewing habits and provides one-button access to your favorite channels. Your preferred volume settings are monitored and set automatically. The set has color PIP and a child timer that turns the set off at the child's bedtime. The preprogrammed 29-key universal remote control can operate almost all VCRs and cable TV boxes, as well as the TV set. The picture has 550 lines of horizontal resolution and will yield a spectacular picture with an S-VHS source. The picture is further enhanced with a wide-band comb filter and video-noise reduction circuits.
Specifications: height, 22¾"; **width,** 25¾"; **depth,** 20½"; **weight,** 84⅛ pounds. **Warranty: parts,** one year; **labor,** one year (in-home service); **picture tube,** two years.

Approx. retail price	Approx. low price
$930	$669

19/20-INCH COLOR TV SETS

RCA F20706FT

The RCA F20706FT has most features of the top-of-the-line big tube models with a more modest size and price tag. The 400 lines of resolution are more than ample on a 20-inch tube, and the added clarity of an S-VHS source provides a reminder that smaller tubes deliver sharper pictures. With optional external speakers, this set delivers surround-sound and SAP (second

Prices are accurate at time of printing; subject to manufacturer's change.

audio program). The 13-jack video/audio monitor panel gives
you a full range of options for connecting to and from external
sources. Yet this unit is small enough to serve as a studio
monitor and for field work. The four-character on-screen
labeling is a nice touch with a multitude of cable channels.
There is a channel block, which could make this a useful
second set. Its price and performance, however, make it worth
considering for your primary unit.
Specifications: height, 18⅞"; **width,** 27⅛"; **depth,** 19"; **weight,**
59 pounds. **Warranty: parts,** one year; **labor,** 90 days (in-
home service); **picture tube,** two years.

Approx. retail price	Approx. low price
$499	$382

PANASONIC CTN-2092S   RECOMMENDED

The Panasonic CTN-2092S is a monitor/receiver with a
wireless remote control. It has a full range of features with
multiple on-screen displays and adjustments. The audio
includes broadcast stereo and SAP. This set provides the
appropriate inputs and outputs to be designated a monitor/
receiver. The use of comb and notch filters insure a solid
picture. While Panasonic offers several 20-inch models, this set
offers a nice balance between features and price. The data-
grade screen can deliver a sparkling image when fed an S-VHS
source.
Specifications: height, 18"; **width,** 21⅜"; **depth,** 18⁷⁄₁₀";
weight, 50 pounds. **Warranty: parts and labor,** one year;
picture tube, two years (one year labor).

Approx. retail price	Approx. low price
$430	$401

SONY KV-20TS27   RECOMMENDED

The Sony KV-20TS27 is the new 20-inch model that offers a
Microblack picture tube coupled with dynamic picture
processors for an exceptionally fine picture. Sony has never
had to take a back seat when it comes to picture quality. This
model includes MTS (multichannel television sound), and the
variable-level audio output allows you to route the TV through a
separate stereo system. The volume can be controlled with the

Prices are accurate at time of printing; subject to manufacturer's change.

Remote Commander wireless remote control. The on-screen displays are comprehensive and useful. There is also a sleep timer, automatic timer, and channel block.
Specifications: height, 20¾"; **width,** 19¼"; **depth,** 19"; **weight,** 51⅝ pounds. **Warranty: parts,** one year; **labor,** 90 days; **picture tube,** two years.

Approx. retail price	Approx. low price
$530	$375

FISHER PC-1520

The Fisher PC-1520 offers MTS and SAP with on-screen displays and control with the wireless remote control. This model even includes an on-screen demonstration of its many features. This monitor/receiver offers fine performance as a flexible stereo TV with most of the features that electronic controls offer.
Specifications: height, 19³⁄₁₀"; **width,** 20³⁄₁₀"; **depth,** 18⁷⁄₁₀"; **weight,** 44¹⁄₁₀ pounds. **Warranty: parts,** one year; **labor,** 90 days; **picture tube,** two years.

Approx. retail price	Approx. low price
$320	$278

JVC AV-2061   RECOMMENDED

The JVC AV-2061 provides both MTS and SAP, along with a number of unusual features. One feature, home sitter, turns the set on and off when you're not home in order to give the appearance of your being there. You can select three channels to be off limits to your kids with channel block. The noise-mute feature replaces snow and hiss on non-broadcast channels with a quiet blue screen. A dual on timer allows the set to be turned on at two different times with up to two different channel settings. The 29-key remote control makes it easy to make adjustments using the on-screen display. There is a sleep timer, a full A/V input, plus a variable-volume output.
Specifications: height, 18⅝"; **width,** 20"; **depth,** 19½"; **weight,** 50⅝ pounds. **Warranty: parts and labor,** one year (carry in); **picture tube,** two years.

Approx. retail price	Approx. low price
$480	$366

Prices are accurate at time of printing; subject to manufacturer's change.

PORTABLE COLOR TV SETS

TOSHIBA CF 1313A

The Toshiba CF 1313A offers most of the convenience features of larger TV sets, such as a 27-key wireless remote and 181-channel capability. The on-screen displays make it easy to adjust picture and sound. This set also includes on-screen channel, volume, and timer displays. The sleep timer and automatic power off make this a handy set for use in the bedroom. Lines of resolution are not a problem on sets of this size, and Toshiba's Blackstripe II picture tube provides good contrast and brightness in a delightful color picture. This is not a monitor/receiver, but it is a very fine portable unit.

Specifications: height, 13¹⁵⁄₃₂″; **width,** 15⅝₃₂″; **depth,** 14³¹⁄₆₄″; **weight,** 20³⁄₁₀ pounds. **Warranty: parts and labor,** one year; **picture tube,** two years.

Approx. retail price	Approx. low price
$299	$216

ZENITH SJ1325W/X   RECOMMENDED

The Zenith SJ1325W/X has a handy TV-only wireless remote control, which allows you to change the channel and adjust the volume while checking the time or channel using the on-screen display. This set has audio and video inputs so that it can be used as a monitor for a camcorder, and the direct A/V input provides much better playback from a VCR than results from using the RF input. This model is available in a white or black walnut Euro-style cabinet. It offers a flashback feature for the channel last viewed.

Specifications: height, 14″; **width,** 14½″; **depth,** 15⅛″; **weight,** 24 pounds. **Warranty: parts,** one year; **labor,** 90 days; **picture tube,** two years.

Approx. retail price	Approx. low price
$330	$252

HITACHI CT 1397B   RECOMMENDED

The Hitachi CT 1397B is a very effective monitor/receiver. While not everyone needs audio and video inputs in a 13-inch

Prices are accurate at time of printing; subject to manufacturer's change.

set, the additional cost is quite modest and the difference in picture quality when using the A/V inputs is significant. The 24-key wireless remote makes this set easy to run in the kitchen or bedroom. This is a very subdued set with anything but a subdued picture.

Specifications: height, 13¹⁵⁄₁₆"; **width,** 14⅜₆"; **depth,** 14¹⁵⁄₁₆"; **weight,** 20 pounds. **Warranty: transistors,** ten years; **parts,** two years; **labor,** one year.

Approx. retail price	Approx. low price
$300	not available

SONY KV-8AD11 · RECOMMENDED

The Sony KV-8AD11 is an 8-inch set that is truly portable and comes complete with a pull-up handle. It can fit into very small spaces and can be powered by either AC or DC power. Yet even in a set this small, there is a Mirrorblack picture tube, a wireless remote control, a sleep timer, and a dynamic picture processor. This is a great deal of technology squeezed into a very tidy package. Even at this size, the tube offers a brighter picture than can be extracted from most LCD (liquid crystal display) technologies.

Specifications: height, 9½"; **width,** 7⅞"; **depth,** 12⅜"; **weight,** 10¹³⁄₁₆ pounds. **Warranty: parts,** one year; **labor,** 90 days; **picture tube,** two years.

Approx. retail price	Approx. low price
$480	$364

SAMSUNG TC3836T(B) · RECOMMENDED

The Samsung TC3836T(B) is available in either a black or a woodgrain cabinet. This set has a 21-key remote control and on-screen channel and sleep-timer displays. Automatic fine tuning (AFT) and autocolor provide a bright, stable picture. Samsung has a very good service network, although modern sets aren't likely to need service often.

Specifications: height, 13¾"; **width,** 14¼"; **depth,** 15"; **weight,** 22¼ pounds. **Warranty: parts and labor,** one year; **picture tube,** two years.

Approx. retail price	Approx. low price
$270	$174

Prices are accurate at time of printing; subject to manufacturer's change.

MITSUBISHI CS-1347R/1348R

The Mitsubishi CS-1347R comes in a black cabinet and the CS-1348R in a white cabinet. Both offer a dark tint, black matrix picture tube. For people who do not require the monitor inputs, this is a very fine choice. It has many on-screen displays, including picture adjustments, a remote control, and an off timer. While ranked last in this group, this is hardly the last set to be considered when shopping for portables.

Specifications; height, 12⅝"; **width,** 13⅞"; **depth,** 15⅛"; **weight,** 21 pounds. **Warranty: parts and labor,** one year; **picture tube,** two years.

Approx. retail price	Approx. low price
$329	$282

MINI TV SETS

CASIO TV-470B

The Casio TV-470B is a tiny set with a 2⅛-inch LCD (liquid crystal display) screen that is enhanced with a high luminance backlight. The color is very good. There is no question that color LCD screens have proven their quality and reliability. This Casio serves to show how solid and viewable this size set has become. Moreover, this set can be run using batteries or an AC adapter.

Specifications: height, 5⁷⁄₁₆"; **width,** 3³⁄₁₆"; **depth,** 1⁷⁄₁₆"; **weight,** 8⅝ ounces. **Warranty: parts,** one year; **labor,** 90 days.

Approx. retail price	Approx. low price
$200	$157

SONY FD-555 WATCHMAN

The Sony FD-555 Watchman is a very sensible and flexible black-and-white mini TV set with an AM/FM radio, a cassette player, and 4-inch speakers flanking a 4½-inch video screen. It can serve as a modified boombox as well as a personal TV. The set can be powered by batteries, AC, or 12-volt DC. It has a sleep timer and deserves its Best Buy rating even if it lacks color. The price is very attractive as well.

Prices are accurate at time of printing; subject to manufacturer's change.

Specifications: height, 8⅜"; **width,** 13¼"; **depth,** 7¼"; **weight,** 9¹¹⁄₂ pounds with batteries. **Warranty: parts,** one year; **labor,** 90 days; **picture tube,** one year.

Approx. retail price	Approx. low price
$200	$168

CASIO TV-1450 `RECOMMENDED`

The Casio TV-1450 is a very compact machine that fits a 2⅞₀-inch diagonal screen into a unit that is just 3³⁄₁₆ inches wide. Amazingly, this compact unit includes a 1⅞₆-inch by 1-inch speaker. The TV-1450 has jacks for external antenna and power hookup, and an earphone jack. The audio/video input jacks make this unit suitable as a remote color monitor.

Specifications: height, 5½"; **width,** 3³⁄₁₆"; **depth,** 1⁷⁄₁₆"; **weight,** 10⅜ ounces. **Warranty: parts,** one year; **labor,** 90 days.

Approx. retail price	Approx. low price
$350	$307

SONY FDL-380
COLOR WATCHMAN `RECOMMENDED`

The Sony FDL-380 Color Watchman has a very bright three-inch LCD screen and the considerable reliability record of the Watchman in its corner. Moreover, this unit includes an AM/FM tuner and an RF booster to provide the optimum signal from off the airwaves.

Specifications: height, 4⅜"; **width,** 8⅝"; **depth,** 2⅞"; **weight,** 2⁵⁄₁₆ pounds with batteries, 1½ pounds without batteries. **Warranty: parts,** one year; **labor,** 90 days; **picture tube,** one year.

Approx. retail price	Approx. low price
$399	$346

REAR-PROJECTION TV SETS

MITSUBISHI VS-4517S

The Mitsubishi VS-4517S provides a picture with 700 lines of resolution—hard to fault that picture. The color PIP (Picture-In-

Prices are accurate at time of printing; subject to manufacturer's change.

Picture) is as clear and as big as the image on some standard TV sets. While it is possible to get rear-projection sets with much larger screens, the VS-4517S combines a very generous 45-inch diagonal screen with a relatively compact cabinet. This unit offers a full range of features from on-screen time-channel display and audio-picture adjustments to channel block and pay-for-view direct dial. There is an on-screen graphic equalizer that allows you to adjust the sound to match the picture. This unit has two S-VHS inputs and front-panel inputs, which you will appreciate in a set this size. The range of adjustments makes it possible to obtain a truly state-of-the-art picture on the Diamond Vision screen.

Specifications: height, 49¼"; **width,** 36³⁄₁₆"; **depth,** 20⅞"; **weight,** 187⅝ pounds. **Warranty: parts and labor,** one year; **screen,** 30 days (in-home service).

Approx. retail price	Approx. low price
$3,299	$2,774

HITACHI 60SX1K   ✔BEST BUY

The Hitachi 60SX1K offers a 60-inch diagonal picture with up to 1,000 lines of resolution. It may not be for everyone, but the 60SX1K provides all the features of a monitor/receiver in a truly spectacular fashion. There are so many features available that in addition to the on-screen autodemonstration, this set comes with two wireless remotes—one programmable and one "easy." As a monitor, this set has a total of 11 A/V inputs. There is a color PIP and Dolby prologic surround-sound. The Insight 2001 on-screen system includes all audio, video, date/time memory, station/channel memory, and message-timer options. A set this large clearly will serve as the anchor of a home theater system. A serious audio system built into this unit will allow you to experience movies with sonic richness rivaling the neighborhood cinema.

Specifications: height, 63¹⁄₁₆"; **width,** 53½"; **depth,** 28³⁄₁₆"; **weight,** 362 pounds. **Warranty: parts,** two years; **labor,** one year; **transistors,** ten years; **lenses,** lifetime.

Approx. retail price	Approx. low price
$4,400	$2,999

TELEVISION SETS AND TV/VCR COMBINATIONS

TOSHIBA TP5580A

 ✓BEST BUY

The Toshiba TP5580A features on-screen displays in your choice of three available languages. The color PIP gets added flexibility from the second built-in tuner. The brightness is very good, and the picture can be viewed from a wide angle. This set has a total of 48 watts of audio output so that any of the four preset digitally processed sound modes can make the rafters ring. The built-in subwoofer helps add even more body to this hefty audio output. The 800 lines of resolution are more than enough to provide an unforgettable video experience on the 55-inch rear-projection screen. This is a very substantial set in every sense of the word.

Specifications: height, 57¾"; **width,** 50⅜"; **depth,** 31⅞"; **weight,** 320 pounds. **Warranty: parts and labor,** one year; **picture tube,** two years.

Approx. retail price	Approx. low price
$3,799	$2,499

FRONT-PROJECTION TV SETS

ZENITH PV890X

 ✓BEST BUY

The Zenith PV890X represents the mature development of the three-tube model that provides a picture from three seven-inch rectangular tubes. The three color-images from these tubes converge on a wall or screen and can provide a picture with a five- to ten-foot diagonal measurement. This unit can be ceiling mounted and can even be used for rear projection on a flat (matte) finish screen. It has all the features found in conventional Zenith digital sets plus an advanced video processor to tweak the big picture even more dramatically. An optional rolling stand is available, so it could be brought forth for big video viewing or tucked away discreetly when not required.

Specifications: height, 10½"; **width,** 31"; **depth,** 25"; **weight,** 106 pounds. **Warranty: parts,** one year; **labor,** 90 days; **picture tubes,** two years.

Approx. retail price	Approx. low price
$3,995	$3,045

Prices are accurate at time of printing; subject to manufacturer's change.

SHARPVISION XV120ZU

✔ **BEST BUY**

The SharpVision XV120ZU represents the newest technology for front projection and can present an image with diagonal measurements from 20 to 100 inches. The three-inch LCD (liquid crystal display) panels provide the three color-images using hundreds of thousands of pixels. A strong projection lamp throws the crisp single image formed from these LCDs onto a wall or screen in the size that is required. The use of a carefully selected screen greatly enhances the image, but any plain flat surface will do in a pinch. The portability and flexibility of this new design makes it very attractive for those who want to show videos to different size groups. This unit can travel to class-rooms, boardrooms, and even campsites if a power source is available. The image is excellent under optimum conditions and quite satisfactory under marginal conditions, such as a yellow concrete block wall with an audience of 30.

Specifications: height, 12⅜"; **width,** 8⅜"; **depth,** 17⅜"; **weight,** 27 pounds. **Warranty: parts and labor,** one year; **projection lamp,** 90 days.

Approx. retail price	Approx. low price
$4,000	$3,350

TV/VCR COMBINATIONS

There are now two distinct types of TV/VCR combinations. The first type provides a VCR combined with a conventional TV set as a single unit. These sets may range in size from 7 to 27 inches and can provide all the features available in the best TVs and VCRs in a single uncomplicated package, without endless connections and setup hassles. The second type provides new hi-tech LCD flat screens in very compact packages designed for portability and flexibility. These units are obviously handy for travelers who want to watch videotapes, but they are also useful for reviewing videotapes when using camcorders in the field. Since the LCD screens are still relatively small and light, they are ideal for real portability but don't do very well for family or large group viewing. In both cases, if there is a problem with either the TV or the VCR, you lose the use of both units until the problem with one is corrected. The trade-off is a matter of cost and convenience with the need for portability or group viewing an additional factor.

SAMSUNG VM7105

The Samsung VM7105 is an economical, simple, and straightforward combination of a basic VCR and a very good 20-inch TV set. The VCR has two heads and uses HQ (high quality) for better VHS pictures. This set has audio and video inputs and outputs so that it can be used as a camcorder monitor. It provides on-screen programming.
Specifications: height, 19½"; **width,** 20¾"; **depth,** 19¼"; **weight,** 55 pounds. **Warranty: parts,** one year; **labor,** three months; **picture tube,** two years (carry-in service).

Approx. retail price	Approx. low price
$740	$559

PANASONIC PV-MS2750

The Panasonic PV-MS2750 is proof that you can get a TV/VCR combination that has all the best features of both technologies in a single unit. This set has a 27-inch color screen and the full complement of comb filters and video-noise reducers. It has MTS (multichannel television sound) as well as S-VHS. The VCR provides high-fidelity stereo sound, four video heads, and two tuners so that you can watch one program while taping another. This unit is a trifle too large for portability, but it certainly qualifies as a high-tech video and as a high-tech VCR without compromising picture, sound, or recording capabilities. If you want a combination that you can operate out of the box that will confound your technosnob friends, this machine will fill the bill. It provides crisp tapes and brilliant no-hassle viewing. It rates as a Best Buy since the equivalent combination would cost more as separates.
Specifications: height, 28⅞"; **width,** 27⅞"; **depth,** 19⅜"; **weight,** 95⁄₁₀ pounds. **Warranty: parts,** one year; **labor,** 90 days; **picture tube, parts,** two years; **labor,** 90 days.

Approx. retail price	Approx. low price
$1,699	$1,433

Prices are accurate at time of printing; subject to manufacturer's change.

Portable TV/VCR Combination

SONY GV 300
VIDEO WALKMAN

 ✓**BEST BUY**

The Sony GV 300 Video Walkman is clearly the leader in a truly portable TV/VCR combination. The picture is superb and can be enjoyed with high-fidelity stereo sound. However, the 8mm tape cassettes cannot be played in VHS or Beta machines. Since it is possible to tape off the air or from a conventional VCR (keeping copyright laws in mind), that needn't be a major drawback. There is a growing library of prerecorded tapes as well. This is an expensive unit, but it represents the cutting edge of video technology.

Specifications: height, 8⅞″; **width,** 5⅛″; **depth,** 2⅞″; **weight,** 2⁹⁄₁₀ pounds. **Warranty: parts,** one year; **labor,** 90 days.

Approx. retail price	Approx. low price
$1,400	$1,010

Videocassette Recorders, Laser Disc Players, and Video Accessories

Over 60 percent of all households in the United States have at least one videocassette recorder (VCR). Unlike VCRs, laser disc players (LDPs) have been slow to catch on because they cannot record and also because the format previously had limited playing time. While they still cannot record, LDPs now have extended playing time, and the new models play all video laser disc formats and all audio compact disc formats. For those who want to record televised programs, copy recorded tapes, or edit tapes made with camcorders, a VCR is still the choice. VCRs also remain the prime choice for many because LDPs are quite a bit more expensive and because rental tapes are widely available for VCRs. The video and audio quality of laser discs is generally superior to tape quality. As laser discs become more available and the price of players comes down, LDP popularity will grow, although they will never become as popular as VCRs until they can record as well as play. In an attempt to overcome this great disadvantage, companies are now producing multiformat disc players at lower prices and introducing such features as automatic play of both sides.

Because a VCR has its own tuner, you can record a program on one channel and use the tuner in your TV to watch a program on another channel. If you want to record from another tape, you need two VCRs, or a VCR and a camcorder.

VCR Formats

There are three basic video formats: 8mm, Beta, and VHS. A fourth format, VHS-C, is a cassette one-fourth the size of a regular VHS cassette that can be played in a VHS VCR with an adapter. A couple of full-size VHS VCRs will soon be available that will also accept VHS-C cassettes without the adapter. Even though the different formats are physically incompatible, you can transfer a recording made on one format to another format by connecting the two different VCRs, or a VCR and a camcorder with the cables supplied with the machines.

The original VCR formats are continuously being improved. VHS units now have HQ (High Quality) circuitry, and Beta now has SuperBeta circuitry. There is also ED Beta (Extended Definition Beta), S-VHS (Super VHS), and Hi-8 with improved horizontal definition. These improved video formats continue to lack wide consumer acceptance because you also need a new, higher quality television set to get improved results with these VCRs. Another problem is HDTV (High Definition Television), a completely new method of broadcasting that will require new TV sets, and most people are not willing to invest in a new video system that may soon have to be replaced.

Choosing Tapes

If you are going to record on a tape only once or twice, and then not play it very often, high standard grade tapes are fine.

But if you plan to record and play back the same tape many times, such as when time shifting (recording at one time to watch later), use the highest grade tape available. You can even use an S-VHS tape in a standard VHS VCR for this purpose. Use brand name tapes such as Fuji, Kodak, Konica, Maxell, Panasonic, Samsung, Scotch, etc., rather than cheap tapes from unknown manufacturers. Many of them are so poorly made that they can quickly cause expensive damage to the heads of your VCR.

Choosing a VCR

One reason shopping for a VCR is so confusing is the array of features and combinations of features. One sales promotion may advertise a VCR's programmability; another, its six heads. Since not every consumer needs or wants every feature, it is important to understand what is available and to know what you want.

Hi-fi sound: There is a difference between stereo sound and high fidelity sound. Stereo means that the sound is recorded and played back through two channels. Hi-fi refers to high-quality sound, whether stereo or monaural.

Index search: Many VCRs now record an electronic index code at the beginning of each recording. To scan your recording on a tape, you press index search; the VCR then stops at each index mark and plays back a few seconds of the recording. Some VCRs now even allow you to tell them which index mark to go to and it will start playing that section back.

Number of heads: To record and play back a tape, you only need two video heads. Additional heads are used for special effects, such as freeze frame and clear on-screen search.

Programmability: If you are buying a VCR primarily to record television broadcasts, programmability is an important consideration. Almost all VCRs can be programmed to record at least one program. The simplest programming uses a built-in clock timer that you set to start and stop within the next 24 hours. More elaborate programming allows you to record several different programs over a period of a month or more. Other program operations let you record the same program every day or every week.

Quick access/quick play: Many VCRs now provide quick play from the stop position. There are also VCRs that provide quick access from fast forward or fast rewind to visual scanning, and quick access from visual scanning to play.

Tape speeds: Most VCRs let you choose between two or three different recording speeds; playback speed is automatically set, and even VCRs that record in only two speeds play back all three speeds. The faster the tape moves, the less total time it records, but the faster the tape moves, the better the quality of the recording.

Best Buys '92

Our Best Buy and Recommended VCRs, LDPs, and video accessories follow. They were evaluated on the basis of their performance when they were connected to a Toshiba CZ2697 26-inch stereo monitor/receiver. All units were tested directly through the monitor as well as through the receiver. The units were evaluated on the basis of their recording and playback images and on their sound quality, as well as their features and overall operational design. Within each format designation, the best of the Best Buys is listed first, followed by our second choice, and so on. A Best Buy or Recommended designation applies only to the model listed, not to other models by the same manufacturer.

VHS VIDEOCASSETTE RECORDERS

MITSUBISHI HS-U54

The Mitsubishi HS-U54 is a four-head hi-fi stereo VHS VCR with rapid-access tape transport, digital tracking, and a multifunction shuttle ring and adjust dial conveniently located on the palm-size infrared remote control. The unnecessarily complicated method of programming Mitsubishi VCRs has been eliminated in the HS-U54. The four-event/four-week programming is easy to set up—the shuttle ring and adjust dial takes you through each program step by step. Corrections and cancellations are also made simple with these controls. One-touch recording (OTR) is handled by the record button on the VCR, with recording time programmable in 15-minute increments. The shuttle ring and adjust dial are also used for playback, special effects from pause and single-frame advance to slow motion, and high-speed forward and reverse. The adjust dial can also be used to select channels when the tape is not running. When you put a tape in the HS-U54, the rapid-access tape transport starts recording or playback in about ³⁄₁₀ second. When you press the play button on the VCR or the wireless remote, the digital-tracking system adjusts the tape moving across the heads to provide the best possible picture. There is two-speed search in fast forward and rewind, normal-speed search, and high-speed search, which is ten times faster in SP (standard play) and 30 times faster in EP (extended play) than normal play. Even switching from high-speed search to play takes only a second. In fast forward or rewind, you can switch to visual search by pressing and holding the fast forward or rewind button to scan the tape. Along with index search, the HS-U54 has time search. You enter the amount of plus or minus time from zero of the real-time counter where you want to start playing back, and the VCR goes to that time and starts playing. There is also a child lock to prevent children from putting foreign objects in the tape receptacle. The Mitsubishi HS-U54 is an excellent and easy-to-operate VCR that produces high-quality recordings.

Specifications: height, 3¹³⁄₁₆″; **width,** 16⅝″; **depth,** 13⁷⁄₁₆″; **weight,** 13 pounds. **Warranty: parts,** one year; **labor,** six months.

Approx. retail price	Approx. low price
$599	$518

TOSHIBA M-651 ✓BEST BUY

The Toshiba M-651 is a four-head hi-fi stereo VHS VCR with a quick-access tape transport system in all modes, a tape-remain display in real-time, and foolproof programming. During timer recording, the M-651 checks the tape-remaining time and switches from SP to SLP (if there is not enough tape left to record your program). There is a 181-channel cable compatible frequency synthesized (FS) tuner that is always in its autoscan mode, so that whenever you press the up or down button, it goes to the next channel that is broadcasting. The Quick Access System loads the tape as soon as you insert the cassette into the M-651. With the tape preloaded, it takes about a second to start recording or playback after you press the function button on the VCR or on the wireless remote. The Quick Access System provides instantaneous switching between fast forward or rewind and visual search, and immediate switching from visual search to play. Switching directly to play from fast forward or rewind takes about 2½ seconds. When rewinding or fast forwarding the tape, the M-651 has a brake system that slows the high speed down as it nears its stopping point to reduce strain on the tape and the VCR mechanism. The real-time tape counter keeps track of lapsed time in hours, minutes, and seconds. The on-screen programming allows you to set up to eight events over a one-year period. There is also a one-touch timer that lets you quickly set up one timer recording. The one-touch timer can also be used to program a recording in progress to shut off in up to four hours in 30-minute increments. The M-651 has automatic indexing that puts a signal on the tape at the start of every recording. The automatic digital tracking has a manual override for those rare tapes that the automatic digital cannot lock on. It also features normal and accelerated visual search, frame-by-frame picture advance, and slow play at ½ or ⅒ of normal speed. The M-651 is a fast and user-friendly VCR.

Specifications: height, 3¾"; **width,** 14¹²⁄₁₃"; **depth,** 12¾"; **weight,** 13⁹⁄₁₀ pounds. **Warranty: parts,** one year; **labor,** 90 days.

Approx. retail price	**Approx. low price**
$550	**$394**

PANASONIC PV-4164 ✓ BEST BUY

The Panasonic PV-4164 is a sophisticated four-head hi-fi stereo VHS VCR with quasi S-VHS playback, shuttle control, and front (line 2) and rear (line 1) audio and video inputs and outputs. The PV-4164 is designed for those who have another VCR and a camcorder, and who do a lot of editing and re-recording. The shuttle ring on the front panel of the VCR is used to control the forward or reverse speed of the tape from still to slow to normal to fast scan. This is useful when searching for the exact frame where you want to start your recording. The front-mounted A/V jacks make it easy to hook up your camcorder to copy or edit a tape. The front jacks are inputs when you are in the record mode and output jacks when

Prices are accurate at time of printing; subject to manufacturer's change.

you are in the playback mode. The PV-4164 has no channel selectors—all channel selections are on the remote. The remote commander, which can also control select Panasonic TV sets, has many sophisticated functions, from a manual override for those rare tapes that the automatic-digital tracking cannot handle to a bookmark search for an unrecorded section of a tape. There is also a time search, where you enter the time to be fast forwarded or rewound before the unit begins playback. During playback, a monitor button pauses the tape and displays the TV channel. The 4-event/30-day on-screen timer recorder is programmed with the remote commander. There is also 24-hour delayed recording and one-touch timed recording activated from the remote with the time on and/or time off appearing on-screen. The PV-4164 has a rapid-access system that starts to play or record about 1½ seconds after the command button is pressed. The reaction time is just as quick when switching from play to forward or reverse search and back to play. A built-in head cleaner keeps dust and dirt from marring your picture. The Panasonic PV-4164 is a versatile unit designed for those who want to do a lot of copying.

Specifications: height, 3½"; **width,** 15⅞"; **depth,** 11¼"; **weight,** 9⅛ pounds. **Warranty: parts,** one year; **labor,** 90 days (carry-in service).

Approx. retail price	Approx. low price
$529	$419

RCA VR334

The RCA VR334 is a monaural two-head VHS VCR with high speed rewind and auto-channel tuning. After pressing the program button, select the VCR setup, and then press autoprogram—the VCR tunes in all the broadcast or cable channels in your area. On-screen programming of the four-event/one-year timer is done with the wireless remote control, as are all other on-screen operations, such as immediate or delayed express recording (XPR). The remote can also control basic functions of compatible television sets as well as a second RCA VCR. The real-time counter is well suited for the VR334's time-search operation. Just enter the amount of time you wish to skip before play starts, then press either fast forward or rewind. The VR334 has autoplay and autorewind.

When you insert a cassette with the record protected tab removed, the tape automatically starts to play. At the end of the tape, it is automatically rewound and the VCR shuts off when the power button is pressed during rewind. Automatic tracking during playback will adjust for most tapes whether prerecorded or made on another machine. For problem tapes, manual tracking adjustments can be done from the remote. The RCA VR334 is an attractive, modestly priced monaural VCR with many fine features.

Specifications: height, 3½"; **width,** 14"; **depth,** 11¼"; **weight,** 8⅝ pounds. **Warranty: parts,** one year (carry-in service); **labor,** 90 days.

Approx. retail price	Approx. low price
$319	$299

PANASONIC PV-4127 ✔BEST BUY

The Panasonic PV-4127 is a four-head HQ VHS VCR with digital automatic tracking and automatic head cleaning. The PV-4127 comes with a liquid crystal display (LCD) program director that is the simplest and most logical programming device we have ever seen. Program dials are rotated to enter the date, start time, stop time, and channel in the LCD panels: Press the transmit button to transfer the program to the VCR. Up to eight programs can be programmed for the PV-4127. The LCD program director PV-PC100 is available separately for those who own other Panasonic VCRs. Programming can also be done with the unified VCR/TV remote commander, including one-touch instant or delayed recording. A real-time counter displays hours, minutes, and seconds. A time-search feature lets you enter the time in hours and/or minutes; then the VCR fast forwards or rewinds to that time and starts playback. The bookmark button sets the VCR to search for an unrecorded section of the tape. A monitor button puts the tape in pause and displays the channel set on the VCR. The quick-start feature starts playback or record about one second after the play or one-touch record buttons are pressed. Playback special effects include frame-by-frame advance, variable slow motion, double-speed playback, instant search, and rapid search. On the front panel is a shuttle control that handles all playback special effects in one control. Automatic programming of the 155-

Prices are accurate at time of printing; subject to manufacturer's change.

channel quartz tuner locks in all broadcast or cable channels in your area. There are both front and rear line inputs and outputs, which make it easy to hook up another VCR permanently, and you can quickly connect a camcorder at the front of the PV-4127. Finally, a child lock switch prevents children from putting foreign objects in the tape compartment. The Panasonic PV-4127 is a fine, reasonably priced monaural VCR with many features.

Specifications: height, 3½"; **width,** 15⅞"; **depth,** 11¼"; **weight,** nine pounds. **Warranty: parts,** one year; **labor,** 90 days.

Approx. retail price	Approx. low price
$429	$369

SAMSUNG VR3901   ✔ BEST BUY

The Samsung VR3901 is a reasonably priced HQ VHS VCR with a linear-time counter, index search, and quick-start full-loading tape system. The time counter in the LED display on the VCR only displays hours and minutes, but the on-screen display shows hours, minutes, and seconds. When you put a cassette in the VR3901, it immediately loads the tape so that when you press the play button, you are watching a picture in less than two seconds. Shifting from normal or fast search to play also takes less than two seconds, while going to play from fast forward or rewind takes only three seconds. The VR3901 puts an index signal on the tape at the beginning of every recording and also allows you to manually enter or erase index marks. An automatic-program feature cycles through the 181-channel tuner and locks in every channel in your area. A monitor switch lets you quickly check a channel during tape play by putting the tape in pause and switching to the TV tuner. There are both front and rear video and audio jacks for connecting another VCR or a camcorder. The jacks are set up so that when you plug a unit into the front jacks, the rear input jacks are inoperative to eliminate interference. The wireless remote is used for on-screen programming of the eight-event/one-year program timer, while the one-touch recording button is on the VCR. Electronic tracking, which is controlled from the remote, is usually found only on expensive machines. The remote can also be used to control most TV sets by holding down the TV button on the remote and pressing the

Prices are accurate at time of printing; subject to manufacturer's change.

number that corresponds to your brand of TV. The Samsung VR3901 is an inexpensive monaural VCR that is packed with features, including a head cleaner that removes dust particles every time you load or unload a cassette.

Specifications: height, 3½"; **width,** 15"; **depth,** 12¼"; **weight,** 13 pounds. **Warranty: parts,** one year; **labor,** 90 days.

Approx. retail price	Approx. low price
$380	$239

PANASONIC PV-2101 — RECOMMENDED

The Panasonic PV-2101 is an inexpensive no-frills two-head VHS VCR. The no-frills means that there is no fluorescent display panel on the VCR, just four small lights: power on, VCR tuner on, timer programmed, and record indicators. All readouts for time of day, real-time counter, one-touch recording, channel select, and timer programming are displayed on-screen. The PV-2101 has a digital-quartz tuner that can automatically program itself to receive all broadcast or cable channels in your area. Digital tracking will automatically track most recorded and prerecorded tapes. If you occasionally come across a rental tape that it cannot track, the tracking can be adjusted with the tracking buttons on the remote control. The quick-play mechanism starts play two seconds after pressing the play button. Special playback effects include double-speed playback, still picture, and slow-motion play. Automatic functions include autoplay with record tab removed, autorewind at end of tape, and memory rewind with VCR shutoff.

Specifications: height, 3½"; **width,** 14⅛"; **depth,** 11¼"; **weight,** 8¹⁄₁₀ pounds. **Warranty: parts,** one year; **labor,** 90 days (carry-in service).

Approx. retail price	Approx. low price
$269	$225

8mm VIDEOCASSETTE RECORDER

SONY EV-S550

The Sony EV-S550 is an 8mm VCR with edit and synchro-edit capabilities, edit shuttle, hi-fi stereo, and PCM audio recording.

The EV-S550 can be connected to any VCR or camcorder with a LANC control jack for synchro editing. This allows you to control the start and pause of both units by the controls of the one unit with an edit switch; this produces the best possible re-recording. Recordings on the EV-S550 can be made at either the single-play or long-play tape speeds. The EV-S550 has a linear time counter that keeps track of lapsed time in hours, minutes, and seconds at either speed, making it easy to keep track of your recordings and to locate exact scenes on your tapes. The jog shuttle and the linear counter make it very easy to locate your already completed tape via audio dubbing on the PCM track without affecting either the video or standard sound track. Playback special effects include still picture, frame-by-frame advance, slow-motion playback at ⅒- or ⅕-normal speed, two-times normal speed playback with or without sound, and momentary-picture viewing during fast forward and reverse. It is also capable of high-speed picture search in fast forward and reverse. Almost all playback special effects are controllable from either the VCR or the remote control. The commander has an LCD (liquid crystal display) panel, which makes it easy to set the clock and to program the six-event/one-month timer. Once the time or program displayed on the screen is correct, you press the transmit button, which transfers the information to the VCR. The tuner has an automatic-preset mode that scans the channels in your area, either broadcast or cable, and locks in the channels that are live. The Sony EV-S550 is a full-featured and versatile VCR for those who want to expand their 8mm capabilities.

Specifications: height, 4⅞"; **width,** 16⅞"; **depth,** 11⅞"; **weight,** 8¹⁄₁₀ pounds. **Warranty: parts,** one year; **labor,** 90 days.

Approx. retail price	Approx. low price
$850	$659

LASER DISC PLAYERS

A laser disc is an optical medium for playing video and digital audio recordings. Pits cut in the disc are read by a laser beam. Because there is no physical contact, the acrylic-coated discs will virtually last forever. Laser discs also produce excellent image quality with ordinary hookups to your television set, and are capable of producing superb images with nearly twice the horizontal resolution of standard videotapes when hooked up to new TV sets that have S-VHS connections. The newer laser disc players, known as multidisc players, play all available formats of audio and video discs.

One of the peculiarities of laser discs is the different types of counters used for CAV and CLV (see below) recorded discs. A frame counter is used to keep track of the recording on standard CAV discs, while long-play CLV discs use elapsed-time counters. The counters are recorded on the discs, and the players automatically display the counter recorded on the disc being played.

Laser Disc Terminology

LD: Laser disc

LDP: Laser disc player

CD: Compact (audio) disc

CDV: Compact disc with video

CAV: Constant angular velocity: LDs spin at a constant speed of 1,800 rpm with a playing time of 30 minutes per side; all CAV discs can be played back with special effects.

CLV: Constant linear velocity: LDs spin at speeds varying from 1,800 rpm for the inner tracks to 600 rpm for the outer tracks with a playing time of 60 minutes per side. Special effects with CLVs are only possible with players that have digital frame memory.

Random access: All laser disc players have random access, which lets you quickly find a particular spot on a disc.

Chapter numbers: These numbers recorded on discs are used to indicate sections or chapters, and are used to find scenes with a chapter-search function. For example, a symphony with four movements will have four chapters. The movie *Batman* will have chapters such as: Chapter 1—Main title/credits; Chapter 2—Robbery in Gotham City, "I'm Batman"; Chapter 3—Press conference, etc.

PIONEER CLD-2090

The Pioneer CLD-2090 is a multidisc player with an alpha-turn system and twin one-bit DLC digital-analog (D/A) converters.

The alpha-turn system plays both sides of a laser disc automatically, going directly to side two and beginning play when side one is finished. This eliminates the need to turn the disc over when the first side is completed. Either side and any chapter of either side of an LD can be accessed at any time, so that you are not limited to playing the sides and chapters in sequence. The D/A converters, one for each channel, have double-step noise shaping that theoretically eliminates all noise and distortion in the process of converting digital sound to rich, full analog sound. The CLD-2090 has two sets of audio and video outputs for direct connection to any TV/monitor or amplifier with pin-plug jacks, and an S-video output for TV sets with an S-video input for the highest image quality. There is also a CD-deck synchro jack for synchro editing, which can be used with a Pioneer tape deck equipped with a synchro jack. Automatic-program editing selects and programs the songs that can be played back within a specified time. A last-memory function for laser discs allows you to turn the player off part way through a disc and turn it on later to start where you left off. A motor opens and closes the disc table for easy loading. Once a disc is loaded, the CLD-2090 automatically detects and displays the type of disc loaded on the front panel. The scan controls on both the player and the infrared remote allow you to vary the forward or reverse scan rate from approximately 3-times to 30-times normal speed. Variable-speed playback from 3-times to ⅟₆₀-times and single-frame advance is available with CAV discs. There are eight repeat modes from chapter repeat to full repeat of either or both sides of an LD. There are a number of video displays that range from simple time or frame and chapter display for video discs to audio output level meters with elapsed time and total chapter display. The Pioneer CLD-2090 is a fine multidisc player that gives you both sides of the story.

Specifications: height, 5⁵⁄₁₆"; **width,** 16⅜"; **depth,** 17¼"; **weight,** 18½ pounds. **Warranty: parts and labor,** one year.

Approx. retail price	Approx. low price
$800	**$576**

PANASONIC LX-101 RECOMMENDED

The Panasonic LX-101 is a laser multidisc player with a shuttle dial that has fast, clear cue, review playback, and editing

Prices are accurate at time of printing; subject to manufacturer's change.

capabilities for transferring CDs to audiotape. The shuttle dial allows you to vary the image-scan rate of laser discs and the audio-scan rate of compact discs. With the scan buttons on the remote control, the scanning is slow for the first two seconds, then rapid until the button is released. Special playback effects such as autoplay when the disc is placed in the drawer, scanning, chapter-intro scan (ten seconds of the beginning of each chapter is played back), skip to following chapter, and direct chapter access are available for both CAV and CLV discs. Direct access by time is only available with CLV discs. All other special effects, such as direct access to a frame number, image still, frame-by-frame advance, and multispeed playback variable from ⅟₉₀ normal speed (each frame displayed about 3 seconds) to 3-times normal speed, only work with CAV laser discs. The motorized disc drawer can be opened and closed with a button on the remote or on the player. For CDs, there is random playback of tunes, programmed playback of tunes, repeat playback, direct access, skipping, and intro-scan. Editing capabilities include programming for 30-, 60-, and 90-minute tapes and editing in programmed order. There are video on-screen displays of chapters, time, or frame lapse. The LX-101 features an S-VHS output, standard pin plug, and F cable connections for standard hookups. The Panasonic LX-101 is a fine multidisc player with excellent audio and video quality.

Specifications: height, 4⁷⁄₁₆″; **width,** 16¹⁵⁄₁₆″; **depth,** 15¾″; **weight,** 18 pounds. **Warranty: parts and labor,** one year.

Approx. retail price	Approx. low price
$600	not available

VIDEO ACCESSORIES

Video accessories can make operating your video equipment easier and better. Video editors allow you to enhance and improve a copied image, and add music and narration. But until now, they have been frightfully expensive. A videocassette rewinder saves you wear and tear on your VCR and camcorder. A video headcleaner will keep your picture sharp and extend the life of your video heads. If you have trouble programming your VCR, there are now machines that make your life easier.

Prices are accurate at time of printing; subject to manufacturer's change.

SIMA PRO ED/IT 3 (SED-3)

The Sima Pro Ed/it 3 (SED-3) is a video-processing center that includes color processing, signal enhancement, editing, and sound mixing stereo and/or monaural sources. There are two switchable video/stereo inputs, a stereo music input, and a stereo microphone input. Two video/stereo outputs let you make two copies simultaneously. Sliding volume controls provide easy sound mixing and fading of one sound source into another. A fade button allows you to add three-second fade-outs and fade-ins if you forgot to do so in the original recordings. The enhancement control adds brightness to dim recordings and brightness reduction of recordings made in contrasting light. A detail control allows you to increase or decrease the sharpness of the image, and a pic-set control optimizes a cross-formatted picture, such as copying an 8mm onto VHS. Separate color intensity and tint controls provide excellent manipulation of even very faded and color shifted recordings. The color intensity control also provides you with visual effects such as fading a color image to black and white.
Warranty: parts and labor, 90 days.

Approx. retail price	**Approx. low price**
$300	**$130**

VIVITAR VRW-1

The Vivitar VRW-1 is a basic unit that only rewinds a tape. Just open the cassette compartment, insert the tape, and close the cover. The machine begins rewinding. A T-120 tape is fully rewound in about 2½ minutes. When rewinding is complete, the cassette compartment reopens, and the VRW-1 turns off.
Warranty: parts and labor, one year.

Approx. retail price	**Approx. low price**
$30	**not available**

SCOTCH HEADCLEANING VIDEOCASSETTE ✔BEST BUY

The Scotch Headcleaning Videocassette is the best designed headcleaner. It has a unique prerecorded message that tells you when your video heads are clean and an audible signal that tells you when your audio heads are clean. Video and audio heads should be cleaned after about every 30 hours of playing time, and after about 15 hours if you play a lot of rental tapes. Unless your heads are very clogged, a couple of seconds will thoroughly clean them. The headcleaning videocassette will give you 240 cleanings.

Warranty: six months.

Approx. retail price	Approx. low price
$13	$11

GEMSTAR VCR PLUS+

✓ BEST BUY

The Gemstar VCR Plus+ is a palm-size battery-powered instant programming system that turns programming your VCR into a one-step operation. The VCR Plus+ is programmed by simply entering the PlusCodes for the shows you want to record. These codes are listed after each show in the *TV Guide* and newspaper TV sections. Then place the VCR Plus+ near your VCR, where it will start and stop recording each program you have selected at the appropriate times. The VCR Plus+ operates both remote-operated VCRs and cable boxes at the same time for easy multiprogramming of cable channels.

Warranty: parts and labor, 90 days.

Approx. retail price	Approx. low price
$60	$56

Camcorders

The camcorder, which combines a video camera and a videocassette recorder in one unit, allows you to capture live action on tape and immediately play it back on your television. The hit TV show *America's Funniest Home Videos* attests to the popularity of camcorders. Most of the videos from the 1991† Gulf War were shot with consumer-model camcorders, showing their professional picture quality. Rapid advances in technology are responsible for that quality, along with an ever-increasing number of features. Major advances include models with stereo hi-fi sound, the improved resolution of "super" and "hi-band" models, ultralow-light recording capability, and even a few models with color viewfinders.

Although increasingly longer (more powerful) zoom lenses are being offered on camcorders, they serve little purpose. An eight-power zoom lens is the maximum for steady shooting with a handheld camcorder. Only if you have firm support, such as a monopod or tripod, can you effectively use a 12-power zoom lens.

In the past year, camcorder prices fell as the market became more competitive. The VHS formats offered the greatest discounts, but even the popular 8mm models became more affordable. While picture quality between models in similar categories varies only modestly, the feel and operational ease differ substantially.

CAMCORDERS

When traveling overseas with your camcorder, be aware that outside of Japan, Korea, and Taiwan, you cannot watch your tapes on local TV sets. Most of the world uses a different video standard than we do. Airport security devices, unless grossly defective, will NOT damage your camcorder or your tapes. When flying with your camcorder, always be sure that its battery is charged. Airport security will often ask you to turn it on to prove that what you are carrying is actually a camcorder.

The tide dramatically turned this year beaching the full-size VHS models and carrying forward the VHS-C and 8mm compact formats. The U.S. finally joined the rest of the world in preferring smaller camcorders. The change was so noticeable that JVC, which formerly marketed mostly full-size models, now sells only compact models. Of the compact formats, the 8mm is pulling ahead.

Camcorder Formats

VHS camcorders have a longer recording capacity (up to eight hours at the slow EP, extended play, speed with T-160 tapes) than recorders using other formats. Full-size VHS is the only format directly playable in home VHS VCRs. However, the bulky size of the VHS cassette with its ½-inch-wide tape requires a relatively large, often heavy camcorder. Camcorders without the hi-fi option record low-fidelity audio. An upgraded VHS format, S-VHS (Super VHS), uses a specially formulated, much more expensive tape that records up to 400 lines of resolution and far outperforms conventional VHS tapes.

VHS-C is a variation of the VHS format that uses cassettes about the same circumference as audio cassettes, but twice as thick. VHS-C records signals fully compatible with full-size VHS. This allows VHS-C cassettes to record and play on any VHS VCR with the use of an adapter. Some new VCRs play these small tapes without an adapter. VHS-C tapes record for 30 minutes at SP (standard play) and 90 minutes at EP. A new tape expected in 1992 will increase that time to 40 minutes at SP and 120 minutes at EP. S-VHS-C camcorders are also available. VHS-C has been losing market share to the 8mm format.

8mm cassettes are thinner than other videocassettes because the tape is only about ⅛ inch wide. By using metal tape technology to increase recording density, 8mm tapes reproduce an image equal to or better than most ½-inch VHS tapes. Camcorders that use this format, like those that use the VHS-C, are becoming increasingly more compact and lightweight, with many models weighing less than two pounds. An 8mm camcorder records for two hours at the fast (SP) speed. The slow (EP) speed is not available for recording on most camcorders, but permits four hours of recording on home VCRs.

Hi Band 8mm (Hi8) offers the same resolution as S-VHS (about 400 lines), but Hi8 records with slightly less color noise, so the picture quality is subtly better than S-VHS. Standard 8mm tapes will record and play on Hi8 machines, but tapes recorded on Hi8 will not play back on conventional 8mm machines. Hi8 camcorders require special tape, and two new metal tape formulations have been developed: a premium metal evaporated tape (Hi8-ME), and an improved metal particle tape (Hi8-MP). Both are more expensive than the standard tape. Hi8-ME records with slightly less picture noise than Hi8-MP. Hi8 camcorders, like S-VHS, include "S" jacks for maximum signal transfer quality to another VCR or TV. However, much of the Hi8 advantage can still be realized with ordinary cables.

The standard 8mm mono soundtrack is high fidelity, unlike VHS. Until recently, the only stereo hi-fi soundtrack for 8mm was a complex digital system available only on one or two of the most expensive models. Now many 8mm camcorders also use the simpler AFM (audio frequency modulation) stereo hi-fi soundtrack.

Unlike VHS, the 8mm format was designed for camcorder use since its inception. Perhaps this explains its continuing surge in popularity. The 8mm cassettes are more robust and less susceptible to damage and mishandling than the VHS-C cassettes. These reasons account for our expanded listings of 8mm camcorders.

The VHS and 8mm formats are electronically compatible. This allows you, for example, to connect your 8mm camcorder to your VHS VCR and copy your 8mm videos onto VHS tape. Front panel input jacks for this purpose are becoming nearly standard on VHS VCRs. You can also connect your 8mm camcorder directly to your TV for viewing. You do not have to buy a camcorder that uses the same format as your VCR.

Features and Terminology

Before shopping for a camcorder, you should be familiar with the following terms:

Aperture designation tells you the maximum opening of the iris, or the greatest amount of light that can be admitted. The designation is given as an f-stop rating, such as f/1.6. The iris automatically adjusts in all camcorders. Some offer a desirable manual adjustment as well.

Autofocus describes a feature that focuses the lens as the distance between the camcorder and the subject changes. Some camcorders also have manual focus. Each company uses a proprietary autofocus system, with varying degrees of speed and accuracy. While most companies have switched to some form of a computerized through-the-lens (TTL) system, the simpler infrared system often works better. Be sure to try out the autofocus when evaluating a camcorder.

CCD (charge-coupled device) is a solid-state imaging device that replaces the pickup tube. CCDs eliminate most image lag, which looks like a streaking highlight on a moving subject. CCDs function well in a broad range of lighting conditions and are rarely damaged by excessive light. All CCDs used in camcorders are based on MOS (metal-oxide semiconductor) devices. The CCD is a system by which electrons are collected and moved through the imaging device. The MOS is the type of light-sensitive transistor making up the CCD. References to CCD or MOS in camcorder specifications are arbitrary and bear little relationship to the quality of the product.

Character generators allow you to add the time, date, titles, or other written information to the images you are recording.

Continuous white balance is used to keep the color of video images true to life. An inaccurate white balance can result in a picture that is too red or too blue.

Fade-in/fade-out is a feature of some camcorders that automatically takes the image to or from a blank screen.

Flying erase head is an erase head mounted on the spinning video head drum, rather than mounted in a stationary position along the tape path. Because it spins with the other heads, the flying erase head allows you to make smooth transitions when you stop and start the tape between scenes, eliminating noise bursts. The flying erase head is particularly desirable if you plan to edit your tapes.

High-speed shutter alters the method that the camcorder uses to collect light from its CCD imaging device. This results in the equivalent of allowing less light into the camcorder. As with a still camera, the high-speed shutters operate at speeds up to $\frac{1}{40,000}$ of a second. Unless you plan to shoot sports events, this is not an essential feature, although most camcorders now include it.

Lux is a method of measuring the amount of light that is falling on a photo subject. Many camcorders have a low light level rating of around 10 lux; this is the amount of light on a subject about 12 feet from a single 60-watt light bulb. While sensitive camcorders deliver a picture signal with 2 lux, you are more likely to get a good image with 80 lux. The best color and depth of focus require several hundred lux.

Microphones are built into all camcorders, and most can be connected to external mikes as well.

Minimum illumination tells you the minimum amount of light, stated in lux, that you need to record a clear picture. Many camcorders deliver a picture signal with about four lux and can be used with ordinary indoor lighting.

Pixels, which is short for picture elements, are the tiny points that make up the video image. In general, a high pixel count produces a more detailed video image, but because the size and type of imaging devices vary, comparing pixel counts between two different devices doesn't always determine which one yields the more detailed image.

Resolution is the ability to produce fine detail in a video picture. It is usually measured in horizontal lines. A good video monitor produces more than 500 lines; TV broadcasts are about 340 lines; conventional VHS reproduces 240 lines; and 8mm yields slightly more.

Superimposer is a digital memory function that can store images or titles. At the push of a button, you can superimpose the stored image over the picture that is currently being recorded.

Best Buys '92

Our Best Buy and Recommended camcorders follow; they were all evaluated on their performance from tapes recorded under a variety of conditions and played back directly on a Sony 32-inch XBR color television/monitor. The camcorders are listed within each category according to their quality, features, and value. The unit we consider the best of the Best Buys is first, followed by our second choice, and so on. Keep in mind that a Best Buy or Recommended rating applies only to the model listed, not to other models by the same manufacturer or in the same product line.

8mm CAMCORDERS

SONY CCD-TR81

✓ BEST BUY

The Sony CCD-TR81 is a Hi8 camcorder that resembles the other models in Sony's "TR" (travel) line of camcorders. In performance, it's light years ahead of any model in its ultra-miniature size category. The CCD-TR81 is the first super-compact hi-band (Hi8) model. Hi8 recording captures the full high resolution of its ½-inch, 410,000-pixel CCD imager. In addition to outstanding picture quality, the CCD-TR81 records in stereo hi-fi sound. The special design of the built-in microphone reduces wind noise. The CCD-TR81 comes with an eight-power zoom lens and a seven-position high-speed shutter, and it requires two-lux minimum illumination. The one-page superimposer allows you to scroll the image from the bottom to the top of the screen. With the fader you can fade to black. The built-in clock/calendar changes time zones at the push of a button. The camcorder comes with a miniature wireless remote control with a belt clip. The optional SPK-TRX Sports Pack water-resistant housing ($250) increases the versatility of the CCD-TR81.

Specifications: height, 4⅛"; **width,** 4⅜"; **length,** 7"; **weight,** 1¾ pounds without battery and tape. **Warranty: parts,** one year; **labor,** 90 days.

Approx. retail price	Approx. low price
$1,500	not available

SONY CCD-TR51

RECOMMENDED

The Sony CCD-TR51 8mm camcorder is so ultracompact that it breaks the weight record for a camcorder. It's almost a quarter of a pound lighter than the previous CCD-TR4 model. The

---

Prices are accurate at time of printing; subject to manufacturer's change.

CCD-TR51's ⅓-inch, 270,000 pixel CCD imager is coupled with a 6-power zoom lens. It has a three-lux light sensitivity. While the original Sony TR models encountered some autofocus difficulties, this new model is definitely improved. However, Sony's through-the-lens autofocus still fails to match the best infrared autofocus models. The CCD-TR51 includes six high-speed shutter settings and a one-page superimposer. An added bonus with this basic model is stereo hi-fi sound. Simply pushing a button adjusts the built-in clock/calendar to any time zone in the world. Sony supplies a wireless remote with the CCD-TR51. This camcorder records great videos, includes plenty of features, and fits in the palm of your hand.

Specifications: height, 4″; **width,** 4¼″; **length,** 6⅝″; **weight,** 1³⁄₁₀ pounds without battery. **Warranty: parts,** one year; **labor,** 90 days.

Approx. retail price	Approx. low price
$1,200	$1,050

RCA PRO860 RECOMMENDED

The RCA PRO860 8mm camcorder is an ultra-compact, full-featured design. Not much larger than a large hand, the PRO860 uses digital signal processing for improved automated functions, such as autoexposure. The use of artificial intelligence aids when adjusting the iris and white balance. The PRO860's ⅓-inch, 250,000-pixel CCD is coupled with an 8-1 power zoom lens and a 6-position high-speed shutter. The PRO860 requires a minimum illumination level of three lux. The infrared autofocus is accurate and extremely fast. This unit includes a two-page superimposer. The electronic viewfinder displays tape time remaining.

Specifications: height, 4½″; **width,** 4½″; **length,** 6⅞″; **weight,** 1⅘ pounds without battery and tape. **Warranty: parts,** one year (carry-in service); **labor,** 90 days.

Approx. retail price	Approx. low price
$1,100	not available

CANON E40 RECOMMENDED

The Canon E40 8mm camcorder combines ruggedness, durability, ease of use, and good performance in a moderately

Prices are accurate at time of printing; subject to manufacturer's change.

compact package. A ⅓-inch, 270,000-pixel CCD is coupled with an 8-power zoom lens and a highly accurate infrared autofocus. It focuses within two feet of the subject, even when fully zoomed. It has two high-speed shutter positions. Canon's autoexposure and automatic white balance are slightly more sophisticated than many competing models. This comes from Canon's long experience in making cameras. Automatic backlight compensation adjusts for objects in front of bright backgrounds. The 180-degree FlexiGrip allows the camcorder to rotate around the grip/viewfinder for a continuous range of comfortable shooting angles. A gain-up mode increases sensitivity to two lux. The E40 has automatic fade-in/fade-out to white. A built-in titler and clock/calendar allow you to document your videos.

Specifications: height, 4¹⁵⁄₁₆″; **width,** 4⁵⁄₁₆″; **length,** 11⁷⁄₁₆″; **weight,** 2½₀ pounds without battery and tape. **Warranty: parts,** one year; **labor,** 90 days.

Approx. retail price	Approx. low price
$1,250	$836

FULL-SIZE VHS CAMCORDERS

PANASONIC PV-704

The Panasonic PV-704 is a full-size VHS camcorder with an innovative design that makes it easy to use and that reduces the burden of size and weight associated with most full-size models. The Switch Hitter locates the grip with controls in the center under the lens barrel for equal convenience of right- or left-handed people. To complement this, the viewfinder flips from one side to the other. The PV-704 couples its ⅓-inch, 270,000-pixel CCD with an 8-power zoom. It has a six-position high-speed shutter. In addition to two-lux light sensitivity, the PV-704 comes with a small video light, acknowledging that even camcorders with good sensitivity need extra light for a good picture. A flying erase head provides smooth edits, and edit search and bookmark search offer quick and easy access to the beginning of recorded segments for faster edits. The digital autofocus adjusts quickly and accurately. The camcorder fades in and out to black. The PV-704 includes a clock/

Prices are accurate at time of printing; subject to manufacturer's change.

calendar, which is visible in the electronic viewfinder and is recordable. Panasonic supplies an attache-style carrying case with the PV-704.
Specifications: height, 8⅛"; **width,** 3⅜"; **length,** 14½"; **weight,** 4⅕ pounds without battery and tape. **Warranty: parts,** one year; **labor,** 90 days.

Approx. retail price	**Approx. low price**
$1,000	$898

SHARP VL-L50U "SLIMCAM" ✓**BEST BUY**

The Sharp VL-L50U "Slimcam" full-size VHS camcorder is the first full-size model to directly compete with compact models. It's the lightest full-size camcorder on the market. Sharp compressed the camcorder's width to make it competitive with VHS-C. The VL-L50U is slim, but long enough to support with your shoulder for steadier videos. You'll need that support when using the full magnification of the twelve-power zoom lens. You can zoom that lens at a wide range of speeds from 6 to 20 seconds. There's a five-position high-speed shutter. Behind the shutter is a ⅓-inch CCD with 270,000 pixels. A Cat's Eye feature permits shooting in as little as one lux. Rather than simple automatic functions, Sharp employs a degree of artificial intelligence in white balance and exposure settings to adjust for optimum recording. The flying erase head permits seamless edits. The VL-L50U has a clock/calendar.
Specifications: height, 7⁵⁄₃₂"; **width,** 3⁵⁄₃₂"; **length,** 13⅞"; **weight,** 3⁷⁄₁₀ pounds without battery and tape. **Warranty: parts,** one year; **labor,** 90 days.

Approx. retail price	**Approx. low price**
$1,880	not available

VHS-C CAMCORDERS

JVC GR-AX2U ✓**BEST BUY**

The JVC GR-AX2U VHS-C camcorder is the budget model of the ultracompact JVC VHS-C camcorders, matching the smallest 8mm models in size and weight. It strongly resembles last year's breakthrough GR-AX7U VHS-C model. Its 6-power zoom lens is coupled with a ⅓-inch CCD with 270,000 pixels, with 4 high-speed shutter settings. It requires a minimum of one-lux illumination. It has automatic backlight compensation. We like this unit because its size and shape make shooting easy and fun. It's an affordable first camcorder that has everything the novice home videomaker needs to get started. **Specifications: height,** 4⅝"; **width,** 6¹¹⁄₁₆"; **length,** 4¹³⁄₁₆"; **weight,** 2 pounds without battery and tape. **Warranty: parts,** one year; **labor,** 90 days.

Approx. retail price	Approx. low price
$1,000	not available

PANASONIC PV-41 "PALMCORDER"

✓ **BEST BUY**

The Panasonic PV-41 "Palmcorder" is a reworking of last year's PV-40, incorporating user feedback for an improved model. One improvement is a small detachable video light. The PV-41, with its slightly improved performance, is easier to hold and more sleek and elegant than the boxy PV-40. The PV-41 represents the top-of-the-line of Panasonic's aptly named "Palmcorders." Although not quite as small as the JVC GR-AX2U, its under-two-pound weight makes it easy to tote. It comes loaded with features. The PV-41's ⅓-inch, 270,000-pixel CCD is coupled with an 8-power zoom lens. However, digital circuitry within the PV-41 can magnify this electronically to a twelve-power zoom lens. It incorporates a seven-position high-speed shutter, a flying erase head for seamless edits, and a one-page superimposer. The clock/calendar is powered by a rechargeable lithium battery that automatically recharges from the main battery. The time and date, as well as the real-time tape counter, are displayed in the viewfinder. The circuitry that provides a digital freeze-frame on playback also supplies a digital strobe function when recording. With digital strobe you can record a progression of momentary still-frame images, giving the camcorder the versatility of an electronic still-frame camera. What makes the PV-41 unique is a proprietary Panasonic feature called Digital Electronic Image Stabilization (Digital E.I.S.). This reduces distracting jitter from unwanted camcorder movement, such as shaky hands or vehicle movement. It aids in shooting while walking and riding, reducing the

Prices are accurate at time of printing; subject to manufacturer's change.

irritating unsteadiness that usually accompanies shooting while in motion. Some resolution is lost with Digital E.I.S., and it does not work in all situations, but most people will find it a desirable feature.

Specifications: height, 4½"; **width,** 3⅞"; **length,** 7¾"; **weight,** 1½ pounds without battery or tape. **Warranty: parts,** one year; **labor,** 90 days.

Approx. retail price	Approx. low price
$1,300	$1,065

JVC GR-SX90U   ⬚ RECOMMENDED

The JVC GR-SX90U S-VHS stereo hi-fi camcorder is the first ultracompact S-VHS camcorder. It's barely larger and no heavier than the basic GR-AX2U, but it has the features of larger models. The 8-power zoom of the GR-SX90U is coupled with a ½-inch, 360,000-pixel CCD, which has a sensitivity of 3 lux. It has six high-speed shutter settings. A unique feature is its cinema mode. At the push of a button, the camcorder electronically letterboxes the video to give it the same aspect ratio (shape) as a movie. This is useful because future TV sets will use this wide-aspect ratio. You can digitally superimpose in eight colors and switch superimposition from positive to negative for special effects. The GR-SX90U incorporates a flying erase head and a master edit control system for easy, glitch-free editing. The camcorder records stereo audio in VHS hi-fi for excellent sound quality. JVC supplies a wireless remote control.

Specifications: height, 4⅜"; **width,** 4⁵⁄₁₆"; **length,** 6¹⁵⁄₁₆"; **weight,** 1⁹⁄₁₀ pounds without battery and tape. **Warranty: parts,** one year; **labor,** 90 days.

Approx. retail price	Approx. low price
$1,200	not available

Stereo Components

Home theater describes the merger of audio and video systems. Stereo components now complement entertainment systems, which include a TV and VCR. VCRs and laser disc players that play (and in the case of VCRs, record) soundtracks in true stereo high fidelity, as well as stereo TV broadcasts, increase the desire for improved audio for video. The success of the CD (compact disc) and the arrival of DAT (Digital Audio Tape) more than ever justify a good stereo component system.

While some manufacturers offer special audio systems to complement their video products, most standard audio components mate easily with TVs and VCRs equipped with stereo output jacks. Just be careful not to place the speakers too close to the TV screen. Unless they were specially designed for this kind of placement, the speaker magnets can distort the color of the picture.

Buying stereo components instead of a prepackaged or all-in-one system allows you to upgrade your equipment at any time without having to discard the entire system. It also allows you to add new technologies as they come along. If you cannot afford all the components you want (or the quality of components you want), you can begin with just a stereo receiver (which combines an amplifier and tuner) and two speakers. That will provide a high fidelity AM/FM stereo radio. Later you can add a CD player, cassette deck, and/or DAT.

During 1991, two new music recording/reproduction formats were broached. These are MD (mini disc), a 2½-inch CDlike disc, and DCC (digital compact cassette). Neither will make CDs obsolete, so feel free to buy a CD player. Neither MD nor DCC promises the same absolute sound quality as CD or DAT, but they aim to replace DAT, and ultimately analog compact cassettes as the mass market record/play medium of the future. MD and DCC will probably not be on the market before the end of 1992.

Over the past 25 years, technology has continuously raised the performance level of audio components while lowering the prices. The relatively stable dollar and low price of computer memory chips during the past year reaffirm this trend. When CD players were introduced in 1982 they cost $1,000. Now a better sounding player than the first players costs $150. Stereo components represent one of the best values in consumer goods.

Best Buys '92

Our Best Buy and Recommended stereo components follow. They are presented in the following categories: loudspeakers, headphones, receivers, compact disc players, turntables, phono cartridges, cassette decks, and DAT recorders. (Stereo systems and portable audio products are discussed in other chapters.) Within each category, components are listed by quality; the item we consider the best of the Best Buys is first, followed by our second choice, and so on. Remember that a Best Buy or Recommended designation applies only to the model listed; it does not necessarily apply to other models made by the same manufacturer or to an entire product line.

LOUDSPEAKERS

Choose loudspeakers more carefully than other components in your sound system. Speakers determine the personality of the system much more than the electronics do. Often it is advantageous to select speakers first, because some speakers require more power than others. This will influence your choice of a receiver. Speakers are the most subjective component in a stereo system. Thus, the advice of friends, magazine reviews, and speakers recommended here should serve only as the starting point for your listening. There are over 360 speaker companies flooding the market with multiple models. Discerning the sonic difference between two electronic components often requires intense concentration, but the differences between similarly priced speakers come through loud and clear. Insist on the right to return speakers that do not meet your expectations. Speakers interact dramatically with room acoustics. What sounds splendid in the store may sound tinny or muddy in your home. The size of the speaker enclosure and the number of individual speakers (woofers, tweeters, and midrange) do not always correlate with sound quality. We base our speaker rating on quality of construction, reputation, and listening tests.

Features and Terminology

The following are some terms you should know when shopping for speakers.

Power requirements: Different speakers apply different laws of physics to produce sound. High-efficient ported systems, also known as ducted or reflex systems, are most common among larger speakers. They take advantage of the resonance of the port, allowing the air inside the speaker to move in and out, acoustically amplifying the bass frequencies. Ported speakers use the amplifier or receiver's power efficiently and require modest power to produce ample sound levels. Low-efficiency acoustic-suspension (sometimes referred to as air-suspension) speakers, which are most common among bookshelf-size speakers, seal the enclosure tightly and force the speaker to fight the air within. In a well-designed system this results in good, tightly controlled bass. Large floor-standing speakers can produce throbbing levels with 24 watts of power, while compact bookshelf models sometimes require twice that much power.

Too much power can damage speakers, but speaker ratings and amplifier ratings do not always match. Speakers rated at 100 watts maximum may be powered safely by 300-watt amplifiers, but if you force all 300 watts into the speaker the sound would become so loud that it would cause you pain as well as damaging the speakers.

Speaker Impedance: Speaker impedances are commonly listed from 4 to 8 ohms, with some ranging from 2 to 16 ohms. This is a technical description of the amount of resistance the speaker offers to the flow of electrical signals. Under normal circumstances, impedance makes little difference to sound quality, but many receivers need a minimum of four ohms to work properly. Two pairs of four-ohm speakers connected to play at the same time equal two ohms as far as the receiver is concerned. A good receiver may work with two ohms, but other receivers will automatically shut off or blow a fuse. A two-ohm load can actually destroy a poorly designed receiver. If you intend to use two pairs of speakers, choose loudspeakers rated at eight ohms.

Woofers, tweeters, and other speaker elements: The woofer is the largest speaker component. It reproduces bass notes and often the lower midrange sounds. The tweeter is the smallest speaker component. It reproduces treble notes and often the upper midrange. Some speakers include a midrange speaker component that reproduces the range of sound between the woofer and the tweeter, the range of the human voice. Where a speaker component starts and finishes varies from one speaker to another.

The crossover network is a series of resistors, capacitors, and coils that divide the incoming sound from the receiver, ensuring that the bass goes to the woofer and the treble to the tweeter. These individual speaker components are "drivers." The size of the driver and the material from which it is manufactured offer no intrinsic advantages. An 8-inch woofer sometimes reproduces more bass than a 12-inch woofer, and paper surpasses some plastics in the quality of the speaker cone.

NHT ONE A

The NHT One A (NHT stands for Now Hear This) is an unconventionally attractive small bookshelf speaker. An angled front baffle is responsible for the distinctive appearance of this nonrectangular speaker. The 6½-inch woofer and 1-inch dome tweeter produce a smooth, natural sound with good bass for such a small box. (A matching sub-woofer is available for super-low bass.) The NHT One A comes finished in real oak veneer, although other optional finishes are available. The stereo image is lifelike. The speakers come magnetically shielded, making them an ideal choice for a high-quality video system. NHT is now owned by International Jensen.

Specifications: height, 12"; **width,** 7"; **depth,** 10"; **weight,** 11 pounds each. **Warranty: parts and labor,** five years.

Approx. retail price	Approx. low price
$350/pair	$279/pair

B&W DM-310

The B&W DM-310 represents the bargain in a new line of B&W speakers, which use components similar to much more expensive models without the elaborate and costly matrix enclosure. The ported enclosure holds an eight-inch polypropylene woofer and a one-inch metal dome tweeter. The enclosure comes finished in simulated walnut or black ash veneer. B&W pays attention to small details, such as the precise flare of the woofer cone, and molding nonconcentric grooves around the tweeter for the clearest possible sound. The DM-310 reproduces rich, full sound with good clarity. The frequency response ranges from below 60 hertz in the bass to over 20,000 hertz in the treble. Distortion is low.

Specifications: height, 19"; **width,** 10"; **depth,** 8¾"; **weight,** 15⅝ pounds. **Warranty: parts,** five years.

Approx. retail price	Approx. low price
$500/pair	$463/pair

CELESTION 5 ✓BEST BUY

The Celestion 5 is a good small speaker system. There's nothing fancy about these speakers. Their plain wood cabinets are finished in simulated oak or black ash veneer with a black cloth grille. Inside the sealed acoustic-suspension enclosure is a six-inch felted-fiber cone woofer in a polycarbonate basket and a one-inch titanium dome tweeter. The Celestion 5 is the response to the complaint of a lack of bass in the company's excellent, smaller Celestion 3. To realize full bass from the Celestion 5, it should be used on a bookshelf or a rigid stand near the wall. These speakers are pleasingly low in distortion and withstand large amounts of power, while they need relatively little power (as little as ten watts) for good sound. The frequency response ranges from below 70 hertz in the bass to 20,000 hertz in the treble. Versatile recessed rear binding posts secure bare wire, banana plugs, or lugged wire.

Specifications: height, 13⅝"; **width,** 8¹⁰⁄₁₀"; **depth,** 9⅝"; **weight,** 10⅜ pounds each. **Warranty: parts and labor,** five years.

Approx. retail price	Approx. low price
$400/pair	$329/pair

ALLISON ACOUSTICS AL-115   ✔BEST BUY

The Allison Acoustics AL-115 bookshelf speakers reproduce sound with pleasing accuracy and satisfying bass from a moderate-size enclosure. Roy Allison, who designed these speakers, pioneered the acoustic suspension bookshelf speaker design and is credited as one of the popularizers of the bookshelf speaker. The AL-115 uses an eight-inch woofer specially treated with a proprietary energy-absorbing compound that soaks up spurious vibrations, and a one-inch ferro-fluid cooled dome tweeter. The speakers are average in sensitivity, and can reproduce good sound from an amplifier with as little as 15 watts per channel. The AL-115 cabinets come finished in a choice of walnut, oak, or black woodgrain vinyl.

Specifications: height, 20"; **width,** 11⅛"; **depth,** 10¹⁄₁₆"; **weight,** 22 pounds. **Warranty: parts and labor,** five years.

Approx. retail price	Approx. low price
$460/pair	$443/pair

TANNOY 609   RECOMMENDED

The Tannoy 609 large bookshelf loudspeakers reproduce an impressively transparent sound. These speakers from this well-established Scottish company recreate a convincing stereo image. For optimum bass they should be placed near a wall. The hexagonally shaped enclosure (which looks more like a trapezoid), with ultra rigid mineral reinforced top and bottom, reduces sound reflections inside the cabinet. This contributes to the clarity of sound. What Tannoy calls Differential Material Technology (DMT) joins the different parts of the cabinet and the drivers using special energy-absorbing compounds that

Prices are accurate at time of printing; subject to manufacturer's change.

damp out spurious vibrations. Each 609 consists of an eight-inch woofer with a one-inch aluminum dome tweeter mounted inside the woofer, a design Tannoy calls Dual-Concentric. This improves the perception that the sound originates from a single point. A soundwave guide, shaped like a tulip, helps project the sound forward. Only a slight shyness of bass prevent these speakers from being a Best Buy. The speakers come finished in black ash or walnut veneer.

Specifications: height, 19½"; **width,** 12⅜"; **depth,** 8⁹⁄₁₀"; **weight,** 22 pounds. **Warranty: parts and labor,** five years.

Approx. retail price	**Approx. low price**
$599/pair	not available

MB QUART 390MCS `RECOMMENDED`

The MB Quart 390MCS are mini-tower floor standing speakers with a wide sonic range. They have impressive bass, clear treble, and a very good stereo image. Music sounds solid with a great deal of depth. The 390MCS speakers achieve extended bass response through an innovative design called Moving Control System (MCS). A specially designed port allows air to move in and out at desired frequencies. This allows deep but highly controlled bass, the best combination of ported and acoustic suspension speaker systems. Each 390MCS speaker consists of an eight-inch woofer and a one-inch titanium dome tweeter. The cabinet consists of several different densities of particle board to minimize cabinet resonances, and is impressively finished in high-quality black ash. Imitation granite and imitation marble are optional, extra-cost finishes. Quart speakers are built to exceptional quality standards, and are hurt competitively by the exchange rate between the dollar and the deutsche mark. Their high cost disqualifies them as a Best Buy.

Specifications: height, 31½"; **width,** 9⅜"; **depth,** 10⅜"; **weight,** 29⅘ pounds. **Warranty: parts and labor,** five years.

Approx. retail price	**Approx. low price**
$1,100/pair	$1,099/pair

POLK 5JR+ `RECOMMENDED`

The Polk 5jr+ are three-way speakers that offer good value. Each speaker uses a 6½-inch woofer, 6½-inch midrange, and 1-

inch dome tweeter. A bass radiator acoustically couples with the mid-bass driver to reinforce bass response between 30 and 60 hertz. The overall frequency range is 30 hertz to 25 kilohertz. The high sensitivity of the Polk 5jr+ requires only 20 watts of amplifier power. The cabinet is available in black or oak finish.

Specifications: height, 19½"; **width,** 10"; **depth,** 10"; **weight,** 20 pounds each. **Warranty: parts and labor,** five years.

Approx. retail price	Approx. low price
$370/pair	not available

HEADPHONES

Like speakers, headphones are best judged according to how they sound. But unlike speakers, headphones are unaffected by room acoustics, and their sound quality needs to please no one but their owner. The general criteria for good headphone performance include a full bass response with accurate tonal definition and balance from the midrange frequencies up to the highest frequencies.

A headset must also be comfortable. Weight and fit should be considered carefully. There are three basic designs for headphones. **Circumaural phones** cover your entire outer ear and block out all external sound. **Supra-aural phones** do not completely block external sound. **Open-air phones** rest lightly against the outer ear and usually have a foam pad that separates the actual phone from your head, so that almost all outside sounds can be heard while wearing them.

As a general rule, circumaural phones provide the best bass while open-air phones usually provide the least bass. Another style of headphone inserts directly into the ear. These tend to be difficult to keep in the ear and are uncomfortable. They also tend to have less fidelity than other types of headphones.

AUDIO-TECHNICA ATH-M4X

The Audio-Technica ATH-M4X headphones are a terrific bargain. They produce smooth, full-bodied sound with great bass. Audio-Technica uses copper-clad aluminum wire for the voice coil and a powerful samarium cobalt magnet for the best com-

Prices are accurate at time of printing; subject to manufacturer's change.

bination of conductivity, low mass, and strong magnetic field. The round ear cups sit lightly and directly on the ear. The cushion material is a crepelike leatherette that feels quite comfortable. The well-padded headband is a single band of metal that provides the ear cups with adequate movement for a good fit. Although considerably more substantial than the phones supplied with headphone stereos, the ATH-M4X phones weigh only four ounces. The 10-foot straight cord terminates with a stereo mini-plug, and comes with a ¼-inch snap-on adapter for standard stereo jacks.

Warranty: parts and labor, one year.

Approx. retail price	Approx. low price
$50	$35

KOSS PRO/4XL

The Koss PRO/4XL represents the latest evolution of the company's classic PRO/4 series stereo headphones. They certainly are the most comfortable of the PRO/4 line-up. Breathable crepe-type vinyl cushions firmly surround the ear, supported by a broad, well-padded headband. The PRO/4XL, although full-size headphones, weigh only 12 ounces. A titanium coating on the diaphragm improves transient response and high clarity. The wide frequency response serves all music well. Koss supplies three- and eight-foot detachable cords, with gold-plated plugs, as well as a carrying case. The lifetime limited warranty makes these headphones particularly attractive.

Warranty: parts and labor, lifetime, limited.

Approx. retail price	Approx. low price
$130	not available

KOSS TNT-88

The Koss TNT-88 circumaural headphones have titanium nitride-coated diaphragms that are stronger and more rigid than titanium, but extremely lightweight. These diaphragms produce greater clarity throughout the midrange and treble. These headphones are rated for a high-frequency response of up to 30,000 hertz. The TNT-88 headphones weigh five ounces. Soft pneumalite ear cushions fit over the ear and seal out external sounds, as well as aiding good bass response. The TNT-88

Prices are accurate at time of printing; subject to manufacturer's change.

uses a double headband with a rigid outer band supporting the ear cups and a soft inner band resting on the head. The ear cups swivel in multiple planes for maximum comfort. The TNT-88 comes with a ten-foot straight cord, which employs DuPont Kevlar fibers that make the cord nearly indestructible. The cord has a gold-plated ⅛-inch mini stereo phone plug and a gold-plated ¼-inch adapter.

Warranty: parts and labor, lifetime.

Approx. retail price	Approx. low price
$70	not available

SONY MDR-V6 [RECOMMENDED]

The Sony MDR-V6 are full-size but lightweight stereo headphones, weighing seven ounces. They show good attention to detail and quality of construction. The large, oval crepelike leatherette ear cushions fit over and around the ear. They provide a good but breathable seal and are very comfortable on the ear, although the padded headband could use a little more padding. The MDR-V6s have a wide frequency response with excellent dynamic range. The 3-meter cord is a nice feature, terminating in a well-machined metal-jacketed stereo mini-plug, with a screw-on ¼-inch adapter provided. The MDR-V6 comes with a carrying pouch, into which the phones collapse.

Warranty: parts and labor, one year.

Approx. retail price	Approx. low price
$100	$78

RECEIVERS

A receiver combines a radio tuner with a preamplifier and a power amplifier on a single chassis in a well-matched system. The receiver provides radio reception, selects among inputs from other components, adjusts tone, and amplifies the selected audio signal.

The preamplifier section serves as a kind of switchboard for the entire system. It contains the program, or function, switch; volume and tone controls; and input and output terminals for program sources, such as turntables, cassette decks, and

Prices are accurate at time of printing; subject to manufacturer's change.

compact disc players. The preamplifier also boosts the level of electrical signals to a level suitable for the power amplifier section of the receiver.

The power amplifier boosts the signal it gets from the pre-amplifier to levels that are strong enough to cause the loud-speakers to deliver undistorted sound.

Features and Terminology

Here are some of the terms that you should know before you purchase a receiver:

Quieting (in dB, decibels) tells you the amount of signal that is needed at the antenna terminals to provide noise-free, acceptable reception. The lower the number, stated in microvolts (millionths of a volt) or dBf (femtowatts), the better.

Frequency response should be uniform, or "flat," over the entire range of human hearing from 20 to 20,000 hertz.

Power output is stated in watts. Be sure that the wattage applies to each channel and not to the sum of both stereo channels. Most amplifiers deliver higher power when hooked up to four-ohm speakers than they will when they are driving eight-ohm speakers. When you compare power outputs, make sure that they are referenced to the same speaker impedances.

Selectivity is the ability of a tuner to pick up and isolate stations that are close in frequency to each other. It is quoted in dB; the higher the number, the better. Look for at least 60 dB.

Sensitivity is usually stated in microvolts or in dBf. Excellent sensitivity figures of 2.0 microvolts or 10 to 12 dBf are typical. Sensitivity concerns you if you are attempting to receive weak radio stations or live in a fringe area.

Signal-to-Noise ratio (S/N) is a measure of how much background noise, or hiss, is present along with even, strong signals. S/N is stated in dB; the higher the number, the better, but anything above 75 dB is adequate for normal listening.

Stereo separation is the amount of separation between left and right stereo channels when receiving stereo FM broadcasts. While manufacturers often list separation figures as high as 50 dB, anything above 30 dB is adequate (the best phonograph cartridges rarely exceed 30 dB in separation).

Tape monitor (Loop) is a set of output and input jacks that allows you to interpose an external audio component in the signal path of an amplifier to monitor recordings as you make

Prices are accurate at time of printing; subject to manufacturer's change.

them or to process the signal through a device, such as a graphic equalizer.

SONY STR-AV570

The Sony STR-AV570 receiver is an upgrade from Sony's previous budget model, at the same price. The STR-AV570 produces 60 watts per channel, and its quartz-frequency synthesized tuner has direct access tuning. A numbered keypad lets you tap in the exact station frequency. For example, if you want to tune in a station at 98.7, you just press 9-8-7. You can also scan up and down. Once tuned, you can assign the station to one of 30 presets and recall it at the push of a single button. The STR-AV570 includes a video input as well as four audio inputs. A "matrix surround" button widens the breadth of the stereo image, giving the illusion of surround-sound while using only stereo speakers. A dynamic bass feedback system improves bass response. Sony supplies the STR-AV570 with remote control. We like the STR-AV570 because of its ease of operation, good performance, and reliability. A similar, but slightly inferior model with 20 watts less per channel and without remote is the STR-AV270, for about $30 less.

Warranty: parts and labor, two years.

Approx. retail price	Approx. low price
$240	$199

ONKYO TX-904

The Onkyo TX-904 tuner/amplifier is rated at 60 watts per channel, but can deliver considerably greater power on musical peaks because of its oversize power supply coupled with its high-current output transistors. The quartz-frequency synthesized AM/FM stereo tuner has 40 station presets, with a memory that needs no battery backup. The presets can be divided into six categories, such as rock, jazz, classical, etc. You can then select and scan each category. The TX-904 also has direct-access tuning with a numbered keypad that lets you key in the desired station frequency by number. Automatic Precision Reception (APR) monitors the FM reception and switches between stereo/mono, local/distance, and hi-blend

Prices are accurate at time of printing; subject to manufacturer's change.

on/off as needed for the best sound. This receiver also includes a CD direct mode, which bypasses the preamp, and a video input. An unusual extra is a sleep timer that shuts off the receiver automatically after a set amount of time. The tone controls are more precise than on many receivers, and are designed for the way your perception of high and low frequencies varies at different volumes. The bass boost is limited to deep bass, so it does not muddy the midrange. It comes supplied with wireless remote control and can be used with Onkyo's optional multiroom remote.

Warranty: parts and labor, two years.

Approx. retail price	Approx. low price
$400	$359

TECHNICS SA-GX505   ✓ BEST BUY

The Technics SA-GX505 receiver, with 110 watts per channel, incorporates a multitude of features. At first, its control-studded front panel may seem confusing, but basic functions such as volume, balance, and quartz-frequency synthesized tuning are controlled with old-fashioned big knobs. The different-sized knobs identify at a glance which adjustments you are making. The SA-GX505 includes four audio and two video inputs, including a front panel VCR input for a camcorder. There are 30 AM/FM radio station presets, plus rotary tuning. A versatile, precise tone-control system, called parametric equalization, provides greater control over tonal adjustments than ordinary tone controls. The SA-GX505's parametric equalizer permits adjusting four different user selectable points in the sound spectrum. The parametric equalization can be bypassed for the most natural sound. Technics includes Dolby Pro Logic, the most advanced Dolby surround-sound decoder for video. Pro Logic helps keep voices centered on the video screen by sending them to a center speaker. The SA-GX505 provides three additional ten-watt amplifiers to power the center and two rear channels. However, this is really insufficient. If you're serious about surround-sound you'll need additional amplifiers, since the center and rear channels should have at least one-third of the power of the front channels. A large fluorescent display fills the center third of the front panel. It shows relative frequency levels of what you're listening to, as well as the

levels and actions of the tone controls. The supplied 58-key remote operates other Technics and Panasonic components.
Warranty: parts and labor, one year.

Approx. retail price
$400

Approx. low price
$383

PIONEER VSX-4800 | RECOMMENDED |

The Pioneer VSX-4800 receiver includes three video inputs and four audio inputs. A large amber and red fluorescent display fills the center half of its front panel. The VSX-4800 produces 100 watts per channel for the left and right front channels, 20 watts per channel for the front center channel, and 18 watts per channel for the rear channels. The sensitive tuner section has a very good signal-to-noise ratio, and also should do a good job separating stations on a crowded dial. Pioneer's Hyper Intelligent Tuning System (HITS) stores settings and names for 30 radio stations. Using the custom memory function you can categorize stations into five groups: rock, pop, jazz, news, and party. A sleep timer turns the unit off after a 90-, 60-, or 30-minute period. The front panel display dims when you set the sleep timer. The VSX-4800 not only features Dolby Pro Logic, but the latest enhancement to Pro Logic called Time-Link. This lets you fine-tune the Pro Logic to your room. The return key is a convenient feature. Should someone in your household leave the receiver in an abnormal setting, the push of a button returns everything to normal status. While this Pioneer is a notch above the Technics in performance, it is not quite as versatile and is substantially more expensive, which is why it is not a Best Buy. The VSX-4800 comes with the standard Pioneer wireless remote. The VSX-4900S is the same receiver, but it is supplied with Pioneer's elaborate programmable Smart Remote, which controls other brands of equipment, for about $65 more.
Warranty: parts and labor, one year.

Approx. retail price
$520

Approx. low price
$357

JVC RX-305TN | RECOMMENDED |

The JVC RX-305TN receiver is a simple, solid, entry level 50-watts-per-channel receiver. It is comparable to the Sony STR-

Prices are accurate at time of printing; subject to manufacturer's change.
CONSUMER GUIDE®   131

AV570 in performance, but includes fewer features, which is why it is Recommended rather than a Best Buy. JVC imbues the RX-305TN with very attractive styling in the newly popular titanium finish, rather than black. The receiver has 40 AM/FM station presets. A simple synthesized surround-sound circuit provides a surroundlike effect when used with an additional stereo amplifier and speakers. The tuner of the RX-305TN matches the specifications of JVC's most expensive models, and the amplifier has specifications similar to more expensive models. JVC supplies a wireless remote control with the RX-305TN.

Warranty: parts and labor, two years.

Approx. retail price	Approx. low price
$260	$182

LUXMAN R-115   RECOMMENDED

The Luxman R-115 receiver performs exceptionally well, but its escalating price prevents it from being a Best Buy. However, classic design, excellent reliability, and outstanding sound continue its Recommended status in our listings. This expensive receiver performs so well that it justifies its price. While rated at 70 watts per channel, it can actually produce twice that much power during loud musical passages. The R-115 is very stable and can drive the most unstable speakers. The digitally synthesized tuner delivers superb, low-noise FM stereo reception and reasonably good AM as well. This receiver features 20 presets. Another desirable feature is CD straight circuitry, which routes the input from a compact disc player directly to the power amplifier section for the utmost sonic accuracy.

Warranty: parts and labor, five years.

Approx. retail price	Approx. low price
$800	$646

COMPACT DISC PLAYERS

Compact discs (CDs) have revolutionized home sound reproduction. Until a few years ago, all home audio equipment stored and reproduced sound in analog form. The minute wiggles in the grooves of a vinyl record replicate actual sound vibrations; they are analogous to the original sound they

Prices are accurate at time of printing; subject to manufacturer's change.

represent. For instance, louder sounds increase the depth of the groove.

CDs store sound as a string of numbers. A digital recorder samples the sound thousands of times each second and assigns each sample a numerical value, based on a binary code of zero and one. These numbers represent electrical voltage pulses (one) or the absence of pulses (zero) that can be read and converted into sound by computer chips in CD players. The CD stores this digital information as a series of microscopic depressions, or pits, arranged in a continuous spiral pattern below its clear plastic surface. The player reads the reflection of a laser beam that tracks these pits, so nothing but a beam of light actually touches the CD while it plays.

CDs surpass the sound quality of LPs and analog tapes in many ways. Besides having virtually inaudible distortion and flat (uniform) frequency response, CDs do not produce the annoying noise and hiss of analog recordings. When you hear hiss on a CD, you are actually hearing the hiss from the original analog master tape (some CDs originate from analog recordings). In addition, CDs add no wow and flutter, the annoying speed variations that cause a wavering of pitch.

CD players usually ignore small scratches and dust specks on the disc, although larger flaws can cause problems. Since CDs have no grooves to be worn away, with proper care they should last indefinitely. Always store your discs in their plastic boxes in a cool place. If you leave a CD in your car on a hot summer day, it can warp. The label side of a CD is more fragile than the silver data side, and writing on the label can damage the aluminum film.

Beware of CD gimmicks. Use no labels, adhesive rings, chemicals, or markers on the disc itself. The past years have seen a rise in such "magic" accessories that at best fail to improve performance and at worst harm the disc.

During the past couple of years, CD changers rapidly increased in popularity. The five-disc carousel model allows easy adding of and removing of discs from a giant platter, even as one disc is playing. This is the ideal changer for most home situations. The magazine or cartridge changer holds six or ten discs, depending upon the manufacturer, providing greater uninterrupted playing time. The magazines are not standardized. People with CD car changers benefit from being able

Prices are accurate at time of printing; subject to manufacturer's change.

to use the same magazines at home or on the road, providing their car changer is compatible with their home changer. We recommend the two highest quality brands that also have the largest number of changers already on the road.

In 1991, CDs completely supplanted LPs. Most record stores now stock only CDs and cassettes, and some record companies have discontinued pressing LPs.

Programmability

The noticeable difference between CD players is in programming capabilities. **Programming** is a machine's ability to store instructions in its electronic memory and execute them.

CDs are divided into **tracks**. A disc that offers a dozen songs will have 12 tracks, numbered 1 through 12. For classical music, such as a symphony, track numbers are used to separate the piece's movements. Some CDs have other divisions. For example, a symphonic movement may have more than one melodic theme; such themes can be assigned index numbers in a given track.

A programmable CD player can, at the very least, play specific tracks in ascending sequence, such as tracks 1, 4, 7, 9, and 12, in that order. More sophisticated units can play tracks in a random but specified order, such as tracks 5, 2, 4, 3, and 9, in that order. A few CD players also let you program index numbers. Some machines can store only six instructions in memory; others accept 30 or more.

Many CD players also offer **repeat play.** If you press a button they will play a disc or certain programmed tracks until the instruction is canceled. Many machines randomly shuffle the order in which tracks are played. A newly available programming feature permanently memorizes your favorite tracks on a disc. Some players with this feature store several hundred selections.

Features and Terminology

AAD to DDD: Virtually all discs now display a code indicating the origin of the program material. The letter *A* stands for an analog source, and the letter *D* stands for digital. The first letter indicates the nature of the original tape. The second letter reveals how the original recording was processed and mixed. The final letter shows that the material on the CD is digital.

Digital-to-analog (D/A) converters are microchips that translate digital numbers back to an analog form. The CD standard uses 16 bits, meaning that all discs contain blocks of 16-bit information. However, manufacturers encountered great difficulty in producing large quantities of perfect 16-bit D/A chips. Thus, many use 18- and 20-bit chips to retrieve information from the disc. They cannot retrieve additional sound, but often provide a greater margin of error for improved accuracy in the decoding process. The improvement is not always audible. A bad 20-bit converter is not always better than a good 16-bit converter.

Recently, engineers developed a method of converting digital information to analog in a rapid stream of single bits. This one-bit system is often known by its trade name of Bitstream. Each company proclaims a proprietary version of this technology, such as MASH, PEM, or PWM, along with a number-crunching technique called noise shaping that shifts what would have been audible noise outside the range of human hearing. One-bit D/A conversion improves sound at a lower cost than other methods, generally improving the sound of low-cost CD players. However, even among one-bit conversion systems there are differences in quality, so this alone does not guarantee the best sound quality.

Error correction and tracking: Some manufacturers claim that a three-beam laser system is superior to a single-beam system. Both systems use only one laser, which is either split with lenses and prisms into three beams or used as a single beam. While either system can be effective, there are differences in tracking accuracy and stability between various CD players that are not due to how many beams are used.

If a CD player cannot read one or more numbers on a disc, an error may result, producing a crashing sound. If several errors occur in a short time, the sound becomes very distorted. Fortunately, CD players use error-correction systems, so you will not hear anything wrong. Dropouts (missing or obscured numbers) may be caused by a scratch or dirty area on the disc's surface. In testing CD players, we used a disc with calibrated dropouts that simulate scratches, dust, and fingerprints.

You can judge a CD player's tracking stability, as well as its resistance to external vibration and shock, by tapping lightly on the top and sides of the player's cabinet with your finger. CD players with superior tracking stability will play through such testing without missing a beat.

Is Your Stereo Digital Ready?

You can connect a CD to most stereo systems, but you may not get the sound quality you expect. While you probably will not want to play your CDs any louder than you play LPs or tapes, the occasional peaks that occur in music will be 10 to 15 dB louder than if you were playing an LP or tape. So your amplifier must deliver 10 to 15 dB more power when playing CDs. A 10 dB increase represents a ten-to-one increase in power rating. This means your 30-watt receiver must deliver 300 watts per channel. Since most receivers do not usually operate at their maximum limit, you may not need to purchase a new amplifier for your CD player.

Another way to increase acoustic power is to switch to more efficient speakers. **Efficiency** is the amount of acoustic power you can get from a speaker that is fed a given amount of electrical audio power. If you own acoustic (air) suspension speakers or if your speaker enclosures are small, sealed boxes, you probably have low-efficiency units. Speakers with openings on their front surfaces are usually more efficient.

Sensitivity ratings can give you an idea of a speaker's efficiency. Low-efficiency speakers have sensitivity ratings of 80 to 85 dB per watt; medium-efficiency models have ratings between 86 and 89 dB; and high-efficiency units offer ratings higher than 90 dB, some as high as 98 dB or more.

A CD player must be connected to a receiver's high-level inputs, which are usually labeled Aux or Tuner. If these inputs are not available, "Tape" or "Tape Play" may be suitable. Before connecting a CD player, check out the maximum input level permitted at the input jack. If the rating is less than two volts, choose a CD player that has an output level control.

Compact Disc Players

TECHNICS SL-PS700

The Technics SL-PS700 compact disc player excels in tracking ability and banishes noise. Technics' new digital servo system

keeps the laser focused on the right place on the disc, even when the disc is grossly defective. The servo system reads ahead on the disc and anticipates problems. Analog servo designs often are foiled by disc defects. In addition to superior tracking, the SL-PS700 reduces noise well below inaudibility with a signal-to-noise ratio of 114 decibels (dB), which is about six dB better than most other machines in its price class. Technics designed the SL-PS700 for greater user convenience. Its Function Management System lets you customize the player by selecting 5 from the 17 possible functions and assigning them to a single button. The player makes copying CDs to tape easy by locating the loudest portion of the CD for setting recording levels and calculating which songs from the CD should go on which side of the tape for maximum tape economy. The player can even calculate optimum track arrangements for copying multiple discs onto a single cassette. The SL-PS700 uses four Technics MASH one-bit D/A converters with four-times oversampling for crystal clear sound. You can program 20 tracks. Direct track access is available from the front panel or the supplied remote control. The player shows good resistance to shock and external vibration.
Warranty: parts and labor, one year.

Approx. retail price	Approx. low price
$300	$265

ONKYO DX-700/DX-702 ✓BEST BUY

The Onkyo DX-700 and DX-702 CD players are sonically and mechanically identical. The DX-702 comes supplied with a wireless remote control and an optical digital output, for an additional $30. This bargain-priced player includes most of the features of more expensive players, as well as very good sound quality. The DX-700 uses dual AccuPulse one-bit D/A converters with an eight-times oversampling digital filter. It has 20-track programmability, with direct-track access from either the front panel or the remote control. A music calendar on the fluorescent display aids in programming. The display shows three time modes, plus track number. The time-edit function helps arrange tracks for optimum tape use when copying CDs to tape. The player operates smoothly, and resists shock and vibration.
Warranty: parts and labor, one year.

Prices are accurate at time of printing; subject to manufacturer's change.

Approx. retail price	Approx. low price
$200 (DX-700)	$181
$230 (DX-702)	$205

SONY CDP-X555ES

✓ **BEST BUY**

The Sony CDP-X555ES CD player continues Sony's tradition of top-of-the-line sound from a CD player at a little more than half the cost of the premier model. Many experts feel that Sony sets the standard for CD players every year. There are better models on the market, but they often use the sound of the top Sony as a reference point. We list this $900 CD player as a Best Buy because it shares most of the same internal components with Sony's more expensive, top-of-the-line models, while eliminating the professional output, esoteric material, and hand-selected parts. The CDP-X555ES operates with remarkable speed and precision, skipping from one end of the disc to the other in less than the blink of an eye. Its mechanical design is nearly bullet-proof. The player uses eight of Sony's High Density Linear Converter one-bit D/As operating at extremely high speed, combined with an eight-times oversampling digital filter with its own 45-bit noise-shaping circuitry. Digital sync circuitry cleans up digital nuisances, such as jitter. The CDP-X555ES even includes user conveniences missing from the more expensive model. A Custom File feature memorizes your favorite tracks on up to 185 discs, and includes a memo on the display of the title about the disc that is playing. The display also shows track and timing information, plus a music calendar for ease of programming. The player offers 24-track programming, remote control, and shuffle player. The player will locate peak levels for recording.
Warranty: parts and labor, three years.

Approx. retail price	Approx. low price
$900	$900

JVC XL-V141TN/XL-V241TN

RECOMMENDED

The JVC XL-V141TN and XL-V241TN compact disc players are identical, except that the XL-241TN comes with wireless remote control. In this case we recommend spending the extra $20 for the remote, since this provides direct track access, which is not

available from the front panel. The players use JVC's Pulse Edge Modulation one-bit D/A converter with the company's proprietary noise-shaping circuit in conjunction with an eight-times oversampling digital filter. This provides good, clean sound. A newly upgraded servo system, which JVC calls Y Servo, improves tracking and handles discs without problems. The XL-V141TN permits 32-track programming, with a 15-track program chart on its amber fluorescent display. The player is smartly styled with a minimum of confusing buttons and keys.
Warranty: parts and labor, one year.

Approx. retail price	Approx. low price
$180 (XL-V141TN)	$128
$200 (XL-V241TN)	$137

PIONEER PD-31 `RECOMMENDED`

The Pioneer PD-31 CD player goes to great lengths to prevent vibration of the disc within the player. The company's stable platter disc drive supports the disc more evenly and completely, reducing mistracking from warped discs and player vibration. The PD-31 uses Pioneer's high-density pulse flow one-bit D/A converters with noise shaping for clean, smooth sound. A peak search mode locates the loudest portion of the disc to aid in setting recording levels when making a copy. A computer editing system arranges tracks in optimal order to make best use of each side of the cassette. The player can even be programmed to fade a song out at a pre-selected time. The PD-31 offers direct track selection from the front panel or the supplied wireless remote control. The large display shows track number and selectable timing, plus a 20-track music calendar.
Warranty: parts and labor, one year.

Approx. retail price	Approx. low price
$450	not available

Compact Disc Carousel Changers

SONY CDP-C515

The Sony CDP-C515 drawer-loading carousel CD changer comes with the sound of Sony's most expensive changers, but

Prices are accurate at time of printing; subject to manufacturer's change.

without all the frills. It uses Sony's one-bit High Density Linear Converter D/A system with an eight-times oversampling digital filter. The digital sync circuit reduces jitter for cleaner sound. We like this Sony changer because it is very fast and accurate in its disc handling. You can program 32 tracks from any and all of the five discs on the carousel. Direct disc and track access is available from both the front panel and supplied remote control. The fluorescent display shows complete operating information, including a music calendar to aid in programming. The CDP-C515 will automatically find the peak level on a disc for setting recording levels, and will arrange tracks for optimal tape usage. **Warranty: parts and labor,** one year.

Approx. retail price	Approx. low price
$330	$275

TECHNICS SL-PC705/SL-PC505 ✔ BEST BUY

The Technics SL-PC705/SL-PC505 top-loading CD changer twins differ only in that the SL-PC705 comes with wireless remote control and costs about $20 more than the SL-PC505. These Technics CD changers offer the same features as last year's models with better performance at a lower price, making them an exceptional Best Buy. These full-featured bargains use four of Technics' one-bit MASH D/A converters with four-times oversampling. The players offer 32-track programming and random play. A unique playback feature is the new spiral play, which plays the first track from each of the five discs, followed by all the second tracks, etc. It also will mix spiral and random play, selecting discs and tracks from those discs randomly. The top-loading design allows adding or removing of any of the four other discs while the fifth plays. Direct disc and track selection is available from the front panel or remote. Technics' digital servo system plays a large number of damaged and imperfect discs that may not play on other players. The Edit Guide feature arranges tracks for optimal tape usage when copying. The blue and amber fluorescent display confirms programming. **Warranty: parts and labor,** one year.

Approx. retail price	Approx. low price
$220 (SL-PC705)	$213
$200 (SL-PC505)	$193

Prices are accurate at time of printing; subject to manufacturer's change.

PIONEER CLD-M90   RECOMMENDED

The Pioneer CLD-M90 is a one-of-a-kind drawer-loading five-disc carousel CD changer. It also is a combination laserdisc player, playing all kinds and sizes of videodiscs, as well as CDs. You can even play a laserdisc without removing the CDs (although you must remove the laserdisc to play the CDs). In addition to the amber with red highlights front panel fluorescent display, you can also see all functions and programming on your TV screen if you have the player connected to a TV. The CLD-M90 plays CDs with uncompromised sound quality. You can even switch off the video section for the purest CD sound quality. Pioneer uses its one-bit D/A converters for low distortion and low noise. A unique and desirable feature is the automatic digital level controller (ADLC). It does not reduce the dynamic range of discs, but equalizes the output of different discs, so that each plays at the volume level you set. You can program 24-tracks on any of the CDs (or 24 chapters on a laser disc). The CLD-M90 automatically arranges tracks on CDs for optimum tape usage when copying. Direct disc and track access is available from the front panel or supplied remote control.

Warranty: parts and labor, one year.

Approx. retail price	Approx. low price
$700	**$609**

Compact Disc Cartridge Changer

PIONEER PD-TM1   ✓**BEST BUY**

The Pioneer PD-TM1 cartridge CD changer is a unique machine that enables you to have a home jukebox for the price of an ordinary CD changer. The PD-TM1 holds three 6-disc cartridges, or magazines, as Pioneer calls them. These are the same magazines that work with Pioneer car CD changers and those of several other manufacturers. In addition to supplying the magazines, Pioneer includes a single-disc loader. Direct disc and track access is available from the front panel or supplied remote control. The PD-TM1 uses Pioneer's one-bit

D/A converter with eight-times oversampling digital filters for good sound quality. A large fluorescent display has symbols for all 18 discs, and shows all functions and timings. The automatic digital level controller (ADLC) automatically adjusts output levels from each of the 18 discs for a uniform user preset volume level. This is a great boon for taping as well as listening. These levels as well as programmed tracks can be stored in memory. The player arranges tracks for optimum tape usage when recording. The PD-TM1 can play randomly from all 18 discs.

Warranty: parts and labor, one year.

Approx. retail price	Approx. low price
$510	**$423**

TURNTABLE

Compact discs and cassette tapes with improved sound have replaced conventional records. Most people purchasing turntables are music lovers with large collections of LPs and a desire to play them on a good turntable. Virtually all turntable purchasers today are buying replacement turntables.

The function of a turntable is simple. All it has to do is rotate at a constant speed while introducing no audible noise or vibration via the tonearm and mounted cartridge that trace the minute undulations found in a record groove. Turntables are either direct driven or belt driven. In a belt-driven turntable, a rubber or neoprene belt couples the motor shaft to the platter. In a direct-driven turntable, the shaft of a slow-speed motor revolving at the required revolutions per minute (rpm) actually forms the center spindle of the turntable platter. The method of drive is less important than the performance specifications that result from a particular design.

BANG & OLUFSEN
BEOGRAM TX-2 TANGENTIAL RECOMMENDED

The Bang & Olufsen Beogram TX-2 Tangential semi-automatic belt-driven turntable is an elegant record-playing machine, certain to impress you for its styling as well as its performance. Rather than a tonearm that pivots from the corner of the platter,

Prices are accurate at time of printing; subject to manufacturer's change.

the TX-2 uses a motor-driven straight-line tracking arm that travels on a hidden track across the rear of the base. This system, perfected by Bang & Olufsen, reduces tracking error and record wear to almost zero. The ultrasmooth motor coupled with the belt drive results in extremely low rumble (-80 dB). The two-speed TX-2 (33⅓ and 45) contains virtually no adjustments. The cartridge comes as an integral part of the tonearm, although you can exchange it for more expensive Bang & Olufsen cartridges (which are quite good). The TX-2 is designed so that you never touch the tonearm. Pressing a key controls all operations.

Warranty: parts and labor, one year.

Approx. retail price	Approx. low price
$400	$399

PHONO CARTRIDGES

A phonograph cartridge is a transducer; it translates one kind of signal into another, converting the movement of the stylus into electrical signals. There are three basic phono cartridge designs:

P-mount cartridges plug into sockets in the front of tonearms that are designed to accept them.

Moving-magnet cartridges use magnetic induction, and all preamplifiers, integrated amplifiers, and receivers have inputs that can deal with signals from them.

Moving-coil cartridges are more expensive than moving-magnet cartridges, and some listeners insist they offer superior sound quality. Most moving-coil cartridges must be sent to an authorized service center when the stylus, or needle, needs to be replaced. Some preamplifiers, integrated amplifiers, and receivers need a special pre-preamplifier, or a step-up transformer, to use signals from this type of cartridge.

SHURE VST V

The Shure VST V is the last phono cartridge that you will ever need to buy. Twenty-five years of engineering are evident in the performance of this budget-priced cartridge. It is basically the scaled-down version of the famed Shure V15 Type V-MR. It

Prices are accurate at time of printing; subject to manufacturer's change.

simply costs about $120 less. The VST V comes without the fancy box, the printed individual response curve, and all the frills. You still get the incomparable MicroRidge (MR) stylus shape and beryllium cantilever. The VST V will track the most difficult records with a clean, clear, neutral sound. The user-replacement stylus makes future stylus replacement easy. Shure remains committed to replace any defective stylus for the life of the company. The easy-to-install VST V will provide indefinite hours of listening pleasure.

Warranty: parts and labor, one year.

Approx. retail price	Approx. low price
$180	$167

SHURE V15 TYPE V-MR   ✔ BEST BUY

The Shure V15 Type V-MR is a moving-magnet cartridge that has exceptional tracking ability. The MR suffix stands for MicroRidge, which means that the stylus tip is shaped to hug the walls of any record groove. This cartridge weighs 6⅜ grams and uses a stylus tip that measures ¹⁵⁄₁₀₀mm in its narrowest dimension and 3mm along its longer axis.

Warranty: parts and labor, one year.

Approx. retail price	Approx. low price
$297	$231

AUDIO-TECHNICA AT120E   RECOMMENDED

The Audio-Technica AT120E is a moving-magnet cartridge that employs a titanium-bonded stylus. It has an overall frequency response capacity from 15 to 25,000 hertz. Special dual-magnet construction provides excellent response and good separation. The tracking force range is from 1 to 1⅜ grams.

Warranty: one year, limited.

Approx. retail price	Approx. low price
$95	not available

CASSETTE DECKS

An audiocassette recorder is nearly as common in most households as a television or telephone. However, before you shop for a single- or dual-transport cassette deck for your stereo system, read through this brief explanation of the major specifications that you may want to evaluate when choosing a deck.

Frequency response, distortion, and signal-to-noise ratio are closely related. *Frequency response* sometimes is improved at the expense of distortion and signal-to-noise ratio. But achieving the true hi-fi range of 20 to 20,000 hertz may not mean that the overall sound quality is better, since most humans (especially as they get older) cannot hear much above 15,000 hertz and few instruments other than a grand pipe organ produce tones that go much below 30 hertz. When you compare the frequency response of two machines, be sure that the response of each is accompanied by a tolerance, usually stated as plus or minus a certain number of decibels (dB); otherwise the frequency response statement is meaningless.

Distortion is quoted by tape manufacturers for a 0 dB recording level, the maximum level at which you will want to record. This specification depends on the type of tape, but it should be no higher than one percent.

Signal-to-noise ratios for cassette decks should be a prime consideration. Once you have selected a tape deck, you should use one of the types of tape recommended by the manufacturer of that recorder. Avoid bargain brand tapes for all but voice-taping applications.

Wow and flutter is a measurement of tape-speed fluctuation. It is usually listed as a percentage, followed by the acronym WRMS. For example, a wow and flutter specification might read 1/10 percent WRMS. Look for the lowest percentage available within your budget limitations.

Bias, equalization, and level setting adjustments are not available on all cassette decks, but some tape decks offer fine-tuning controls that let you adjust for slight differences in the bias of recording tapes. Other decks control adjustments with microprocessor chips. These circuits test the tape and adjust for the optimum bias, equalization, and sensitivity to provide the best performance from a tape.

Three-head cassette decks have one head for erase, another for recording, and a third for playback. This arrangement provides the same sort of rapid off-the-tape monitoring capability found on professional open-reel machines.

Types of Tape

Several different types of recording tape are used by cassette recorders. The different types of tape require different levels of recording bias voltage, which is a high-frequency signal that must accompany all audio signals being recorded on tape to achieve low levels of distortion and high levels of output.

Normal tape (Type I) is coated with ferric oxide and requires a moderate amount of recording bias voltage. **Chrome tape** (Type II) refers to either a formulation of chromium dioxide particles or ferric oxide tape that has been treated with cobalt particles. This kind of tape requires a higher level of bias. **Metal tape** (Type IV) requires the highest bias level of any of these three kinds of tape. It offers better high-frequency recording capability, particularly at high volume levels, and better overall frequency response. A little-known benefit is that it is less subject to gradual erasure from magnetized tape heads and stray magnetic fields. Recently the cost of metal tape has declined, making it a good choice for most music recordings. Many companies now offer metal tapes (Type IV) at chrome (Type II) prices.

Tape Brands

The brand of tape you choose determines the quality of recording as much as the machine you buy. For ultimate performance, pick one representative of each tape type (normal, chrome, metal) and have a service technician adjust the deck for that tape. Then stick with it. The instruction manuals of some decks specify the tapes for which the machine comes adjusted. We recommend three tape brands for the most reliable service and highest fidelity: Maxell, TDK, and Sony. We also find Fuji and Scotch acceptable. These brands employ the most sturdy, high-tech shells and internal mechanisms for superior mechanical stability.

Noise-Reduction Systems

Even with the very best cassette tape and the very best cassette recorder, you will probably notice some tape hiss, or noise, when playing back your recordings. Hiss is especially noticeable during playback of softer musical passages. Several electronic techniques are available to reduce the audible effects of tape noise.

Dolby B reduces high-frequency noise by a factor of 5 to 10 dB; this is equivalent to the noise having been reduced by about half of its perceived intensity. Dolby B may be played back on non-Dolby equipped decks with only slight sonic aberration.

Dolby C reduces both midrange and high-frequency noise by about 10 dB, but sounds subjectively like it reduces noise twice as much as Dolby B. It also lowers distortion on high-frequency peaks. While Dolby C-encoded tapes can be played back with some success using Dolby B, they sound unpleasant when played back on decks that lack any Dolby decoding.

Dbx noise reduction offered the greatest amount of noise reduction (up to 30 dB) of any consumer system. However, it created sonic aberrations and it had to be reproduced on a dbx-equipped deck. Because of these reasons and the failure of its parent company, dbx is no longer available on cassette decks.

Dolby HX-Pro is a headroom-expansion (HX) system that, unlike noise-reduction systems, works only while recording. Dolby HX-Pro adjusts the recording current, or bias, to allow higher levels of high frequencies (treble) on the tape. With more signal on the tape, the signal-to-noise ratio is improved. A deck with HX-Pro will make superior tapes.

Dolby S is a consumer version of the professional Dolby SR system. It provides the greatest degree of noise reduction on the market, up to 20 dB, with the least adverse side effects. Dolby S-encoded tapes can be decoded by Dolby B-equipped machines with only minor sonic aberrations. Several companies now market Dolby S-equipped decks. Because of the expense of designing the integrated circuit chips for Dolby S, retail prices rival those of DAT machines. Music recorded using Dolby S approaches DAT quality, but does not rival it.

Single-Transport Cassette Decks

SONY TC-K677ES

The Sony TC-K677ES cassette deck records and plays with audiophile performance at a moderate price. When you invest in this tape deck, all the money goes toward performance, very little goes toward gimmicks and frills. The ruggedly built TC-

K677ES employs three motors for smooth, assured tape handling and deck longevity. Three heads permit tape/source monitoring, with the Sony laser amorphous record and play heads optimized for their functions. A very high recording bias frequency, which Sony calls Super Bias, eliminates the possibility of bias noise on the tape and interaction with the sound. A special damping material holds the cassette in place, reducing vibration that interferes with sound quality. The TC-K677ES includes Dolby B and C noise reduction, plus Dolby HX-Pro headroom extension. Users cannot only make fine bias adjustments for optimum matching between tape and deck, but also recording sensitivity level calibration. Large, logically arranged controls make this deck easy to operate. The deck includes a real-time tape counter as part of its large fluorescent display. The automatic music sensor (AMS) skips forward or backward to locate individual songs on the tape.

Warranty: parts and labor, three years.

Approx. retail price	Approx. low price
$400	$400

ONKYO TA-201

The Onkyo TA-201 two-head cassette deck uses two motors for smooth, fast tape handling, but retains a bargain price. Contributing to smooth tape motion is full-logic control, which means the function keys control the motors via a computer chip. The TA-201 includes Dolby B and C noise reduction, plus Dolby HX-Pro, another bonus on this budget-priced deck. The easy-to-read fluorescent display with peak-level indicators includes a peak-hold function. It also has a four-digit electronic tape counter, although the counter does not display the tape play in real-time.

Warranty: parts and labor, one year.

Approx. retail price	Approx. low price
$230	$209

PIONEER CT-M66R

The Pioneer CT-M66R is a unique cassette deck that makes quality recordings; it also is an autoreverse cassette changer. This updated version of the original CT-M66R incorporates

Prices are accurate at time of printing; subject to manufacturer's change.

some minor upgrades at a slightly lower price, making it an even better Best Buy than last year. It can record or play any of the six cassettes you load, which means up to nine hours of uninterrupted recording or unrepeated playback. The deck makes little compromise in recording quality. It incorporates Dolby B and C noise reduction, coupled with Dolby HX-Pro for low noise and wide dynamic range. This deck's many automatic features include cassette-scan, which plays the first 10 seconds of each cassette to remind you of its contents, and music skip search for up to 15 selections in either direction. The fluo—orescent display includes a real-time tape counter. The deck automatically senses tape type, which is a necessity since it holds six tapes. When used with a Pioneer CD changer, the CT-M66R can automatically copy multiple discs while rearranging tracks in the best order to make optimum use of the tape, and never missing a song. The CT-M66R comes with a wireless remote control.

Warranty: parts and labor, one year.

Approx. retail price	Approx. low price
$440	**$303**

PIONEER CT-41   RECOMMENDED

The Pioneer CT-41 cassette deck is one of the first to include the new Dolby S noise-reduction system, as well as Dolby B and C, plus HX-Pro. This three-head deck far surpasses the only other Dolby S equipped decks on the market in performance, and at an equal or lower price. Pioneer makes few compromises in building this smoothly operating cassette deck, which approaches DAT in fidelity. Most important is Pioneer's Auto BLE system, which automatically adjusts bias, level, and equalization for the specific tape you insert in the machine. The computerized adjustment takes only a few seconds and dramatically improves the sound quality of recordings by finding the perfect match between tape and machine. The fluorescent display has very accurate level meters, and a real-time tape counter.

Warranty: parts and labor, one year.

Approx. retail price	Approx. low price
$800	**not available**

Prices are accurate at time of printing; subject to manufacturer's change.

Dual-Transport Cassette Decks

TECHNICS RS-TR515

The Technics RS-TR515 dual-transport autoreverse cassette deck brings full-featured versatility to a lower price point. This is the lowest-priced quality machine that plays and records on both transports. That means you can record the same program on two tapes simultaneously or record a long program sequentially first on one transport and then automatically switching to the next. It records on either transport with impressively high fidelity and low noise using Dolby B or C noise reduction, plus Dolby HX-Pro headroom extension. To further optimize fidelity, the second transport includes a manual fine-bias adjustment to match the specific tape you choose. High-speed copying between transports cuts tape copying time in half, and the synchro-start feature allows you to operate both transports at the touch of a button. The quick-reverse mechanism minimizes turnaround time between sides. The fluorescent level display shows tape position for each transport in arbitrary numbers, not real-time. The large controls are simple to operate.

Warranty: parts and labor, one year.

Approx. retail price	Approx. low price
$260	$253

AIWA AD-WX515

The Aiwa AD-WX515 cassette deck offers essential recording features at a very good value. It's a simple budget deck, but still includes Dolby B and C noise reduction. It offers high-speed dubbing, continuous playback, and automatic tape-type selection. An anti-modulation tape stabilizer, normally found in more expensive decks, improves tape drive stability.

Warranty: parts and labor, one year.

Approx. retail price	Approx. low price
$200	$152

SONY TC-WR87ES

The Sony TC-WR87ES dual-transport cassette deck represents an excellent mid-priced value. It incorporates Sony's Super

Bias and Laser Amorphous heads for very clean sound with extended high frequency response. The TC-WR87ES includes Dolby B and C noise reduction plus Dolby HX-Pro. A fine-bias adjustment permits precise matching to specific tapes. This autoreverse deck plays and records on both transports, permitting you to make two copies at once from another source or sequential recordings that start recording on transport B when transport A is finished. Each deck has two motors for durability. A real-time tape counter on the fluorescent display tells you the tape position in minutes and seconds. As with most dual-transport machines, you can copy tapes at double speed. The TC-WR87ES also includes automatic sensing for the type of tape loaded and an automatic music sensor that can skip forward or backward to find a desired selection.

Warranty: parts and labor, three years.

Approx. retail price	**Approx. low price**
$430	$430

PIONEER CT-W51 RECOMMENDED

The Pioneer CT-W51 has a slightly higher price, which prevents this unique dual-transport cassette deck from rating a Best Buy. Pioneer builds its automatic bias/level/equalization circuitry into the CT-W51, making it the only dual deck that automatically custom-matches to specific tapes. This desirable feature assures the utmost fidelity no matter which brand or type of tape you use. Both autoreverse transports record using the ABLE calibration circuit. Pioneer includes Dolby B and C noise reduction and Dolby HX-Pro. Other standard features are high-speed dubbing, quick-reverse, and music search that skips forward or back to locate a desired selection. The fluorescent display includes real-time tape counters. A cassette stabilizer keeps the tape firmly in place to reduce spurious vibrations.

Warranty: parts and labor, one year.

Approx. retail price	**Approx. low price**
$570	not available

JVC TD-W805TN RECOMMENDED

The JVC TD-W805TN dual-transport cassette deck offers good sound quality with ample features at a reasonable price. Both

Prices are accurate at time of printing; subject to manufacturer's change.

quick-reverse transports play and record, allowing you to make two copies at once or extended length copies using both tapes. JVC includes Dolby B and C noise reduction plus Dolby HX-Pro. The deck automatically senses the type of tape loaded. A fine-bias control allows you to adjust transport B for specific tapes. The TD-W805TN operates smoothly and elegantly. The soft-touch function keys engage operation via small motors. The powered cassette doors open gently. Behind the doors, cassette stabilizers damp out spurious vibrations that interfere with recording quality. The fluorescent display incorporates real-time tape counters. JVC's Dynamics Detection Recording Processor automatically adjusts the record level when used with JVC receivers and CD players, a most convenient feature. The logically positioned control keys are clearly marked and easy to operate. JVC cosmetically finishes the TD-W805TN in a titanium gun-metal color, an attractive alternative to the standard black.

Warranty: parts and labor, one year.

Approx. retail price	Approx. low price
$370	$293

DIGITAL AUDIO TAPE (DAT)

Digital Audio Tape (DAT) is to the analog cassette as CD is to the analog LP record. It records digitally using a system nearly identical to CD. DAT records using 16-data bits, but with a choice of sampling rates of 48,000 hertz (for recordings originating on DAT), 44,100 hertz for copies from CD, and 32,000 hertz for long play and special applications—at the cost of some fidelity. Because it is digital, DAT requires no noise-reduction system.

The reason the record industry fought DAT's arrival was that the system is capable of recording with fidelity virtually identical to the source material. Whereas regular tapes lose a bit of fidelity with each copy, you can digitally copy from one DAT to another DAT to another, etc., with the final copy still sounding like the original—assuming that you make all the copies digitally. DAT decks can also make unrestricted copies with their analog inputs and outputs, but the results are not as perfect as when using digital inputs and outputs, because the signal must first go through a D/A converter and then back again through an A/D (analog-to-digital) converter.

The record industry and DAT manufacturers reached a compromise during the summer of 1989. Dutch electronics giant Philips, which invented the analog compact cassette, developed a microchip that would limit digital copying without affecting sound quality. This chip, called Serial Copy Management System (SCMS), allows you to make a digital DAT copy from a digital source. For example, you can copy a CD onto DAT using the digital output from the CD player and the digital input on the DAT, but you can't make digital copies of that copy. You can copy that same CD as many times as you like onto DAT. You can also copy DAT to DAT digitally one time. Analog sources such as LPs or radios can be recorded on DAT, and then be digitally copied from DAT to DAT once, but no more.

DAT not only far surpasses the fidelity of conventional cassettes, it also offers superior tape handling. Any selection on a tape can be located within a minute by the touch of a button. DAT cassettes are about half the size of analog cassettes, and come in lengths of up to two hours.

SONY DTC-57ES

The Sony DTC-57ES represents Sony's third generation digital audio tape deck, while most other companies are still on their first or second generation. Sony engineered a new, higher quality analog to digital converter for this deck using one-bit technology. For playback, the DTC-57ES incorporates eight 1-bit D/A converters. Sony managed to improve performance while reducing cost by developing large-scale integrated circuits (LSI) that combine multiple functions in a single chip. The deck can search for selections at up to 400-times normal playback speed, and it permits 60-track programming. The sophisticated fluorescent meters are specially calibrated for digital recording, unlike most other DAT decks. Accurate metering is essential for good digital recording, since over-recording causes catastrophic distortion. Once you record using this deck, you will never be satisfied with analog recordings again. Sony supplies a remote control. The deck also

includes the serial copy management system (SCMS).
Warranty: parts and labor, three years.

>   Approx. retail price   Approx. low price
>   not available   not available

JVC XD-Z507TN   RECOMMENDED

The JVC XD-Z507TN DAT recorder matches the preceding
Sony very closely, but its slightly higher price prevents it from
being a Best Buy. JVC is a natural for building DAT recorders,
since the technology is quite similar to VCRs and camcorders.
What makes the XD-Z507TN stand out is JVC's proprietary
one-bit P.E.M. D.D. D/A converter and the related one-bit A/D
converters. These circuits operate with exceptionally low noise.
In addition to the normal versatility of DAT editing, the XD-
Z507TN permits varying edit points in quarter seconds. The
fluorescent meters are calibrated for digital recording, with a
numeric readout of your decibel margin. The large, clearly
marked controls make operating this deck easy. JVC supplies a
remote control. The XD-Z507TN comes with SCMS.
Warranty: parts and labor, one year.

>   Approx. retail price   Approx. low price
> $1,000   not available

Stereo Systems

Stereo systems, which are often called rack systems, are audio component systems that are designed to work well together. When you shop for a stereo system, consider which components it includes, its audio power, and its sound quality. Additional features you may wish to consider are remote-control selection of program source and automatic shutoff of one component, such as the tuner, when another program source, such as the tape player, is selected. The speakers are usually the weakest component of rack systems. Most electronics manufacturers do not make good loudspeakers. If possible, you should select different speakers than the ones supplied with the system. A recent trend has been toward compact, or mini, systems. These fit big sound into stylish downsized components. In some cases, all the components of a mini system are only slightly larger than a conventional receiver.

For additional information about stereo components, please refer to the preceding chapter.

Best Buys '92

Our Best Buy and Recommended stereo systems follow. They are divided into full-size stereo systems and compact stereo systems. Within each category, systems are listed by quality; the item we consider the best of the Best Buys is first, followed by our second choice, and so on. A Best Buy or Recommended designation applies only to the model listed; it does not necessarily apply to other models made by the same manufacturer or to an entire product line.

FULL-SIZE STEREO SYSTEMS

TECHNICS SC-S2200

✔ **BEST BUY**

The Technics SC-S2200 stereo system packages a five-disc carousel CD changer, integrated amplifier with Dolby surround-sound, a seven-band graphic equalizer, dual-transport cassette deck, quartz-synthesized AM/FM stereo tuner, and speakers featuring ten-inch woofers and one-inch dome tweeters. The CD changer is similar to the separate model recommended in our CD changer listings. You can change four discs while the fifth plays. The carousel operates in either direction. The player has 32-track programming, and uses Technics' MASH one-bit D/A converter. The powerful integrated amplifier produces 130 watts per channel for the front two channels, and 15 watts per channel for the two rear surround channels. The tuner has 24 station presets, shown along with the station frequency on a large fluorescent display. The dual-transport, autoreverse cassette deck plays on both transports but only records on one. The recording transport records with Dolby B or C noise reduction. It includes high-speed copying, sequential playback from one transport to the other, and feather-touch controls. The CD changer and cassette deck are electronically linked so that the press of a single button begins copying. To take advantage of the surround-sound feature, you must buy the optional SBS-15 rear speakers for $50. An optional turntable, model SL-BD20A, is available for an additional $130. Technics includes a lot of performance in this simulated-wood rack system for a reasonable price. The supplied remote control also operates Technics/Panasonic video components. The equipment is reliable and provides almost as much versatility as separate components.

Warranty: components, parts and labor, one year; **speakers, parts and labor,** three years; **cartridges, parts and labor,** 90 days.

Prices are accurate at time of printing; subject to manufacturer's change.

Approx. retail price	Approx. low price
$1,000	$884

JVC GX-8730CD   RECOMMENDED

The JVC GX-8730CD rack system performs well, while economizing a bit of convenience. Rather than a changer, it includes a single-disc CD player. Otherwise, it almost matches systems costing $200 more. Its 110-watts-per-channel amplifier section includes a five-band graphic equalizer, with a light emitting diode (LED) bar graph power display. Although the tuner appears to be a separate unit, it is actually attached to the amp, making it a receiver. The quartz-locked tuner section, which features good sensitivity, has 40 station presets. The CD player has 32-track programming. The dual-transport cassette deck provides only Dolby B noise reduction. It features sequential play and high-speed copying. The floor standing tower speakers include 12-inch woofers. The rack comes finished in black with a glass door. JVC provides a remote control with the system. An optional belt-drive turntable is available.

Warranty: parts and labor, one year; **receiver, parts and labor,** two years; **speakers, parts and labor,** three years.

Approx. retail price	Approx. low price
$800	$681

COMPACT STEREO SYSTEMS

YAMAHA YST-NC1 "UNITY"   ✓ BEST BUY

The Yamaha YST-NC1 "Unity" represents the third generation of Yamaha's YST compact systems. Yamaha led the way in developing small, refined systems with full features and big sound. This year's model resembles last year's model, with the same performance and features at a lower price. The main difference between last year's model and the current design is that the YST-NC1 is now a two-piece system allowing you to stack the components vertically or side-by-side for space flexibility. The contemporary styling immediately catches your eye. The system combines an amplifier featuring Yamaha's active servo technology, AM/FM stereo tuner, dual-transport autoreverse cassette deck, seven-band graphic equalizer, and a CD player in a petite package. Each component is competitive with the performance of many components found in full-size systems. The active servo technology custom matches the speakers to the amp, and by using special feedback circuitry, produces low, accurate bass from these miniature speakers. The system includes a phase-locked-loop synthesized AM/FM stereo tuner with direct station access and 30 station presets. Direct track access is also available on the CD player. The dual-transport autoreverse cassette deck with Dolby B noise reduction records on only one transport. The CD player has 20-track programming capability.

Warranty: parts and labor, one year.

Approx. retail price	Approx. low price
$800	$624

ONKYO PCS-05

The Onkyo PCS-05 is a personal component system of stackable mini-components in a brushed aluminum titanium finish. They look stunning and perform on a par with full-size separate components. The receiver produces 45 watts per channel into two-way, bass reflex magnetically shielded speakers. The shielding means that you can use the system in conjunction with your TV as the audio center of a video system. The synthesized AM/FM stereo tuner section has 30 station presets. The CD player uses a one-bit D/A converter with a four-times oversampling digital filter. The outstanding dual-transport autoreverse cassette deck incorporates two motors (unusual in this size and price range), Dolby B and C noise reduction, plus Dolby HX-Pro.

Warranty: CD and tape deck, parts and labor, one year; **receiver and speakers, parts and labor,** two years.

Approx. retail price	Approx. low price
$1,000	$885

JVC MX-50 ✔BEST BUY

The JVC MX-50 compact component system provides a good sounding, full-featured compromise from more expensive

systems. JVC divides the components into two modules, the amplifier/CD player and the tuner/cassette deck. These can be stacked or placed side-by-side. When stacked, the speakers are the same height when standing on end; when side-by-side, the speakers are the same height when placed on their sides. The ported speakers use an internal labyrinth design to squeeze maximum bass from a small enclosure. The amp produces 35 watts per channel and includes a seven-band graphic equalizer. It comes with six pre-programmed EQ settings, such as rock, jazz, etc., and can store one of your own EQ settings. The amber and red fluorescent display shows relative frequency levels and the action of the equalizer settings, as well as the CD player programming functions. The CD has 32-track programming. The tuner holds 40 station presets. The amplifier has four preset volume levels, and includes a clock/timer, which allows it to function as a clock radio. The dual-transport cassette deck plays on both transports but records only on one, and includes only Dolby B noise reduction. It features high-speed copying. The interconnection of components fosters very easy copying of CDs onto tapes. JVC supplies a system remote that can also control the company's DAT machines and VCRs.
Warranty: parts and labor, one year.

Approx. retail price	Approx. low price
$750	$538

DENON POINT COMPO 7.5 RECOMMENDED

The Denon Point Compo 7.5 system offers a cross between a prepackaged compact system and the flexibility of choosing separate mini-components. It rates as the closest to an audiophile compact system you can buy. The basic system starts with the 50-watts-per-channel PMA 7.5 integrated amplifier, which has six inputs plus a CD/DAT direct mode that bypasses unnecessary circuitry for the clearest sound. The TU-7.5 tuner stores 30 station presets in its memory, as well as offering three tuning modes. It displays station frequency and other tuning information on an LCD (liquid crystal display). The DRR-7.5 cassette deck includes Dolby B and C noise reduction plus Dolby HX-Pro. The deck's music search function can search for your desired selection through up to 99 tracks. The

Prices are accurate at time of printing; subject to manufacturer's change.

DRR-7.5 automatically selects tape type. The DCD-7.5 CD player uses Denon's 20-bit, eight-times oversampling digital filters with dual D/A converters. Unlike most other compact systems, the player comes with digital outputs for optimal interconnection with future digital components. The player offers easy and ample programming functions. Its LCD shows track, timings, and other status information. The matching SC-7.5 speakers employ 6½-inch woofers and are magnetically shielded, allowing them to be used near your TV set. However, any speakers may be used with the system. The system is controlled by the remote control supplied with the amplifier. Because these are separate units, they can be arranged in any configuration, and adding future components such as a DAT are easy. The silver anodized front panels have gold accents for an attractive appearance. A great advantage of this system is that you only purchase the components you want.
Warranty: two years.

Approx. retail price	Approx. low price
$500	not available
PMA-7.5 amplifier	
$300	not available
TU-7.5 tuner	
$400	not available
DRR-7.5 cassette deck	
$400	not available
DCD-7.5 CD player	
$500/pair	not available
SC-7.5 speakers	

BOSE ACOUSTIC WAVE MUSIC SYSTEM SERIES II

RECOMMENDED

The Bose Acoustic Wave Music System (AWMS) Series II is unique among compact systems. In concept and size, it resembles a boombox; in performance and styling it's like a component system. The original Bose AWMS, which has been on the market for almost a decade, has not been included in our previous listings because of its limited flexibility—it lacked additional inputs. The new model corrects this oversight with the optional AWMS Pedestal that offers four additional inputs.

Prices are accurate at time of printing; subject to manufacturer's change.

This unit docks with and sits atop the slim pedestal for no compromise in size or styling. The Bose Acoustic Wave technology that gives the model its name sets it apart from all other systems on the market. The breadbox-size enclosure contains a series of waveguides, which are tiny square tunnels, that acoustically amplify the bass frequencies. This permits small woofers to deliver enormous bass sound. The system combines an amplifier, AM/FM stereo tuner, an equalizer, speakers, and your choice of a cassette deck or CD player. Conventional specifications fail to define the performance of the Bose AWMS, which is startlingly impressive. No other system matches its ease of operation, which is the same (or easier) as an ordinary radio. An optional carrying case, battery pack, and automobile power cord make the system portable. This unit sells nationally for a fixed price, and is not available through conventional retail channels. It is sold by a door-to-door sales force, a few catalog outlets, and directly from Bose. A two-week free trial is provided. For further information on ordering, call 1-800-282-2673.

Warranty: parts and labor, one year.

Approx. retail price	Approx. low price
$997	**$733**

Personal Stereos

Personal stereos are everywhere. Commonly known by the Sony trademark of Walkman (Sony invented the category in 1979), personal stereos are also called headphone stereos and personal portables. The large all-in-one portable stereo systems, called boomboxes, have flourished. The personal stereo can be as small as a set of headphones with an integral radio, while the boombox can be as large as a suitcase. Personal stereos can combine radios, tape players (and recorders), or CD players. The even more versatile boombox can contain any combination of radio, tape player(s), and/or CD player, and even tape-dubbing dual-cassette transports.

Various portable models offer a variety of the following features: Dolby B and Dolby C noise reduction, autoreverse, automatic music search (AMS), a graphic equalizer for fine-tuning frequency response, bass boosters, water resistance, and recording capability. Portables may also supply integral rechargeable batteries, solar power, TV sound (on units with radio tuners), and digitally synthesized tuning. Many of these features are marketing ploys rather than performance enhancements. However, you may find autoreverse and digitally synthesized tuning with preset station buttons a great convenience.

Choosing a Portable

Most major brand-name portable stereos perform impressively under ideal conditions, but the true test of a portable is how it performs when it is in motion. Listen for tape skewing (a varying amount of treble) and wow and flutter (warbling or off-speed sound) while you shake and vibrate the unit to simulate jogging or cycling.

The critical test of FM reception occurs in cities where the unit may overload from nearby transmitters. This is often compounded by multipath distortion caused by signals bouncing between tall buildings. A stereo/mono switch or a local/distant switch helps in these situations. Some FM-only models use automatic stereo/mono blending to help smooth out the rapid and distorting change between stereo and monaural sound that can occur when you are downtown.

Another test of reception occurs inside steel and concrete buildings that shield the stereo's antenna from radio signals. The length of the headphone cord determines the quality of FM reception in units where the cord acts as the FM antenna. A few inches more or less than the ideal 31 inches makes a great deal of difference.

Upgrading Your Portable System

Even though the electronics used in portable stereos are constantly being improved, many units come with inferior headphones. The only remedy is to purchase better phones. You may also want to consider small, powered speakers that allow you to turn your portable into a system that can fill a room with sound.

Best Buys '92

Our Best Buy and Recommended portable stereos follow. They are divided into portable CD players, personal radio-cassette player/recorders, personal radio-cassette players, personal cassette players, personal radios, personal headset radios, and boomboxes. In each category, the units are arranged in order of preference. The best of the Best Buys is listed first, followed by our second choice, and so on. Remember that a Best Buy or Recommended designation applies only to the model listed; it does not necessarily apply to other models made by the same manufacturer or to an entire product line.

PORTABLE CD PLAYERS

SONY D-35

The Sony D-35 is one of the most expensive portable CD players on the market, yet it qualifies as a Best Buy. Even though it is one of the smallest, lightest portable CD players, it's also the only one that can fully double as a home player. Exactly one inch thick, this tiny player's lid contains nearly every control found on a full-size CD player, including a numbered keypad for direct track access. An LCD (liquid crystal display) screen, much larger than found on other portable CD players, presents the same information commonly found on the fluorescent displays of home players. The D-35 calculates the best track arrangements for optimal dubbing onto cassettes. The D/A converter uses an eight-times oversampling digital filter. The sound quality is quite good. Its built-in rechargeable battery powers the D-35 for two hours. Two alkaline AA cells in the outboard detachable battery compartment power the unit for about 3½ hours. The rechargeable and outboard batteries can be used together for about 5½ hours. A separate lithium button cell maintains the D-35's memory and clock functions. The clock, besides displaying time of day on the LCD, can be programmed to stop and start the D-35 and even fade in and out at desired times. You can program up to 22 tracks. Sony's Mega Bass circuit boosts bass, a useful feature for headphones. A remote control module is in the middle of the headphone cord. Remote control only operates when using the supplied in-the-ear headphones.

Specifications: height, 1″; **width,** 5″; **depth,** 5⁷⁄₁₆″; **weight,** 13⁷⁄₁₆ ounces without batteries. **Warranty: parts,** one year; **labor,** 90 days.

Approx. retail price	Approx. low price
$400	$288

PANASONIC SL-NP500

The Panasonic SL-NP500 portable CD player closely resembles its Technics cousin (SL-XP700). The SL-NP500 includes the XBS bass-boost circuit for dramatic low frequencies, and a high-cut filter to reduce treble. You can program 24 tracks, and choose among three play modes: normal, random, and resume from the last track played. The LCD shows track number, operating mode, memory, track time elapsed, and disc time remaining. A single-button wired remote operates all major functions. The unit operates for about 2½ hours on internal rechargeable batteries or two AA batteries. Panasonic provides an AC adapter and soft carrying case with strap. This unit sounds very good, but lacks immunity to motion shock, as do virtually all portable CD players.

Specifications: height, 1⅛"; **width,** 5"; **depth,** 5¹¹⁄₁₆"; **weight,** 10⅝ ounces without batteries. **Warranty: parts and labor,** one year.

Approx. retail price	Approx. low price
$210	$185

TECHNICS SL-XP700 ✔BEST BUY

The Technics SL-XP700 is the realization of the promise of portable CD players. It is the same size as a slice of white bread, but far more stylish. The player is less than an inch thick, less than a pound in weight, but more than ample in sound quality. The S-XBS circuit boosts bass, while a high-cut filter reduces treble on poorly recorded discs. The player has three play modes, plus 24-track programming. The remote control, which is a bulge in the headphone cord, controls half a dozen functions with a single button, and has a volume adjustment control. A series of beeps heard in the phones confirm your commands. The unit functions on internal rechargeable batteries, or a screw-on battery pack holding two AA batteries. The sloping control panel on the top front of the player has seven differently sized buttons, the largest being play/pause. In the center, a small LCD shows function, track numbers, elapsed track time, and battery status. Slide switches on the left side select a safety hold that deactivates the top buttons and a play-mode selector. Similar switches on the right side select the bass boost and high cut. The headphone jack is next to the bass-boost switch. The rear contains the AC power adapter jack, line output, and connectors for the battery pack. With the battery pack installed, the AC and line out jacks are inaccessible. You also cannot change batteries without removing the battery pack. Battery life is about two hours. A

Prices are accurate at time of printing; subject to manufacturer's change.

long, narrow window on the top of the unit allows you to see the disc. The SL-XP700 is sensitive to shock and not intended for jogging and bicycling. It works fine in cars and airplanes.
Specifications: height, 1⁄16″; **width,** 5⅛″; **depth,** 5¹⁄₁₆″; **weight,** 10³⁄₁₀ ounces without batteries. **Warranty: parts and labor,** one year; **earphones,** 90 days.

Approx. retail price	Approx. low price
$280	$253

PERSONAL RADIO-CASSETTE PLAYER/RECORDERS

SONY WM-GX35

 ✔BEST BUY

The Sony WM-GX35 sounds great in its versatile role of radio-cassette player/recorder. The AM/FM stereo radio portion includes the newly extended AM band, and a local/distance switch for improved FM reception. In the tape mode, the autoreverse operates in play and record. Tape playback benefits from Dolby B noise reduction and equalization for chrome/metal tapes. The supplied one-point stereo microphone, which can be aimed for better pickup from a desired direction, performs well for live recordings. The WM-GX35 resists vibration and shock. The adequately sized buttons along this unit's spine make it easy to operate. An old-fashioned slide-rule tuning dial on the front of the case aids in tuning. Sony supplies a belt clip and conventional headphones.
Specifications: height, 4⅝″; **width,** 3½″; **depth,** 1⅝″; **weight,** 9⅖ ounces without batteries. **Warranty: parts,** one year; **labor,** 90 days.

Approx. retail price	Approx. low price
$165	$129

AIWA HS-J707
RECOMMENDED

The Aiwa HS-J707 radio autoreverse cassette player/recorder offers more features and better sound at an admittedly substantial price. If this unit were just a little less expensive, we'd rate it a Best Buy. The improved, supplied headphones

sound very good and are reasonably comfortable. You can play tapes back with Dolby B noise reduction. An LCD (liquid crystal display) screen shows time or radio station frequency. There are five AM and five FM station presets. The HS-J707 will also sample all local radio stations and program the five strongest AM and FM signals, in addition to your presets. This is a nice feature when traveling. The digital tuner adjusts to broadcast standards around the world, and offers wide-band AM for higher AM fidelity. The clock stores five different time zones. The quick-charge battery plays two hours on a 15-minute charge. Aiwa supplies a detachable stereo microphone.
Specifications: height, 4¼"; **width,** 3¹⁄₁₆"; **depth,** 1"; **weight,** 6⁷⁄₁₀ ounces. **Warranty: parts,** one year; **labor,** 90 days.

Approx. retail price	Approx. low price
$270	not available

PERSONAL RADIO-CASSETTE PLAYERS

SHARP JC-510

The Sharp JC-510 radio-cassette player breaks the mold of inexpensive players by looking stylish, not cheap. This unit, finished in titanium gray, has an easy-to-read slide-rule radio tuning dial on the top front. The tape player has autoreverse, or you can change tape sides at the push of a button. The AM/FM stereo radio includes the newly extended AM tuning band. An anti-rolling mechanism reduces tape warbling when the unit is in motion. The JC-510 comes with comfortable, on-the-ear stereo headphones and a belt-clip. It operates on two AA batteries. The sound output is ample, and the quality is pleasing for the price.
Specifications: height, 5⁵⁄₁₆"; **width,** 3¹⁄₁₆"; **depth,** 1¹⁄₁₆"; **weight,** 9½ ounces without batteries. **Warranty: parts,** one year; **labor,** 90 days.

Approx. retail price	Approx. low price
$40	$38

AIWA HS-T65

The Aiwa HS-T65 radio-cassette player not only includes the newly extended United States AM band, but also the ability to

Prices are accurate at time of printing; subject to manufacturer's change.

tune AM and FM anywhere in the world. Some countries do not use the same spacing between stations as the United States, thwarting some digital tuners. You can store five AM and five FM station presets in the frequency synthesized tuner's memory. The LCD (liquid crystal display) shows not only local time, but multiple time zones at the push of a button. The autoreverse cassette player includes Dolby B noise reduction and equalization for chrome/metal tapes. In addition to bass and treble tone controls, the HS-T65 includes a variable super-bass control. Two AA batteries power the unit. The good-sounding, on-the-ear headphones include a tuned chamber for what Aiwa calls the Power Bass Pipe-Phone.

Specifications: height, 4¾"; **width,** 3⅜"; **depth,** 1½"; **weight,** 8½ ounces without batteries. **Warranty: parts,** one year; **labor,** 90 days.

Approx. retail price	Approx. low price
$110	$93

SONY WM-FX50   RECOMMENDED

The Sony WM-FX50 is super compact and comes loaded with features. Foremost among these is a dual-battery compartment. Most headphone stereos require you to clip on an external battery compartment to supplement the internal rechargeable battery, a clumsy nuisance. The WM-FX50 accepts either the supplied gumstick rechargeable battery, or a single AA cell in its battery compartment. Sony also supplies the battery charger. The rechargeable battery powers the unit for four hours on a three hour charge. The radio includes the newly extended AM band, as well as a local/distant switch for improving stereo FM reception. The autoreverse cassette player has Dolby B noise reduction and equalization for chrome/metal tapes. The variable Mega Bass control can double the amount of mid-bass sound. The comfortable over-the-ear headphones are designed to reproduce maximum bass.

Specifications: height, 4¼"; **width,** 2¹⁵⁄₁₆"; **depth,** 1¹⁄₁₆"; **weight,** 8¹⁄₁₀ ounces without batteries. **Warranty: parts,** one year; **labor,** 90 days.

Approx. retail price	Approx. low price
$170	$126

Prices are accurate at time of printing; subject to manufacturer's change.

PERSONAL CASSETTE PLAYERS

SONY WM-EX30

The Sony WM-EX30 cassette player provides features and performance formerly available only on players twice its price. In fact, in actual sound quality, it surpasses Sony's original Walkman, which sold for four times the price of the WM-EX30. The compact autoreverse player incorporates an anti-rolling mechanism for steady sound, and equalization for chrome/metal tapes. The WM-EX30 is more compact than many other models in this price range. It operates on two AA batteries. The on-the-ear headphones are comfortable and deliver good sound.

Specifications: height, 4⁷⁄₁₆"; **width,** 2¹¹⁄₁₆"; **depth,** 1⁹⁄₃₂"; **weight,** 4⅘ ounces without batteries. **Warranty: parts,** one year; **labor,** 90 days.

Approx. retail price	Approx. low price
$160	$130

SHARP JC-K99

RECOMMENDED

The Sharp JC-K99 may be the world's lightest personal cassette player, weighing only about 3½ ounces with the battery. The black carbon fiber body is not only light, but strong. That makes the JC-K99 not only easy to carry, but durable as well. Few compromises are made in the quality of tape playback. It includes Dolby B noise reduction and proper equalization for all tape types. The autoreverse player includes the standard anti-rolling mechanism to keep the tone steady while the player is in motion. A multifunction wired remote control makes operation easy. The earbud-style headphones (two earpieces without a headband) employ a dual element design that sounds fairly good if you can fit them in your ears properly. The JC-K99 operates on a supplied rechargeable battery. Sharp also supplies the battery charger.

Specifications: height, 2²⁷⁄₃₂"; **width,** 4⁷⁄₃₂"; **depth,** ¾"; **weight,** 3½ ounces with battery. **Warranty: parts,** one year; **labor,** 90 days.

Approx. retail price	Approx. low price
$270	$210

Prices are accurate at time of printing; subject to manufacturer's change.

PERSONAL RADIOS

SONY SRF-4

The Sony SRF-4 is a basic, nearly indestructible FM stereo radio with a rugged, water-resistant design. Its on/off buttons, volume knob, and tuning knob are easily distinguishable both by touch and by shape. A small light-emitting diode (LED) on the front acts as a stereo indicator light and shows the condition of the batteries. The bright yellow case is resistant to moisture. The radio circuit is based upon a single computer chip for simplicity, dependability, and good reception. The radio comes with water-resistant in-the-ear headphones. Two AAA alkaline batteries power the unit for 30 hours.

Specifications: height, 4¼"; **width,** 2¼"; **depth,** $^{27}/_{32}$"; **weight,** 3³⁄₁₀ ounces. **Warranty:** one year.

Approx. retail price	Approx. low price
$45	$36

AIWA CR-12

RECOMMENDED

The Aiwa CR-12 is a no-frills personal radio that offers fine performance at a modest price. A good-size, easy-to-read slide-rule tuning dial occupies the top quarter of the unit's front. A stereo/mono switch can select mono for cleaner reception of noisy signals. A super-bass switch can boost low frequencies. It operates over 30 hours from two AA batteries. Aiwa supplies comfortable on-the-ear headphones.

Specifications: height, 4⁷⁄₁₆"; **width,** 2⅝"; **depth,** 1"; **weight,** 3½ ounces without battery. **Warranty: parts,** one year; **labor,** 90 days.

Approx. retail price	Approx. low price
$35	$23

PERSONAL HEADSET RADIOS

SONY SRF-H2

The Sony SRF-H2 personal headset radio stays on your head because of its unusual double headband. You won't mind its

Prices are accurate at time of printing; subject to manufacturer's change.

tenacity because it is extremely lightweight and it has reasonably comfortable on-the-ear cushions. A flexible short-whip antenna resists breaking, yet pulls in stations loud and clear. The reflective fluorescent yellow tip of the antenna is a safety feature that increases visibility, especially useful when jogging at night. The SRF-H2 tunes in the newly extended AM band, and includes a local/distant switch for improving FM reception. Radio reception is quite good, although an overload is possible in the immediate vicinity of powerful transmitters. The unit operates for about 70 hours on a single AAA alkaline battery.
Specifications: weight, 4⅕ ounces including battery.
Warranty: one year; **labor,** 90 days.

Approx. retail price	Approx. low price
$35	$34

AIWA HR-S20

✔**BEST BUY**

The Aiwa HR-S20 is one of the lightest headset radios on the market. For carrying, the headband collapses, making it quite compact. Aiwa still found space to include its Super Bass circuitry to enhance low frequencies. The on-the-ear earphones provide good sound, but the built-in antenna may not be adequate for reception in some fringe locations. Although it looks fragile, the HR-S20 can take a fair amount of beating without damage. It operates for about 60 hours on a single AAA alkaline battery.
Specifications: weight, 3⁹⁄₁₀ ounces including battery.
Warranty: parts, one year; **labor,** 90 days.

Approx. retail price	Approx. low price
$48	$35

BOOMBOXES

HITACHI CX-W700H

✔**BEST BUY**

The Hitachi CX-W700H includes an acoustic super woofer and can provide dynamic surround-sound. There is a built-in CD player, and it has a flexible four-band tuner for AM/FM/SW1/SW2. This unit has twin cassette bays with standard and high-speed dubbing. It can be powered by AC or batteries. The
Prices are accurate at time of printing; subject to manufacturer's change.

CX-W700H is a good size. It can serve as a great sound system in a dormitory or efficiency apartment.
Specifications: height, 8⅞₁₆″; **width,** 24¹³⁄₁₆″; **depth,** 10⅞₁₆″; **weight,** 17 pounds with batteries. **Warranty: parts and labor,** one year.

Approx. retail price	Approx. low price
$400	$365

SHARP CD-S77

RECOMMENDED

The Sharp CD-S77 has a 38-key wireless remote control, which makes it a home audio system as well as a portable sound source. The CD player is augmented by dual autoreverse cassette decks with autoedit features and a digital timer. The active servo technology enhances bass and linear response. This is a space-efficient shelf or portable stereo system.
Specifications: height, 7¹¹⁄₁₆″; **width,** 22¹³⁄₁₆″; **depth,** 9⅜″; **weight,** 14⅜ pounds. **Warranty: parts,** one year; **labor,** 90 days.

Approx. retail price	Approx. low price
$350	$333

JVC RC-X220CD

RECOMMENDED

The JVC RC-X220CD provides a CD synchro start for taping CDs and has an AM/FM tuner. This unit uses six D batteries, which is a comparatively modest number for these machines. It can also be run with AC power. The sound produced by the two four-inch speakers is very good, even if not true high fidelity. But for economy, flexibility, and portability, the RC-X220CD is effective as a source of music or news.
Specifications: height, 6⅞₁₆″; **width,** 16⅜₁₆″; **depth,** 8¹⁵⁄₁₆″; **weight,** 7⁷⁄₁₀ pounds. **Warranty: parts and labor,** one year.

Approx. retail price	Approx. low price
$200	$170

PANASONIC RX-DS45

RECOMMENDED

The Panasonic RX-DS45 can serve as a shelf system or as a portable, and it features an attractive modern design. It has a separate amplifier for each of its four loudspeakers. This

machine has a Fit Edit feature that facilitates taping CDs that can run up to 70-some minutes onto cassettes that can hold a maximum of 60 minutes per side. This unit uses a total of ten D batteries, but it also runs on AC power. The RX-DS45 has a headphone jack, an external mike jack, and two input jacks.
Specifications: height, 6⅞"; **width,** 25½"; **depth,** 9⅞"; **weight,** 13⅔ pounds. **Warranty: parts and labor,** one year.

Approx. retail price	Approx. low price
$350	$301

PANASONIC RX-CT840   RECOMMENDED

The Panasonic RX-CT840 may lack a CD player, but it has a wide range of features that make this unit a good buy. It can serve as a compact stereo system, a recording machine, and a portable music system. The built-in five-band equalizer makes it possible to optimize the sound provided by four speakers with their own amplifiers. The detachable speakers can be wall mounted or placed apart for greater stereo separation. Features include CD/line-in jacks, two cassette decks, synchro start, headphone jack, and autoreverse playback.
Specifications: center unit, height, 7⅞"; **width,** 12"; **depth,** 6¹¹⁄₁₆"; **speakers, height,** 7¹³⁄₁₆"; **width,** 5⅝"; **depth,** 6¹⁄₁₆"; **total weight,** 8⁷⁄₁₆ pounds. **Warranty: parts and labor,** one year.

Approx. retail price	Approx. low price
$120	not available

SAMSUNG RCD995   RECOMMENDED

The Samsung RCD995 has only one cassette mechanism but comes with a CD player that will handle both three- and five-inch discs. While machines without CD players are available, this unit demonstrates that the added cost of the CD player is quite modest and well worth the money. It has a streamlined design and weighs a modest eight pounds. The four-inch speakers provide a warm, friendly sound.
Specifications: height, 7⅜"; **width,** 21⅞"; **depth,** 7⅞"; **weight,** eight pounds. **Warranty: parts and labor,** one year (carry-in service).

Approx. retail price	Approx. low price
$240	$153

Prices are accurate at time of printing; subject to manufacturer's change.

Clock Radios

While there are lots of innovations available in clock radios, nothing is more important than finding a product that will let you have a good night's sleep. Some models emit sound called white noise that blocks out sounds that might keep you awake, such as traffic noise and barking dogs. If you're the worrisome type, many models have a battery backup system to make sure the alarm goes off in time even if there is a power failure while you sleep. Look for a clock radio with simple and easily accessible controls that can be operated in the dark. Get one that is sturdy enough so that you don't push it off your nightstand when fumbling for the controls. The best product has features that match your needs.

Clock Radio Features

The **doze** or **snooze bar** lets you catch a few minutes of extra sleep after the alarm goes off by waking you up a second time. The **sleep feature** lets you fall asleep to music, which plays for a preset period and then shuts itself off automatically. **Dual alarms** let you awaken at a different time than your spouse or roommate. A **backup system** ensures the alarm will sound in time in case of a power failure; most backup systems require a 9-volt battery. **Ramp-up volume** awakens you with a gradual increase in music or alarm volume instead of clicking on at high volume.

Best Buys '92

Our Best Buy choices follow. The unit we consider the best of the Best Buys is listed first, followed by our second choice, and so on. Remember that a Best Buy designation applies only to the model listed, not necessarily to other models by the same manufacturer or to an entire product line.

PANASONIC RC-X250

The Panasonic RC-X250 is an AM/FM stereo clock radio that looks like a small, black boombox. Its two three-inch diameter dynamic speakers are located on each side of the unit. This model produces unusually good sound quality in FM stereo. It has a cassette tape player/recorder so you can fall asleep to or wake up to tapes. It can also be used as a personal message center; an LED message indicator lets you know a message is waiting. The RC-X250 has doze/snooze and sleep functions, a green LED time display, a headphone jack, a booster switch, dual alarms, and a battery backup system.

Specifications: height, 4¼"; **width,** 13⅛"; **depth,** 5¹¹⁄₁₆".
Warranty: parts and labor, one year.

Approx. retail price	Approx. low price
$85	$78

PROTON 325 ✔BEST BUY

The Proton 325 is the successor to the boxy-looking perennial Best Buy, the Proton 320, which has been discontinued. The 325 also offers rich, high-fidelity sound in a moderately priced digital AM/FM clock radio. Other brands with comparable sound cost much more. This black wedge-shaped model has a three-watt amplifier, dual alarm, and a four-inch speaker.

Specifications: height, 4¾"; **width,** 10⅞"; **depth,** 4¾".
Warranty: parts and labor, one year.

Approx. retail price	Approx. low price
$110	$100

SONY ICF-C303 ✔BEST BUY

The Sony ICF-C303 is an AM/FM clock radio that you can set to wake you at different times each day of the week. The Sony

Prices are accurate at time of printing; subject to manufacturer's change.

CLOCK RADIOS

ICF-C303 also has a dual alarm, date display, digital tuner with seven station presets, and four-hour power backup without battery. It comes in black.

Specifications: height, 2⁷⁄₁₆"; **width,** 7¹⁵⁄₁₆"; **depth,** 6⅛".
Warranty: parts and labor, 90 days.

Approx. retail price	Approx. low price
$50	$47

PANASONIC RC-6099

The Panasonic RC-6099 is a compact AM/FM clock radio. It has dual alarm, doze and sleep functions, battery backup, ramp-up volume, an earphone jack, and a three-inch dynamic speaker.

Specifications: height, 2⅜"; **width,** 9⅛"; **depth,** 6¹⁄₁₆".
Warranty: parts and labor, one year.

Approx. retail price	Approx. low price
$33	$32

SONY ICF-IR7

The Sony ICF-IR7 is a brand new model that offers very good sound quality and true stereo separation without cluttering your room with wires. The Sony ICF-IR7 consists of two Mega Bass speakers that can be placed anywhere in your room and a small control clock that fits on a headboard, nightstand, or desktop. The control clock uses infrared technology to transmit audio to the remote speakers. This model has a digital AM/FM stereo tuner with ten presets, memory scan tuning, battery backup, and dual alarm. In addition, you can plug in a portable CD player and awaken to CD sound. Each speaker comes with a stand and contains a 3⅛-inch full-range speaker and a 3⅛-inch woofer. This model comes in black.

Specifications: control module, height, 2⅞"; **width,** 5⅞"; **depth,** 5⁵⁄₁₆"; **speakers, height,** 18⁷⁄₁₆"; **width,** 4¾"; **depth,** 5⅜".
Warranty: parts and labor, 90 days.

Approx. retail price	Approx. low price
$220	$213

Cameras

Some sixty billion pictures are taken every year around the world. At least 85 percent of those sixty billion pictures are taken with color-negative film, partly because of the rapid growth of minilabs, and partly because you no longer have to be an expert to operate most modern cameras. Many of these cameras automatically focus the lens, meter the available light, set the correct aperture and shutter speed, and even activate the built-in or attached flash if the light level is too low for a good exposure. Some of the more sophisticated models will allow you to use them as fully automatic cameras, or let you take control to make your own picture taking decisions. There are also full manual cameras. Photography is an enjoyable way to record the many important things that will happen in your life. The choices are getting harder because camera manufacturers have turned their attention to producing high-quality lenses, accurate exposure systems, and wide-ranging exposure controls even in less expensive models.

Types of Cameras

With a **single-lens reflex (SLR) camera,** you view the subject of your picture through the lens that takes the picture so that you see exactly what the camera sees.

With a **viewfinder camera,** you see the image you are going to photograph through a window, or viewfinder.

With a **range finder camera,** you view your subject through a viewfinder, and the range finder projects a second image of the subject in the viewfinder. The lens is in focus when the two images coincide.

A **zone-focus camera** is a viewfinder camera that uses symbols or a distance scale to focus the lens. You estimate the distance and set the lens according to your estimate. Some autofocus cameras use zone-focus symbols in the viewfinder to indicate where the camera is focused.

A **fixed-focus camera** (usually called a point-and-shoot camera) is a viewfinder camera that has its focus fixed at a certain point, so that everything from a specified minimum distance to infinity is in focus.

An **autofocus camera** is any kind of camera that uses one of several different methods to focus the lens automatically when you touch the shutter-release button.

Features and Terminology

Aperture, or **f-stop,** is listed as a ratio of the diameter of the lens opening to the focal length of the lens. All lenses are identified by their focal length and their largest aperture. A standard, or normal, lens for a 35mm camera is usually listed as a 50mm f/2 lens (a normal lens produces a picture that approximates the perspective and degree of magnification that is seen by the human eye, excluding peripheral vision). The f-stop is a function of the lens aperture setting. The standard series is f/1.4, f/2, f/2.8, f/4, f/5.6, f/8, f/11, f/16, f/22, and f/32. The smaller the number, the larger the aperture and the more light that will strike the film. For example, a 50mm f/1.8 lens is able to let in more light and is a faster lens than a 50mm f/2 lens. Most lenses do not cover the full range of settings, and some may extend higher or lower.

A **dedicated hot shoe** is a shoe, or clip, found on most 35mm SLR cameras that interfaces accessories—such as electronic flashes—with the camera's electronics. Some dedicated systems provide through-the-lens-off-the-film (TTL-OTF) flash control.

DX coding imparts information about the film directly to the camera. The 35mm film cassette has metal strips on it that make contact with the pins in the camera, and tell the camera the film speed, exposure latitude, and the number of exposures on the roll. Most SLRs offer both DX coding and manual film-speed settings. Compact 35mm cameras offer only DX coding.

EV compensation corrects the automatic exposure of subjects that are either very light or very dark. One EV (exposure value) is equivalent to one full f-stop.

A **focal-plane shutter** uses curtains or blades that travel either vertically or horizontally across the film plane to make an exposure. Almost all 35mm SLR cameras use this shutter because it allows the camera to use interchangeable lenses.

ISO (International Standards Organization) is a numerical system that indicates the relative speed of film. The higher the ISO number, the faster the film records an image. To take photographs in low light, use a high-speed film.

A **leaf shutter** uses a series of blades arranged in a circle that open and close to make an exposure. Compact 35mm cameras with fixed lenses use leaf shutters.

A **self-timer** is a switch found on most 35mm cameras that delays the operation of the shutter for about ten seconds, allowing the photographer to get in the picture.

Viewfinder information is a visual display in the camera's viewfinder of the exposure information you need to take good pictures. Autofocus SLR cameras also have signals that indicate when an image is in focus, and some signal out-of-focus conditions. Most cameras also provide flash signals that tell you when the flash is needed for good exposures.

Exposure Systems

Most 35mm SLR cameras have built-in TTL exposure meters that allow for accurate exposures no matter which lens you have on the camera. These meters use silicon photodiodes, which react instantly to light and are not blinded by very bright light. Most SLR cameras provide both automatic and manual-exposure operation.

Most 35mm autofocus and compact cameras also have built-in meters that parallel the lens to meter the image area. These parallel meters are now so sophisticated that they provide accurate exposures even for zoom lenses.

There are three basic kinds of automatic-exposure (AE) systems in cameras that provide automatic exposures:

Aperture-priority AE lets you set the lens opening (f-stop), and the camera's metering system selects the shutter speed.

Shutter-priority AE lets you select the shutter speed, and the camera selects the lens opening automatically.

Programmed AE automatically selects both the aperture and shutter speed that will give you the appropriate exposure for the film in use. A microcomputer connected to the metering cell determines the correct settings. Programmed AE is used in most 35mm autofocus cameras, 35mm compact cameras, and instant-print cameras.

Best Buys '92

Our Best Buys and Recommended cameras follow. These are presented in seven categories: 35mm manual-focus SLR cameras, 35mm autofocus SLR cameras, 35mm autofocus cameras, 35mm compact cameras, an underwater camera, a snapshot 110 cartridge camera, instant-print cameras, and 35mm single-use cameras. Within each category, products are listed according to overall quality. The best of the Best Buys is first, followed by our second choice, and so on. Recommended cameras follow our Best Buy selections. Remember that a Best Buy rating applies only to the model listed and not to other models made by the same manufacturer or to an entire product line.

35mm MANUAL-FOCUS SLR CAMERAS

The 35mm SLR camera is probably the most widely used professional camera. Newspaper, combat, and sports photographers use 35mm SLRs, as do fashion and nature photographers, scientists, and doctors. The research and development that has perfected professional SLR systems is passed on to amateur photographers in the form of advanced, but less expensive, 35mm SLRs. Our manual-focus SLR selections provide TTL exposure metering with manual-exposure adjustment so that you have full control over your images. Unless specified, prices quoted are without lenses.

NIKON N6000

The Nikon N6000 is a sophisticated manual-focus SLR with a built-in motor drive. The N6000 has two types of light meters built in: center-weighted metering can be used with all Nikon lenses, and Matrix metering analyzes five areas of the image for brightness and contrast to determine the best exposure for the total scene. Manual exposure and aperture-priority AE can be used with all lenses, while shutter-priority AE and multiprogram AE operate only with AF and P lenses. The N6000 has exposure compensation of +/- 5 EV, automatic-exposure lock for changing composition after metering your main subject, and automatic-exposure bracketing of three- and five-frame sequences to insure you get the best exposure in difficult or tricky lighting situations. The high eye-point viewfinder gives you a full view of the image on the briteview focusing screen and the LCD (liquid crystal display) exposure information, even when wearing glasses. DX coding and manual film-speed settings provide for film-speed settings of ISO 6 to ISO 6400. The built-in motor drive loads the film to the first frame, advances the film after each exposure, and rewinds the film at the end of the roll. The motor-drive operation can be set for single-frame advance, and for 1⅛ or 2 frames-per-second for rapid shooting. With Nikon Speedlights, the N6000 provides matrix-balanced fill-flash, center-weighted fill-flash, slow-synch fill-flash, flash-exposure compensation, and rear-curtain shutter synch for exciting long exposures of moving objects. The Nikon N6000 is the versatile manual-focus SLR for those photographers who want automation while having full control over their pictures.

Warranty: parts and labor, one year.

Approx. retail price	Approx. low price
$510	**$353**

RICOH KR-5 SUPER II

The Ricoh KR-5 Super II is a compact 35mm single-lens reflex camera that uses all popular K-mount lenses from wide angle to telephoto. The KR-5 Super II has mechanical shutter speeds from one second to ½₀₀₀ second, plus B for long exposures, and a flash synchronization of ¹⁄₁₂₅ second. The shutter speeds and apertures are coupled to a built-in, through-the-lens, center-weighted meter. There are three LEDs in the viewfinder: a green circle for correct exposure, a red plus that indicates overexposure, and a red minus that indicates underexposure.

Prices are accurate at time of printing; subject to manufacturer's change.

To take an exposure reading, you move the film-advance lever to its 30-degree standoff position, then depress the shutter-release button part way to activate the meter. Film speeds are manually set from ISO 25 to ISO 1600 on a collar around the rewind knob. The only other control is a self-timer. A well-designed finger grip gives you a firm hold of the camera. The KR-5 Super II is a basic, reliable SLR that gives you full control over your pictures at a reasonable price.

Warranty: parts and labor, two years.

Approx. retail price	Approx. low price
$240	$165
$310 (with 50mm f/2 Rikenon lens)	not available

35mm AUTOFOCUS SLR CAMERAS

Autofocus (AF) SLR cameras have CCD (charge-coupled device) sensors that use subject contrast to achieve the correct focus. Some CCDs are so sensitive that they can focus on low-contrast subjects in light so low that you can hardly see the AF frame in the viewfinder. Many AF SLRs now have built-in near-infrared AF illuminators that automatically project a focusing pattern so that the camera can focus on subjects with no contrast, and even on subjects in total darkness. Highly efficient microprocessors and micromotors have made autofocusing very fast and accurate, even with long telephoto lenses.

The **ZLR** (zoom-lens reflex) is a new and growing breed of AF SLR. The ZLR is so named because it is a single-lens reflex with a permanently attached zoom lens. A ZLR gives you the best of both worlds: viewing through the lens in a compact, unified camera/lens design.

MINOLTA MAXXUM 8000i

The Minolta Maxxum 8000i is a sophisticated AF SLR with intelligent autofocus and intelligent metering. The 8000i has multiple AF sensors that give you an autofocus area that is up to 12 times wider than that of other AF SLRs, allowing you to focus on off-center subjects. The multiple AF sensors provide focusing on vertically, horizontally, and diagonally oriented subjects. A built-in AF illuminator, with a range of 30 feet, automatically switches into predictive focus control when it detects a moving subject, and continues to focus up to the instant of exposure. The 8000i has three metering systems: spot for pinpoint metering; standard center-weighted average; and AF Integrated Multi-Pattern, which has six metering segments and also uses autofocus information to determine the best exposure for each subject. There is also automatic-contrast compensation that corrects for backlit and spotlit situations. The 8000i uses the Maxxum Creative Expansion Card System with 13 software cards that produce controls for special effects and automatic operation of complicated photographic procedures, such as exposure bracketing and highlight/shadow metering. The top shutter speed is $\frac{1}{8000}$ second, and the top flash synch speed is $\frac{1}{200}$ second. The long eye-relief viewfinder is one of the best we have ever seen for providing a complete view of the image frame and the information panel below it for eyeglass wearers. In spite of its many operations, the 8000i is user friendly, with all major controls set up so that they can be used with the camera at eye level, and all necessary information appears in the uncluttered viewfinder. Simply put, the sophisticated Maxxum 8000i is easy to use.

Warranty: parts and labor, two years.

Approx. retail price	Approx. low price
$812	**$556**

CANON EOS 10S   ✓ BEST BUY

The Canon EOS 10S is the first AF SLR to use the innovative flexible autofocus system. Three sensors, capable of working individually or together, are spread across half the frame, and the location of each one is marked in the viewfinder. The beauty of the flexible AF system is that it automatically evaluates your subject matter for accurate focusing even for off-center subjects, and the focus mark or marks where the focus is determined is lightly illuminated in red. The flexible AF system is particularly good at predicting the actual focus point of moving subjects at the instant of exposure. The flexible-focus system will also focus on any subject no matter what its orientation. In the 10S depth-of-field mode, the flexible-focus

Prices are accurate at time of printing; subject to manufacturer's change.

marks are placed over the near and far focus points, and the microcomputer sets the right aperture for a sharp picture of the scene. For special focus situations, you can elect to use only one focus mark. There is a built-in focusing aid light that automatically projects a pattern in low light for any of the three AF sensors to focus on. The novel eight-zone metering is coupled to the flexible AF system so that the meter always knows the location of your main subject, then evaluates the brightness levels around it to produce the best exposure for the composition. There is also partial metering for tricky lighting situations, which meters only the central 8½ percent of the scene. The 10S is also the first advanced camera to have a built-in pop-up flash for fast-flash illumination when there is not enough time to attach a separate flash. Other convenient features of the 10S are automatic program shifting for different focal lengths; camera-shake compensation, which automatically shifts to a higher shutter speed to avoid blurred pictures; automatic-exposure bracketing to vary the exposure rendition of a subject; multiple-exposure control; an interval timer for time-lapse photography; five-frames-per-second film advance; four programmed image-control settings; and custom-function control for setting up the camera the way you want it to operate. In spite of having too many operations, the EOS 10S is one of the very best AF SLRs available because of its flexible autofocus, eight-zone meter, built-in flash, and five-frames-per-second motor drive.

Warranty: parts and labor, one year.

Approx. retail price	**Approx. low price**
$730	**$510**

OLYMPUS IS-1

The Olympus IS-1 is a ZLR and is the first camera with a permanently attached 35 to 135mm f/4.5-5.6 zoom lens that uses ED (Extraordinary Dispersion) glass. ED glass, only found in expensive SLR lenses until now, greatly improves the sharpness, contrast, and color purity of your photographs. The IS-1 is uniquely designed with an L-shaped design, M-pattern viewfinder, and S-wrap film system that makes it a slender, portable camera. The IS-1 also has fuzzy logic ESP (Electro-Selective Pattern) metering. Fuzzy logic is a new type of

Prices are accurate at time of printing; subject to manufacturer's change.

computer that operates more like the human mind than standard computers. ESP metering reads contrast information of the whole scene, and the fuzzy logic microcomputer instantly interprets even the smallest contrast differences to make the best settings for the image. The ESP meter pattern is used in the programmed AE mode, while in aperture-preferred AE and metered manual, a center-weighted averaging meter pattern is employed. Spot metering is also available for all metering modes. The flip up, dual-strobe intelligent flash uses one strobe for wide-angle and close-up photography, and the other one for telephoto pictures. The flash has both normal and auto-S operation, which eliminates red-eye by omitting a series of low-power flashes before making the exposure. The low-power flashes close the pupils of your subjects so that there is no red reflection from the retinas of the eyes reflected back to the film. The flash can also be used with the night-scene mode for well-exposed dim backgrounds and foregrounds illuminated by flash. Three portrait modes zoom the lens to the proper focal length to produce either head and shoulder, half-length, or full-length portraits. Wide-angle and telephoto macro modes provide focusing down to two feet. Other features are a double-exposure mode, continuous-film advance, +/- 4 EV exposure compensation in ⅓ steps, and zoom memory, which includes macro. Accessories include a powerful and versatile dedicated shoe-mount flash, a 28mm converter lens, a 200mm converter lens, and a macro lens that comes with a diffuser for soft-flash lighting for extreme close-ups. The Olympus IS-1 is a unique camera in many ways, and its many unique features help you to produce superb photographs.

Warranty: parts and labor, one year.

Approx. retail price	Approx. low price
$800	**$540**

CHINON GENESIS III   RECOMMENDED

The Chinon Genesis III is an ergonomically designed AF SLR with a fixed 38mm-to-110mm power zoom lens. Slipping your hand through the hand strap, the camera nestles in your palm and your fingers rest in the finger grip on top of the camera, with your forefinger on the shutter-release button. The ergonomic design allows you to take sharp pictures even with

Prices are accurate at time of printing; subject to manufacturer's change.

one hand. The Genesis III features both a through-the-lens contrast autofocus system and a three-beam infrared autofocus system for accurate focusing in all situations—from distant subjects to subjects in total darkness. Zooming can be controlled by the photographer via the telephoto and wide buttons on top of the camera. For snapshooting, you can let the automatic composition system zoom the lens for you in any one of three modes: landscape mode for scenic and large group shots, sport/portrait mode for action and people shots, and standard-program mode for general shooting. The sport/portrait mode also has automatic close-up operation when your subject is from 33½ to 39⅝ inches from the camera. The focal plane shutter has speeds from 1 to ¹⁄₁₀₀₀ second, plus long-time exposures for nighttime scenic shots. The pop-up flash, which stands 2½ inches above the film plane to reduce red-eye, normally sets the shutter speed to ¹⁄₁₀₀₀ second, but it can be overridden to produce balanced ambient and flash pictures by holding the flash button down while you press the shutter-release button. DX coding handles film speeds from ISO 25 to ISO 3200. The silicon photo diode produces very accurate exposures for all types of film. Film speeds can be fine tuned with the +/- 2 EV control, which is also used to compensate for unusual lighting situations without using a flash. The Chinon Genesis III is an excellent camera for those who want an autofocus SLR, but do not want to bother with changing lenses.
Warranty: parts and labor, two years, limited.

Approx. retail price	Approx. low price
$500	$356

35mm AUTOFOCUS CAMERAS

The 35mm leaf-shutter autofocus (AF) camera is popular because it is an easy way to shoot high-quality 35mm film. An AF camera does more than focus the lens automatically. It loads the film, advances it after each exposure, and rewinds the film after the last exposure. Many AF cameras have a sophisticated meter that activates a built-in flash in difficult lighting situations, such as backlight, to produce a well-lit subject that is balanced with the background exposure. Some models, called dual-lens cameras, have both a normal and mod-

Prices are accurate at time of printing; subject to manufacturer's change.

erate telephoto lens. Others have a zoom lens, which gives you a variety of focal lengths. Some cameras now have special flash operations that reduce or eliminate red-eye, a problem caused by the flash being too close to the film plane. The most recent trend, one that you will notice here, is the return to compact designs that give you both high quality and high portability.

OLYMPUS INFINITY STYLUS

The Olympus Infinity Stylus is a sleek, shirt-pocket-size AF compact with sophisticated autofocus, exposure, and flash operation. The Stylus has a clamshell cover that becomes a comfortable finger grip when open. There are no yellow lines in the full-image viewfinder to distract you because you are seeing exactly what the lens sees. The 35mm f/3.5 lens focuses from 13⅛ inches to infinity with pinpoint accuracy because the active-infrared system has an amazing 100 zones of focus. The Electro-Selective Pattern (ESP) metering system is also very accurate; it reads the central and surrounding areas for the image separately, then makes the best exposure for the lighting ratio. If the lighting is too contrasted, such as when your subject is backlit, the ESP meter activates the built-in flash to maintain exposure accuracy. The built-in flash has a range of 13⅛ inches to 11½ feet with ISO 100 film, and 13⅛ inches to 23 feet with ISO 400 film. The Infinity Stylus also features the Olympus Auto-S flash operation, which sends out a rapid series of low-level flashes that close down the pupils of your subjects before the exposure is made, thus eliminating red-eye. Along with automatic flash and S-flash operation, there is a fill-in flash, which fires the flash regardless of the lighting, and flash-off for natural-light pictures. The programmed electronic shutter has speeds from ⅟₁₅ second to ⅟₅₀₀ second. The built-in winder automatically advances and rewinds the film, DX coding is set for speeds from ISO 50 to ISO 3200, and the autofocus light in the viewfinder blinks to tell you that your subject is too close. The Olympus Infinity Stylus is as attractive as it is easy to use, with its black finish and three silver operating buttons on top.

Warranty: parts and labor, one year.

Approx. retail price	**Approx. low price**
$225	**$146**

KONICA BIG MINI

The Konica Big Mini, a successor to our top-rated A4 last year, is a compact, shirt-pocket-size 35mm autofocus camera that has superior optics and an accurate exposure system that produces excellent images. The Big Mini has a 35mm f/3.5 lens with a focusing range of 13¾ inches to infinity; focusing is done by an active-infrared system with 23 points of focus to provide sharp images over its entire focusing range. When not in use, the lens slides into the body to make a small package that can fit into a shirt pocket or small purse. The electronic shutter has stepless speeds from 3⅗ seconds to ⅟₅₀₀ second that provides you with a range that can take accurate exposures in bright light to time exposures in very dim light. The built-in flash has a range of 13¾ inches to 12½ feet with ISO 100 film, and 13¾ inches to 24⁹⁄₁₀ feet with ISO 400 film. The new automatic-variable flash produces accurate close-ups by automatically reducing its output when the lens moves into its close-up range of 13¾ inches to 24 inches. The Big Mini has five-exposure modes: automatic flash; flash-on for slow-shutter synch for well-exposed backgrounds with flash-illuminated foregrounds and to fill-in shadows; flash-off for available-light pictures; +1½ apertures to compensate for backlighting; and -1½ apertures for subjects in front of a dark background. The built-in winder loads the film to the first frame automatically, advances the film after each exposure, and rewinds the film after the last exposure. The Konica Big Mini is small in size, but it delivers a big performance.

Warranty: parts and labor, one year.

Approx. retail price
$290

Approx. low price
$218

PENTAX IQZOOM 60-X

The Pentax IQZoom 60-X is the most compact autofocus zoom-lens camera available. It can easily be carried in a jacket pocket or small purse because the 38mm-to-60mm f/4.5-6.7 zoom lens retracts into the body of the camera when the power switch is turned off. Even though it is small, the IQZoom 60-X is big in performance, producing brilliant, colorful pictures with its accurate exposure system and high-quality multicoated six-element zoom lens. An active-infrared autofocus system, with 23 zones of focus, produces sharp pictures from two feet to infinity. The green autofocus lamp in the viewfinder glows when correct focus has been achieved, and flickers when you get too close to your subject. The built-in flash has a range of 2 to 10 feet at 38mm, and 2 to 6⅝ feet at 60mm with ISO 100 film. With ISO 400 film, the flash range is 2 to 20 feet at 38mm, and 2 to 13 feet at 60mm. There are four exposure modes: automatic flash; daylight synch for fill-flash and slow-shutter synch; flash-off for available light photography; and bulb for exposures from one to eight seconds. The IQZoom 60-X has three self-timer modes: single shot, dual frame that takes two pictures, and dual zoom that takes the first picture at your selected focal length and the second one at 38mm. There are two zoom controls: a continuous zoom control, and an instant tele/wide that quickly zooms the lens to 60mm or 38mm. The Pentax IQZoom 60-X is a superb compact AF zoom camera.

Warranty: parts and labor, one year.

Approx. retail price	Approx. low price
$245	$200

FUJI DISCOVERY 3000 ZOOM DATE

✔**BEST BUY**

The Fuji Discovery 3000 Zoom Date is a binocular-style camera with a three-time zoom and an accessory flash for extended flash operation. The 38mm-to-115mm power zoom lens is multicoated to produce sharp, accurate color exposures. The power zoom has two methods for zooming: a standard-zoom lever for exact framing of your subject, and three quick-zoom buttons that set the lens to 38mm, 70mm, or 115mm. The real-image viewfinder shows you only the scene being photographed, and also zooms along with the lens to give you a correctly magnified image of what the lens sees. Dioptric adjustment is provided so that you can adjust the viewfinder for your eyesight. The active-infrared focusing system has 164 focus zones that produce accurate focusing both in the normal range of 4³⁄₁₀ feet to infinity, and in its close-up range of 31½ to 51 inches at 115mm. A landscape button defeats the AF operation for accurate focus on distant subjects, even when

Prices are accurate at time of printing; subject to manufacturer's change.

photographed through a window. The 3000 Zoom Date has four exposure modes: automatic flash, flash-fill, flash-off for available light pictures, and +2 exposure compensation for backlit subjects. The self-timer can be programmed to take one, two, or three exposures to capture those unguarded moments. The built-in flash has a range of 4³⁄₁₀ to 16½ feet at 38mm, and 4³⁄₁₀ to 11½ feet at 115mm with ISO 100 film. The accessory flash, which attaches to the top of the 3000 Zoom Date, extends your flash-working range by 60 percent. The accessory flash also has a preflash mode, which sends out a short burst of light to close down the pupils of your subjects before the exposure is made, thus minimizing red-eye. The accessory flash folds down to be out of the way when not in use. The green autofocus confirmation lamp in the viewfinder warns you that you are out of focusing range in the close-up mode by blinking, and also blinks in the normal photography mode when your subject is out of the range of either the built-in or accessory flash. The 3000 Zoom Date prewinds the film to the last exposure, and the LCD (liquid crystal display) frame counter on the back indicates the number of exposures left on your roll of film. The autodate imprinting can be turned on or off at any time. The Fuji Discovery 3000 Zoom Date is a versatile camera that produces sharp, accurately exposed, and colorful pictures. **Warranty: parts and labor,** five years, limited.

Approx. retail price	**Approx. low price**
$430	$357

OLYMPUS INFINITY ZOOM 200

The Olympus Infinity Zoom 200 introduced the innovative Auto-S-mode flash operation that eliminates the red-eye effect in most subjects. Red-eye happens when you take pictures of people in low-light levels with a flash that is too close to the film plane. When light levels are low, the pupil opens up, and the retina reflects back the red spectrum of the flash. In the S-mode, the Infinity Zoom 200 emits about 15 low-level preflashes that effectively close the pupil down before the shutter opens and the full-power flash exposure is made. With the pupil closed, not enough red light is reflected back to be recorded on film. The flash has variable power, putting out less light for close subjects than for far subjects, so that subjects

Prices are accurate at time of printing; subject to manufacturer's change.

even as close as two feet are properly exposed. There is also a Multi Flash mode that makes four flash exposures in ⅙ second on one frame. The Infinity Zoom 200 makes both spot and average readings to measure contrast, and it will automatically fire the flash in situations such as backlighting. You can shift to spot metering, which also switches autofocus operation from multifocus to spot focus. The optical real-image viewfinder shows only the image that is being seen by the 38mm-to-80mm zoom lens. The Infinity Zoom 200 also features automatic-zoom framing for portraits and a remote control that allows you to trip the shutter from up to 16 feet away.

Warranty: parts and labor, one year.

Approx. retail price	Approx. low price
$400	$276

CHINON AUTO 4001 ✓BEST BUY

The Chinon Auto 4001 has a motorized 35mm-to-70mm f/3.7-6.9 zoom lens with an innovative two-stage automatic-composition system for daylight and flash photography. The on/off switch has two on positions: power and automatic. The power position lets you power the lens to select your own composition with the zoom lever on the back of the camera. The automatic position selects the focal length for you with its new powerful microcomputer that analyzes data from the infrared-multibeam autofocus system and the CdS cell to determine the most pleasing composition for the subject matter. Daylight program favors the longer focal lengths, while the program that takes over when the built-in flash is activated in low-light levels favors the short focal lengths. A spring loaded automatic-flash sensor switch on the front panel has two positions: the fill position is used in contrast lighting to fill in the shadows, while the off position takes advantage of shutter speeds down to ¼ second for available-light photography. The built-in winder automatically advances the film to the first frame, advances the film after each exposure, and rewinds the film after the last exposure. DX coding is set for ISO films of 100, 200, 400, and 1000. With its high-quality multicoated lens and accurate exposure system, the Chinon Auto 4001 is a fine AF zoom camera.

Warranty: parts and labor, two years.

Prices are accurate at time of printing; subject to manufacturer's change.

Approx. retail price **$275** | **Approx. low price** **$190**

MINOLTA FREEDOM ZOOM 105i

RECOMMENDED

The Minolta Freedom Zoom 105i is the first 35mm autofocus camera to have eye-start operation. The 105i has a 35mm-to-105mm f/4-6.7 zoom lens that is controlled by an advanced program zoom (APZ) system that automatically sets the lens to the correct focal length for the subject. The continuous APZ control range is $2\frac{3}{10}$ to 36 feet, with the lens being set to 105mm when the focus is beyond 36 feet. Eye-start operation ties into the APZ operation: An infrared sensor next to the viewfinder eyepiece detects an object when it is about three inches or closer and activates the APZ so that the lens begins to zoom by the time you are looking at your subject in the viewfinder. When you take your eye from the viewfinder, the APZ system is switched off to conserve battery power. There are telephoto and wide buttons that provide you with manual override of the APZ system, either for one shot or for continuous manual zooming. The 105i uses a through-the-lens AF phase detection, which provides continuous focusing from $2\frac{3}{10}$ feet to infinity. The built-in flash has a range of $2\frac{3}{10}$ to 18 feet at 35mm, and $3\frac{9}{10}$ to $10\frac{4}{5}$ feet at 105mm with ISO 100 film. There are four flash modes: automatic flash; automatic preflash, which emits a low-level flash before the actual exposure to minimize red-eye; fill-flash for filling in shadows that would not be detected by the metering system in the automatic modes; and flash-off for available light photography down to ½ second. Film advance and rewind is automatic. The Freedom Zoom 105i is perfect for those who want a fully automatic, high-quality autofocus zoom.
Warranty: parts and labor, one year.

Approx. retail price **$444** | **Approx. low price** **$343**

RICOH SHOTMASTER AF SUPER

RECOMMENDED

The Ricoh Shotmaster AF Super is a pocket-size camera with multimode operation. The 35mm f3.5 lens has a focus range of

Prices are accurate at time of printing; subject to manufacturer's change.

2⅖ feet to infinity, and the LED AF monitor lamp in the viewfinder blinks if your subject is closer than that. The built-in flash automatically pops up in low-light levels; it also pops up when the meter detects a backlit scene to provide fill-in lighting. There are six other modes besides the autoflash mode: the panorama mode sets the lens to infinity for sharp landscape pictures, even when taken through windows; the night mode sets the lens to infinity and uses shutter speeds down to 1⅖ second for evening panoramas; the TV mode sets the camera so that it synchronizes with the scanning lines of television screens and computer monitors; the continuous mode allows you to take sequences of moving subjects, and when combined with the self-timer, you will get two sequential frames; the interval mode makes an exposure every 60 seconds until the end of the roll is reached or you turn the mode off; and multiple exposures, which allows you to put two or more exposures on one frame. The camera uses DX-coded film from ISO 100 to 1600. The Ricoh Shotmaster AF Super is a fine pocket-size AF camera for the snapshooter who wants quality images.

Warranty: parts and labor, one year.

Approx. retail price	Approx. low price
$230	$177

35mm COMPACT CAMERAS

The 35mm compact is a relatively inexpensive camera with a fixed lens. Many 35mm compact cameras are simple point-and-shoot cameras with simple exposure systems designed for color-negative films. Some compacts are more versatile and take high-quality photographs. These cameras demand more input from the photographer than the point-and-shoot autofocus compacts, but they often produce excellent results.

MINOX 35 GT-E

The Minox 35 GT-E is a sophisticated, high-quality compact that weighs only seven ounces with its lithium batteries, and fits in a shirt pocket. It has a folding flatbed that protects the 35mm f/2.8 multicoated Minoxar lens when you are not taking pictures. Zone focusing is from 28 inches to infinity, with a

Prices are accurate at time of printing; subject to manufacturer's change.

CAMERAS

footage scale on the focusing ring. The 35 GT-E is an aperture-priority AE camera with f-stops from f/2.8 to f/16, and the meter selects shutter speeds from 8 seconds to ¹⁄₅₀₀ second. The shutter-speed scale in the viewfinder has a shaded area below ¹⁄₃₀ second to remind you to use a tripod or flash. An optional 35 FC-E flash has two automatic-exposure ranges as well as manual. Film speeds from ISO 25 to ISO 1600 are manually set with a dial on the camera base. On the top of the camera is a +2 EV switch used to compensate for backlighting, a self-timer switch, and a battery-check switch.

Warranty: parts and labor, two years, limited.

> **Approx. retail price**
> **$595**

> **Approx. low price**
> **$423**

KONICA KANPAI   ✓**BEST BUY**

The Konica Kanpai is named after the Japanese word for "cheers," which is just what you'll say to the camera once it is set up at a party or family gathering. It is the world's first sound-activated compact camera. The sound trigger has three sound level positions: low for a moderate sound level of ⅛ second or longer, medium for a ³⁄₁₀-second duration, and high for a ½-second duration. A built-in timer controls the rate of frames exposed, extending the completion of a 24-exposure roll of film to between 20 and 40 minutes. The Kanpai comes with a special mini tripod that will aim the camera at one area or will let the camera operate in free-swing framing to cover an area of 100 degrees. In free-swing framing, the Kanpai takes a picture, swings about 40 degrees, takes another picture, then swings back to its original position, and so on until the last frame. Sound still activates each exposure as set by the sound level and is still governed by the timer. To make subject framing easier when placing the camera near a wall for sound-activated operation, a second viewfinder is located on top of the camera. The Kanpai is a fully automatic point-and-shoot camera with automatic flash, flash-on for fill-flash, flash-off for low-light pictures, and self-timer operation. The Kanpai is a fun camera.

Warranty: parts and labor, one year.

> **Approx. retail price**
> **$216**

> **Approx. low price**
> **$168**

Prices are accurate at time of printing; subject to manufacturer's change.

RICOH YF-20 SUPER RECOMMENDED

The Ricoh YF-20 Super is a simple, inexpensive point-and-shoot camera that goes one step further than most cameras in this price range. When taking pictures of distant subjects such as landscapes, you slide and hold the infinity switch in the infinity position while you take the picture. The infinity switch, which is located below the 35mm lens, is spring-loaded so that the lens returns to its snapshot position when you release it. The camera's flash and automatic winder are powered by either two AA alkalines, or one three-volt lithium battery, which gives you fast recycling times. A red LED lights up in the viewfinder telling you when to turn on the flash for correctly exposed pictures. A switch on the front panel is used to set the camera for the film speed in use—color-negative films of ISO 100, 200, 400, and 1000. The Ricoh YF-20 Super is a better-than-average point-and-shoot snapshot camera.

Warranty: parts and labor, one year.

| **Approx. retail price** | **Approx. low price** |
| $90 | $85 |

KODAK STAR 935 RECOMMENDED

The Kodak Star 935 is a focus-free 35mm camera with infinity. The electronic flash is built into the protective flip-up lens cover so that the flash is located a good distance away from the film plane in order to reduce red-eye. The Sensalite flash automatically fires when the light level is too low for correct exposures without flash. The flash has a range of 4 to 11 feet with ISO 100 film, and 4 to 16 feet with ISO 400 film. The Star 935 has a built-in winder that advances the film after each picture. The Kodak Star 935 is a slim snapshot camera designed for easy operation for the occasional photographer.

Warranty: parts and labor, one year.

| **Approx. retail price** | **Approx. low price** |
| $90 | $62 |

UNDERWATER CAMERA

An underwater camera is waterproof. Waterproof means that all areas of the camera where water could enter under pressure

Prices are accurate at time of printing; subject to manufacturer's change.

have O-rings that compress under pressure to seal the areas. The depth to which an underwater camera can be used is listed in the instruction booklet that comes with the camera.

MINOLTA WEATHERMATIC DUAL 35

The Minolta Weathermatic Dual 35 is an autofocus dual-lens camera that is waterproof to a depth of 16 feet. Lens selection of 35mm or 50mm is done by a push button on top of the camera. As the lens changes, the viewfinder changes to give you the proper framing for the lens in use. Since water bends light rays, the autofocus operation only works above water. It becomes a fixed-focus camera with a range of 4 to 11⅚ feet at 35mm, and 4 to 10½ feet at 50mm. An underwater close-up button shifts the focus from 1⁷⁄₁₀ to 4³⁄₁₀ feet at 35mm, and 2 to 3³⁄₁₀ feet at 50mm. The built-in flash automatically fires in low-light levels. The Weathermatic Dual 35 uses DX-coded film from ISO 100 to 1000, and is designed to be used with color-negative film. Film loading, film advance, and film rewind are automatically handled by the camera's built-in autowinder. Because it is waterproof, the Weathermatic Dual 35 is also an excellent all-weather camera that is fully protected from dust and sand, as well as snow and water.

Warranty: parts and labor, one year.

Approx. retail price	Approx. low price
$303	$236

SNAPSHOT 110 CARTRIDGE CAMERA

The 110 cartridge camera used to be the most popular snapshot camera, but most people now prefer 35mm compact cameras. The only advantage to a cartridge camera is that you never have to touch the film.

KODAK EKTRALITE 10

RECOMMENDED

The Kodak Ektralite 10 is a basic 110 cartridge camera for taking snapshots with color-print film. The 25mm f/8 lens has a fixed focus from 5 feet to infinity. The built-in flash, activated by a switch on top of the camera, has a range of 5 to 14 feet with 100/200 film, and 5 to 20 feet with 400 film. The flash is powered by two AA batteries. The film is advanced by a two-stroke thumb lever, and the shutter release is locked until film advance is completed to prevent double exposure.

Warranty: parts and labor, one year.

Approx. retail price	Approx. low price
$20	$18

INSTANT PRINT CAMERAS

Instant print cameras produce a finished black-and-white or color print in anywhere from 15 seconds to a few minutes.

MINOLTA INSTANT PRO

The Minolta Instant Pro is a versatile instant-print camera with many features that give you both image control and creative control. The Instant Pro produces rectangular pictures with an image area that measures 3⅜ by 2⁹⁄₁₀ inches. On the back of the Instant Pro is the LCD information panel, system-control buttons, and flash-status LEDs. The modes are automatic flash, with a normal shooting range of 2 to 15 feet, which can be turned off for available-light pictures; sonar autofocus system, which can be switched to manual focus for special-focus situations; audio signals for focus, self-timer, and film-pack empty, which can be turned on or off; automatic exposure, which can be adjusted to lighten or darken the picture; time-exposure mode, which provides long exposures beyond the automatic-exposure range of six seconds; backlighting mode to provide exposure adjustment for backlit scenes; sequential mode, which allows you to take a series of pictures at various time intervals from 3 minutes to 20 minutes; and finally, multiple exposure, which allows you to make two or more exposures on one picture. An automatic-reset button returns the camera to its basic automatic modes when pressed. The normal shooting range of the Instant Pro is two feet to infinity, but a close-up lens supplied with the camera allows you to take pictures at ten inches; a built-in measure provides the exact measurement for

Prices are accurate at time of printing; subject to manufacturer's change.

close-ups. The Minolta Instant Pro is a sophisticated instant-print camera that gives you great control over your images.
Warranty: parts and labor, five years.

Approx. retail price	Approx. low price
$197	$186

POLAROID PROPACK
✓ **BEST BUY**

The Polaroid ProPack is a folding camera that uses ten kinds of instant pack film: four color, one color-positive transparency, and five black-and-white. The ProPack is used in any application where instant prints are needed, such as real-estate displays of houses for sale. Though called a pro camera, it is easy to operate. Focusing from 3½ feet to infinity is done via a distance scale on the focusing lever. There is a film-type selector for ISO 80 or ISO 3000 film used outdoors, and a 3000 ER (extended range) setting for indoor available-light photography. A lighten/darken switch is used to control the brightness of your prints. Development takes from 15 to 60 seconds, and a built-in timer beeps when print is ready.
Warranty: parts and labor, one year.

Approx. retail price	Approx. low price
$165	$143

POLAROID IMPULSE
RECOMMENDED

The Polaroid Impulse is an instant-print point-and-shoot camera that produces 3⅛ by 3¹⁄₁₆-inch pictures on Polaroid 600 Plus film. The Impulse has a normal picture range of 4 feet to infinity outside, 4 to 10 feet inside with flash, and a close-up range of 2 feet to 4 feet. To use the close-up lens, you slide the close-up lever on the top of the camera to the close-up position and hold it there while you take the picture; the lever returns to the normal range when you release it. To open the lens cover, just touch the top of the flash and it pops up, the lens cover opens, and all circuits are activated. The flash has a range of 4 to 10 feet. A soft-touch viewfinder shows 100 percent of the picture.
Warranty: parts and labor, one year.

Approx. retail price	Approx. low price
$106	$71

Prices are accurate at time of printing; subject to manufacturer's change.

35mm SINGLE-USE CAMERAS

Single-use cameras were formerly known as disposable cameras, but because of the growing concern for the environment, processors now return these cameras to the manufacturers after processing your film, where the parts are then recycled. Although single-use cameras are very inexpensive, they produce excellent pictures within their limits. The first single-use cameras to be introduced were the Fuji Quicksnap and the Kodak Fun Saver 35, both of which must be used in sunlight or cloudy bright conditions. These cameras were so successful that a flash was added to the Quicksnap and the Fun Saver 35 because picture opportunities do not always happen outdoors in bright light. All four models are still available for those times you forget to bring your camera and need to take pictures.

FUJICOLOR QUICKSNAP PANORAMA

The Fujicolor Quicksnap Panorama produces 12 3½- by 10-inch panoramic prints with a 25mm f/11 lens that has a 75-degree angle of view, which is about twice the angle covered by a standard 50mm lens. Because the lens is wide angle, it is protected from stray light by a built-in lens shade. The focus is fixed to produce sharp pictures of everything from three feet to infinity. The Panorama has an optical viewfinder that gives you a good view of the scene it is recording. Loaded with Fujicolor Super HG 400, the Panorama is designed to produce good exposures in bright sunlight to partially cloudy days. When you bring the camera to your lab, make sure you tell them you want stretch prints.

Approx. retail price	Approx. low price
$14	$11

KODAK FUNSAVER WEEKEND 35

The Kodak Funsaver Weekend 35 has a transparent housing that is waterproof up to a depth of 18 feet. The waterproof housing also makes the Weekend 35 a good camera to use when taking pictures at the beach and when boating. The

Prices are accurate at time of printing; subject to manufacturer's change.

focus-free Weekend 35 has a fixed-focus from four feet to infinity. Because it will be used underwater, the Weekend 35 has a viewfinder that is easy to use with goggles, a large film-advance knob that is easy to use even with gloves on, and a wrist strap for safety. The Weekend 35 is loaded with a 24-exposure roll of Kodacolor Gold 400.

Approx. retail price	Approx. low price
$15	$12

KONICA FILM IN

✔ **BEST BUY**

The Konica Film In is a single-use camera loaded with a 24-exposure roll of Konica Super SR 400 film designed to take pictures in bright sunlight and cloudy bright days. The Film In is designed to be used when you forget to bring your camera with you to fun places, including an amusement park, a picnic, or a holiday trip. The Film In has a plastic lens and it produces sharp pictures from 3⅗ feet to infinity, and from edge to edge.

Approx. retail price	Approx. low price
$8	$7

Telephones and Answering Machines

In the past few years, telephone technology has become highly advanced. For the consumer, this means greater options and more versatility; it can also mean greater confusion when it comes to picking a phone with just the options you need! Getting what you need or want from a phone, no more and certainly no less, is the key to making an intelligent telephone purchase. A buyer needs to know what each feature does and whether or not it's necessary for his or her purposes. It doesn't pay to purchase a phone that is full of complex features when all that is needed is a basic model. There are top-quality telephones available in all categories.

A telephone depends on the kind of service the local telephone company supplies. This can be either UDK (universal dialing keyset), more commonly called pulse (or rotary) dialing, or it can be DTMF (dial tone multiple frequency), known as tone dialing. If your area is wired for tone, you can use either a pulse or tone phone. About half the United States is wired for the tone system; the rest still uses the pulse system.

Many phones are tone/pulse switchable, so they can use either system. These phones can also be used for long-distance services in pulse-dialing areas: First dial the number of the system, then switch to tone dialing. Tone dialing allows you to access beeperless-remote answering machines, computer information, and telephone banking systems.

Telephone Features

Automatic last-number redial automatically redials the last number dialed if you've reached a busy signal. It will redial the number a set number of times (10 to 15) at regular intervals (usually once every minute or 45 seconds) until the party is reached. If the number being called is busy, the telephone automatically hangs up. If the number is free, the caller will hear it ringing and take the call. This feature is usually found on telephones that have speakerphones so you do not have to lift the receiver to make a call.

Hearing-aid-compatible telephones provide distortion-free conversations for people who wear hearing aids.

Hold temporarily cuts off the line so that neither party can speak to or hear the other.

Last-number redial temporarily stores the last number dialed in the phone's memory so you can redial that number by pressing one or two buttons.

Memory stores phone numbers so they can be called by pushing one or two buttons. Almost all new phones have some memory. Basic models can store about 10 numbers, while feature phones can retain 30, 40, or even 100 numbers.

Mute is similar to hold. By pressing the mute button, you can have a conversation with someone in the room without the person on the other end of the line hearing you.

Speakerphone means that, like the handset, the base of the telephone has a microphone and a speaker. You don't have to lift the handset to send and receive calls; you just speak in the direction of the phone. Almost all speakerphones are simplex, rather than duplex, which means that both parties cannot speak at the same time.

Best Buys '92

Our Best Buy and Recommended telephones and answering machines follow. They are categorized as follows: basic telephones, feature telephones, cordless telephones, cellular mobile and portable telephones, and answering machines. The best of the Best Buys is listed first, followed by our second choice, and so on. Recommended products follow our Best Buys and may be substituted if their features meet your needs. Remember that a Best Buy or Recommended designation applies only to the model listed.

BASIC TELEPHONES

AT&T TRIMLINE 210

The AT&T Trimline 210 is a top-quality table or wall phone. It is fully modular, comes in six colors, and features a lighted keypad, receiver and ringer-volume controls, mute, last-number redial, and switchable tone/pulse dialing.
Warranty: parts and labor, two years, limited.

Approx. retail price	Approx. low price
$50	$31

RADIO SHACK ET-174

The Radio Shack ET-174 is a fully modular model that will suit folks with special needs. It's a desktop phone that features an amplified handset in an easy-grip K configuration. The buttons and numbers are extra big—they are easy to see and dial. The phone is hearing-aid compatible. The ET-174 features switchable tone/pulse dialing and comes in almond.
Warranty: parts and labor, one year.

Approx. retail price	Approx. low price
$50	$50

CODE-A-PHONE STYLELINE I   RECOMMENDED

The Code-A-Phone Styleline I is a desk or wall phone that's fully modular. It features a compact design with bigger buttons and easy-to-read numbers and letters. The dialpad is backlit as well, to make dialing easier. It has a ringer-volume control, last-number redial, and is available in white and cream.
Warranty: parts and labor, one year.

Prices are accurate at time of printing; subject to manufacturer's change.

Approx. retail price	Approx. low price
$30	$25

GENERAL ELECTRIC 2-9210 RECOMMENDED

The General Electric 2-9210 telephone is a desktop model that features a good-looking design that sets it off a bit from other basic phones. It's equipped with last-number redial, hearing-aid compatibility, ringer-volume control, and a 12-number memory. Three of the 12 memory numbers are accessed by one touch. The 2-9210 is fully modular, and comes with a 10-foot cord.

Warranty: parts and labor, two years, limited.

Approx. retail price	Approx. low price
not available	$27

FEATURE TELEPHONES

AT&T MEMORY TELEPHONE 710

The AT&T Memory Telephone 710 is a good choice if you want a bit more capability than a basic model. Besides ringer-volume control, last-number redial, and switchable tone/pulse dialing, this desk or wall-mount model offers a 16-number one-touch dialing memory feature, hold with remote release, flash for custom calling, and pause.

Warranty: parts and labor, two years, limited.

Approx. retail price	Approx. low price
$60	$55

PANASONIC KX-T2335

The Panasonic KX-T2335 offers more than the usual 16 one-touch memory numbers—it offers 28. In addition, the phone has one-touch redial, a save button for temporary numbers you'd like to redial, and the ability to transfer numbers from the temporary to the permanent memory. The memo dial allows you to enter a number into the phone's memory while on a call. It's a wall-mountable, switchable tone/pulse phone with hold, ringer-volume control, flash, and pause.

Warranty: parts and labor, one year, limited.

Prices are accurate at time of printing; subject to manufacturer's change.

Approx. retail price	Approx. low price
$55	$46

CODE-A-PHONE 4060 `RECOMMENDED`

The Code-A-Phone 4060 is a two-line phone that offers a 20-number memory dialer, last-number redial, flash for call waiting, adjustable ringer, switchable tone/pulse dialing, redial, save, and pause. The two lines give you conferencing capability. There is a hold button and each line has a distinctive ring. The phone is wall mountable.

Warranty: parts and labor, one year.

Approx. retail price	Approx. low price
$70	$54

AT&T TWO-LINE SPEAKERPHONE 722 `RECOMMENDED`

The AT&T Two-Line Speakerphone 722 features a 16-number one-touch dialing memory, hold, and LED indicators for the speakerphone and to show what line is in use. It also features an incoming call identification, last-number redial, mute, flash, and pause.

Warranty: parts and labor, two years, limited.

Approx. retail price	Approx. low price
$100	$98

SONY IT-A4000 `RECOMMENDED`

The Sony IT-A4000 features an integrated TAD (telephone answering device) that is completely digital. The digital advantage eliminates time spent rewinding and fast forwarding, and it allows for selective save or erase of individual messages. Until now, the disadvantage of a digital was the limited recording time available. With this machine, you receive a full 16 minutes of recording time, just as much as the C-30 cassette offers. The speakerphone offers redial, flash, hold, pause, and 13-number memory. It's fully modular and has switchable tone/pulse dialing. The built-in answering device features beeperless remote, remote turn-on, automatic disconnect, and a voice time/day stamp. It has a digital message

Prices are accurate at time of printing; subject to manufacturer's change.

counter and an automatic message transfer that forwards important messages to a preprogrammed number.
Warranty: parts and labor, one year.

Approx. retail price	Approx. low price
$350	not available

CORDLESS TELEPHONES

Mobility is the number one feature of cordless telephones. Whether you are working in the garage or barbecuing with the neighbors, you can always be ready to place or receive a call.

Cordless telephones use a special radio, not a cord, for transmissions between the base and handset. The transmissions carry the voice signals and operate the telephone's functions. Cordless phones have many features, such as memory, hold, mute, and last-number redial. However, the most important feature to look for is clear transmission between the base and the handset. Security features and channel selections are used to deal with interference and static. The FCC (Federal Communications Commission) allocated ten different channels in the frequency range used by cordless phones. Phones are equipped to use from one to ten channels, allowing you to search for the clearest transmission.

Although manufacturers cite a maximum distance between the base and the handset, which is usually between 700 and 1,500 feet, clear reception is based upon several factors. Electrical storms, dense trees, and other cordless phones in use in your area can have an impact on the operation of your unit.

Two other features found on cordless phones are **intercom** and **paging.** Intercom allows you to speak between the base and the handset. Paging lets you send a tone signal between the base and the handset. If two-way paging is offered, the signal can be sent either way. With one-way paging, the signal can be sent only from the base to the handset. The paging feature can be used to locate your handset.

CODE-A-PHONE 7010

The Code-A-Phone 7010 has fewer features than other cordless models and for that reason is very affordably priced.

Prices are accurate at time of printing; subject to manufacturer's change.

It's an attractive, ultracompact phone that offers one-way paging, large easy-to-read buttons, user replaceable battery and antenna, ringer-volume control, pause, flash, and last-number redial.

Warranty: parts and labor, one year.

Approx. retail price
$75

Approx. low price
$56

AT&T 5500 — RECOMMENDED

The AT&T 5500 cordless telephone features an extended battery life—up to one week between charges. From the handset, you can select from ten channels for best reception. You can dial from the base or the lighted handset keypad. It also features a two-way page and intercom, hold buttons on both base and handset, security system, redial, and replaceable battery and antenna. The phone has a nine-number memory and a portable holder for the handset.

Warranty: parts and labor, one year.

Approx. retail price
$200

Approx. low price
$172

COBRA INTENNA AN-8525 — RECOMMENDED

The Cobra Intenna AN-8525 is a cordless phone with an integrated telephone answering system. The handset features Cobra's built-in antenna, noise-reduction circuitry, digital security coding, and a nine-number memory. The beeperless-remote answering device uses a digital voice-chip for the outgoing message and records incoming messages on a microcassette. With the handset, you can screen messages that are being left on the tape and interrupt and take the call if you like.

Warranty: parts and labor, one year, limited.

Approx. retail price
$250

Approx. low price
not available

SONY SPP-320 — RECOMMENDED

The Sony SPP-320 is a combination cordless phone and full-function base telephone. From the base you can place and receive calls using a receiver or the speakerphone. The cordless handset is designed to deliver seven-day standby time. It features a dual battery system, noise-reduction circuitry, a ten-number memory, a channel button, and a two-way intercom. Both the handset and base unit feature switchable tone/pulse dialing, flash, last-number redial, and ringer-volume control.

Warranty: parts and labor, one year.

Approx. retail price	**Approx. low price**
$340	**$279**

CELLULAR MOBILE AND PORTABLE PHONES

The mobile telephone is an essential business tool for anyone who needs to be in continuous contact with clients. Cellular telephone service is now widely available, and prices are coming down. If you live near a major city, you probably have a choice between two carriers. The FCC regulates cellular services and allocates cellular licenses to two carriers in each area.

The cellular system divides each area into a number of cells with one central mobile telephone switching office (MTSO) that ties the cells to a conventional phone system. When you dial a number from your cellular phone, this signal is transmitted to an MTSO that transmits it to the telephone system. As you drive around, you move from one cell to another. Each cell site has a radio receiver/transmitter that hands you off to an adjacent cell. If you move from one cellular service area to another, you are switched automatically to the service in the new area.

For cellular phone service you pay both fixed and ongoing access and usage fees. The fixed costs are the cost of the phone itself and the initial installation and service activation fee.

In addition to standard cellular phones installed in your automobile or boat, transportable and portable cellular phones are also available. These three kinds of cellular phones differ not only in size, but also in price and the amount of power. Standard and transportable models transmit at three watts, while portables operate at ⅗ watt.

Cellular telephones offer most of the features of standard phones including memory dialing, last-number redial, and speakerphone. Many offer on-hook dialing, which lets you dial a

Prices are accurate at time of printing; subject to manufacturer's change.

number without picking up the handset. One difference between cellular and standard phones is that the cellular service charges you for both the calls you send and the calls you receive.

DIAMONDTEL 92M

The Diamondtel 92M is a deluxe compact cellular telephone with a duplex speakerphone. It has a 99-number memory with a directory scan, last-number redial, and a silent scratch pad that lets you enter a number into a temporary memory instead of jotting it down. It's a car phone that can be converted into a transportable with an optional kit. A turn-off override feature lets you continue talking once the car ignition is off. There's a call timer and counter, and an electronic lock that prevents unauthorized calls. It also has full 832-channel capacity. **Warranty: transceiver,** three years; **accessory parts,** six months.

Approx. retail price	Approx. low price
$695	$514

RADIO SHACK TANDY CT-102

The Radio Shack Tandy CT-102 is a low-priced mobile phone that offers all the basic features. It has a permanent car mount that offers hands-free operation. A 30-number memory, last-number redial, and recall features are also included. There's a call-in-absence indicator, as well as a call-lock feature that prevents unauthorized calls. It also has a backlit LCD (liquid crystal display).
Warranty: parts and labor, one year.

Approx. retail price	Approx. low price
$300	$200

CELLULAR PORTABLE PHONE

RADIO SHACK TANDY CT-302

The Radio Shack Tandy CT-302 is a handheld portable cellular phone that weighs only 15⁹⁄₁₀ ounces and is very affordable. The

---

Prices are accurate at time of printing; subject to manufacturer's change.

phone comes with a rechargeable battery, desktop charger, and carrying case. It has an 832-channel capacity and illuminated LCD with backlit controls for night driving. The CT-302 also features last-number redial, electronic lock, scratch-pad memory, signal strength and status indicators, and call timer. Forty numbers can be stored for fast two-digit dialing. It comes with a built-in antenna and an extendable antenna.

Warranty: parts and labor, one year.

Approx. retail price	**Approx. low price**
$400	$300

ANSWERING MACHINES

Answering machines offer the convenience of never having to miss a phone call. They are easy to install: simply plug one into a modular phone jack and an electrical outlet. Two-line answering machines are especially convenient for someone who has a small business at home and needs both the home and business numbers answered.

Most answering machines include two tapes, one for your outgoing messages (OGM) and one to record the incoming messages (ICM). These tapes can be either standard C-cassettes or microcassettes. The only difference is in size—microcassettes allow manufacturers to make smaller machines.

Less expensive, smaller single-tape machines put both the outgoing and the incoming messages on one tape. These units are designed for someone who does not get many messages. The machine sits in position at the beginning of the outgoing message and waits for a call. When the phone rings, it plays the outgoing message and then moves over any already-received calls while sounding a beep tone. It is then ready to record another incoming call. If there are many messages, the beep tone can last as long as a couple of seconds and be annoying to callers. Some single-tape machines use digital recording voice chips for the outgoing message. Since the tape is only for incoming messages, there is plenty of capacity and no problem with the beep tone. Some manufacturers offer machines that record incoming and outgoing messages on chips, but the number of incoming messages is limited to 15-second messages.

Prices are accurate at time of printing; subject to manufacturer's change.

Features and Terminology

Autodisconnect allows you to pick up any telephone in your home while the answering machine is taking a message and stop the answering machine automatically.

Beeperless remote lets you call in to get your messages from any touch-tone phone. You access your machine with a security code.

Call screening allows you to listen to a call as it comes in.

Memo lets you put a message on the machine while you are at home for someone who is coming home later. When that person listens to the phone messages, your memo will be heard.

Remote turn on allows you to turn on your machine, usually by calling it and letting it ring about ten times.

Toll saver lets you call long distance for your messages and not pay for the call if there are no messages. The way this works is that the answering machine will ring more often before answering the first message (usually four times) and then only once before answering subsequent calls. When you call your phone number, if the phone rings more than once, you know there are no messages and you can hang up.

VOX allows the incoming message to be any length, up to the maximum capacity of the tape. The machine continues recording as long as the person keeps speaking. It will not chop off the end of the message or leave a dead space or dial tone at the end of a message.

COBRA AN-8568

The Cobra AN-8568 is a dual-microcassette system answerer that features VOX and a time and date voice stamp. It's a beeperless remote with autodisconnect, a digital call counter, memo, and two-way record.

Warranty: parts and labor, one year, limited.

Approx. retail price	Approx. low price
$140	**not available**

AT&T 1306   RECOMMENDED

The AT&T 1306 is a basic answering machine that's perfect for someone who doesn't get a lot of calls. It is a beeperless remote system with autodisconnect, toll saver, an LED message-receive indicator, and personal memo feature. It can also record a two-way conversation.

Warranty: parts and labor, one year, limited.

Approx. retail price	Approx. low price
$70	$63

GENERAL ELECTRIC 2-9882 | RECOMMENDED |

The General Electric 2-9882 dual-microcassette system offers 17 touch-tone remote functions and is meant for someone who gets many messages and relies heavily on accessing messages remotely. The day/time speech function records the day and time each message is received. A remote voice menu guides you through remote functions. The unit itself features a message counter and built-in clock. There's a user selectable three-digit security code, VOX, toll-saver, memo, two-way recording, autodisconnect, and call monitor.

Warranty: parts and labor, one year, limited.

Approx. retail price	Approx. low price
not available	$95

PANASONIC KX-T1740 | RECOMMENDED |

The Panasonic KX-T1740 is a beeperless-remote answering machine that has answering capabilities for a two-line phone, which allows you to leave a different outgoing message for each line or to receive a message on one line while using the other. Playback/reset, skip forward and answer back are remotely accessible features. VOX, autodisconnect, personal memo, and toll saver are also included.

Warranty: parts and labor, one year.

Approx. retail price	Approx. low price
$170	$147

Computers

There are hundreds of computers from which to choose. To help you find the right one, our reviews are divided into five categories: under $1,000; $1,000 to $2,000; $2,000 to $3,000; over $3,000; and portable computers. We usually describe computers without any extras, but some "extras" are required. For example, some systems are sold without video monitors, but you must have one to use the computer. An incomplete system may cost less initially, but better-equipped systems may offer superior value if they have the extras you need.

The Ratings

Ratings at the end of each review use a scale of one (worst) to ten (best) to rate the computer's overall value, performance, ease of use, documentation, software (how much is offered for that computer), and expandability (the availability of and capacity for add-ons). Portable computers are rated for portability, not expandability.

The Overall Value rating measures how well the computer's price compares to its performance, ease of use, and features. An overpriced system will not have a high rating. The Performance rating tells how well the computer functions. The Ease of Use rating measures how easy the computer is to learn to use. The Documentation rating tells how well the manuals explain the computer's functions and if the manuals are well organized.

Understanding Computer Terminology

You do not need a technical understanding of computers to select and use one. But you do need to know some terms.

A computer's "brain," the **central processing unit (CPU)** or **microprocessor**, resides on one **chip**, which is a tiny silicon wafer with thousands of electronic parts. The CPU and the **operating system software** regulate the data transfer between the computer's parts as well as between the computer and a peripheral such as a printer. The CPU does math and tests hypotheses that are "true" or "false," which it indicates by allowing or preventing electricity to flow through a circuit.

The CPU usually receives data from a disk drive (see below), a keyboard (as on a typewriter), a **modem** (a device used to send data over telephone lines to another computer), or a **mouse**, which is a small device that you roll on a desktop or a special pad to move the **cursor** (the on-screen pointer that shows where a character will be inserted, deleted, or moved). The mouse's button(s) lets you access on-screen functions. Another input device is a **joystick**, which is a small box with a vertical lever that you tilt to move an on-screen figure or cursor.

The CPU uses **random-access memory (RAM)** to manipulate data and programs. **Read-only memory (ROM)** may store the operating system, utility programs, and/or applications, such as word processing, that will be sent to the RAM. The contents of RAM are usually lost when the electricity is shut off; ROM retains its memory. RAM changes constantly; ROM does not. Peripherals also use RAM and ROM. For example, printers use RAM **buffers** to store data received from the computer until it can be printed.

RAM and ROM are measured in **bytes**, which are made up of **bits**. A bit (*Bi*nary dig*IT*) is the smallest unit of data. Its value is either one or zero (yes or no). A group of bits, usually eight, make up one byte that represents a letter, number, or symbol. A byte is treated as a unit of data. Roughly 1,000 bytes are equal to one **kilobyte (K or Kb or K byte)**. A **megabyte (M or Mb or M byte)** is about one million bytes.

The more RAM in a computer, the better. This allows for larger, more powerful programs that run faster. Some programs hide in RAM until you need them. These **RAM-resident programs** steal RAM from the main program in use, reducing the amount of data you can create. The operating system also uses RAM, unless it exists in ROM. A computer's RAM often can be increased by chips or add-ons.

Programs and data are saved on magnetic **disks** and **tapes**. **Floppy disks** (or **diskettes**) are circular and flexible, although they have square, stiff housings. **Hard disks** are rigid and hold more data than floppy disks. Hard disks also speed up the loading of software into RAM and make programs run faster.

Single-sided floppies use one side of the disk; double-sided floppies use both sides. High-density (or quad-density) disks hold more data than double- and single-density disks. You must know how many sides and the density your computer needs when you buy blank disks. Avoid no-name bargain-priced disks.

A **disk drive** transfers data and programs between RAM and a disk. A **disk operating system (DOS)** is an operating system that stores data on disks. The most common one is Microsoft's MS-DOS and its IBM version, PC-DOS; both systems are used by IBM-compatible computers (or clones). A **proprietary operating system** is used by only one manufacturer, so programs written for other computers cannot normally be used. If you work closely with other computer users, you should use the same operating system.

The CPU sends the data it has processed to an output device, such as a video monitor, printer, modem, or disk drive. The CPU, RAM, ROM, other chips, and connecting circuits are on the main circuit board, called the **motherboard**. This board often has slots for **expansion cards** (smaller circuit boards) that add functions, speed, or memory to the computer.

A computer's **ports** (connectors for peripherals) and operating system limit the devices and programs a computer can use. Software is often sold for only one operating system. In addition, a computer with an RS-232C port can only use devices that have RS-232C **interfaces** (software and hardware that permit the transfer of data). The words "port" and "interface" are often used interchangeably. There are many varieties of the two most common interfaces, RS-232C serial and Centronics parallel.

Prices

Manufacturers often change their prices or add "free" items to their systems. Prices also vary in different parts of the country. Plus, the fluctuations in the value of the U.S. dollar may affect prices. Therefore, the retail and low prices in this buying guide may not be the same as offered locally or by nationwide mail-order. Compare prices from several dealers, and check ads.

Where to Buy

Computers are sold primarily by department stores, computer stores, and mail-order firms. Department store prices can be low, but their clerks often cannot give you technical help. Such stores do not offer a wide selection, and they usually send items to the manufacturer for repair, which may take a long time.

A computer store usually offers a wider selection, hands-on evaluations, knowledgeable salespeople, training, technical help, and factory-trained repair service, which eliminates shipping time. Discounts will vary greatly, but you can often obtain a sizable discount when you buy a complete system.

Mail-order firms advertise in computer magazines. They offer a wide selection and low prices. A few companies promote new items before they are released or fail to ship items for which your credit card has been billed, so check out the firm by contacting a satisfied client and the Better Business Bureau. Use the firm's toll-free number to confirm the product's description, price, and compatibility. Accept brand names only. Place your credit-card order cautiously. Make your first order a small one. When a shipment arrives, report any damage to the box *before the driver leaves* on the receipt. If a box is severely damaged, don't accept it, and immediately call the mail-order firm to ask for a new shipment.

Best Buys '92

Our Best Buy and Recommended computers follow. Within each category, the Best Buys are listed first, followed by our Recommended choices in order of decreasing overall value. If ratings for two items are identical, reviews appear alphabetically. A Best Buy or Recommended designation applies only to the model listed.

COMPUTERS UNDER $1,000

APPLE MACINTOSH CLASSIC

The Apple Macintosh Classic strongly resembles the older Macintosh SE. The Classic retains the old size and shape, but it has new styling and a greatly reduced list price.

You can expand the Classic's one megabyte of RAM to 4Mb. Although it uses the same 7.83-MHz Motorola 68000 CPU as previous models, it performs well. Apple's graphic user interface is built into the Mac; it's not an afterthought. Thus, the Classic performs similarly to a 10-MHz IBM AT-compatible computer running Microsoft Windows 3.0. However, Apple's interface feels smoother and is much easier to use.

The $999 base Mac Classic has one 1.4Mb 3.5-inch microfloppy disk drive that can also read and write data in IBM's format. In the $1,495 Classic, the memory is expanded to 2Mb and a quick 40Mb internal hard drive is added.

The Classic lacks expansion slots, but large-screen monitors, accelerators, larger internal hard drives, and memory expansion kits are sold by other companies.

The 9-inch black-and-white screen displays only 512 by 342 pixels (dots), but it appears sharper due to its small size. There are ports for a modem, printer, external microfloppy drive ($399), and up to seven SCSI (Small Computer System Interface, pronounced "scuzzy") devices, like external hard disks, CD-ROM drives, and scanners. The 81-key keyboard features a much improved overall feel.

Apple's manuals are easy to understand, and the Desktop Tour programs offer excellent introductions to the Mac.

The operating system can run in one of two modes: Finder and MultiFinder. Finder is used for normal operations, MultiFinder for multitasking, allowing you to use more than one program at the same time. For instance, you can sort a database file in the background (off-screen) while using a word processing program on the screen. HyperCard software can create applications that integrate text, graphics, animation, music, voice, and/or video. With one megabyte of RAM, HyperCard and MultiFinder cannot run simultaneously.

Icons (on-screen images depicting files and commands) remain the basis of the Mac's user-friendly interface. Using the mouse, you move the cursor to an icon and press the mouse's button to access the desired function. While most Mac software will run on the Classic, many new programs require more than a megabyte of RAM.

The Mac's four-voice sound generator supports very-good-quality digitized sound and music software. A $99 interface lets

Prices are accurate at time of printing; subject to manufacturer's change.

you attach MIDI (musical instrument digital interface) devices (such as keyboards, synthesizers, and electronic drum boxes) for music composition and live performances.

The Classic is suitable for personal and light business use. For greater power, consider Apple's new Macintosh LC ($2,499) and Macintosh IIsi ($3,769), which offer color graphics, higher performance, and greater expandability.

Specifications: RAM, one megabyte (1,024Kb); **operating system,** proprietary; **included hardware,** system unit with CPU and integral monochrome monitor, keyboard, one 1.44Mb microfloppy disk drive, video display circuitry, mouse, clock/calendar, two RS-232/RS-422 serial ports, external microfloppy disk drive port, SCSI port, two Desktop Bus ports, sound port; **included software,** Finder and MultiFinder operating systems, Apple File Exchange, Guided Tour, HyperCard, Tools, utilities. **Warranty:** one year. **Ratings: overall value,** 10; **ease of use,** 10; **software,** 10; **performance,** 9; **documentation,** 9; **expandability,** 9.

Approx. retail price	Approx. low price
$999	$922

COMPUADD 212 ✔ BEST BUY

The low-profile CompuAdd 212 delivers IBM AT-class computing, fine performance, and good flexibility at a very reasonable price. The $595 base model includes a dual-speed (8 or 12 MHz) Intel 80286 processor, 101-key keyboard, 512Kb of RAM, a 1.2Mb 5.25-inch floppy or 1.44Mb 3.5-inch microfloppy drive, a parallel port, and two serial ports.

This system can support two more data storage devices, and it has three 16-bit (AT-type) full-size expansion slots and two 8-bit (XT-type) half-size slots. The main circuit board contains the parallel and serial ports and the floppy and hard drive controller. Thus, four slots will be free after a video display card is added. Built-in circuitry for a joystick requires a $10 cable.

Adding 512Kb of RAM to the standard 512Kb costs $65. The main circuit board can hold four single in-line memory modules (SIMMs). That translates to one to four megabytes, depending on the type of SIMMs used. An expansion card can add more RAM. Though the keyboard lacks crisp tactile response, it feels better than those of other low-cost PCs.

Prices are accurate at time of printing; subject to manufacturer's change.

The CompuAdd 212 performed over one and a half times faster than an 8-MHz IBM AT; that's about six times faster than the original IBM PC. Our 212's speed was complemented by a 40Mb IDE (Integrated Drive Electronics) hard drive ($429) that was a bit noisy but performed well.

CompuAdd packages add a hard drive, a house-brand display card, and a monitor to the 212. Systems with basic monochrome displays are priced according to the hard drive's capacity: $1,149 with a 40Mb drive, $1,419 with an 80Mb drive. VGA color graphics adds another $310 to these prices. CompuAdd monitors and display cards are of good quality. The firm also discounts brand-name peripherals.

MS-DOS 4.01 comes pre-installed on 212s purchased with a CompuAdd hard drive, but a DOS manual costs $49. No software is included with the base model 212, but CompuAdd sells MS-DOS 4.01 (including a manual) for $89. The 212's construction is excellent, and its manuals are complete, easy to follow, and clearly illustrated.

CompuAdd systems are available from CompuAdd retail outlets in most metropolitan areas or by telephone from the company's mail-order facility. Free assistance is available from stores as well as a toll-free support line.

Computer hardware sold by CompuAdd carries a 30-day no-questions-asked money-back guarantee. Warranty service can be obtained from dealers or at CompuAdd's Texas facility.

Specifications: RAM, 512Kb; **operating system,** MS-DOS, MS OS/2; **included hardware,** system unit with CPU, keyboard, 1.44Mb microfloppy or 1.2Mb floppy disk drive, clock/calendar, Centronics parallel port, two RS-232C serial ports, game port interface; **included software,** none. **Warranty:** one year. **Ratings: overall value,** 10; **ease of use,** 8; **software,** 10; **performance,** 8; **documentation,** 10; **expandability,** 9.

Approx. retail price	Approx. low price
$595 (Part No. 64776)	**$595 (Part No. 64776)**

ALR POWERFLEX MODEL 1   RECOMMENDED

The PowerFlex Model 1 from Advanced Logic Research (ALR) offers good performance and value and an easy upgrade path that postpones the prospect of obsolescence. Its compact sys-

Prices are accurate at time of printing; subject to manufacturer's change.

COMPUTERS

tem unit packs a lot of expandability and power. The 1.44Mb 3.5-inch microfloppy disk drive and optional 40Mb hard disk drive ($300) are mounted vertically, leaving room for two more 5.25-inch data storage devices. With a 16-bit (AT-type) display card installed, there are one 8-bit (XT-type) and four 16-bit expansion slots open.

On the main circuit board are the serial and parallel ports and disk controller circuitry. Adding memory modules to the main circuit board can expand the one megabyte of RAM to 5Mb. A memory card can increase the RAM to 16Mb.

The usual processor is a 12.5-MHz Intel 80286. A slot on the main circuit board allows you to upgrade to an 80386SX or 80486 chip. Upgrade modules simply plug in. The computer reconfigures itself automatically when turned on again. The CPU in our stock PowerFlex performed about 1.8 times faster than an 8-MHz IBM AT. Adding a 16-MHz 80386SX card ($395) increased the performance by ten percent. That's not much, but it lets you use software that requires an 80386 (such as Microsoft Windows 3.0 in its 386 enhanced mode). ALR also offers a 20-MHz 80386SX processor card ($595), which boosts the performance to almost three times that of a stock IBM AT. ALR's 25-MHz 80486 processor card raised the performance of the PowerFlex to about 8.5 times the power of the original IBM AT. At $1,995 retail, this i486 card is costly, but we expect the price to drop.

The 40Mb hard drive performs very well, especially when using the supplied disk caching software. (Caching employs RAM to store data often accessed from a disk.) ALR's comfortable 101-key keyboard lacks a solid sense of touch.

Our ALR Model 1414 Super VGA monitor ($699) yielded good color and reasonable sharpness. Its image quality was much improved from the model 1413 that it replaced. ALR's combination of the 1414 monitor and a 16-bit Paradise VGA card ($199) supports images with resolutions of up to 800 by 600 pixels (dots). If possible, we recommend buying a monitor-card combo that displays 1,024 by 768 pixels.

Although not for novices, the quick-reference guide is straightforward, easy to follow, and clearly illustrated. A more detailed reference guide is available at extra cost.

You may have to go out of your way to find an ALR dealer, but it's worth it.

Prices are accurate at time of printing; subject to manufacturer's change.

Specifications: RAM, one megabyte (1,024Kb); **operating system,** MS-DOS, MS OS/2; **included hardware,** system unit with CPU, keyboard, 1.44Mb microfloppy disk drive, clock/calendar, Centronics parallel port, RS-232C serial port; **included software,** setup, utilities. **Warranty:** one year. **Ratings: overall value,** 9; **ease of use,** 9; **software,** 10; **performance,** 9; **documentation,** 8; **expandability,** 10.

Approx. retail price	Approx. low price
$795	$692

COMPUTERS FROM $1,000 TO $2,000

COMPUADD 320SC ✔BEST BUY

The CompuAdd 320sc supplies a speedy (20-MHz) Intel 80386SX processor in a sturdy, low-profile unit that offers highly capable computing at a very good price. It has a 5.25-inch 1.2Mb floppy or 3.5-inch 1.44Mb microfloppy disk drive and two 8-bit (XT-type) half-size and three 16-bit (AT-type) full-size expansion slots. With a hard drive installed, there's room for one more data storage device.

One megabyte of RAM is standard. The main circuit board has eight slots for RAM modules, which can support up to 32Mb. The 320sc's 101-key keyboard, which inconveniently plugs into the back of the system, has an adequate feel.

CompuAdd has incorporated its Hi-Rez VGA circuitry and disk controllers into the 320sc's main circuit board, eliminating the need for two expansion cards. The 320sc has 512Kb of VGA video RAM; an upgrade to a full megabyte costs $29 when purchased with the 320sc.

The 320sc's metal chassis is very sturdy, and the metal used throughout the system unit and cover is of a heavy gauge.

In our tests, the 320sc ran about 30 percent faster than most 16-MHz 386SX systems. This was due to the 320sc's 20-MHz processor and to its 32Kb of cache memory. Frequently used data gets stored in the cache, so it can be accessed quickly. Our unit turned in an overall CPU performance that averaged 2.8 times faster than an 8-MHz IBM AT.

Our $2,129 test system came with a 40Mb hard drive and CompuAdd's High-Resolution VGA color monitor. The hard disk

Prices are accurate at time of printing; subject to manufacturer's change.

was noisy but quick. Higher-capacity hard drives (up to 200Mb) are available. The monitor produced sharp, colorful images with almost no distortion, and the 320sc's display circuitry was the quickest and most capable we have tested.

The user manual combines a straightforward style with helpful illustrations and a quick-start section. Advanced users will find the manual short on technical content. The utilities and diagnostics are handy and well documented. If you buy a CompuAdd hard drive with the 320sc, CompuAdd throws in MS-DOS 4.01 and CompuAdd (Microsoft) Windows 3.0, and installs the software on the hard disk.

CompuAdd systems are available at CompuAdd retail stores in most metropolitan areas or by telephone from the mail-order facility. Local stores and a toll-free support line offer free assistance. Hardware sold by CompuAdd carries a 30-day no-questions-asked money-back guarantee. Warranty service can be obtained at CompuAdd dealers or repair facility in Texas.

Specifications: RAM, one megabyte (1,024Kb); **operating system,** MS-DOS, MS OS/2; **included hardware,** system unit with CPU, keyboard, 1.2Mb floppy or 1.44Mb microfloppy disk drive, video display circuitry, clock/calendar, Centronics parallel port, two RS-232C serial ports; **included software,** MS-DOS 4.01, CompuAdd Windows 3.0, diagnostics, setup, utilities. **Warranty:** one year. **Ratings: overall value,** 10; **ease of use,** 9; **software,** 10; **performance,** 10; **documentation,** 9; **expandability,** 9.

Approx. retail price	Approx. low price
$1,295	$1,295
(Part No. 66720)	(Part No. 66720)

COMPUADD 325 · RECOMMENDED

The CompuAdd 325 is a complete 80386-based computer that offers an impressive amount of power and expandability at a low price. With a hard drive and your choice of a 1.2Mb 5.25-inch floppy or a 1.44Mb 3.5-inch microfloppy drive, there is room for three more data storage devices. The one megabyte of memory resides on a card attached to a special slot on the main circuit board. This card accepts up to 16Mb of RAM. With a graphics board and the standard floppy disk controller card installed, one 8-bit (XT-type) and five 16-bit (AT-type) expansion slots remain free.

Prices are accurate at time of printing; subject to manufacturer's change.

The feel of the 101-key keyboard isn't very crisp, but it's better than average. The serial mouse provided with the system is comfortable to use, and it works well.

CompuAdd's VGA-16 display card ($149) offers up to 800 by 600 pixels (dots). However, CompuAdd's Hi-Rez VGA card ($179) is twice as fast as the VGA-16, and it supports a resolution of 1,024 by 768 pixels. A $29 memory upgrade for the Hi-Rez card increases the video RAM to one megabyte and the maximum number of simultaneous on-screen colors from 16 to 256 in the high-resolution mode.

CompuAdd's low-cost color VGA (CVGA) monitor retails for $359, but its maximum resolution is only 640 by 480 pixels. At $409, CompuAdd's High-Resolution VGA Monitor, which can display up to 1,024 by 768 pixels, is a much better value. CompuAdd also carries brand-name peripherals and software.

Like other 25-MHz 80386 machines, the 325 was over three times faster than an 8-MHz IBM AT. The 40Mb hard disk ($429) performs well, though it's noisier than average. We also tried CompuAdd's 80Mb ($699), 120Mb ($799), and 320Mb ($1,759) hard disks.

The 325's construction is good although the chassis uses lighter-gauge metal than more costly systems. The serial and parallel ports on the back are not labeled.

At $1,495, the base 325 system is an excellent buy. CompuAdd also offers complete systems. For example, the package price for a CompuAdd 325 with an 80Mb hard drive, Hi-Rez VGA card, and High-Resolution VGA color monitor is $2,659. CompuAdd sweetens the pot by throwing in MS-DOS 4.01 and CompuAdd (Microsoft) Windows 3.0.

The well-illustrated documentation is adequate for expert users but a bit tough for novices. Local CompuAdd dealers and a competent toll-free technical support line provide free assistance. CompuAdd provides free on-site warranty service in 250 metropolitan areas.

CompuAdd systems can be purchased at CompuAdd retail outlets in most metropolitan areas or by phone from the company's mail-order facility. Hardware sold by CompuAdd carries a 30-day no-questions-asked money-back guarantee.

Specifications: RAM, one megabyte (1,024Kb); **operating system,** MS-DOS, MS OS/2; **included hardware,** system unit with CPU, keyboard, 1.2Mb floppy or 1.44Mb microfloppy disk

Prices are accurate at time of printing; subject to manufacturer's change.

drive, mouse, clock/calendar, Centronics parallel port, two RS-232C serial ports; **included software,** MS-DOS 4.01, CompuAdd Windows 3.0, setup, utilities. **Warranty:** one year. **Ratings: overall value,** 10; **ease of use,** 8; **software,** 10; **performance,** 9; **documentation,** 9; **expandability,** 10.

Approx. retail price	Approx. low price
$1,495	$1,495
(Part No. 64834)	(Part No. 64834)

ALR BUSINESSVEISA 386/33 MODEL 101

RECOMMENDED

When IBM introduced its PS/2 line of computers, their new Micro Channel Architecture (MCA) was supposedly superior to the expansion bus (electrical pathway for data flow) used in the IBM AT-compatibles (referred to as the Industry Standard Architecture, or ISA). However, embracing the MCA meant throwing out all of your old expansion cards.

As an alternative, several computer makers drafted a new standard that offered higher performance while maintaining compatibility with older cards. It became the Extended Industry Standard Architecture (EISA, pronounced "ee sah"). Few expansion boards use the higher data-transfer capability and other features in the EISA standard. True EISA computers and boards are normally very expensive.

Advanced Logic Research's BusinessVEISA 386/33 Model 101 makes EISA compatibility affordable. Its performance, features, and price make it an excellent base upon which to build a fast, fairly priced PC that avoids obsolescence.

The ALR Model 101's compact system unit has one 8-bit (XT-type) slot, one 16-bit (AT-type) slot, and three 32-bit (EISA-compatible) slots. The EISA slots can also accept AT- and XT-type expansion cards. The Model 101's floppy/hard drive controller circuitry, parallel port, serial port, and mouse port are built into the main circuit board.

The 101's 33-MHz Intel 80386 processor resides on a card that plugs into a special slot. Our system provided over four times the power of an 8-MHz IBM AT. Upgrading the Model 101 to a higher-powered system takes only a few minutes. For $1,995, you can swap the 33-MHz 80386 for a 25-MHz 80486 processor. While that upgrade doubles the cost of the base

Prices are accurate at time of printing; subject to manufacturer's change.

system, it provides less than a 60-percent boost in processor power. ALR plans to offer a 33-MHz 80486 upgrade as well. The price of 80486 chips is likely to drop soon. If the cost of the 486 upgrade is reduced, the Model 101's upgradability may be a real plus. Another special slot accepts a high-speed cache card ($595), which boosts the base Model 101's performance by about 15 percent.

One megabyte of RAM resides on the main circuit board. Sockets let the board hold up to 2, 5, or 17 megabytes, depending on the type of memory modules used. ALR's VEISA Memory Card ($199 with no RAM) lets you expand the RAM up to 49Mb without using one of the 101's expansion slots.

The ALR 101 comes with one 1.2Mb 5.25-inch floppy disk drive. There's room to install a hard drive in the back of the chassis. That leaves a vertical bay for a 3.5-inch microfloppy disk drive and a 5.25-inch bay for an internal CD-ROM drive or tape backup unit. The system expandability is good, and the construction quality is excellent.

No reset button is provided. The Model 101 has a smoked plastic dustcover built into the front of the system unit. To use the floppy drives, the hinged cover must be flipped down. If the keyboard is positioned close to the system unit, it must be moved to access the floppy drives.

The enhanced IBM layout keyboard provided with our evaluation unit had a slightly vague feel that was a bit on the light side but otherwise satisfactory.

ALR has been promoting a 486 system based on the Model 101. The BusinessVEISA Model 486/25-80 included a Model 101 with a 25-MHz 80486 CPU card, 2Mb of RAM, one 1.2Mb floppy drive, one 1.44Mb microfloppy drive, and a fast Quantum-built 80Mb hard disk. With a Paradise Systems VGA adapter and an ALR 800-by-600-pixel (dot) Super VGA color monitor, the package retails for $4,195. If you don't like ALR's packages, dealers can use components of your choosing.

Specifications: RAM, one megabyte (1,024Kb); **operating system,** MS-DOS, MS OS/2; **included hardware,** system unit with CPU, keyboard, 1.2Mb floppy disk drive, Centronics parallel port, RS-232C serial port, mouse port; **included software,** setup, utilities, diagnostics. **Warranty:** one year. **Ratings: overall value,** 10; **ease of use,** 8; **software,** 10; **performance,** 10; **documentation,** 8; **expandability,** 9.

Prices are accurate at time of printing; subject to manufacturer's change.

Approx. retail price	Approx. low price
$1,995	$1,807

COMPUTERS FROM $2,000 TO $3,000

COMPUADD 333T   ✓ BEST BUY

CompuAdd's Model 333T is the M1 Tank of 33-MHz 80386-based computers. Its expandability, options, and construction make it a standout. The *T* in 333T means that it uses a vertical tower cabinet rather than a horizontal desktop chassis. After installing a 1.2Mb 5.25-inch floppy drive, 1.44Mb 3.5-inch microfloppy drive, and hard drive, there's still room for six more data storage devices. The system's 4Mb of RAM reside on a card that plugs into the main circuit board and accepts up to 16Mb of RAM.

With a graphics card and disk controller card installed, one 8-bit (XT-compatible) and four 16-bit (AT-compatible) expansion slots remain free. The 101-key keyboard does not feel very crisp, but it is better than average.

We recommend CompuAdd's very fast Hi-Rez VGA card ($179), which supports resolutions of up to 1,024 by 768 pixels (dots). A $29 memory upgrade increases the maximum number of simultaneous on-screen colors from 16 to 256. CompuAdd's fairly sharp 14-inch High-Resolution VGA monitor can display up to 1,024 by 768 pixels. At $409, it is a good value. If your budget allows, a high-quality 16-inch monitor is a better match for the 333T's capabilities. Besides its own line, CompuAdd carries brand-name monitors.

In our tests, the base 333T was about 4.5 times faster than an 8-MHz IBM AT. A $675 SRAM (static random-access memory) card adds 640Kb of high-speed memory for conventional DOS memory, without using an expansion slot.

The 333T's chassis components are of very high quality, and the 333T's frame is made of very heavy-gauge metal.

At $2,775, the basic 333T provides a rock-solid base for building a dream machine. CompuAdd's Enhanced 333T system includes a speedy 150Mb hard drive, high-performance hard drive controller with one megabyte of cache RAM, two floppy drives, and a SRAM card. (Cache RAM stores data that is frequently accessed from a disk, thus speeding up the sys-

Prices are accurate at time of printing; subject to manufacturer's change.

tem.) The Enhanced 333T system also provides a High-Resolution VGA monitor and a Hi-Rez VGA card with one megabyte of display RAM at a package price of $5,375.

Setup and utility software is included. CompuAdd 333T computers purchased with a hard drive also come with MS-DOS 4.01 and Microsoft Windows 3.0. The documentation is fine for experienced users but a bit tough for novices.

Help is available from local dealers and a toll-free support line. During the warranty period, CompuAdd provides free on-site service for its 300-series systems in 250 metropolitan areas. Systems may also be dropped off at local outlets or shipped to a repair facility in Texas.

CompuAdd systems may be purchased at CompuAdd retail outlets in most metropolitan areas, or by phone from the company's mail-order facility. Hardware sold by CompuAdd carries a 30-day no-questions-asked money-back guarantee.

If you prefer a desktop system, consider the CompuAdd 333. It lists for $180 less than the tower and has four fewer expansion bays, a 230-watt power supply (versus the tower's 300-watt unit), and a lighter chassis frame.

Specifications: RAM, four megabytes (4,096Kb); **operating system,** MS-DOS, MS OS/2; **included hardware,** system unit with CPU, keyboard, 1.2Mb floppy or 1.44Mb microfloppy disk drive, mouse, clock/calendar, Centronics parallel port, two RS-232C serial ports; **included software,** MS-DOS 4.01, CompuAdd Windows 3.0, setup, utilities. **Warranty:** one year. **Ratings: overall value,** 10; **ease of use,** 8; **software,** 10; **performance,** 10; **documentation,** 9; **expandability,** 10.

Approx. retail price	Approx. low price
$2,775	**$2,775**
(Part No. 66656)	(Part No. 66656)

APPLE MACINTOSH LC ✓BEST BUY

The Apple Macintosh LC combines an easy-to-use interface, a quick Motorola 68020 processor, and color graphics. LC stands for both Low-profile Compact and Low-cost Color. At 3 inches high, a bit over 12 inches wide, and 15 inches deep, its small size belies its capabilities.

Most programs run three to four times faster on the LC than on the low-cost Mac Classic. However, the LC lacks a PMMU

Prices are accurate at time of printing; subject to manufacturer's change.

(Paged Memory Management Unit), a chip found on more costly Macs. PMMU circuitry is required for Apple's version of the UNIX operating system and for a few advanced features of Apple's newest System 7.0 software.

The Mac LC has a 40Mb internal hard drive and a 1.4Mb 3.5-inch microfloppy drive that can also read and write data in IBM's format. The LC's chassis cannot hold another internal floppy drive, but you can attach an external unit.

Mac computers use SCSI (Small Computer System Interface) hard drives. Our Mac LC's hard drive was the same 40Mb internal hard disk drive that Apple uses in upscale versions of the Mac Classic. Apple does not currently offer other hard drives as standard equipment on the LC. An external SCSI port allows up to seven external SCSI-based peripherals, including hard disks, optical scanners, and CD-ROM drives.

Expansion cards designed for the Mac SE and SE/30 and NuBus cards for the Mac II series will not fit the LC's one expansion slot. Apple announced a $199 card that will let the Mac LC run Apple IIe software and a $199 card for businesses that want to tie Mac LCs into computer networks. Other manufacturers have announced products that will use the LC's expansion slot, such as accelerator cards and graphics boards for large-screen monitors.

Apple designed two new 12-inch monitors for the Mac LC. Our $299 monochrome monitor's 640-by-480-pixel (dot) resolution yielded a sharp, bright image. However, the maximum resolution of Apple's new $599 RGB (red-green-blue) color monitor is 512 by 386 pixels. Its coarse pixel size resulted in an inferior color display. We recommend Apple's 13-inch high-resolution RGB color monitor ($999) instead.

Video display circuitry on the Mac LC's main circuit board can display 256 simultaneous colors or shades of gray on the $599 RGB monitor, 16 shades of gray on Apple's $299 monochrome display, and 16 colors or shades of gray on Apple's $999 high-res RGB monitor. A video memory upgrade ($199) increases the number of simultaneous colors or shades of gray that the LC can display on the monochrome monitor and high-res color monitor from 16 to 256.

The LC's 81-key keyboard feels good and is comfortable even after extended use. Left-handed users will like the fact that the mouse plugs into either side of the keyboard.

Prices are accurate at time of printing; subject to manufacturer's change.

Apple includes a small microphone that plugs into a jack in the back of the Mac LC. A simple program allows you to record, store, and play back your voice, music, or other sounds. An increasing number of programs might add support for voice response and playback now that Apple has made the facility standard on its two newest Macs, the LC and IIsi.

Although clear and easy to follow, the manuals lack details. Two programs cover the basics of using the LC.

The Mac's operating system can run in one of two modes: Finder and MultiFinder. Finder is used for normal operations; MultiFinder for multitasking, which means you can use more than one program at a time. For instance, you can sort a database file in the background (off-screen) while using a word processing program on your screen.

HyperCard software provided with the Mac LC can create interactive programs that integrate graphics, animation, text, music, voice, and video. And thousands of HyperCard programs (stacks) are available at little or no cost.

Exploiting MultiFinder and HyperCard can take up lots of RAM. The LC has 2Mb of RAM on its main circuit board. Two empty SIMM (single in-line memory module) sockets allow the system memory to be expanded up to 10Mb. However, 2Mb of RAM is barely acceptable.

The Macintosh LC is priced to compete with most high-performance, brand-name 80386SX IBM clones. It offers superior power and a user interface that is easier to use and smoother than Microsoft Windows 3.0. The Mac's diverse software base equals that of the MS-DOS world; in some respects (e.g., ease of learning and use), it is superior.

Specifications: RAM, two megabytes (2,048Kb); **operating system,** proprietary; **included hardware,** system unit with CPU, 1.4Mb microfloppy disk drive, 40Mb hard disk drive, mouse, video display circuitry, clock/calendar, two RS-232/RS-422 serial ports, external microfloppy disk drive port, SCSI port, Desktop Bus port, audio output port; **included software,** Finder and MultiFinder operating systems, Apple File Exchange, Guided Tour, HyperCard, Tools, utilities. **Warranty:** one year. **Ratings: overall value,** 10; **ease of use,** 10; **software,** 10; **performance,** 10; **documentation,** 9; **expandability,** 8.

Approx. retail price	Approx. low price
$2,499	$1,948

COMPUTERS OVER $3,000

ZEOS '386-33 MHZ
VERTICAL SYSTEM

 ✓ BEST BUY

The Zeos '386-33 MHz Vertical System is the least-expensive fully equipped 80386 tower computer we've used. Its tower case contains eight expansion bays, four of which are internal. One internal bay houses the system's 130Mb hard disk. Two of three expansion bays that are accessible from the front of the tower case are occupied by floppy disk drives. Both a 1.2Mb 5.25-inch drive and a 1.44Mb 3.5-inch drive are standard. The reset, on/off, and keylock switches are conveniently front-mounted.

On the main circuit board resides a 33-MHz Intel 80386 processor and 4Mb of RAM. The system memory can be expanded to 32Mb without using an expansion slot. The parallel port, two serial ports, and a joystick port are all contained on a half-size expansion card. With this card and the 16-bit VGA color graphics card installed, six 16-bit (AT-type) slots remain available. The expandability is outstanding.

The Zeos '386-33 computer is almost five times faster than an 8-MHz IBM AT computer. Part of that power comes from the 128Kb (more than most systems) of fast cache RAM, which greatly speeds up the time it takes to access frequently used data. The '386-33's 130Mb hard drive is an excellent match for the 33-MHz 80386 processor. The hard drive was one of the fastest units we've ever tested. The 16-bit VGA video card is fast as well. It has 512Kb of display RAM; 128Kb or 256Kb is the norm in other systems. The 512Kb of display RAM let us access the extended resolutions (up to 1,024 by 768 pixels) of the Zeos's Super VGA color monitor.

Zeos's superb user manuals are easy to follow, with plenty of illustrations. They cover the system's setup and basic operations and offer technical data for experts.

Prices are accurate at time of printing; subject to manufacturer's change.

Zeos maintains excellent toll-free technical support and sales assistance 24 hours a day. During the warranty period, Zeos will ship replacement parts for next-business-day delivery. If you're not comfortable with replacing the defective part yourself, you must ship the system back to Zeos, unless you've purchased on-site service.

Be aware that prices and features change fairly often in the direct sales channel. However, that almost always means more performance and/or features at a lower price.

Zeos sells over the telephone (800-423-5891) and ships directly to its customers. Any Zeos system can be returned within 30 days for a full refund, no questions asked.

Specifications: RAM, four megabytes (4,096Kb); **operating system,** MS-DOS, MS OS/2; **included hardware,** system unit with CPU, keyboard, 1.2Mb floppy disk drive, 1.44Mb microfloppy disk drive, 130Mb hard disk drive, color monitor, video display adapter, mouse, clock/calendar, Centronics parallel port, two RS-232C serial ports, joystick port; **included software,** MS-DOS 4.01, Microsoft Windows 3.0, diagnostics, setup, utilities. **Warranty:** one year. **Ratings: overall value,** 10; **ease of use,** 9; **software,** 10; **performance,** 10; **documentation,** 10; **expandability,** 10.

Approx. retail price	Approx. low price
$3,195	not available

DELL SYSTEM 433P

RECOMMENDED

Dell's compact System 433P is based on a high-speed (33-MHz) Intel 80486 CPU. This speed demon has over eight times the computational power of an 8-MHz IBM AT. While not inexpensive, the price of a complete Dell System 433P is thousands of dollars less than most 33-MHz 80486 systems.

In the 433P's system unit resides 2Mb of RAM. Sockets on the main circuit board can hold up to 16Mb of RAM. Dell lets you choose a 1.2Mb 5.25-inch floppy drive or a 1.44Mb 3.5-inch microfloppy. The 433P comes with a very quick 100Mb hard drive. Dell also offers 190Mb and 320Mb drives.

The 433P's two serial ports, parallel port, and floppy/hard disk controller circuitry reside on the main circuit board. One free bay can support an additional internal data storage device. Though there are only three 16-bit (AT-compatible) slots, the ex-

Prices are accurate at time of printing; subject to manufacturer's change.

pandability is adequate. The 101-key keyboard has a light but comfortable feel. A keyboard lock prevents unauthorized access.

Don't look for a VGA card; the circuitry is built into the main circuit board. The 512Kb of video RAM supports resolutions of up to 800 by 600 pixels. An upgrade to one megabyte ($39) takes the Dell SuperVGA Color Plus monitor up to its maximum resolution of 1,024 by 768 pixels. This monitor yielded very good sharpness and rich color.

The documentation is written in simple language with clearly presented concepts. MS-DOS 3.3 ($100) and 4.01a ($119) come with GW-BASIC and some handy enhancements.

The jackrabbit-quick Dell 433P is a joy to use. While somewhat expensive, the Dell System 433P offers far more power per dollar than any of its brand-name competitors.

Dell systems are available by telephone (800-426-5150; 512-338-4400) and at CompUSA (formerly Soft Warehouse), a nationwide chain of computer stores. Dell computers have a 30-day money-back guarantee, toll-free technical support, and a one-year warranty with next-day on-site service by Xerox within a 100-mile radius of 200 U.S. locations.

Specifications: RAM, two megabytes (2,048Kb); **operating system,** MS-DOS, MS OS/2; **included hardware,** system unit with CPU, keyboard, 1.44Mb microfloppy or 1.2Mb floppy disk drive, 100Mb hard disk drive, color monitor, video display circuitry, clock/calendar, Centronics parallel port, two RS-232C serial ports; **included software,** system setup (in ROM), diagnostics, VGA utilities and drivers. **Warranty:** one year. **Ratings: overall value,** 10; **ease of use,** 9; **software,** 10; **performance,** 10; **documentation,** 10; **expandability,** 8.

Approx. retail price	Approx. low price
$4,999 (2Mb RAM)	$4,999 (2Mb RAM)

PORTABLE COMPUTERS

TRAVELMATE 2000

Weighing only 4.4 pounds, the Texas Instruments TravelMate 2000 notebook computer packs a good amount of power into a tiny package. It's hard to believe that there's a 20Mb hard drive and a 12-MHz Intel 80C286 processor in a computer that mea-

Prices are accurate at time of printing; subject to manufacturer's change.

sures only 1.4 inches high, 11 inches wide, and 8.5 inches deep. The TravelMate 2000's performance is 1.5 times faster than that of an 8-MHz IBM AT. One megabyte of RAM is standard in the TravelMate 2000. It can be filled out to 3Mb by adding a memory expansion kit ($549).

Unlike most laptops, the TravelMate 2000 does not have a built-in microfloppy disk drive. This is not a big problem. Files can be transferred to and from the 2000's hard drive using the built-in LapLink file-transfer software. Simply hook up the cable to the 2000's serial port, attach the other end to the serial port of any other IBM-compatible, and enter a few simple commands. Voila! You're ready to move data quickly between the two systems. If that seems too cumbersome, an external 1.44Mb 3.5-inch microfloppy drive retails for $219. This drive also adds an IBM PS/2-type connector for a 101-key keyboard. MS-DOS 4.01, which is built into the TravelMate's ROM chips, is loaded into memory when the system is powered on.

The black-and-white sidelit liquid crystal display (LCD) screen is one of the best VGA displays we've seen on a laptop. It was readable under all lighting conditions. Convenient controls allow the contrast and brightness to be easily adjusted. The screen has a resolution of 640 by 480 pixels (dots), and it can display 16 shades of gray. A $109 adapter allows the TravelMate 2000 to drive an external VGA color monitor at resolutions up to 1,024 by 768 pixels.

At the back of the TravelMate are several ports, which are covered by flimsy plastic caps that tend to get lost. A special adapter provided with the 2000 must be attached to the TravelMate whenever the parallel port is used; that's not very convenient. A connector on the back is for a $799 expansion box that allows one or two XT- or AT-compatible expansion cards to be used with the TravelMate.

The 79-key keyboard has a very light touch, and the keys bottom out quickly. Typing on the 2000 after using a desktop computer often felt disconcerting. However, the more we typed on the 2000, the less difference we noticed.

Depending on how often we accessed the hard drive, the internal battery powered our 2000 for up to two hours, which isn't very long. According to Texas Instruments (TI), a $179 clip-on battery extends the operating time to a maximum of five hours. The hard drive and display can be set to shut off when the system

Prices are accurate at time of printing; subject to manufacturer's change.

is inactive. An indicator light and warning beep signal when the battery power gets very low. Recharging the internal battery usually took a little over two hours using the system's AC adapter.

The 2000's light weight makes it seem much more fragile than heavier laptops. We didn't give our unit any special treatment, and the TravelMate survived our occasionally rough handling with flying colors. However, consider buying TI's fitted carrying case ($99) just to be safe.

With the exception of those pesky plastic caps for the ports, the TravelMate 2000's fit and finish was impressive. TI offers an internal 2400-bps (bits per second, or baud) fax/modem ($299) that can send (not receive) faxes. It adds only an ounce or two to the system's weight.

The instruction manuals are models of clarity, with easy-to-follow system setup procedures and helpful tips.

Texas Instruments and Sharp Electronics jointly developed the TravelMate. Sharp's PC-6220 and CompuAdd's Companion laptops are basically the same as the TravelMate 2000. If you want an ultralightweight computer that's unobtrusive in transit, the 2000 is up to travel, mate.

Specifications: RAM, one megabyte (1,024Kb); **operating system,** MS-DOS, MS OS/2; **included hardware,** system unit with CPU and keyboard, 20Mb hard disk drive, liquid crystal display, clock/calendar, Centronics parallel interface, RS-232C serial interface, external numeric keypad connector, external floppy disk drive/expansion bus interface; **included software,** MS-DOS 4.01, LapLink, Battery Watch, file manager, system diagnostics, utilities. **Warranty:** one year. **Ratings: overall value,** 10; **ease of use,** 9; **software,** 10; **performance,** 8; **documentation,** 10; **portability,** 10.

Approx. retail price	Approx. low price
$2,369	$1,928

ALR VENTURE/16

Advanced Logic Research's Venture/16 packs a 386SX punch into a small, affordable, feature-laden package. It is about the same length and width as a sheet of typing paper, and it is only two inches thick. When you pick up a Venture/16, you're likely to underestimate its weight. Our fully loaded Venture/16 with a battery weighed a bit over eight pounds, a bit heavy for a notebook computer. However, the added weight provides features that eliminate most of the compromises associated with notebook computers.

Our Venture/16's 16-MHz Intel 80386SX processor churned out two times the processing power of an 8-MHz IBM AT. We tested a Venture/16 Model 20 ($2,795), which had a 1.44Mb 3.5-inch microfloppy disk drive and a 20Mb hard drive. The Model 40 ($3,295) substitutes a 40Mb hard drive. Our hard disk was a better-than-average performer.

The Venture/16 comes with one megabyte of RAM. A slot in the battery compartment has room for one memory module. Filling that slot brings the system up to 2Mb or 5Mb.

On the back panel are two serial ports and a parallel port that also attaches to an external 5.25-inch floppy drive. However, ALR doesn't offer one. A video output for an external VGA monitor is provided. One connector attaches to an 80Mb external hard drive ($995), and another attaches to a full-size external keyboard ($75). Our Venture/16's 82-key keyboard felt very pleasant. Other accessories available from ALR include a carrying case ($79), a 2400-bps (bits per second, or baud) pocket fax/modem ($695), and a rechargeable battery pack.

The backlit LCD is bright and clear. Its 8.5-inch (diagonal) screen maintains a proper aspect ratio for graphics; that is, circles appear normal rather than squashed. This monochrome display supports VGA (Video Graphics Array) graphics with a resolution of 640 by 480 pixels. With a Super VGA monitor attached, the Venture/16 can support up to 800 by 600 pixels.

The battery lasted about three hours in our system. It took us only a little over two hours to recharge a depleted battery. The battery operating time is maximized by an automatic shutdown of the screen and hard drive after they have been inactive for a period of time that you can set. A smart sleep feature allows shutting off the Venture while in the middle of a program and returning to where you left off when you start it up again. This mode can be invoked manually or automatically after a user-specified period of system inactivity. Unfortunately, it tends to shorten the amount of operating time you can squeeze out of a battery.

The Venture/16 has a setup program and many useful utilities, including one for password protecting the Venture/16. This is the first computer we've tested that comes with Digital

Prices are accurate at time of printing; subject to manufacturer's change.

Research's DR-DOS, an operating system that is compatible with MS-DOS. We didn't have any problem with DR-DOS 5.0. In fact, we liked its ability to be loaded into expanded memory on a Venture/16 equipped with more than a megabyte of RAM. This left all 640Kb of DOS's work space for applications and RAM-resident utilities.

The manuals were the best we've seen yet from ALR. A Quick Setup Guide helps novice users get started. The reference manual is exceptionally complete. A lightweight PortaGuide summarizes the system's features and operation.

Considering its numerous features and 386SX performance, the Venture/16 is a noteworthy notebook bargain.

Specifications: RAM, one megabyte (1,024Kb); **operating system,** DR-DOS; **included hardware,** system unit with CPU and keyboard, 1.44Mb microfloppy disk drive, 20Mb disk drive, liquid crystal display, clock/calendar, Centronics parallel/external floppy drive interface, two RS-232C serial interfaces, external video interface, external storage module interface, numeric keypad port; **included software,** DR-DOS 5.0, system utilities. **Warranty:** one year. **Ratings: overall value,** 10; **ease of use,** 9; **software,** 10; **performance,** 9; **documentation,** 10; **portability,** 9.

Approx. retail price	Approx. low price
$2,795 (Model 20)	**$2,380 (Model 20)**

DELL SYSTEM 320LT [RECOMMENDED]

The Dell 320LT is a powerful IBM AT-compatible for people who need a laptop computer with better-than-average expandability. It features a 20-MHz Intel 80386SX processor that yields approximately 2.5 times the power of an 8-MHz IBM AT. The 15-pound system unit also includes a megabyte of memory (expandable to 8Mb) and an 83-key keyboard with a firmer-than-average, but comfortable, touch. A 1.44Mb 3.5-inch microfloppy drive and 20Mb hard drive are standard.

The 320LT's backlit LCD offers good legibility under a variety of lighting conditions. This VGA (Video Graphics Array) display has a resolution of 640 by 480 pixels. It can simulate up to 16 levels of gray. To obtain the best clarity, we often had to adjust the brightness and contrast when changing video modes. The display has a reasonably wide viewing angle, and it is a bit larg-

Prices are accurate at time of printing; subject to manufacturer's change.

er than average. On-screen images exhibit none of the squeezed characters or graphics of many laptop screens. The external video port can attach to any VGA display.

A fully charged battery will operate the system for about two hours, depending on the screen's brightness setting and the usage of the disk drives. The 320LT has the standard power-conservation features: powering down of the hard disk and screen when the computer is unused, and a sleep mode. (The main difference between these two is that a program can't perform unseen operations, such as sorting a database, while the sleep mode is in effect.) However, while the 320LT is running on battery power, its battery can be swapped for a fresh one without turning off the computer. It normally takes about eight hours to recharge the battery using the system's large and heavy (two-pound) AC adapter. A quick-charge mode does the job in two hours.

The Dell 320LT is much heavier than today's notebook-sized computers, but it offers something those systems lack. Besides a proprietary slot for an optional internal modem, the 320LT has another slot that accepts most half-size 8-bit (XT-compatible) expansion cards. Other notebook computers offer this capability only through the added expense and hassle of an external expansion box.

The overall construction and quality is first rate, and Dell's documentation is well organized, complete, and clearly written. MS-DOS 3.3 ($100) and 4.01a ($119) both come with GW-BASIC and some handy enhancements as well.

Dell also markets the 316LT, which uses a 16-MHz 386SX chip. The only difference between the two computers is in their CPU speeds; the 320LT is about 25 percent faster. Both models come with a 40Mb or 120Mb hard disk. With one megabyte of RAM and a 20Mb hard disk, the 316LT retails for $2,899, a 40Mb system lists for $3,099, and a 120Mb 316LT goes for $3,899. Similar 320LT units cost $600 more.

Dell systems are available by telephone (800-426-5150; 512-338-4400) and at CompUSA (formerly Soft Warehouse). Dell computers are backed by a 30-day money-back guarantee. You also get toll-free technical support and a one-year warranty with next-day on-site service by Xerox within a 100-mile radius of 200 U.S. locations.

Specifications: RAM, one megabyte (1,024Kb); **operating system,** MS-DOS, MS OS/2; **included hardware,** system unit

Prices are accurate at time of printing; subject to manufacturer's change.

with CPU and keyboard, 1.44Mb microfloppy disk drive, 20Mb hard disk drive, liquid crystal display, clock/calendar, Centronics parallel interface, RS-232C serial interface, external video interface; **included software,** diagnostics, utilities. **Warranty:** one year. **Ratings: overall value,** 9; **ease of use,** 9; **software,** 10; **performance,** 10; **documentation,** 10; **portability,** 7.

Approx. retail price	Approx. low price
$3,499	**$3,499**
(20Mb hard drive,	**(20Mb hard drive,**
1Mb RAM)	**1Mb RAM)**

TOSHIBA T1000LE   RECOMMENDED

The Toshiba T1000LE has a moderate price and many useful options. At 6.5 pounds, it is light enough to travel with. Measuring 12 by 10 inches and only 2 inches thick, the T1000LE is easy to carry in a briefcase or in its carrying case ($99). Like its predecessor, the T1000SE, the T1000LE employs a 9.54-MHz Intel 80C86 processor.

Its large liquid crystal display is very good. The shape of its blue-on-white characters appears strange at first, but their unique shape improves their readability. The sidelit display is legible in poor light, even when viewed at an angle. This display is CGA-compatible (Color Graphics Adapter), and its 640-by-400-pixel mode is supported by some popular software, including Microsoft Windows 3.0. The keyboard is very comfortable to use.

The T1000LE comes with a megabyte of memory. You can add up to 8Mb of RAM using memory cards: 1Mb ($449), 2Mb ($599), 4Mb ($1,099), or 8Mb ($2,199). Given the high cost of Toshiba's memory, we recommend less-costly third-party cards. Memory above 640Kb can be used as a nonvolatile RAM disk (part of memory that mimics a very fast disk drive).

A 1.44Mb 3.5-inch microfloppy drive and 20Mb hard drive are standard. The parallel port can also connect to an external 360Kb 5.25-inch floppy drive ($499). There is no external video output. There is room for a 2400-bps (bits per second, or baud) internal modem ($349). When used with a $295 interface, a new modem ($449) allows the T1000LE to receive and transmit data over a cellular phone system. Toshiba offers a chassis

Prices are accurate at time of printing; subject to manufacturer's change.

($1,199) that holds one or two 8-bit (XT-type) or 16-bit (AT-type) expansion cards.

A battery-conserving feature allows the screen to turn off at a time interval you select. A resume feature lets you shut off the T1000LE in the midst of a program and return to where you left off when it is turned back on.

The T1000LE's battery lasted almost three hours before a beep and light told us to replace or recharge it. The battery is light enough to make carrying a spare ($99) feasible. Recharging the battery using the AC power supply/recharger takes around eight hours. A quick-charger unit ($349) can recharge up to three batteries at a time.

Toshiba's manuals are very well organized and complete, except for a few errors in the reference manual's index. On-disk versions of the MS-DOS and system manuals make carrying the paper versions unnecessary. Toshiba supplies MS-DOS in ROM, a setup program, diagnostics, and MultiSoft's PC-Kwik Power Pak, a set of handy utilities.

Toshiba promises a two-business-day turnaround on repairs made while the T1000LE is under warranty. Help is available from a toll-free support number, a bulletin board system (BBS), and a support area on CompuServe.

Specifications: RAM, one megabyte (1,024Kb); **operating system,** MS-DOS; **included hardware,** system unit with CPU and keyboard, 1.44Mb microfloppy disk drive, 20Mb hard disk drive, liquid crystal display, video display circuitry, clock/calendar, Centronics parallel port, RS-232C serial port; **included software,** MS-DOS 3.3 (in ROM and on diskette), PC-Kwik Power Pak, setup program, utilities, on-disk reference manuals. **Warranty:** one year. **Ratings: overall value,** 9; **ease of use,** 9; **software,** 10; **performance,** 7; **documentation,** 10; **portability,** 9.

Approx. retail price	Approx. low price
$1,799	**$1,581**

Home Office Products

There is a wide range of typewriters, word processors, copiers, and fax machines made specifically for home use. Those that are more reasonably priced very often produce the same quality output as those that are higher priced, but they may not hold up well under constant use. The higher-priced home office models have features similar to commercial-use models.

Best Buys '92
Our Best Buy and Recommended home office products follow. They are categorized into word processors, electronic typewriters, desktop copiers, and fax machines. Within each category, products are listed by quality; the best of the Best Buys is first, followed by our second choice, and so on. A Best Buy designation applies only to the model listed; it does not necessarily apply to other models made by the same manufacturer.

WORD PROCESSORS

A word processor is a computer that is designed primarily for producing letter-quality reports, manuscripts, correspondence, and other documents. The differences between a computer and a word processor have decreased in the past few years. Some word processors can also be used to create spreadsheets and perform some of the other functions of a computer. Some advanced word processors can even interface with computers.

Most home office word processors are portable and produce letter-quality correspondences. They vary considerably in weight, number of features, and cost. Your choice of a word processor depends on your anticipated needs and your budget. Before you buy a word processor, you should consider whether a laptop or desktop computer or an electronic typewriter might better suit your needs. If you decide to purchase a word processor, buy the most advanced model available.

PANASONIC KX-W1555

The Panasonic KX-W1555 is a full-featured word processor with a built-in ten-inch cathode-ray tube and a daisy-wheel printer in a cabinet with a separate keyboard. Its print speed of 16 characters per second is significantly faster than the speed of most other word processors, so it gets the job done faster, especially with big jobs. The display shows 80 characters on 25 lines as green characters on a black screen. The unit's built-in text memory can store up to 58,000 characters (about 30 pages), including 2,000 characters of user-programmed phrases. A 3.5-inch floppy disk drive provides unlimited external storage. This model has a 63,000-word spelling checker, which can be programmed for 120 additional words. It also has a thesaurus of 45,000 root words and 500,000 synonyms. The KX-W1555 allows you to store up to 999 names, addresses, and phone numbers on a floppy disk, and its mail merge/list built-in software lets you generate individually typed letters to each person on the list. Lists can be organized by zip code and state. The disk drive can read ASCII files produced by computer-generated word processing software, and data encoded on disks by the KX-W1555 can be read as ASCII files by certain computers, the manufacturer claims. Other features include spreadsheet capability, lift-off correction, and a variety of electronic word processing functions such as search/replace, bold, underline, centering, and justification.

Specifications: height, 10⅝₆″; **width,** 17⁵⁄₃₂″; **depth,** 12″; **weight,** 21⅞₆ pounds. **Warranty: parts,** one year; **labor,** 90 days.

Approx. retail price	Approx. low price
$930	$423

BROTHER WP-760D

The Brother WP-760D is a full-featured word processor with a seven-line LCD (liquid crystal display), daisy-wheel printing, and unlimited memory through its built-in 3.5-inch floppy disk drive. While the LCD is limited, it lets you type and scroll through up to three pages of text before printing. Print-out speed is 13 characters per second. The built-in spelling checker signals when you incorrectly spell any of 70,000 words and suggests correct spellings. You can also program 204 words of your choice into the checker. A 45,000-word thesaurus disk is optional. The WP-760D will also alert you to punctuation errors and to words typed twice. Other features include lift-off correction, capability to merge names and addresses, justification, bold, underline, centering, and stop code. An optional spreadsheet and personal organizer is available.

Specifications: height, 5⅝″; **width,** 15⁷⁄₁₀″; **depth,** 16⁹⁄₁₀″; **weight,** 14⅗₀ pounds. **Warranty: parts,** one year; **labor,** 90 days.

Approx. retail price	Approx. low price
$600	$360

SMITH CORONA PWP 8000LT ✓BEST BUY

The Smith Corona PWP 8000LT has sophisticated word-processing capabilities in a truly portable laptop priced lower than most laptop computers. The unit uses six standard C-size nickel cadmium batteries or is AC powered. The edgelit LCD screen shows 16 lines of 80 characters. The user interface in this new model is friendlier than in previous models. It features icons, a mouse, windowing, and a WYSIWYG screen (What You See Is What You Get). The PWP 8000LT has 128K of internal memory and unlimited storage capability using standard 3.5-inch double-sided, double-density diskettes in the built-in disk drive. It creates files compatible with MS-DOS files and has many of the advanced electronic features of personal word processors, including a 90,000-word dictionary, thesaurus, punctuation checker, address merge, search/replace, and envelope format. A special program lets you produce spreadsheets. You also get an expansion card slot, a parallel port, and an RS-232 port providing fax and modem capability. To generate documents, this model must be connected to either a matching daisy-wheel printer, Model DWP I, or a matching high-resolution transfer printer, Model HRT 100 (both are optional). The DWP I operates at 18 characters per second and uses the maker's widely available printwheels and supplies. The HRT 100 prints at 48 characters per second and has letter-quality resolution.

Specifications: height, 2⅜"; **width,** 14"; **depth,** 10½"; **weight,** 76½ pounds. **Warranty: parts,** one year; **labor,** 90 days.

Approx. retail price	Approx. low price
$699	$605

ELECTRONIC TYPEWRITERS

Prices of full-featured electronic typewriters have plummeted as electronic technology has made manual and electric typewriters obsolete.

When you shop for an electric typewriter, think about the ways in which you plan to use it. A basic model may suit your needs, or you may need a typewriter that has many features of a word processor. If you plan to use the typewriter to address letters produced by a computer, make sure the typewriter and your computer printer have the same pitch (characters per inch), size of print characters, and font (print style).

SMITH CORONA XL 2800

The Smith Corona XL 2800 is a good value because it has simple-to-operate, basic features at a good price. Also, supplies are widely available. This dual-pitch, daisy-wheel machine has a built-in 75,000-word spelling checker, lift-off correction, automatic center, automatic underlining, automatic superscript and subscript, and bold print. The spelling checker beeps when you type a word with a spelling not found in its dictionary.

Prices are accurate at time of printing; subject to manufacturer's change.

Specifications: height, 4⁹⁄₁₀"; **width,** 16³⁄₁₀"; **depth,** 14³⁄₈";
weight, 12 pounds. **Warranty: parts,** one year; **labor,** 90 days.

Approx. retail price	Approx. low price
$259	$210

BROTHER GX-7000

The Brother GX-7000 is a good value in a basic electronic typewriter. Its 56,000-word spelling checker alerts you to incorrectly
typed words. It has lift-off correction, automatic center, automatic underline, bold print and superscript and subscript. It
uses daisy wheels in several fonts for 10- or 12-pitch typing. A
clear-plastic shield minimizes the sound of typing, which is
important in close quarters. It runs on AC power.
Specifications: height, 5¹⁄₁₀"; **width,** 16¹⁄₅"; **depth,** 14³⁄₅";
weight, 9⁹⁄₁₀ pounds. **Warranty: parts,** five years; **labor,** 90
days.

Approx. retail price	Approx. low price
$250	$173

SMITH CORONA XD 5800

The Smith Corona XD 5800 is a portable electronic typewriter
that has a 24-character LCD (liquid crystal display) and a
7,000-character (about four pages) internal memory. Although
the screen size is limited, you can see your work and review it
for errors before it is printed on the page. The 75,000-word
spelling checker beeps when it detects a word it cannot recognize and then displays alternative, correctly spelled words.
Other features include lift-off correction, automatic center, automatic underline, stop codes, three pitches, and end-of-page
warning. The XD 5800 is AC powered.
Specifications: height, 5"; **width,** 16⁹⁄₁₀"; **depth,** 16½"; **weight,**
13⁷⁄₁₀ pounds. **Warranty: parts,** one year; **labor,** 90 days.

Approx. retail price	Approx. low price
$329	$229

BROTHER GX-9000

The Brother GX-9000 is a full-featured portable electronic typewriter with lift-off correction and a 22,000-character memory

Prices are accurate at time of printing; subject to manufacturer's change.

(about ten pages). This model displays what you type on an LCD consisting of 2 lines of 40 characters each. This makes it possible to review and edit stored documents without printing them out. Its word processing features include search/replace, block move/copy/delete, stop codes, justification, bold, automatic centering/underlining, and end-of-page warning. Its 70,000-word spelling checker will alert you when you type a word it cannot recognize. To prevent it from beeping when you type proper nouns and other words not already programmed, you can add up to 255 words of your own. We like the clear plastic sound shield because it reduces typing noise. The GX-9000 is AC powered.

Specifications: height, 5⅒"; **width,** 16⅛"; **depth,** 14⅝"; **weight,** 9⅒ pounds. **Warranty: parts,** five years; **labor,** 90 days.

Approx. retail price	Approx. low price
$400	$230

DESKTOP COPIERS

Three factors have made photocopiers popular for use in the home. Most importantly, they are built and designed to be simply serviced by the user, unlike office copiers, which typically require periodic servicing by a technician. When the toner runs out, you simply replace the old cartridge with a new one. Second, they are small enough to fit on a desktop. And third, they are more convenient and cost-effective than running out to a print shop or coin-operated copier every time you need copies.

Before you buy a copier, test a floor model in the store to make sure it produces clear copies.

CANON PC-3

The Canon PC-3 produces excellent copies. Its price makes it a very good value. It is a single-sheet, manual-feeding machine capable of making copies from business-card size to 8½ by 11 inches. Its easily replaceable cartridge is available in black, brown, blue, green, or red toner and sells for under $100. The cartridge contains toner for about 1,500 copies. The Canon PC-

3 is small enough to tuck away in a closet when not in use. **Specifications: height,** 5⅜"; **width,** 14⅜"; **depth,** 16⅜"; **weight,** 25½ pounds. **Warranty: parts and labor,** 90 days.

Approx. retail price	Approx. low price
$795	$451

CANON PC-7

The Canon PC-7 is a versatile desktop photocopier that produces excellent quality copies. You can make copies up to 8½ by 14 inches from originals up to 10 by 14 inches. This model offers zoom reduction down to 70 percent and enlargement up to 122 percent. A stationary platen makes it easy to copy bulky originals such as books and magazines. A paper cassette lets you run up to 99 copies at a time. The exposure control is automatic, or you can set it manually. The PC-7 uses toner cartridges for black, brown, blue, or green copies. Each cartridge makes about 3,000 copies and sells for under $150. **Specifications: height,** 10⅜"; **width,** 20"; **depth,** 18⅜"; **weight,** 44½ pounds. **Warranty: parts and labor,** 90 days.

Approx. retail price	Approx. low price
$1,695	$911

DESKTOP FAX MACHINES

Fax is the commonly used term for a facsimile machine and electronic facsimile transmission of a document. Faxing has become known as electronic mail, as everything from orders for goods and deli food to love letters and song requests are faxed. At least 100,000 fax machines are being bought each month because desktop faxes have become even less expensive, with a number of them now listing for less than a thousand dollars. Desktop faxes use heat-sensitive paper to record transmissions and to make copies of personal documents. Fax machines transmit over ordinary telephone lines, and most include a telephone. Fax transmissions and receptions can be done manually or automatically, and most machines can be programmed for delayed transmission to take advantage of low night phone rates. Most machines have various reproduction modes for transmitting different types of documents, and

Prices are accurate at time of printing; subject to manufacturer's change.

many now have half-tone reproduction for transmitting photographs.

TOSHIBA FACSIMILE 4400

The Toshiba Facsimile 4400 is an inexpensive, basic fax machine that provides automatic FAX-TAD (telephone answering device) switchover that permits automatic answering of a telephone call or fax transmission using a single telephone line. The fax machine is connected to the incoming phone line, the answering machine is connected to the fax, and the 4400 is then set for FAX/TAD reception. The ring delay can be set for two, three, or five rings before the 4400's automatic-receiving mode is activated, allowing you to pick up the phone if you wish. The 4400's LCD (liquid crystal display) and journal print-out can be programmed for Spanish or English. Journal reports, usually found in expensive machines, can be automatically set to be printed after ten transmissions or receptions. Errors are displayed on the LCD panel to alert you to problems such as paper supply empty or a communication error during transmission or reception. Up to seven pages can be automatically fed for transmission or copying. Fifty speed-dial fax and phone numbers can be stored along with the transmission speed for each number. Transmission modes include 16-shade gray scale, normal, fine, and ultrafine resolution. The Toshiba Facsimile 4400 is a user-friendly fax that is very affordable.
Specifications: height, 4³⁄₁₀"; **width,** 14⅛"; **depth,** 10½"; **weight,** 10⅝ pounds. **Warranty:** one year.

Approx. retail price	Approx. low price
$899	$562

PANASONIC KX-F110

The Panasonic KX-F110 is a desktop communications center that is a facsimile, a telephone, and an answering machine. There is built-in automatic switching so that it can receive both voice and fax transmissions while you are out. When another fax machine calls, the KX-F110 senses the signal and switches into its fax mode. You record your outgoing message (OGM) to tell the caller to start transmission if they want to send a fax, or to wait for the tone to leave a voice message. An automatic cut-

Prices are accurate at time of printing; subject to manufacturer's change.

ter cuts each page that is transmitted or copied, and deposits each sheet in a tray. The document feeder holds up to ten pages, and a delayed transmission program allows you to send documents automatically when the phone rates are low. Transmission controls include resolution, contrast, and a 16-shade gray scale for sending photographs. Setting up and using the KX-F110 is easy as both the machine and the instruction booklet are user friendly. For example, the KX-F110 records your OGM on a microchip, and also records it on the tape that records your incoming messages. If there is a power outage, you lose the OGM on the chip, but when the power is restored, the KX-F110 automatically re-records your message on the chip from the tape. You can also access the answering machine from any phone, and remote access is restricted to you because you program your own access code. The KX-F110 features seven-page reception and transmission memory, multicopier function, memory for 20 one-touch and 100 speed-dialing numbers, and journal reports of transmissions and receptions. The Panasonic KX-F110 is a sophisticated, yet user friendly communications center.

Specifications: height, $4^{29}\!/_{32}''$; **width,** $16^{7}\!/_{8}''$; **depth,** $12^{9}\!/_{32}''$; **weight,** 12 pounds. **Warranty: parts and labor,** one year.

Approx. retail price	Approx. low price
$1,150	**$865**

RICOH FAX77 ✔ BEST BUY

The Ricoh Fax77 is a sophisticated desktop fax with high-quality 64-tone gray scale photo reproduction, an automatic paper cutter, and side exit trays on its left side for copies and originals. The quality of photographic reproduction depends only on the sending machine, so the 64-tone gray scale capabilities of the Fax77 make it the fax machine for those who want to transmit photographs. The photos can be sent quickly with rough detail, or a bit more slowly with very fine detail. Drawings, blueprints, and small print can also be accurately transmitted using either the detail or fine modes. The Fax77 has both manual and automatic reception and transmission, with a document feeder that sends up to 20 pages automatically, even by delayed transmission, which allows you to send documents unattended during night rates. The Fax77 has 15 one-touch

Prices are accurate at time of printing; subject to manufacturer's change.

and 30 two-touch speed dialing numbers for frequently called telephone and fax numbers. Redial memory stores the last ten numbers called for quick redial access. Besides the standard printout of transmissions and receptions, the Fax77 prints out an error report as soon as an error occurs so that you know what went wrong and how to correct it. The heavy-duty Ricoh Fax77 is a versatile and sophisticated fax machine.

Specifications: height, 6⁹⁄₁₀"; **width,** 12⅖"; **depth,** 14⅖"; **weight,** 20 pounds. **Warranty: parts and labor,** 90 days.

Approx. retail price	Approx. low price
$1,495	$1,092

Personal Care Appliances

Consumers have never had it so easy when it comes to taking care of personal needs. In a difficult economy, appliance manufacturers have taken special pains to give buyers a reason for spending money. Personal care appliances are easier than ever to use and are often loaded with special features. As an added inducement, a proliferation of models allow consumers to choose just what features they want to spend money on. In addition, more attention is now paid to the design of personal care items. The newest products are often ergonomically designed, making them easier than ever to use. Electric razors, for example, are shaped to fit more comfortably in the hand and many are now lighter in weight. With storage a problem, appliances are often attractive enough to be kept in the open.

Manufacturers know that hectic schedules have us traveling more these days. Whether you are dashing from office to health club to home, or from continent to continent, the newest personal care appliances have been designed to follow you. Many offer such helpful features as compact design, cordless operation, dual voltage, and fast heat-up times.

Safety is an important consideration in personal care appliances because so many are used in damp or wet bathrooms.

Most electric appliances include a reminder that electrical parts are electrically live even when the switch is off, and warns users to unplug the unit immediately after use to eliminate any risk of electric shock. When you shop for any personal care appliance, make sure that it has a UL seal. This is your guarantee that the product meets the most stringent, current safety specifications of Underwriters Laboratories (UL).

Prices for personal care products are reasonable, and you may be tempted to buy on the basis of price alone. But a low price does not necessarily mean that a product is a good value. Reject products that have weak plastic housing, rough edges where flashing was not trimmed thoroughly after it was molded, or sections that don't fit together properly. Check the balance and the way the product feels in your hand, and make sure that a particular model is designed to handle the job you want it to do. In addition, be certain that the retailer has a reasonable return policy if the product does not perform as you expected.

Best Buys '92

Our Best Buy and Recommended personal care appliances follow, divided into the following categories: makeup mirrors, men's and women's electric shavers, full-size and travel irons, garment steamers, and table-top air cleaners. In each category, products are listed by quality. The best of the Best Buys is first, followed by our second choice, and so on. A Best Buy or Recommended designation applies only to the model listed, not to other models made by the same manufacturer.

MAKEUP MIRRORS

Makeup mirrors are designed to help you look your best in any light. Select a mirror that offers multiple light settings, including those that duplicate daylight, fluorescent, and incandescent lighting. The light output should be consistent and evenly spaced around the mirror to eliminate shadows. Look for a sturdy, adjustable frame that lets you set the mirror at an angle that's most comfortable for you when applying makeup. A magnifying mirror, in addition to a regular mirror, is especially helpful for makeup application. A convenience outlet for use with other beauty appliances is an added plus on some mirrors.

PERSONAL CARE APPLIANCES

CLAIROL TRUE-TO-LIGHT
LIGHTED MAKEUP MIRROR LM-7

The Clairol True-to-Light Lighted Makeup Mirror LM-7 provides four lighting filters to simulate day, fluorescent, evening, and incandescent lighting. Strips of light on both sides of the mirror illuminate the glass entirely so there are no shadows to mar makeup application. The 8½- by 6½-inch mirror swivels for regular or magnifying glass. A sturdy wire fold-out stand on the back of the unit easily adjusts to the desired angle. An outlet on the frame can be used with other appliances.
Warranty: one year, limited.

Approx. retail price	Approx. low price
$30	$25

WINDMERE MIRROR GO
LIGHTLY MGL-8

✔ BEST BUY

The Windmere Mirror Go Lightly MGL-8 makeup mirror is a tri-view mirror that has two adjustable mirrored side panels that permit panoramic viewing for better makeup application. The center mirror swivels from regular to triple magnification. This unit has two 9-inch glare-free fluorescent bulbs that can be set to simulate day, office, evening, or home lighting situations. Conveniences include an adjustable folding backstand and an outlet for use with other beauty appliances.
Warranty: one year.

Approx. retail price	Approx. low price
$30	$18

ELECTRIC SHAVERS

The newest men's and women's shavers more closely adhere to the principles of ergonomic design, with slimmer shapes that are contoured to fit the hand more comfortably. Regardless of shape, there are two basic methods of operation for electric shavers: those with rotary heads that have two or three spring-mounted guards and turn in a circular pattern, and those with foil heads that have a thin, flexible screen over the cutting edges. Shavers come in both corded and cordless

Prices are accurate at time of printing; subject to manufacturer's change.

rechargeable models, as well as shavers that are corded or cordless that are not rechargeable.

Top-of-the-line men's shavers have precision-hardened blades, rugged motors, and a selection of closeness settings. These shavers also include a mechanism to stretch the skin before the whiskers are cut, an ultrathin screen covering the blades, and rechargeable power. A growing number of electric shavers are fully immersible and are cleaned by rinsing in water. Some charger stands never need recharging. Most shavers include a coiled cord, a pop-up trimmer, and a miniature cleaning brush. Many have international dual-voltage capability.

Standard women's shavers are designed specifically for women and are not simply smaller versions of men's shavers. Most are easy to handle and pack well for travel. Increasingly, manufacturers are offering dual-voltage models. Another desirable option on some shavers is a pop-up trimmer specially designed to shave the bikini line and other sensitive areas.

Men's Shavers

REMINGTON MICRO SCREEN RECHARGEABLE XLR-3000NE

The Remington Micro Screen Rechargeable XLR-3000NE shaver has an extremely powerful motor, twin ultrathin screens, and cutters with 120 diamond-honed edges for quick, close, comfortable shaves. The shaver comes with a convenient charger stand with indicator light. The stand never needs charging, and the shaver stays fully charged when stored in it. The shaver has dual voltage for worldwide use and comes with a convenient travel case.

Warranty: one year.

Approx. retail price	Approx. low price
$60	$50

PANASONIC SMOOTH OPERATOR ES326SK

The Panasonic Smooth Operator ES326SK is a rechargeable wet/dry shaver that is totally immersible and shaves either wet

Prices are accurate at time of printing; subject to manufacturer's change.

with lather or dry. This unit, which can be used in the shower, has durable ultrathin titanium-coated foil for close shaving. The foil is sharply angled to allow more of the hair root to be exposed to the cutting edge. A wide slide-up trimmer neatly trims sideburns and moustache. The shaver is ergonomically designed with a T-shaped body and comes with a charger stand with automatic voltage conversion. This unit, which can be fully charged in just one hour, also features a reserve power system so that if the main battery should run out of power, a flip of the reserve power switch provides for extra shaves. It comes with a deluxe hard case with mirror.

Warranty: parts and labor, one year.

Approx. retail price	Approx. low price
$135	$99

NORELCO RECHARGEABLE CORDLESS RAZOR 805RX

✓**BEST BUY**

The Norelco Rechargeable Cordless Razor 805RX, with its angled shaving head for easier shaving, has a patented Lift and Cut shaving system, which features 3 floating heads, 45 lifters, and 45 self-sharpening cutters. The one-piece razor head is easy to clean and reduces the chance of interchanging cutters and combs. This unit has a pop-out trimmer for beard, moustache, and sideburns. Other features include a charging stand, recharge indicator light, and locking on/off switch. Perfect for traveling, this lightweight, compact shaver has a worldwide voltage selector and travel pouch.

Warranty: parts and labor, two years.

Approx. retail price	Approx. low price
$93	$67

BRAUN SYSTEM 1-2-3 MODEL 3510

✓**BEST BUY**

The Braun System 1-2-3 Model 3510 is a cord/cordless rechargeable shaver with platinum-coated foil and ice-hardened steel blades for close cutting. The shaver has three positions for precise shaving. The first, for routine shaving, uses the foil screen blade. The second, for awkward areas, uses the trimmer and blade, and the third, for moustache and sideburns,

Prices are accurate at time of printing; subject to manufacturer's change.

uses the fully extended trimmer. The 3510 has automatic dual-voltage adjustment capability and a built-in one-hour recharger with an indicator light showing the level of recharging. The shaver can be quick-charged in five minutes for touch-up shaving. A 12-volt car/boat charging cord is available. A cleaning brush is conveniently fitted in the storage case. This unit comes with a 30-day, money-back guarantee.
Warranty: two years, limited.

Approx. retail price	Approx. low price
$110	$61

Women's Shavers

LADY REMINGTON ULTIMATE ELECTRIC SHAVER ULTW-2

✔**BEST BUY**

The Lady Remington Ultimate Electric Shaver ULTW-2 is a corded shaver that features a combination head with Micro Screen slotted cutters, diamond-honed blades, and grooved Hair Lifter for smooth, close shaves. The lightweight, slim shape is comfortable in the hand and the sliding on/off switch is textured for easy use. This shaver comes with a soft travel case.
Warranty: one year, limited.

Approx. retail price	Approx. low price
$45	$45

PANASONIC SMOOTH OPERATOR ES179DK

✔**BEST BUY**

The Panasonic Smooth Operator ES179DK is a rechargeable wet/dry women's shaver that can be used with shaving foam or in the shower or tub. It can also be used as a dry shaver. An angled shaving head is designed so the cutting system rests against the skin regardless of whether you are standing, sitting, or laying in the tub while shaving. The cutting system features an ultrathin shaving foil and precision trimmer aligned on the same flat surface so both cutting systems work simultaneously. In this way, longer hairs are cut by the trimmer, while the foil system smoothly finishes off the shaving. A pop-up trimmer for

Prices are accurate at time of printing; subject to manufacturer's change.

shaving the bikini line is released with the push of a button. The shaver is totally immersible for quick and easy cleaning. This unit, which comes with a charging stand that features automatic voltage conversion for worldwide use, is housed in a hard case. **Warranty: parts and labor,** one year.

Approx. retail price	Approx. low price
$135	not available

LADY REMINGTON SHOWER STYLE WET/DRY LWD-1000 BP

The Lady Remington Shower Style Wet/Dry LWD-1000 BP shaver is a rechargeable unit that can be used with lather or foam in the shower or tub or as a dry shaver. Stainless-steel twin cutters and screen are housed in a hinged head that opens for easy cleaning. This unit comes with a charging stand that can be wall-mounted and is adaptable for worldwide voltage. **Warranty:** one year.

Approx. retail price	Approx. low price
$42	$42

FULL-SIZE IRONS

Although ironing may not rank among your favorite pastimes, the newest irons have so many features to speed things along that the task can now be done in a fraction of the time it used to take. Electronic controls to maintain consistent heat ranges, spray mist to spot dampen wrinkles, multiple steam settings, and an extra burst of steam for problem areas are just a few of the options that take the pressure out of pressing clothes.

Safety, too, has become a major concern and an increasing number of manufacturers are paying attention to consumer demands in this area. Automatic shut-off is no longer found on just top-of-the-line models. An added safety feature on some irons is a switch-off mechanism that shuts the iron off in 30 seconds if left unmoved on the soleplate. A large heel base and a ready light are other safety features to look for.

Non-stick soleplates, self-cleaning vents, a wide range of temperature settings to accommodate many different types of fabrics, a body that remains cool to the touch, and a cord that ad-

Prices are accurate at time of printing; subject to manufacturer's change.

apts to right- or left-handed users are other options worth considering. Finally, there are the cord/cordless models that allow for more freedom of movement than conventional irons. If you are interested in this expensive option, keep in mind that these irons are best suited for small jobs since they work at an optimum temperature for a relatively short time—about ten minutes.

PROCTOR-SILEX ELECTRONIC SHUT-OFF MEMORY IRON 12736   ✓ BEST BUY

The Proctor-Silex Electronic Shut-Off Memory Iron l2736 offers two of the most wanted features in a steam iron—automatic shutoff and spray mist—at a bargain price. The iron will shut off if left unmoved on the soleplate for 30 seconds or on the heel rest for 15 minutes. The spray-mist feature allows you to spot dampen difficult wrinkles as you iron. A fabric guide helps you to set the iron at the proper temperature for a variety of fabrics. The water window lets you know when you need to refill the iron. The soleplate has 53 self-cleaning steam vents for a steady source of steam. Other features include button grooves and a reversible cord for right- or left-handed use.
Warranty: one year, limited.

Approx. retail price	Approx. low price
$50	$36

ROWENTA SURFLINE TITAN PLUS DE-42   ✓ BEST BUY

The Rowenta Surfline Titan Plus DE-42 iron features a unique tank-within-a-tank steam system that maintains a steady pressure within the iron to produce a constant level of steam regardless of the amount of water left in the reservoir. The see-through water gauge prevents overfilling. Ten steam settings allow for greater flexibility when ironing a variety of fabrics and thick layers at seams and waistbands. An atomized spray allows you to lightly mist stubborn wrinkles as you iron. The non-stick, scratch-resistant soleplate glides easily over fabrics. Other features include a deep-button groove, transparent water tank, center cord, and an on light.
Warranty: parts and labor, one year.

Prices are accurate at time of printing; subject to manufacturer's change.

Approx. retail price	Approx. low price
$55	$50

TRAVEL IRONS

Travel irons are useful appliances, but they do have their limitations. They lack many features of full-size irons such as heating power, proper weight, and multiple steam and temperature settings. But a travel iron does deliver for the traveler, pressing wrinkles out of suits, dresses, and shirts.

Considering their compact size and light weight, travel irons function remarkably well, providing steam, finger-activated sprays, and thermostatically controlled heat settings. While the dual-voltage and adapter plug features that are practically standard on most travel irons suit the needs of the international traveler, people whose ironing is limited to the occasional once-over might find a travel iron is all they need.

FRANZUS TRAVEL CLASSICS STEAM SPRAY/DRY IRON LT-15B

The Franzus Travel Classics Steam Spray/Dry Iron LT-15B is a compact, lightweight, dual-voltage travel iron that can accomplish many tasks just as well as larger irons. This unit features multiple steam vents on a non-stick soleplate. A power-indicator light glows in the temperature dial when the unit is plugged in—alerting you that the iron is hot. An automatic thermostat maintains the correct temperature throughout use whether the iron is used on dry or steam settings. A finger-operated spray nozzle is good for stubborn wrinkles. The folding handle locks in place. This unit comes with a travel pouch and adapter plug. **Warranty: parts and labor,** one year.

Approx. retail price	Approx. low price
$37	$36

BLACK & DECKER STOWAWAY TRAVEL IRON F56G   RECOMMENDED

The Black & Decker Stowaway Travel Iron F56G is a powerful dual-voltage steam iron with 21 steam vents on a polished alu-

minum soleplate for easy ironing. A see-through handle holds water for steam and then folds down and locks. It comes with a travel pouch and an adapter plug.
Warranty: two years.

Approx. retail price	Approx. low price
$32	$26

GARMENT STEAMERS

Increasingly versatile, garment steamers do far more than just remove wrinkles from clothes. These handheld units are excellent for smoothing wrinkles out of draperies and sheers. Today's units deliver abundant amounts of steam and contain bristle brushes, lint removers, and crease attachments—an innovation that turns steamers into pressing machines for pants, with results approximating those of an iron. On the road, these fast-working units do an excellent job.

FRANZUS TRAVEL CLASSICS DUAL VOLTAGE CLOTHES STEAMING BRUSH WA-6D ✓BEST BUY

The Franzus Travel Classics Dual Voltage Clothes Steaming Brush WA-6D offers penetrating bursts of steam at the push of a button in less than one minute. The detachable see-through water reservoir has a water level window so you can tell at a glance if the unit needs refilling. This steamer comes with a removable lint pad, travel/storage pouch, dual-voltage adapter, and a convenient hanging loop.
Warranty: parts and labor, one year.

Approx. retail price	Approx. low price
$43	$41

ROWENTA STEAMBRUSH DA-56 ✓BEST BUY

The Rowenta Steambrush DA-56 is a powerful steambrush that produces steam in just 90 seconds to quickly remove closet and suitcase wrinkles. A built-in bristle brush opens the fabric weave to allow steam to penetrate. The brush detaches for delicate fabrics. A handle-mounted control releases a strong burst of steam where needed. The DA-56 has a removable water tank, water level gauge, and built-in removable lint brush. It comes with a convenient travel case. An optional crease attachment is available for $10.

Warranty: parts and labor, one year.

Approx. retail price	Approx. low price
$40	$35

TABLE-TOP AIR CLEANERS

As news about the environment continues to cause concern, interest in air cleaners has increased. Table-top models have proven to be effective at trapping airborne dust and pollen. They do not, however, scoop up particles that have settled on the floor or on furniture. And although they can remove smoke particles from tobacco or from the kitchen or fireplace, thereby helping to reduce eye, nose, and throat irritation, they don't have much effect on smoky smells.

Table-top air cleaners use a fan to move the air. Dust and smoke particles are then generally removed either mechanically, using some form of a filter, or by electrical attraction.

An effective form of comparison among units is the "clean air delivery rate," or CADR, the equivalent in cubic feet per minute of how much fresh air the unit is providing. In general, an air cleaner with a higher CADR usually reduces airborne smoke, dust, and pollen particles faster from the same size room than a model with a lower rating.

The more air that is moved, the more effective the unit is at providing clean air. Be sure to check fan speeds and noise levels before selecting a unit, however. Although the noise level climbs at higher speeds, some air cleaners are so noisy at the lowest fan speed that conversation is difficult.

NORELCO CLEAN AIR SYSTEM WITH IONIZER CAM880

✔ BEST BUY

The Norelco Clean Air System with Ionizer CAM880 features a three-stage filtration system, which includes pre-filters, electrically charged pleated filters, and activated charcoal, plus ion-

Prices are accurate at time of printing; subject to manufacturer's change.

ization for maximum air cleaning. In addition, it has two high-volume blower wheel fans to move air efficiently. In a 10- by 12- by 8-foot room, the CAM880 removes 90 percent of the dust particles in about 17 minutes. This air cleaner also has three speed settings to accommodate different cleaning needs. Separate switches indicate when the unit is operating and the ionizer is on.

Specifications: height, 7"; **width,** 8½"; **length,** 16"; **weight,** 8½ pounds. **Warranty: parts and labor,** one year, limited.

| Approx. retail price | Approx. low price |
| $147 | $84 |

POLLENEX PURE AIR "99" ELECTRONIC AIR CLEANER WITH IONIZER

✔**BEST BUY**

The Pollenex Pure Air "99" Electronic Air Cleaner with Ionizer uses a multistage electrostatic air filter to reduce indoor air-borne pollutants. The ionizer can be used alone or in combination with the air cleaner. A red light indicates that the ionizer is working. This unit has a two-speed air-flow control. It is compact and lightweight.

Specifications: height, 9½"; **width,** 6¼"; **length,** 10⅝"; **weight,** 3‰ pounds. **Warranty:** three months.

| Approx. retail price | Approx. low price |
| $80 | $53 |

Home Fitness Equipment

In the past, home gyms were reserved for the rich and famous and the dedicated bodybuilder. But today, a lean, well-toned torso radiating energy and health is a goal to which many people aspire. Workouts have become part of a daily routine, whether it's running four miles or exercising at a gym or health club. While the facilities are usually well-equipped and offer a variety of programs, they are more often than not overcrowded, expensive, inconvenient, and are limited by space.

Until recently, home gyms were not a really viable alternative, since most of the equipment was poorly engineered. But high-quality, well-priced fitness equipment is now being manufactured for home use. The better products combine the latest microcomputer technology with solid performance features to motivate and excite the user. When buying home exercise equipment, invest in products that will meet your expanding needs. The growing array of high-tech options and features are excellent for motivation and monitoring your performance and progress. It is not wise, however, to buy equipment with a lot of options that you will never use. Bargains may not always be the best choice either, due to poorly designed and engineered equipment.

Always remember that even the finest equipment is potentially harmful if you do not work gradually into a regimen suited for you. Consult a physician before beginning any strenuous exercise program.

Equipment placement is crucial to the success of any home gym. If the equipment isn't readily accessible, your use may taper off as the novelty wears off. Basements may be the perfect place, because of the square footage, but exercising with no natural light and wedged between storage cartons may be the quickest way to drive you away from your new home gym. Some exercisers like to have access to a music system. A section of your bedroom, a spare room, or another pleasant location will encourage regular workouts.

Best Buys '92

Our Best Buy and Recommended home fitness equipment products follow. We reviewed products in the following categories: exercise cycles, rowing machines, treadmills, home gyms, climbing machines, and ski machines. Within each category, the products are listed by quality. The best of the Best Buys is listed first, followed by our second choice, and so on. Recommended products follow the Best Buys. Remember that a Best Buy or Recommended designation applies only to the model listed, not necessarily to other models made by the same manufacturer or to an entire product line.

EXERCISE CYCLES

The stationary exercise cycle is a standard feature in many home and professional gyms. The most common models are the upright, but a growing number of manufacturers are producing recumbent units. These models allow the user to lean back in a padded, ergonomically designed chair that distributes weight evenly and eliminates lower back stress and the numbness associated with upright cycles. In the recumbent position, the legs and heart are nearly level, which means blood pressure is lowered and cardiovascular conditioning is more effective. The unit leaves your hands free for reading or for hand weight exercises. When shopping for a cycle, take time to use the models you are considering. Check out their sturdiness, stability, and motivational and performance monitoring electronics. Be sure the seat is adequately padded and is comfortable during a long session. Look for weighted foot pedals with straps to secure feet. Exercise cycles are excellent for cardiovascular conditioning; toning and firming legs, hips, and buttocks; and for weight reduction.

SEARS LIFESTYLER 3500A

The Sears Lifestyler 3500A is a chain-drive upright stationary cycle featuring top-front fanwheel resistance, electronic speedometer and timer, and handlebars with rowing action. The unit has a light-gray plastic and metal frame with a padded 10-inch-wide by 12-inch-long seat.
Specifications: height, 49″; **width,** 25″; **length,** 47″; **weight,** 44 pounds. **Warranty:** 90 days.

Approx. retail price	Approx. low price
$200	$200

TUNTURI EXECUTIVE ERGOMETER (TEE)

The Tunturi Executive Ergometer (TEE) is a venerable unit first introduced in 1968. It has a 40-pound steel flywheel and disc-brake system that provides smooth, quiet, and continuous variable resistance. This unit has an adjustable handlebar and seat post, and an analog energy-expenditure scale providing calorie consumption. Self-righting foot pedals keep feet secure.
Specifications: height, 42″; **width,** 20″; **length,** 37″; **weight,** 75 pounds. **Warranty: electronics,** two years; **structural,** ten years.

Approx. retail price	Approx. low price
$299	$272

PRECOR 825e

RECOMMENDED

The Precor 825e is a sleekly designed upright stationary cycle featuring a horizontal, 25-pound flywheel, direct-drive system, and adjustable pedal resistance. Motivational electronics display revolutions per minute, elapsed time, distance in miles, and more. For comfort, there is a full-size padded seat, non-slip

Prices are accurate at time of printing; subject to manufacturer's change.

foam handgrips, and wide pedals with adjustable foot straps.
Specifications: height, 46″; **width,** 21″; **length,** 37″; **weight,**
65 pounds. **Warranty: parts,** one year; **labor,** 90 days.

Approx. retail price	Approx. low price
$700	$682

ROWING MACHINES

When you test a rowing machine, examine its construction.
Check the tension devices (hydraulic cylinders and wind fan
resistance), which simulate the movement and action of rowing,
and make sure the machine has adjustable resistance settings.
The seat, which should be contoured and cushioned, should
slide smoothly on rollers and ball bearings. The glide distance
should be sufficient to accommodate all users. The foot pads
should be adjustable for different angles and have foot straps.
Rowing machines are an excellent form of non-impact aerobic
exercise. Rowing works all the major muscle areas of the body
but puts little strain on the joints—making it suitable even for
arthritis sufferers. Rowing machines can lead to back strain, so
learning proper rowing form is a must.

TUNTURI ELECTRONIC ROWER R205 ✔BEST BUY

The Tunturi Electronic Rower R205 is equipped with pivoting
handgrips to reduce friction, silent shocks to provide even resistance, seat lock to adapt the unit for anaerobic workouts, and
programmable electronics with LCD (liquid crystal display).
Specifications: height, 8⅝″; **width,** 30″; **length,** 57⅞″; **weight,**
35 pounds. **Warranty: electronics,** two years; **structural,** ten
years.

Approx. retail price	Approx. low price
$249	$211

NORDICTRACK NORDICROW TBX I ✔BEST BUY

The NordicTrack NordicRow TBX I has split resistance to work
the upper and lower body independently. Resistance for the

upper body is provided by a special flywheel; the lower body is worked by a PowerFlex cord with a resistance range of 2 to 11 pounds. A specially designed, contoured, raised seat cradles and supports the back. An optional electronics package (for $49.95) provides readouts on strokes per minute, calories burned, total strokes, cadence, and time elapsed.
Specifications: height, 24″; **width,** 18″; **length,** 81″; **weight,** 85 pounds. **Warranty:** two years (30 day free in-home trial).

Approx. retail price	**Approx. low price**
$499	**$499**

TREADMILLS

Treadmills are reliable, safe, and versatile. For diehard runners, treadmills are excellent for maintaining training schedules during winter and in bad weather. The units are outstanding for brisk walking and light jogging. When shopping for a unit, look for one with stability, range of speeds, handrails, safety shutoff features, and motivational and performance monitoring electronics including miles per hour, minutes per mile, average calories expended, and so forth. For the best quality, look for DC motors, which provide a wider range of speeds and are more durable than AC motors. The more expensive models have electronic elevation for more intense workouts.

TUNTURI J620 ELECTRONIC TREADMILL

The Tunturi J620 Electronic Treadmill has a large walking and running deck powered by a 1⅜ horsepower DC motor, which delivers speeds up to 10 miles per hour. The unit can be elevated electronically up to a 12 percent grade. A fully electronic panel with LED (light emitting diode) readout monitors speed, time, distance, elevation, and calories expended. The control panel has touch-sensitive membrane keys for quick programming of the system. An auto-scan feature gives continuous, accurate feedback on workout progress.
Specifications: height, 47″; **width,** 24″; **length,** 70″; **weight,** 216 pounds. **Warranty: electronics,** two years; **structural,** ten years; **bed and belt,** one year.

Prices are accurate at time of printing; subject to manufacturer's change.

Approx. retail price	Approx. low price
$1,595	not available

AEROBICS PACEMASTER 870XAE ✔BEST BUY

The Aerobics Pacemaster 870XAE is a 1⅛ continuous horse-power treadmill with a range of speeds up to 11 miles per hour. It features a full array of digital displays, including miles per hour, minutes per mile, distance in miles and hundredths of miles, average calories expended, aerobic point and elevation grade, plus automatic warm-up and cool-down modes, pause mode, and four separate memories. This treadmill elevates up to a 10 percent grade and is equipped with safety features. **Specifications: height,** 51″; **width,** 22″; **length,** 64″; **weight,** 139 pounds. **Warranty:** one year; **motor,** two years; **frame,** five years.

Approx. retail price	Approx. low price
$1,795	$1,732

HOME GYMS

Developing a well-defined physique involves working muscle groups through weight lifting and exercising specific muscle groups such as the gluteals, deltoids, pectorals, biceps, and tri-ceps. The home gym category covers a range of products from systems weighing hundreds of pounds to simple resistance units designed to fit into a closet. The units selected here per-mit you to work on massing and shaping different parts of the body. When shopping, keep in mind your available space and the family members who will use the equipment. As with all exercise equipment, safety is paramount; choose only those units that you know you can safely manage. When shopping, look for a gym that allows ease of movement from one station to another with minimal movement of pins to access weight.

NORDICTRACK NORDICPOWER PLUS ✔BEST BUY

The NordicTrack NordicPower Plus features an adjustable workout seat and an arm and leg exerciser that offers more

Prices are accurate at time of printing; subject to manufacturer's change.

than 50 workout routines. It has two-way directional resistance for push and pull motion. Simple and compact, the unit has no attachments, extensions, weights, or rubber bands.
Specifications: height, 62″; **width,** 30″; **length,** 43″; **weight,** 60 pounds. **Warranty:** two years (30-day free in-home trial).

Approx. retail price	Approx. low price
$399	$399

PACIFIC FITNESS MALIBU · RECOMMENDED

The Pacific Fitness Malibu is a cable-ready unit with many extra features, including body contoured upholstery with lumbar supports, built-in grip handles, two low-pulley exercise positions for more efficient use of floor space, a position incline bench, and easy-access weights at every station. It comes with 195 pounds of weight and provides a maximum resistance workout of about 250 pounds due to its pulley configuration. Work stations include incline chest press, shoulder press, and more.
Specifications: height, 83″; **width,** 56″; **length,** 50″; **weight,** 510 pounds. **Warranty:** ten years.

Approx. retail price	Approx. low price
$1,749	$1,672
(base model)	(base model)

CLIMBING MACHINES

Climbing is an excellent low-impact exercise that avoids jarring and pounding joints, yet provides a challenging aerobic/cardiovascular workout. The range of units is wide. Some simulate a staircase while others have the feeling of mountain climbing. Look for variable resistance settings, step heights, proper handrails, motivational electronics, and foot pedal sturdiness. Climbers are particularly effective for strengthening buttocks and lower-body muscle groups.

TUNTURI VARIABLE RESISTANCE CLIMBER C401

The Tunturi Variable Resistance Climber C401 features 12 resistance settings providing a range of workout options for all

Prices are accurate at time of printing; subject to manufacturer's change.

levels of fitness. An electronic monitor measures elapsed time, steps, steps per minute, total calories, and calories per minute. A programming option allows for preset time and total steps for countdown measurement. An auto-scan function views all electronic readouts in five-second intervals.

Specifications: height, 50"; **width,** 19½"; **length,** 33½"; **weight,** 56 pounds. **Warranty: electronics and shocks,** two years; **structural,** ten years.

Approx. retail price	Approx. low price
$249	$243

PRECOR LOW IMPACT CLIMBER 714   ✔ BEST BUY

The Precor Low Impact Climber 714 features multiple tension settings for resistance climbing that works every muscle group in the lower body. Two hydraulic resistance cylinders provide low-impact resistance for smooth, rhythmic adherence.

Specifications: height, 50½"; **width,** 20"; **length,** 35½"; **weight,** 65 pounds. **Warranty: parts,** one year; **labor,** 90 days.

Approx. retail price	Approx. low price
$350	$308

PRECOR INDEPENDENT ACTION CLIMBER 725e   ✔ BEST BUY

The Precor Independent Action Climber 725e features a climber system that continuously works the large muscle groups of the lower body. The motivational electronics display step rate, total steps, and total exercise time. A variable-pacer function sets a step rate from 30 to 150 steps per minute.

Specifications: height, 51"; **width,** 28"; **length,** 38½"; **weight,** 65 pounds. **Warranty: parts,** one year; **labor,** 90 days.

Approx. retail price	Approx. low price
$625	$573

SKI MACHINES

Ski machines offer a combination of upper and lower body exercise with exceptional cardiorespiratory conditioning. Until recently, only cross-country simulators were available. Now, a downhill simulator is on the market, an innovation that is not only fun, but calls on additional muscle groups. In shopping, look for stability, variable two-way resistance for upper and lower body conditioning, elevation device for uphill skiing, and digital readouts for feedback on speed, time, and distance.

FITNESS MASTER FM 340 ✔BEST BUY

The Fitness Master FM 340 is a sleek new cross-country model featuring concealed stainless-steel resistance cable, front end portability wheels, and slip-resistant angled glideskates. It employs frictional two-way resistance for more complete workouts of upper and lower body. Synchronized glideskates and steel arm poles provide stability so special coordination is not required to use the equipment. Resistance settings range up to 15 pounds for arms and to more than 100 pounds for legs. Standard electronics scan step count, time elapsed, and calorie usage. There is an automatic shutoff.
Specifications: height, 8″ (folded); **width,** 24″; **length,** 53″; **weight,** 39 pounds. **Warranty:** two years; **electronics,** one year.

Approx. retail price	Approx. low price
$449	$439

TUNTURI S530 SKIFIT ✔BEST BUY

The Tunturi S530 SkiFit is a unique downhill alpine ski simulator. Adjustable resistance, foam-covered hand grips, and non-slip swivel foot plates make it possible to simulate skiing under various snow conditions and provide both aerobic and anaerobic workouts. A self-starting, multifunction meter scans different functions at four-second intervals, allowing the user to hold the handlebar throughout the exercise.
Specifications: height, 59″; **width,** 67″; **length,** 50″; **weight,** 77 pounds. **Warranty: electronics,** two years; **structural,** ten years.

Approx. retail price	Approx. low price
$699	$631

Prices are accurate at time of printing; subject to manufacturer's change.

PRECOR 515e

The Precor 515e is a cross-country unit. Low-impact, lower-body resistance is provided by a precision-balanced flywheel, which is adjusted by an easy-to-reach knob. Upper-body resistance is controlled by dacron-polyester ropes and plastic pulleys for smooth, fluid operation. A four-position rear elevator simulates uphill skiing. A digital LCD (liquid crystal display) motivator gives speed, time, and distance.

Specifications: height, 70″; **width,** 20½″; **length,** 68½″; **weight,** 70 pounds. **Warranty: parts,** one year; **labor,** 90 days.

Approx. retail price	Approx. low price
$750	$700

Lawn Care Products

Environmental concerns have had a significant impact on the development of lawn care products, especially the lawn mower, one of the most important tools for the home gardener. Once upon a time, you mowed your lawn and then went over it again with a rake to collect grass clippings. Then came the power mower, which blew the clippings into a rear or side bag to be disposed of at a local dump. Now enter the mulching mower, a unit that chops clippings into minute fragments that settle into your lawn. The fragments decompose and return nutrients to the soil. At the same time, the mulched cuttings reduce evaporation, which means fewer waterings, less fertilizing, and significant reductions in the amount of waste deposited in landfills.

Whether considering a mulching, conventional, or convertible mower, either gas or electric, you have a wide variety of models from which to choose.

Like mowers, trimming devices have come a long way from the days when gardeners got down on all fours to cut hard-to-reach areas by hand. Lightweight and highly maneuverable trimmers, which are variously referred to as weed cutters, string trimmers, or weed whackers, are available in gasoline and elec-

CONSUMER GUIDE˙

tric versions and are excellent tools for adding those finishing touches to your lawn and garden.

Best Buys '92

Our Best Buy and Recommended lawn mowers and weed cutters are listed below. They are presented in the following categories: gasoline, electric, and riding lawn mowers; and gasoline and electric weed cutters. The item we consider the best of the Best Buys is listed first, followed by our second choice, and so on. Remember that a Best Buy or Recommended rating applies only to the model listed; it does not necessarily apply to other models made by the same manufacturer.

LAWN MOWERS

When considering the purchase of a mower, always keep in mind the size of your property and the type of terrain, whether flat or steep. Manual reel mowers are inexpensive, but impractical for anything but a small lot. Among power motors, one choice is a rotary, in either electric or gasoline. Rotary mowers are the best choice for heavy, coarse grasses. The cutting action of rotary is produced by a spinning blade 18 to 24 inches long that rotates at approximately 3,000 revolutions per minute.

Electric mowers are easy to use and relatively inexpensive, but they have limited power and range since they require an extension cord. Gasoline mowers are the most versatile and come in conventional and mulching versions, walk-behind, and self-propelled mowers. Gasoline mowers are also made as riding mowers and as lawn or garden tractor units for the largest lots.

Gasoline or Electric

For small, flat plots of about ¼ acre, electric mowers are effective. Quiet, easy to start, lightweight, and maneuverable, they lack the power of gasoline models. This means taller grasses may pose a problem. The units are limited by their cord length and the ever-present danger of accidentally severing the cord with the cutting blade.

Electric mowers are rated in amps instead of horsepower. The most common is the 12-amp motor, which has about 1¾-

horsepower output. These units are reliable and, except for an occasional tune-up, practically maintenance-free.

Gasoline mowers are versatile, portable, and more powerful than electric mowers. New ignition systems and improved carburetors and air filters have significantly reduced maintenance requirements. Gasoline mowers are much larger, with ranges from 23-inch cutting widths to 48-inch triple blade professional units. Ignition systems range from the standard rope-pull, recoil starters to push-button electric starters. Depending on the number of cycles, gasoline engines deliver from 3½ to 14 horsepower, the latter for professional units.

Mulching Mowers

Mulching mowers have a deeper deck and specially designed rotary blades that chop and rechop grass cuttings into tiny fragments that are scattered over the lawn to settle into the grass to decompose. The more powerful mulcher engines have 3½ to 5 horsepower.

Mulchers have not rendered conventional units obsolete by any means. At present, mulchers are only available in gasoline-powered models, so if you prefer electric units, you will have to bag or rake. Mulching mowers won't clip wet or tall grass properly, and too many clippings can smother a lawn.

Push (Walk-Behind) Mowers

Push mowers are the most economical power mowers. As the name indicates, these units are pushed from behind. They are usually lighter weight for greater maneuverability. Walk-behind mowers are available as mulchers, rear baggers, and convertibles, and with rope-pull, recoil, and electric starters.

Power-Propelled Mowers

With power-propelled or self-propelled models, the engine drives either the front or the rear wheels in addition to the blade. For larger properties, and especially for sloped areas, self-propulsion is certainly worth the extra $80 to $100. With most models, you can adjust the speed to your walking pace.

Riding Mowers

Riding mowers are for lawns 15,000 square feet and larger. In shopping for a riding mower, make sure the models have sufficient power, since the engine must drive from one to three blades, power the self-propelling gear train, and carry your weight. The latest models have mulching kits and improved maneuverability, down to a tight 20-inch turning radius. They are obviously limited in terms of trimming, so you'll need either a backup walk-behind unit or a good trimmer.

When selecting a riding mower, which range in power from 5 to 14 horsepower, look for a wide stance, pivoting front axle, and wide tires. These features will ensure stability as well as reduce tire damage to your lawn. Beware of cutting on a moderate slope and do not attempt to cut grass on steep inclines.

Check the range of cutting heights and the location of the adjustment. Be sure to test drive the model you are considering buying.

Safety Features

Safety regulations mandate that cutting blades remain idle when the mower is at rest. To accommodate these requirements, manufacturers equip mowers with one of two systems: a zone-recoil start or a blade-brake clutch. With a zone-recoil system, you start the machine while depressing a blade control bar under the handle. Whenever the bar is released, the engine shuts down. With the blade-brake clutch, only the rotary blade stops when the bar is released. The latter system is more costly than the standard zone-recoil feature.

Gasoline-Powered Mowers

SEARS CRAFTSMAN 37228

The Sears Craftsman 37228 is a two-speed front-wheel drive self-propelled mower with a four-horsepower Craftsman Eager I engine. The silver-and-black mower has a variable cutting height range of from 1⅜ to 3⅜ inches. The cutting swath is 22 inches and it has a bag capacity of two bushels. An optional mulching kit is available (#33232) for $22.78 and a clipping deflector (#33303) for $22.78.

Specifications: weight, 89 pounds. **Warranty:** one year, limited.

Approx. retail price	Approx. low price
$269	$269

Prices are accurate at time of printing; subject to manufacturer's change.

WHITE OUTDOOR 118R

The White Outdoor 118R is a self-propelled mulching mower. It employs a deep deck and a special mulching blade with a 21-inch swath to cut grass into ultrafine particles. The silver-and-black mower features a double-edge cutting blade and 1⅜-inch adjustable mowing height for a wide range of mowing conditions. It is powered by a five-horsepower Briggs & Stratton Quantum engine. It has nine-position fingertip height adjustment and touch speed control with extended rope start.
Specifications: weight, 92 pounds. **Warranty:** two years.

Approx. retail price	Approx. low price
$380	$307

BOLENS 8655 MULCHING MOWER

The Bolens 8655 Mulching Mower is a front-wheel drive self-propelled mulching mower featuring electric start. A single-lever height adjuster sets the mowing height (one to three inches) on all four wheels. This unit has a solid one-piece steel deck and steel rim wheels. A five-horsepower Briggs & Stratton Quantum engine powers this unit, which has a 22-inch cutting swath.
Specifications: weight, 88 pounds. **Warranty:** three years.

Approx. retail price	Approx. low price
$529	$499

Electric Mowers

SEARS CRAFTSMAN 37026

The Sears Craftsman 37026 is a nine-amp side bagger mower featuring a polymer deck and a variable single-height adjuster device to raise all four wheels at the same time. It has a cutting range height of 1¾ to 3½ inches. The blade/brake clutch system stops the blade from revolving when released.
Specifications: weight, 48 pounds. **Warranty:** one year, limited.

Approx. retail price	Approx. low price
$200	$180

Prices are accurate at time of printing; subject to manufacturer's change.

BLACK & DECKER M300

The Black & Decker M300 is a 6½-amp push mower with an 18-inch cutting swath, and one-touch height adjustment. It has a variable cutting range of 1⅜ to 3½ inches. The M300 is a side bagger, with a bag capacity of 1½ bushels.

Specifications: weight, 38 pounds. **Warranty:** two years.

Approx. retail price	Approx. low price
$278	not available

TORO 20564

RECOMMENDED

The Toro 20564 packs a powerful 10-amp, 110-volt Briggs & Stratton electric motor. The rear-bagging push mower features a 3-inch-deep red aluminum deck, a variable cutting height range of 1 to 3 inches, 6-inch diamond tread wheels, zone-start, folding handle, and a 2¼ bushel capacity.

Specifications: weight, 50 pounds. **Warranty:** two years.

Approx. retail price	Approx. low price
$359	$310

Riding Mowers

SEARS CRAFTSMAN 25506

The Sears Craftsman 25506 is a ten-horsepower silver-and-black rear-engine rider with bagger. The 25506 offers rear-wheel drive, electric start, 5-speed transaxle maneuverability, and a 30-inch cutting swath. It also has a variable cutting height range of 1½ to 4 inches and a 7-bushel bag capacity. This unit is equipped with Turf Saver tires. A mulching kit is optional.

Warranty: two years, limited.

Approx. retail price	Approx. low price
$1,000	$1,000

HOMELITE RE1030E

✓**BEST BUY**

The Homelite RE1030E features a 12-volt electric start. The five-speed transmission has variable forward speeds from zero

to five mph (miles per hour) and a reverse speed of 1½ mph. The Briggs & Stratton engine offers ten horsepower. The riding mower has an electric clutch for blade engagement, rack-and-pinion steering, and a turning radius of 30 inches. The cutting swath is 30½ inches. The bagging system holds seven bushels of clippings. An optional twin-blade mulching kit is available.
Warranty: two years.

Approx. retail price	Approx. low price
$1,500	$1,267

TORO RECYCLER 10-32

The Toro Recycler 10-32 is a mulching unit that offers a 32-inch mowing deck. It is powered by a ten-horsepower Briggs & Stratton engine with solid-state ignition and key start. It has an extremely tight 20-inch turning radius. The power train is a Peerless 700 with 5 forward speeds ranging from about 1½ to a little less than 5½ mph, there is also a reverse speed. The recycler feature cuts and recuts grass into fine particles.
Warranty: two years.

Approx. retail price	Approx. low price
$1,800	$1,549

ARIENS RM1232e RECOMMENDED

The Ariens RM1232e riding mower features a 12½-horsepower engine, rear-wheel drive, electric start, and optional rear bagging. It has a 32-inch cutting swath and has 6 forward speeds and 1 reverse speed. It has a preset variable cutting height range of 1½ to 4½ inches and a 26-inch turning radius. Bag capacity is four bushels. Optional accessories include a dethatcher, bagger, 40-inch front blade, front weights, and tire chains.
Warranty: parts, five years; **labor,** two years.

Approx. retail price	Approx. low price
$1,889	$1,780

WEED CUTTERS

Weed cutters, also called string trimmers, use a nylon cord attached to a hub at one end of a flexible or rigid shaft.

Lightweight and highly portable, these units are powered by either a gasoline engine or an electric motor. As the hub turns, the protruding string whips down weeds and grass. The string generally has a cutting swath of 10 to 20 inches. The string, which is on a spool, is advanced by bumping the hub or by manual or automatic systems.

Thoroughly clear an area of debris before using a weed trimmer and wear goggles, leather shoes, and socks when you operate this equipment. The cord, particularly on high-powered units, can turn stones or other debris into dangerous projectiles.

Special Applications

Some weed cutters have a dual function as a brushcutter and come with a machete-style blade and a saw blade. The string trimmer head is replaced by one of the blades for cutting heavier brush and even small trees. Extreme caution must be used to avoid getting the saw blade near hands or feet. Be sure to use only a blade specified for that particular trimmer.

Gasoline or Electric

Like mowers, the gas-powered trimmers are larger, more powerful, and more versatile than electric models. They have two-cycle engines that call for a mixture of oil and unleaded gasoline. A centrifugal clutch engages the hub when the engine accelerates. Gas models have cutting swaths from 16 to 20 inches and range in weight from 10 to 18 pounds.

Electric models, including cordless, are lightweight and easy to maintain. These units range in power from 2 to 5 amps, have cutting swaths of 9 to 16 inches, and weigh from 3 to 6½ pounds. For average yards, the heavy-duty electrics are certainly suitable.

Gasoline Models

HOMELITE ST-285BC

The Homelite ST-285BC is a two-cycle powered trimmer with a 17-inch cutting swath, dual-line head for smooth trimming, and easy-to-advance string. It has a straight drive shaft for accessing hard-to-reach areas under bushes and fences. An adjust-

able J-shaped bar handle offers balance and handling.
Specifications: weight, 10½ pounds. **Warranty:** two years.

Approx. retail price	Approx. low price
$180	not available

SEARS CRAFTSMAN 79716

The Sears Craftsman 79716 trimmer has 32-cubic-inch displacement power, and a 52-inch straight shaft housing designed for easy access under shrubs and bushes and for general maneuverability. The gear drive operation offers greater durability. The unit's centrifugal force generates automatic line feeding, eliminating the need to bump the head. The trimmer has two handles, cuts an 18-inch swath, and has a 40-inch spool.
Specifications: weight, 18 pounds. **Warranty:** two years.

Approx. retail price	Approx. low price
$198	$159

Electric Models

HOMELITE ST-20

The Homelite ST-20 packs two amps of power and has automatic line feed, which adjusts the string length without bumping the head. Extremely lightweight, the device is easy to handle. It cuts a ten-inch path and its comfort handle makes one-handed operation easy.
Specifications: weight, 3½ pounds. **Warranty:** two years.

Approx. retail price	Approx. low price
$36	not available

BLACK & DECKER
GROOM 'N' EDGE 600 ✔BEST BUY

The Black & Decker Groom 'N' Edge 600 is a 3¹⁄₁₆-amp unit that works both as a trimmer, and, when turned over, an edger. The two-handled device has a straight shaft for maneuverability. The Groom 'N' Edge 600 cuts a 12-inch path.
Specifications: weight, 7¼ pounds. **Warranty:** two years.

Prices are accurate at time of printing; subject to manufacturer's change.

Approx. retail price
$80

Approx. low price
$51

TORO CORDLESS 51720

The Toro Cordless 51720 packs a 12-volt, permanent-magnet motor and a 12,000 revolutions-per-minute line speed. It cuts a nine-inch swath. The 51720 has an automatic bump feed that requires tapping the hub to advance the line. It holds an ample charge to trim almost any yard.

Specifications: weight, 3 pounds. **Warranty:** one year.

Approx. retail price
$59
(without battery pack)
$109
(with battery pack)

Approx. low price
$62
(without battery pack)
not available
(with battery pack)

Snow Removal Equipment

Selecting the right snow removal equipment depends on the size of your property and the climate in which you live. Power shovels are for smaller jobs such as porches, steps, decks, and tight spots where larger, more powerful one- or two-stage walk-behind snow throwers cannot reach.

Power shovels are usually electric. The much larger and heavier snow throwers are, with some exceptions, driven by gasoline engines. A power shovel is a single-stage device with a plastic scoop-shaped housing containing a rotating drum fitted with a set of paddles. When the scoop is pushed into the snow, the paddles slice into the snow, whisk it around the scoop, and hurl it up and away through a deflector. Power shovels clear a 12- to 20-inch path and can throw upwards of 200 pounds of snow a minute. Lightweight and small, they are easily stored.

Walk-behind snow throwers are the work horses. They will clear driveways, sidewalks, and other large areas. They come in single- or two-stage thrower versions.

Single-stage snow throwers have a large metal scoop with a rotating auger formed of two reverse-pitch metal spirals, which rotate toward common paddles at the center. The augers break up the snow and force it into the center from both sides, where the paddles lift it and hurl it upward through a discharge chute at the top of the scoop. The chute can be positioned to throw snow to upwards of 40 feet in any direction within a 200-degree radius. These units clear an 18- to 24-inch path in one or two passes, depending on the depth, density, and wetness of the snow. One-stage throwers usually have a three- to four-horse-power engine. The units come in push-type and auger-pro-pelled versions with either recoil or electric starts.

Two-stage snow throwers combine a slow-speed auger with a rotating, high-speed impeller. The augers break and feed snow to the impeller, which throws it up and out of a chute at the top or side of the machine. Two-stage models can usually clear a path 24 to 32 inches wide, and have engines ranging from 5 to 10 horsepower. Most are self-propelled and have transmissions of up to six-forward and two-reverse speeds. The units come in high-traction pneumatic tire versions or rear track-driven systems.

Features

In shopping for snow removal equipment, there are several features to keep in mind. Electric starters are preferable to recoil systems, which become temperamental in deep winter. Many throwers offer electric start as an option and some offer electric with recoil backups. Snow thrower discharge chutes should rotate to more than 180 degrees to permit operation close to foundation walls and garage doors. Units should have at least four forward speeds, especially slower speeds, to help avoid jamming in heavy or wet snow. The skid shoes should be easy to adjust and should range from ground level to about 1½ inches for clearing unpaved areas. Larger throwers should have a variable weight transfer for stability under different snow conditions and for operating on a variety of surfaces.

In compliance with Consumer Product Safety Commission standards, most snow throwers have "deadman" controls that stop the machine when the clutch handles are released. Self-propelled units have two: one stops the auger and one stops the driving wheels.

Tips for Using a Snow Thrower

Fill the fuel tank with fresh fuel in the fall and keep it filled to the top at all times. This helps prevent water condensation caused by sudden temperature changes. Check the engine and gearbox oil levels regularly and wax the inside of your snow thrower's metal discharge chute to facilitate the movement of wet or sticky snow. Change oil at the end of the season.

If your snow thrower has been stored in a heated area, allow it to cool to outdoor temperature. A warm machine will melt snow and the moisture will freeze and jam the controls. If tires are slipping, you can equip your unit with tire chains.

Before you begin clearing operations, consider what is under the snowfall. Gravel, stones, and other debris can be scooped up and thrown by the machine. If you think this may happen, keep the clearing height of the thrower slightly above the ground by adjusting the skid shoes on larger models.

Begin removing snow from the center of the area and work outward. To avoid side spills, overlap each path you make. And remember that snow throwers can scoop up rocks and chunks of ice, which turn into missiles that can inflict real harm. Never operate a thrower when a bystander is nearby.

Best Buys '92

Our Best Buy snow removal equipment listed were chosen on the basis of efficient performance and value. Within each category, products are listed in order of quality. The item we consider the best of the Best Buys is first, followed by our second choice, and so on. Remember that a Best Buy designation applies only to the models listed. It does not necessarily apply to other models made by the same manufacturer or to an entire product line.

POWER SHOVELS

Power shovels are lightweight electric snow throwers that are manually guided and handled in much the same manner as a handheld snow shovel. The action of the paddle or auger displaces the snow so that no lifting is required. They are suitable for clearing steps, porches, patios, and balconies.

SEARS CRAFTSMAN 88201

The Sears Craftsman 88201 is a 4½-amp, 1-horsepower, electrically powered shovel with a 9-inch intake and one forward

speed. It clears a one-foot swath. The shovel has a forward aim with a fixed discharge chute.
Specifications: weight, 13 pounds. **Warranty:** one year.

Approx. retail price	Approx. low price
$100	$100

TORO ELECTRIC POWER SHOVEL 38310

The Toro Electric Power Shovel 38310 has a permanent magnet 6⅜-amp motor with 3 plastic straight blades, which can process up to 200 pounds of snow per minute. The throw distance is 20 feet and the unit will clear a 4-inch-deep driveway that is 50 by 20 feet in about 25 minutes.
Specifications: weight, 12 pounds. **Warranty:** one year.

Approx. retail price	Approx. low price
$129	$100

SINGLE-STAGE SNOW THROWERS

Single-stage snow throwers are excellent units for moderate snowfalls. They clear up to 10 inches of dry snow or 3 to 4 inches of wet snow. They are propelled by pushing and by the pulling action of the augers on the snow and ground.

SEARS CRAFTSMAN 8829

The Sears Craftsman 8829 is a 12-amp, 3-horsepower, electrically powered snow thrower with an 11-inch intake and a single forward speed and a pull reverse. The auger-propelled, steel and high-impact plastic unit cuts a 21-inch swath and has a 190 degree rotation of the discharge chute.
Specifications: weight, 67 pounds. **Warranty:** one year.

Approx. retail price	Approx. low price
$300	$300

WHITE OUTDOOR SNOWBOSS 350

The White Outdoor Snowboss 350 is powered by a three-horsepower Tecumseh gasoline engine with electric start. The spiral auger-propelled design brings snow to the center before throwing it out the freeze-proof poly discharge chute. This unit clears a 21-inch path. Other features include a 190-degree rotation chute, 7- by 1½-inch wheels, vinyl-edged auger for a clean finish, folding handles, and handle-mounted auger clutch. **Specifications: weight,** 75 pounds. **Warranty:** two years.

Approx. retail price	Approx. low price
$450	$372

JOHN DEERE TRS21 SNOW THROWER

The John Deere TRS21 Snow Thrower packs a 2-cycle, 4-horsepower Tecumseh gasoline engine with a rotating discharge chute (up to 190 degrees). The auger-propelled model has folding handles, foam-rubber grip, sealed ball bearings, and eight-inch wheels. It cuts a 21-inch swath.
Specifications: weight, 77 pounds (recoil), 89 pounds (electric). **Warranty:** two years.

Approx. retail price	Approx. low price
$529	$512
(recoil start)	(recoil start)
$599	$569
(electric start)	(electric start)

TWO-STAGE SNOW THROWERS

Two-stage snow throwers are designed for tackling cold-weather climates with frequent and significant snowfalls. These heavyweights cut wide paths and move snow and ice with speed, elevation, and efficiency.

ARIENS ST524

The Ariens ST524 offers a five-horsepower Tecumseh gasoline engine and a transmission with five forward speeds and one reverse speed. This self-propelled unit has rear-wheel drive, adjustable skid shoes, and pneumatic tires. It plows a 24-inch path and directs snow through a 220-degree rotation chute.

Specifications: weight, 160 pounds. **Warranty: parts,** five years; **labor,** two years.

Approx. retail price	Approx. low price
$899	$829

BOLENS 5210

The Bolens 5210 packs a five-horsepower Tecumseh Snow King gasoline-powered engine. This self-propelled unit features rear-wheel drive, three forward speeds and one reverse speed, adjustable skid shoes, 220-degree rotation discharge chute, adjustable snow blowing direction, and 10½-inch wheels. The width of the clearing path is 21 inches.

Specifications: weight, 162 pounds. **Warranty:** three years.

Approx. retail price	Approx. low price
$799	$774

SEARS CRAFTSMAN 88482

The Sears Craftsman 88482 is a five-horsepower model with a Tecumseh-built gasoline-powered engine, six forward and two reverse speeds, a track-propelled 51- by 4¾-inch drive system, adjustable skid shoes, and clutch system. The unit features a weight-transfer system that shifts weight to the front to dig down into hard-packed snow. The discharge chute has a 190 degree rotation. The 88482 cuts a 24-inch swath.

Specifications: weight, 170 pounds. **Warranty:** two years.

Approx. retail price	Approx. low price
$700	$700

JOHN DEERE TRS24

The John Deere TRS24 is a full-featured gasoline-powered unit offering a five-horsepower Tecumseh Snow King engine and rear-wheel drive. This self-propelled unit has six forward and two reverse speeds. Other features include blade/brake-clutch system to halt the blade but not the motor, 200-degree rotating discharge chute, and variable snow blowing directions.

Specifications: weight, 247 pounds. **Warranty:** two years.

Approx. retail price	Approx. low price
$959	$895

Prices are accurate at time of printing; subject to manufacturer's change.

Food Preparation Appliances

Most kitchens in the United States have a coffee maker, a toaster or toaster oven, a food processor, a mixer, and several other standard food preparation appliances. New products that are more efficient, more compact, and easier to use are developed every year. Some are conveniences we use every day; others are passing fads or meet the culinary needs of only a few people.

Best Buys '92

Our Best Buy and Recommended food preparation appliances follow. They are divided into the following categories: food processors, electric mixers, blenders, coffee makers, toasters, toaster ovens, and specialty food preparation appliances. With the exception of toaster ovens, these categories are further divided into appropriate subcategories. Products within a category or subcategory are listed according to quality. The best of the Best Buys is first, followed by our second choice, and so on. A Best Buy or Recommended designation applies only to the model listed; it does not necessarily apply to other models made by the same manufacturer or to an entire product line.

FOOD PROCESSORS

The first home food processor was a basic machine that could handle chopping, mixing, and pureeing with a simple on/off/pulse motion. Considered by many to be nothing more than a sophisticated toy for culinary artists, the food processor has earned its place in the kitchen alongside coffee makers and mixers.

The original idea has been revised upward and downward. Bigger, more powerful machines can now knead dough for two loaves of bread or slice a whole tomato that has been pushed through an expanded feed tube. Smaller models store compactly on the counter and have smaller work bowls that are efficient for processing a single onion, a handful of parsley, or a cup of mayonnaise. Mini mincers dispense with slicing and shredding discs and specialize in chopping such small amounts of food as a clove of garlic or a tablespoon of herbs. Mini mincers also puree a single serving of baby food or grind coffee or spices.

Since food processors range in price from about $30 to about $350, and because each kind of machine has advantages and drawbacks, you should assess your needs and budget before you go shopping. Ask yourself the following questions:

• How much do I cook? Do I bring home take-out food during the work week and cook only under duress on weekends? Or do I spend time in the kitchen baking, trying new recipes, and chopping ingredients?

• How many people do I usually cook for?

• How hard will I work the machine? Will I use it to knead bread dough or only for slicing and chopping?

• Do I want a food processor that does more than the basics? Should it be able to cut French fries, juice oranges, or whip cream?

Once you answer these questions, you are ready to consider the major kinds of food processors. In general, size is related to price, but not necessarily to quality. The largest machines have strong motors for big jobs and hard work. They usually come with an impressive warranty that helps justify the high cost. Most have options and attachments, such as specialty cutting discs, juice extractors, citrus juicers, or whipping whisks. Less expensive machines are not nearly as powerful as the big machines, but they are capable of kneading dough for a single loaf of bread. Some offer labor-saving accessories such as a second work bowl or a continuous feed chute.

Many compact models adequately meet the needs of small families. These models slice, chop, mince, and shred. Some knead bread dough or continuously spew out processed ingredients into a waiting bowl. Mini mincers handle only very small jobs, and many cooks use them with a larger food processor.

Once you have decided which size food processor is best for your kitchen, carefully read all instructions before you begin. You are likely to overprocess food at first, since most jobs take only a few seconds. Because of their power and speed, you must handle a food processor safely. Keep it out of the reach of children, be sure it is stable on the counter and that the cord is out of the way, and be very careful when you handle the blades and discs.

Large Food Processors

CUISINART DLC-7 FPC FOOD PREPARATION CENTER

The Cuisinart DLC-7 FPC Food Preparation Center is a multi-function appliance with a direct-drive motor designed for handling extra-large quantities. This powerful machine can handle all sorts of tasks—from kneading bread dough to slicing carrots and cabbage for coleslaw. Plus, with the additional whisk attachment, the Food Preparation Center virtually becomes a stand mixer, too. Both large and small feed tubes accommodate whole fruits and vegetables, such as apples and potatoes, in addition to long, thin produce. Cuisinart's easy-to-operate on and pulse/off switches make speedy work of everyday tasks. The Center processes up to 14 cups of sliced or shredded produce or enough dough for about 8 dozen cookies. In addition to the whisk attachment, this machine comes with a stainless-steel chopping blade, reinforced plastic dough blade, serrated slicing disc, medium shredding disc, and plastic spatula. Optional attachments include a fine shredding disc; fine and medium julienne discs; a French fry disc; ultrathin, thin, medium, thick, and extra-thick slicing discs; and a citrus juicer attachment.

Warranty: three years, limited.

Approx. retail price	Approx. low price
$350	$310

MOULINEX DELUXE KITCHEN MACHINE MODEL 097

The Moulinex Deluxe Kitchen Machine Model 097, with its many attachments, will not only handle all your processing tasks; it will also blend a frothy milkshake or turn your favorite fruit into a healthy juice beverage. The large, tinted work bowl processes up to seven cups of dry ingredients or up to four cups of liquid puree. An on/off/pulse switch plus variable speed control renders precision results. The Deluxe Kitchen Machine comes with a stainless-steel chopping blade, a plastic dough blade, two reversible slicing/grating discs, a masher/puree attachment, French fry and emulsifier discs, a mini chopper, a blender, citrus juicer and juice extractor attachments, and a spatula. This machine also features convenient cord storage.

Warranty: parts and labor, one year, limited.

Approx. retail price	Approx. low price
$230	$175

Smaller Food Processors

CUISINART CLASSIC DLC 10C FOOD PROCESSOR ✓BEST BUY

The Cuisinart Classic DLC 10C Food Processor is a standard-size food processor with the same capacity as the original Cuisinart food processor. Its off-white base houses a powerful direct-drive motor capable of processing dough for two standard loaves or grinding up to 1¼ pounds of meat in a single batch. A three-position lever lets you switch from off to on to pulse in seconds. Standard parts include a large amber-tinted work bowl, a cover with both large and small feed tubes to handle a multitude of processing tasks, a stainless-steel chopping/mixing blade, a reinforced plastic dough blade, a serrated slicing disc, a medium shredding disc, and a plastic spatula. Optional attachments include a fine shredding disc, fine and medium julienne discs, a French fry disc, a range of slicing discs, and whisk and citrus juicer attachments.

Warranty: three years, limited.

Approx. retail price	Approx. low price
$200	$163

BRAUN MULTIPRACTIC DELUXE VARIABLE-SPEED CONTROL FOOD PROCESSOR UK-240

The Braun Multipractic Deluxe Variable-Speed Control Food Processor UK-240 is a complete food preparation system. The electronic variable-speed control dial lets you select the optimum speed for the job. A unique disc system adjusts from thick to thin slicing as well as coarse and fine shredding, grating, and French fry/julienne cutting. This machine is also equipped with a heavy-duty stainless-steel dough hook. Besides the standard work bowl, the UK-240 also comes with a heavy-duty stainless-steel chopping blade, a whisk attachment, a wide feed tube that swings out to allow easy loading of whole fruits and vegetables, and a stationary feed tube for use during mixing or blending. The large work bowl can accommodate up to 6½ cups of sliced or shredded produce or about 4 cups of slightly liquid ingredients. This unit also features thermostat overload protection and convenient cord storage.

Warranty: one year, limited.

Approx. retail price	Approx. low price
$170	$155

REGAL DELUXE PROCESSOR PLUS K7751

RECOMMENDED

The Regal Deluxe Processor Plus K7751 is a full-size processor that also functions as a mini chopper, blender, and

Prices are accurate at time of printing; subject to manufacturer's change.

coffee/spice grinder. For big jobs, use the large work bowl and base. For small jobs and for grinding spices or coffee beans, use the small work bowl and base. As an added convenience, this unit also comes with a blender carafe, which fits onto the small work base. Other standard equipment for the Deluxe Processor Plus includes a stainless-steel chopping/mixing blade, a reversible stainless-steel slicing/shredding disc, and thick-slice and coarse-shred discs. The chopper unit comes with a specially designed blade and heavy-duty bowl insert for use during grinding. The Deluxe Processor Plus features a sliding electronic variable speed control in addition to an on/off/pulse switch and selector switch that permits independent operation of the small and large work bases. A detachable storage compartment in the back of the unit stores the accessory blades when not in use.

Warranty: one year, limited.

Approx. retail price	Approx. low price
$170	$115

SUNBEAM OSKAR 3000 ELECTRONIC FOOD PROCESSOR 14201   RECOMMENDED

The Sunbeam Oskar 3000 Electronic Food Processor 14201 is a compact and versatile appliance. Its powerful six-speed motor also features a pulse setting for better processing control. Electronic engineering assures consistent results whether you're slicing a potato or making vichyssoise. This unit comes with a stainless-steel chopping blade, two stainless-steel slicing/shredding discs, and a whipping disc for stirring sauces and whipping cream. The unique work bowl has a cone-shaped bottom to prevent smaller quantities from getting lost and underprocessed. You can knead a loaf of bread dough or half a pound of pasta dough or process up to four cups of relish in a single batch. Convenient cord storage saves counter clutter. For added convenience, the bowl and attachments are dishwasher safe.

Warranty: two years.

Approx. retail price	Approx. low price
$80	$49

Prices are accurate at time of printing; subject to manufacturer's change.

Compact Food Processors

CUISINART LITTLE PRO PLUS FOOD PROCESSOR (LPP)

The Cuisinart Little Pro Plus Food Processor (LPP) is designed for those who want full-size performance and features in a compact unit. It is efficient, versatile, and surprisingly quiet. The Little Pro Plus includes two work bowls—clear for chopping or mixing and white with a chute for continuous slicing or shredding. It also includes a stainless-steel chopping/mixing blade, a serrated slicing disc, a medium-fine shredding disc, a spatula, and a juicer attachment with three stackable reamers for juicing lemons, oranges, and grapefruit. The clear work bowl can accommodate up to three cups of sliced or shredded fruit, cheese, or vegetables, or enough dough for two dozen cookies in a single batch. With the continuous slicing chute, the Little Pro Plus can speed through unlimited quantities of produce. A single on/off/pulse control makes operating the unit a snap.
Warranty: three years, limited.

Approx. retail price	Approx. low price
$115	$103

MOULINEX COMPACT FOOD PROCESSOR MODEL 305

RECOMMENDED

The Moulinex Compact Food Processor Model 305 comes with a stainless-steel chopping blade, slicing and shredding blades, an emulsifier disc for high-speed whipping, and a spatula. Slice or shred up to five cups of produce or process up to two cups of slightly liquid puree in the 40-ounce work bowl. Electronic variable speed control lets you choose the perfect setting for the job. On, off, and pulse buttons allow easy fingertip operation.
Warranty: parts and labor, one year, limited.

Approx. retail price	Approx. low price
$95	$73

BRAUN MULTIPRACTIC MC100

RECOMMENDED

The Braun Multipractic MC100 is a space-saving compact food processor that can handle all the basics. This machine has both

Prices are accurate at time of printing; subject to manufacturer's change.

single-speed and pulse settings and comes with stainless-steel chopping, slicing, and shredding blades. You can process up to two cups of sliced carrots or carrot puree, or mix and grind doughs and meats. Liquids and last-minute ingredients can be added directly through the feed tube. This unit is also equipped with thermostat overload protection, non-slip rubber feet, and convenient cord storage.

Warranty: one year, limited.

Approx. retail price	Approx. low price
$76	$69

Mini Mincers

BLACK & DECKER HANDY SHORTCUT II MICRO PROCESSOR HMP60

The Black & Decker Handy Shortcut II Micro Processor HMP60 can handle virtually all of the tasks you would expect from a full-size machine, yet it takes a fraction of the space in your kitchen. The two-cup work bowl is perfect for mincing onions, garlic, and fresh herbs, grinding small amounts of nuts, and pureeing baby food. Plus, thanks to a continuous flow chute attachment, the Handy Shortcut II can also slice and shred directly into your own work bowl. This unit comes with a stainless-steel chopping blade and a reversible slicing/shredding disc. An on/off/pulse button helps prevent overprocessing. A curly, telephone-style cord reduces counter clutter and rubber feet provide stability. All of the parts except the base are dishwasher safe for easy cleanup.

Warranty: two years.

Approx. retail price	Approx. low price
$42	$33

KRUPS "MINIPRO EXTRA" MINI FOOD PROCESSOR 718

The Krups "Minipro Extra" Mini Food Processor 718 is both compact and powerful. The clear, 19-ounce work bowl can accom-

Prices are accurate at time of printing; subject to manufacturer's change.

modate up to one ounce of parsley, a half-cup chopped onion, or about one cup of chopped apples. For extra convenience, this unit comes with a second work bowl allowing you to perform multiple processing jobs or two batches at one time. Its touch-and-release button is easy to use and produces uniform results. The see-through lid is contoured for easy addition of liquids during processing—especially useful when making sauces or mayonnaise. This machine also features wraparound cord storage and a plastic spatula for scraping the work bowl.

Warranty: one year.

Approx. retail price	Approx. low price
$50	$30

CUISINART MINI-MATE PLUS CHOPPER/GRINDER MM-2M

The Cuisinart Mini-Mate Plus Chopper/Grinder MM-2M blends sauces or mayonnaise, purees baby food, grates cheese or chocolates, and minces garlic or herbs in an instant. Its strong motor can also grind coffee beans, nuts, or peppercorns. The motor is housed in a white plastic cover that sits atop the clear work bowl. This unit features two-speed push-button operation and dual blade positions for added versatility. The reversible metal blade is sharp on one side for chopping soft foods, and blunt on the other for grinding, grating, or pureeing. It can process up to two ounces in each batch. Large foods must first be cut into ½-inch pieces, but herbs, spices, nuts, and coffee beans can be processed whole. A tiny spatula is also included for scraping the work bowl. The bowl and blade are dishwasher safe. Rubber feet add stability.

Warranty: two years, limited.

Approx. retail price	Approx. low price
$40	$28

MOULINEX MAXI-CHOPPER MODEL 094

RECOMMENDED

The Moulinex Maxi-Chopper Model 094 comes with a 16-ounce clear work bowl, which has measurements marked in liters as well as ounces to allow you to measure and process the exact amount you need—especially useful for baby foods and for

Prices are accurate at time of printing; subject to manufacturer's change.

those who are dieting. The motor is housed in the Maxi-Chopper's non-slip cover. An easy pulse-action switch operates the machine. Mince herbs and spices, chop nuts, or grind meat in seconds. The machine's uniquely shaped work bowl and large capacity also let you blend a creamy milkshake in seconds. As with other mini mincers, larger foods, such as onions, must first be cut into small pieces for even results.

Warranty: parts and labor, one year, limited.

Approx. retail price	Approx. low price
$35	$35

ELECTRIC MIXERS

When it comes to whipping cream or egg whites, mixing batter for cakes, cookies, or muffins, or blending creamy fudge or frostings, there is still nothing better than a reliable mixer. Frequent and heavy mixing jobs, such as cookie and bread doughs, require a sturdy stand mixer. These powerful workhorses can handle even the most rigorous jobs with ease. Light and occasional mixing can be completed quickly and conveniently with hand mixers. Of course, the ultimate in convenience is a cordless mixer, which can go to work wherever and whenever the need arises.

Portable Mixers

KITCHENAID ULTRA POWER PLUS HAND MIXER KHM5TWH

The KitchenAid Ultra Power Plus Hand Mixer KHM5TWH exhibits many of the features that made its counterpart—KitchenAid's stand mixer—a kitchen tradition. This sturdy five-speed mixer can handle all the basics—from cake batter to whipped cream—and even tough mixing tasks, such as heavy cookie dough. Exclusive self-cleaning TurboBeaters have no center posts for dough to climb and clog mixing action. Made of sturdy wire, these beaters cut cleanly through ingredients for optimum mixing, beating, and whipping action. The smooth, rounded design and angled handle allow for easy cleanup and a comfortable grip. A thumb-operated control lets you adjust speeds in an instant. An electronic sensor automatically adjusts when more power is needed to maintain a consistent speed. This unit also features a heel rest for added stability.

Warranty: parts and labor, one year.

Approx. retail price	Approx. low price
$65	$63

CUISINART CORDLESS HAND MIXER CM-3

✓BEST BUY

The Cuisinart Cordless Hand Mixer CM-3 is ready when and where you want it. This powerful mixer recharges in its own compact base, which can either be wall-mounted or sit on your counter. It beats eggs, blends puddings and frostings, mixes batter for cakes, cookies, and brownies, or whips cream in record time. Best of all, you can do all these things with no bulky cord to get in the way. The beaters are made of stainless steel, so they produce significantly greater volume with egg whites and cream. They can also handle tough mixing jobs such as brownie and cookie batter. Incredibly powerful for a cordless appliance, the Cuisinart Cordless Hand Mixer is also sturdy and well balanced. It has three speeds: high, medium, and a pulse/low setting. A red light in the handle indicates connection.

Warranty: three years, limited.

Approx. retail price	Approx. low price
$70	$55

BLACK & DECKER SPATULA SMART 6-SPEED MIXER M22S

RECOMMENDED

The Black & Decker Spatula Smart 6-Speed Mixer M22S has six speeds to handle a full range of food-preparation tasks. For mixing thin to medium batters, this unit comes with a plastic spatula that snaps onto the beaters and continuously scrapes the bowl sides to help prevent splatter buildup and eliminate the clumps that can form when dry ingredients aren't thoroughly mixed. Without the spatula attachment, this sturdy, well-balanced mixer goes to work on heavier batters. Use of the spatula attachment is also not recommended for use during whipping

Prices are accurate at time of printing; subject to manufacturer's change.

since this may reduce the volume. The mixer's smooth design and closed handle make it comfortable to hold, even during extended mixing tasks. The thumb-operated control switch is easy to use. For added convenience, the beaters can be snapped onto the sides of the mixer for storage.

Warranty: two years.

Approx. retail price	Approx. low price
$30	$22

OSTER 8-SPEED ELECTRONIC HAND MIXER 5310-20 RECOMMENDED

The Oster 8-Speed Electronic Hand Mixer 5310-20 comes with several unique attachments—a whisk, a drink mixing rod, a stir paddle and a blade, in addition to the standard mixing beaters. These make it versatile as well as efficient. Electronic controls adapt power and speed to prevent the motor from slowing or stopping during heavy mixing jobs or racing during light mixing jobs. Beaters are positioned in-line rather than side by side, which creates a narrow profile that works well in small spaces and also allows for easy storage in a kitchen drawer or cabinet.

Warranty: two years, limited.

Approx. retail price	Approx. low price
$52	not available

Stand Mixers

KITCHENAID K5SS

The KitchenAid K5SS is the mixer of preference for many professional chefs. This mixer features a powerful motor with ten speed settings, a sturdy base with rubber feet to protect the countertop, and unique planetary mixing action to ensure thorough blending of ingredients. Standard equipment includes a five-quart stainless-steel mixing bowl with handle, a flat beater, a heavy-duty dough hook, and a stainless-steel wire whip. The mixer is available in white, almond, imperial gray, onyx black, cobalt blue, and empire green. With a number of optional accessories, the K5SS converts to a food grinder, a pasta

---

Prices are accurate at time of printing; subject to manufacturer's change.

maker, a fruit/vegetable strainer, a sausage stuffer, a rotor slicer/shredder, a grain mill, a citrus juicer, and even a can opener.
Warranty: parts and labor, one year.

Approx. retail price	Approx. low price
$400	$296

OSTER EURO 12-SPEED ELECTRONIC MIXER

RECOMMENDED

The Oster Euro 12-Speed Electronic Mixer comes with 1½-quart and 4-quart stainless-steel bowls to accommodate both small and large mixing jobs. Electronic sensors assess load demand and automatically adjust power to maintain a constant speed. A dial control lets you shift settings quickly and easily from folding and light blending to whipping and aerating. Automatic bowl rotation affords hands-free mixing. This machine is also equipped with heavy-duty dough hooks.
Warranty: two years, limited.

Approx. retail price	Approx. low price
$139	$50

BLENDERS

All the newfangled contraptions on the market still haven't replaced the reliable blender for crushing ice, pureeing liquid food items, and, of course, blending frosty beverages. Of the two types available, carafe units provide added power and their own containers for heavy jobs, such as crushing ice. Immersion blenders offer the added convenience of being able to go directly into the container you happen to be working with.

Traditional Blenders

OSTER 10-SPEED OSTERIZER BLENDER 890-28

The Oster 10-Speed Osterizer Blender 890-28 offers seven continuous speeds for smooth blending plus three touch-and-

Prices are accurate at time of printing; subject to manufacturer's change.

release pulse-action speeds for chopping hard food and crushing ice. A powerful motor combines with a tapered carafe that has internal ribs for optimum blending efficiency. Chop, grate, grind, stir, puree, whip, mix, blend, frappe, or liquefy a full range of ingredients. The five-cup shatter-resistant Perma-Glas carafe is marked for easy measuring. This unit also comes with a one-cup Mini-Blend jar and a cover for convenient blending and storing. The cover is useful for do-ahead food preparation jobs, condiments, or baby foods.

Warranty: one year, limited.

Approx. retail price	Approx. low price
$51	$40

WARING VORTEX 10 VB100-1

The Waring Vortex 10 VB100-1 features six continuous and four pulse-blend speeds for quick and easy blending. Simply lock the 45-ounce shatter-resistant carafe onto the motor base, select Lo or High and the desired setting, and go to work. Exclusive vortex action assures even blending. The Strain 'n' Serve lid lets you pour off liquids and a Twist-Loc removable lid insert doubles as a two-ounce measuring cup. This model also features Waring's Sure-Grip handle, Spill-Guard carafe, and tip resistant base.

Warranty: parts, one year; **motor,** five years.

Approx. retail price	Approx. low price
$50	$29

Immersion Blenders

BRAUN MULTIPRACTIC HAND BLENDER PLUS MINCER/CHOPPER MR50

The Braun Multipractic Hand Blender Plus Mincer/Chopper MR50 is an easy-to-use, single-speed immersion blender that performs many of the tasks of a traditional blender yet saves valuable cleanup time by eliminating the need for a carafe. The MR50 consists of a contoured power base and stem fitted with

Prices are accurate at time of printing; subject to manufacturer's change.

a standard chopping blade. The chopping blade can be inserted into a standard mixing bowl or saucepan, or, thanks to its slender design, a tall drinking glass or mug. The multipurpose mincer/chopper attachment converts the MR50 into a mini food processor for chopping and mixing tasks in a convenient splatter-proof container. The mincer/chopper has a dry or liquid capacity of about seven ounces. This unit also comes with a mixing beaker and a wall bracket for convenient off-the-counter storage. To clean, simply rinse the stem under running water. **Warranty:** one year, limited.

Approx. retail price	Approx. low price
$38	$25

CUISINART QUICK PREP HAND BLENDER CSB1

The Cuisinart Quick Prep Hand Blender CSB1 breezes through a variety of food preparation tasks. Three attachments—a stainless-steel chopping/mincing blade, a stainless-steel blending/mixing disc, and a plastic whipping/beating attachment—handle everything from mixing shakes and salad dressings to whipping cream and pureeing vegetables. Simply choose your attachment and insert the stem into your work container. An up-and-down motion delivers fast, uniform results. For added convenience, this unit comes with a see-through Lexan mixing beaker with clearly marked measurements in ounces, cups, and liters. To clean the blender, simply rinse stem and blades under running water. The beaker is both dishwasher and microwave safe. The Cuisinart Quick Prep Hand Blender CSB1 also features cord wrap and a wall bracket for off-the-counter storage. **Warranty:** 18 months, limited.

Approx. retail price	Approx. low price
$60	$57

COFFEE MAKERS

The tradition of starting the day with a cup of coffee has become an American cliche. However, the path divides when it comes to the preparation of the beverage. Some prefer gourmet beans and a chic Euro-styled coffee maker. Others

---

Prices are accurate at time of printing; subject to manufacturer's change.

want the convenience of pre-measured coffee filter packets and a no-nonsense machine that wakes you up to a full pot of automatically brewed coffee.

The key to successful coffee maker shopping starts with an understanding of your needs and habits. If your counter space doesn't allow for this appliance to take up residence, a unit that mounts under the cabinet is the perfect solution. If you only have the time or desire for a quick cup or two in the morning, a mini model may be just right. If coffee is an all-day affair, an insulated carafe that keeps coffee hot away from the brewing stand might be the perfect option. Remember, the variety of choices can be overwhelming, but your needs, in combination with the cost, will lead you to the correct purchase. So, when you scan through this chapter, don't just consider the bottom line, take a look at all of the entries—you might change your mind about the Best Buy for you. Here's an overview of categories and features to service every type of thirst.

The speed of automatic drip units will always keep them in the forefront. They produce excellent coffee and come in a range of sizes, shapes, and colors, with features that range from basic to elaborate. Most low-cost, no-frills models will have an on light and a warming plate. More expensive units will grab your attention with timers, drip-stop (which allows brewing to be interrupted to pour a cup of coffee), automatic shut-off, etc. Small one- to four-cup models will answer the call for fewer cups at home or the office, but the 10- to 12-cup units are still leaders since they have the versatility to serve a couple or a crowd.

Some prefer to sacrifice automatic drip's quick brewing to get the flavor and aroma of perked coffee. Those who like extra-strong coffee often find this method ideal; but, a new generation of percolators have faster brewing cycles. For serving large parties, an over-size electric percolator is the coffee maker of choice. Generous capacity and self-serving taps make them an essential convenience item when serving a crowd. Our reviews of electric percolators follow those of automatic drip units.

Our coffee makers are categorized as follows: large-capacity automatic drip coffee makers, small capacity automatic drip coffee makers, electric percolators, and a large-capacity electric percolator. Espresso/cappucino makers are listed under specialty food preparation appliances.

Large-Capacity Automatic Drip Coffee Makers

MR. COFFEE SRX20

The Mr. Coffee SRX20 is a dependable model that offers a digital clock timer/brewer. Other features include a lighted on switch, two-hour safety automatic shut-off, and pause 'n' serve. The coffee maker base is white with black trim.
Warranty: one year.

Approx. retail price	Approx. low price
$40	$19

PROCTOR-SILEX A8737 ✔BEST BUY

The Proctor-Silex A8737 has beautiful European styling (in black with white trim) and an electronic clock/brewer. The A8737 also boasts an impressive full two-year warranty, pause 'n' serve, and cord storage (to hide extra cord for a neat appearance). This unit has a two-hour automatic shut-off.
Warranty: two years.

Approx. retail price	Approx. low price
$70	$38

BLACK & DECKER SPACEMAKER SDC1G `RECOMMENDED`

The Black & Decker Spacemaker SDC1G is an updated, dependable coffee maker. In contemporary white or gray, this coffee maker offers ten-cup capacity and a removable water reservoir that you can carry to the sink. For counter clearance, the coffee maker measures only 10¼ inches tall.
Warranty: two years.

Approx. retail price	Approx. low price
$55	$42

OSTER 3420-08 `RECOMMENDED`

The Oster 3420-08 is a full-featured model that offers a thermal carafe to keep coffee hot away from the base. In addition, the sleek white 3420-08 has automatic brewing. It has a two- to

Prices are accurate at time of printing; subject to manufacturer's change.

ten-cup capacity, a removable water reservoir (for easy at-sink fill-ups), and automatic shut-off.
Warranty: one year, limited.

Approx. retail price	Approx. low price
$60	$50

KRUPS 150 `RECOMMENDED`

The Krups 150 offers great design and great coffee. The looks are top-of-the-line, but the price is considerably lower. Fancy features are not the point here—classic value is. Basics like a lighted on switch and cord storage are offered. It's available in white or black. The 150 uses paper filters or an optional permanent gold filter that can be purchased for an additional $18.00.
Warranty: one year, limited.

Approx. retail price	Approx. low price
$55	$50

Small-Capacity Automatic Drip Coffee Makers

PROCTOR-SILEX A8004 ✔BEST BUY

The Proctor-Silex A8004 is an all-white, small-scale appliance that is a curvaceous counter show-off. Looks are not the only advantage of the A8004. The one- to four-cup coffee maker offers pause 'n' serve (a feature generally saved for larger top-of-the-line models) and a lighted on switch.
Warranty: one year, limited.

Approx. retail price	Approx. low price
$30	$20

MR. COFFEE JR4 ✔BEST BUY

The Mr. Coffee JR4 has a low price while still providing good quality and great coffee. It's even good-looking and quite portable and storable at only 10½ inches tall and 3⅘ pounds. A no-nonsense mini coffeemaker, the JR4 has one- to four-cup capacity, and an illuminated on switch. It uses cupcake-style fil-

Prices are accurate at time of printing; subject to manufacturer's change.

ters (a starter package of filters is included).
Warranty: one year.

Approx. retail price	Approx. low price
$20	$19

BLACK & DECKER DCM400   RECOMMENDED

The Black & Decker DCM400 is an attractive small-scale coffee maker in white. Fancy features aren't the draw here. Instead, the DCM400 is a quality appliance that simply produces a good cup of coffee for a good price.
Warranty: two years.

Approx. retail price	Approx. low price
$27	$19

Electric Percolators

PRESTO 02811   ✓ BEST BUY

The Presto 02811 is made of sturdy stainless steel and features a ready light (which illuminates when coffee is finished brewing), removable cord, cool-to-touch plastic handles, and traditional styling. This model has a 4- to 12-cup capacity, and uses 800 watts of power to brew a full pot in just 12 minutes. It has quite an extraordinary price for a stainless percolator.
Warranty: two years, limited.

Approx. retail price	Approx. low price
$68	$37

WEST BEND 54129   RECOMMENDED

The West Bend 54129 is a smaller percolator (five- to nine-cup capacity) that has the industry's standard cool-touch plastic handles and lid. But it also features a plastic spout to add a clever extra-measure of safety. The rest of the coffee maker is made of polished aluminum. A twist-and-lock lid prevents accidental spills and the cord is detachable.
Warranty: parts and labor, one year.

Approx. retail price	Approx. low price
$29	$18

Prices are accurate at time of printing; subject to manufacturer's change.

Large-Capacity Electric Percolator

WEST BEND 58030 ✔BEST BUY

The West Bend 58030 is a crowd-size server/brewer (measuring 15 inches high and 9 inches wide) at a sensational price. It produces 12 to 30 cups of coffee. The 58030 has an aluminum pot with black trim that coordinates with any style of table or buffet decor. This percolator features a twist-lock lid (to help prevent accidental spills), a detachable cord (which fits inside the urn for easy storage), a two-way dripless faucet for convenient self-service, and a safety light that turns on when the brewing cycle is complete. The parts are top-rack dishwasher safe, but the base is nonimmersible.
Warranty: parts and labor, one year.

Approx. retail price	Approx. low price
$49	$27

TOASTERS

Toast—plain and simple—is still best prepared in a machine designed exclusively for that purpose. For fast, even toasting, the standard, reliable toaster does the job. Today's toasters also handle an assortment of other breakfast delicacies—from muffins and pastries to bagels and frozen waffles. For more versatility, a toaster oven can bake, broil, and top brown. Dimensions and capacities vary, so determine your needs before you go shopping.

Two-Slice Toasters

FARBERWARE PREMIER TWO-SLICE TOASTER T2220 ✔BEST BUY

The Farberware Premier Two-Slice Toaster T2220 features precision temperature settings to assure consistent results with each use. Toast two hearty slices of bread, bagels, muffins, or pastries. Select a setting—from light to dark—and push down on the wide lever. Stay-cool front and back panels offer safe, convenient handling. A non-stick exterior and hinged-bottom crumb tray provide easy cleanup. The Farberware Premier Two-Slice Toaster is available in white or black (Model T2280). **Warranty: parts and labor,** one year.

Approx. retail price	Approx. low price
$30	$30

KRUPS "TOASTRONIC I" COOL-TOUCH MICROCHIP LONG SLOT TOASTER 124

The Krups "Toastronic I" Cool-Touch Microchip Long Slot Toaster 124 features a triple-insulated housing that stays cool to the touch. Its extra-wide, extra-long slot can accommodate both thick and thin slices. The microchip monitor assures uniform results with each use. Set the control knob between 1 (light toasting) and 6 (dark toasting), insert your bread (or other food), and push the carriage-lever down. Toast pops up automatically and the toaster switches itself off. You can also interrupt toasting by lifting the carriage lever. The easy-care white exterior wipes clean with a damp cloth. This unit also features rubber feet for stability and convenient cord storage.
Warranty: one year, limited.

Approx. retail price	Approx. low price
$65	$63

Four-Slice Toasters

PROCTOR-SILEX T0046 FOUR-SLICE TOASTER ✔BEST BUY

The Proctor-Silex T0046 Four-Slice Toaster features dual controls to allow independent operation of its extra-wide slots. Ideal for toasting, heating, and defrosting breads, pastries, and muffins, the Proctor-Silex T0046 lets you select two different shades at the same time. Choose your settings—from one to five—then push down on the wide toast lever. Fresh or frozen pastry/defrost settings handle even delicate food items. A heat-sensing thermostat adjusts the temperature for perfect results

Prices are accurate at time of printing; subject to manufacturer's change.

time after time. An elegant granite-styled front panel adds style and sophistication. A hinged crumb tray allows easy cleanup.
Warranty: one year, limited.

Approx. retail price	Approx. low price
$50	$30

TOASTMASTER D772 COOL STEEL FOUR-SLICE WIDE-SLOT TOASTER

RECOMMENDED

The Toastmaster D772 Cool Steel Four-Slice Wide-Slot Toaster features cool-to-touch chrome and white panels. Extra-wide toast wells are designed to accommodate thick bread slices, bagels, and muffins. Independent slide controls let you select a light setting for delicate pastries in one well and a darker setting for toast or bagels in the other. Variable heat selectors adjust for delicate pastries as well as muffins and frozen food items. The MasterMind heat/moisture sensor automatically compensates for bread freshness to ensure consistent results. The exterior wipes clean with a damp cloth and a hinged crumb tray simplifies cleanup.
Warranty: parts and labor, two years.

Approx. retail price	Approx. low price
$66	$41

TOASTER OVENS

DELONGHI ALFREDO DELUX BAKE N' BROIL OVEN XU-20

The DeLonghi Alfredo Delux Bake n' Broil Oven XU-20 offers an extra-large interior space capable of handling just about any task you expect from your conventional oven. This unit features a durable, double-wall construction with a scratch-resistant exterior. Three dials individually control oven temperature, toast-color selection, and desired function: toast, bake, or broil. The roomy interior accommodates large food items, such as a whole chicken, meat loaf, or even your favorite casserole dish. This unit comes with its own black-steel baking pan and broil tray. The two-position wire rack adjusts to allow room for taller items. A full-view glass door and interior light let you keep an eye on cooking. The enamel-coated metal surface resists scratches and wipes clean with a damp cloth. Other features include a bell timer for toasting, a continuous-cleaning interior, a removable crumb tray, cool-touch handles, a power light, cord storage, and non-slip rubber feet.

Warranty: parts and labor, one year.

Approx. retail price	Approx. low price
$129	$103

BLACK & DECKER ULTRA OVEN T660G TOAST-R-OVEN BROILER

The Black & Decker Ultra Oven T660G Toast-R-Oven Broiler performs many of the same functions as your conventional oven. This unit toasts, bakes, broils, defrosts, top browns, and reheats foods. The roomy interior is designed to accommodate its own convenient 9- by 12-inch bake/broil pan, a full-size muffin pan, or up to six slices of bread for toasting. This unit also features a continuous-cleaning interior. The easy-to-use dial control includes toast settings from light to dark, standard bake temperatures, and a broil setting. Select the desired setting, then activate the on/off switch. A handy power light reminds you it's working. Recommended cooking times and temperatures for popular food items appear on the front panel.

Warranty: two years.

Approx. retail price	Approx. low price
$101	$72

TOASTMASTER SIX-SLICE TOASTER-OVEN-BROILER 343 RECOMMENDED

The Toastmaster Six-Slice Toaster-Oven-Broiler 343 features 25 percent more capacity than standard-size toaster ovens. The interior is roomy enough to accommodate a nine-inch pie, meat loaf, or a frozen pizza. Two dial settings offer independent control of toast color and bake/broil temperatures. A power on/off switch activates the machine, while a separate bake/broil

Prices are accurate at time of printing; subject to manufacturer's change.

switch and toasting lever determine the function. Heating elements shut off automatically once the toasting cycle is complete; but you must remember to return the oven switch to the off position.

Warranty: parts and labor, one year.

Approx. retail price	Approx. low price
$100	$72

PROCTOR-SILEX 03030 OVENMASTER ELECTRONIC TOASTER OVEN/BROILER

RECOMMENDED

The Proctor-Silex 03030 Ovenmaster Electronic Toaster Oven/Broiler features 40 percent greater capacity than most four-slice toaster ovens yet occupies nearly the same amount of counter space. Its built-in electronic toast sensor automatically adjusts temperature for precision results. The push-button toast control lets you start and stop toasting in an instant. Independent dial controls let you select toast temperatures from light to dark, including delicate pastry settings, and oven temperatures from defrost to broil.

Warranty: two years.

Approx. retail price	Approx. low price
$80	$52

SPECIALTY FOOD PREPARATION APPLIANCES

Waffle Makers

TOASTMASTER FAMILY SIZE COOL-TOUCH WAFFLEBAKER 282

The Toastmaster Family Size Cool-Touch WaffleBaker 282 bakes a golden, delicious, eight-inch square, four-section waffle. Best of all, its cool-touch exterior won't burn you in the process. A ready light indicates when to pour batter and when to remove the finished waffle. Durable MasterCoat nonstick grids inside, scratch-resistant polyester casing outside, and a full perimeter grease channel simplify cleanup. The automatic control regulates the temperature for hassle-free operation. The unit also stands on end for compact storage.

Warranty: parts and labor, two years.

Approx. retail price	Approx. low price
$56	$37

BLACK & DECKER SWEET HEARTS WAFFLEBAKER G12

The Black & Decker Sweet Hearts Wafflebaker G12 is a compact, handy appliance that makes baking golden, delicious waffles easy and fun. Just preheat the unit, pour batter in, and in about five minutes you'll have a crispy, delicious waffle. A ready light indicates when to pour batter and a bell tone signals when the waffle is done. An automatic thermostat ensures consistent results time after time. The Sweet Hearts Wafflebaker bakes a 7½-inch plate-size waffle that divides into four heart-shaped sections. The nonstick cooking surface simplifies cleanup. When not in use, this unit stands on end for compact storage.

Warranty: two years.

Approx. retail price	Approx. low price
$45	not available

Ice-cream Makers

SIMAC IL GELATAIO SC X 2 "DUET" IC-40

The Simac Il Gelataio SC X 2 "Duet" IC-40 is perfect for ice-cream connoisseurs who can never decide which flavor to make. This two-pint ice-cream maker consists of a sealed cooling chamber with two individual freezer compartments, each with its own electrically powered churning motor. Put a different flavor in each side or make a double batch of your favorite. Prefreeze the cooling chamber, pour in ingredients, assemble the motor and mixing blades, and start the automatic churning. The paddles aerate the mixture, producing fluffier ice cream. A unique dipole action automatically reverses the churning direction when resistance is encountered. In about 40 minutes, you'll have your choice of smooth, creamy ice cream, yogurt, sorbet, or mousse. Other features include an insulated outer shell to retain the cold temperature; clear lids with openings for adding chips, nuts, or fruit during operation; and a nonstick coating for easy cleanup in warm, soapy water.

Warranty: parts and labor, one year.

Approx. retail price	Approx. low price
$125	**$95**

WARING ICE CREAM PARLOR II CF810-1

The Waring Ice Cream Parlor II CF810-1 can be either an electric or manual-crank machine, depending on the ice-cream making mood you're in. This model uses a specially designed chilling bucket rather than an ice/salt mixture to freeze the ice cream. Place the bucket in your freezer for at least 16 hours (or overnight), pour in your premixed and chilled ingredients, and attach the paddle of choice. The hand crank requires only a few turns every five minutes. The electric motor does the cranking for you and automatically shuts itself off when the proper consistency is reached. In about 20 minutes, you'll have up to three pints of soft-serve ice cream. For a harder set, simply place the ice cream in your freezer. The unit also features a see-through lid with opening for adding nuts, chocolate pieces, and other last-minute ingredients. The bucket is immersible for easy cleaning.

Warranty: one year.

Approx. retail price	Approx. low price
$68	**$47**

SALTON BIG CHILL ICM-1   RECOMMENDED

The Salton Big Chill ICM-1 is a completely self-contained, manual ice-cream machine. It does not require ice, salt, or electricity. The double-walled aluminum cylinder must be placed in your freezer for a minimum of 15 hours before each use. While the

cylinder is freezing, you can prepare your ice cream or other frozen delight by mixing ingredients and storing them in the refrigerator. Cold, well-mixed ingredients assure consistent results. Once frozen, you can insert the cylinder into its plastic container, pour in prepared ingredients, assemble the crank, cover, and blade, and turn the crank clockwise two or three times every four to five minutes. In about 30 minutes, you'll have a batch of fresh, creamy ice cream. Add-ins, such as chocolate chips, nuts, or fruit, are no problem with the Big Chiller Filler—a sealable opening in the see-through lid. The Salton Big Chill makes up to 1½ quarts in a single batch.
Warranty: one year.

Approx. retail price	Approx. low price
$25	not available

RIVAL 8200 2-QUART COMPACT ICE-CREAM/ FROZEN YOGURT MAKER

RECOMMENDED

The Rival 8200 2-Quart Compact Ice Cream/Frozen Yogurt Maker is a countertop ice-cream/frozen yogurt maker. This compact model consists of an electric motor base, a large plastic bucket, a two-quart steel ice-cream container, cover, and churning paddle. Premix and chill ingredients, pour into ice-cream container, then fill the space between the container and the bucket wall with layers of ice cubes and table salt. The clear plastic lid locks into position and allows easy viewing of the churning process. The motor shuts off automatically when freezing is complete—in about 25 to 40 minutes.
Warranty: parts and labor, one year.

Approx. retail price	Approx. low price
$32	not available

Electric Deep Fryers

DELONGHI ROTO-FRYER D10

 ✓ **BEST BUY**

The DeLonghi Roto-Fryer D10 features a unique rotating basket, which not only produces crispier fried foods with less satu-

ration, but also takes half the amount of oil needed by traditional fryers. The Roto-Fryer circulates its contents in and out of the
oil to produce crisp, golden French fries, onion rings, or batter-
fried shrimp in just minutes. Two changeable filters in the unit's
sealed lid absorb odors and excess steam. A specially
designed handle lets you raise and lower the basket while the
lid is closed to prevent splattering. Fry up to two pounds of
potatoes in a single batch using only one quart of oil. A thermostat dial maintains temperatures from 300°F for delicate food
items, such as mushrooms, to 370°F for fries and chips. The
self-monitoring basket also reverses direction if it encounters
resistance. Other standard features include a 20-minute bell
timer, cord storage, and a ready light.
Warranty: parts and labor, one year.

Approx. retail price	Approx. low price
$190	$143

DAZEY SUPER CHEF'S FRY DCF-55 ✓BEST BUY

The Dazey Super Chef's Fry DCF-55 is a fully immersible, dish-
washer-safe appliance that can perform a number of different frying tasks. The three-quart pot is ideal for frying potatoes, onion
rings, or chicken. Make four family-size servings using only four
cups of oil. This unit comes with a handy fry basket with a cool-
touch detachable handle. A preset, removable thermostat maintains the perfect frying temperature. A non-stick Dazite coating
inside and out makes cleanup a breeze. Dazey's QuickStore lid
snaps on for odor-free oil storage. The Super Chef's Fry DCF-55
also features heat resistant handles and base.
Warranty: one year.

Approx. retail price	Approx. low price
$40	$26

Juicers

OSTER DELUXE CITRUS JUICER 4100-20 ✓BEST BUY

The Oster Deluxe Citrus Juicer 4100-20 comes with a continuous juicing tray that lets you juice oranges or other citrus direct-
Prices are accurate at time of printing; subject to manufacturer's change.

ly into your own pitcher for easy serving and storing. Or, for a quick glass any time, use the convenient juice pitcher provided. An easy press-and-lift motion affords the best results. Standard features include a powerful motor base, a tinted 14-ounce pitcher with handle and pouring spout, a cover, a cone reamer and a strainer.
Warranty: two years, limited.

Approx. retail price	Approx. low price
$30	$20

HAMILTON BEACH CITRUS JUICER MODEL 379W

RECOMMENDED

The Hamilton Beach Citrus Juicer Model 379W is a lightweight convenient appliance. It consists of a motor base, a plastic juice container with pouring spout and handle, a cone and strainer basket, and a dust cover. The wide, grooved juicing cone is perfect for juicing all types of citrus—orange, grapefruit, lemon, or lime. Press down on the cone to start and lift to stop the motor. Juice up to 24 ounces in a single batch.
Warranty: one year.

Approx. retail price	Approx. low price
$24	$15

MOULINEX DELUXE JUICE EXTRACTOR 753

 ✓BEST BUY

The Moulinex Deluxe Juice Extractor 753 uses centrifugal force to transform ordinary fruits and vegetables into a delicious, healthy beverage in seconds. This unit features automatic pulp discharge into its own 32-ounce plastic container for easier cleanup. An easy-to-use on/off switch activates the motor. Prepare the produce to be juiced. Wash and cut larger fruits and vegetables into sections. Peel citrus fruit and bananas. Then feed fruits or vegetables into the top-loading chute for continuous processing through the stainless-steel strainer. Juice flows directly into your own glass or other container.
Warranty: parts and labor, one year.

Approx. retail price	Approx. low price
$70	$60

Prices are accurate at time of printing; subject to manufacturer's change.

Popcorn Popper

PROCTOR-SILEX 5 QUART HOT-AIR POPCORN PUMPER H7340

✔BEST BUY

The Proctor-Silex 5 Quart Hot-Air Popcorn Pumper H7340 uses hot air to produce fresh, delicious popcorn without the added calories that come from oil-popped corn. The Popcorn Pumper yields about five quarts of fluffy popcorn in less than three minutes. The handy popcorn measure can also be filled with butter and placed atop the unit for melting. Simply feed kernels into the machine; the popcorn is automatically ejected into a waiting bowl. This unit pops all types of popcorn and leaves fewer unpopped kernels. Both chute and measuring cup detach for easy cleaning and then stack together with pumper base.
Warranty: one year, limited.

Approx. retail price	Approx. low price
$25	$17

Pasta Makers

ATLAS PASTA MACHINE 170   ✔BEST BUY

The Atlas Pasta Machine 170 is a manual-crank unit that can produce superior, fresh ¹⁄₁₆-inch spaghetti or ¼-inch fettucini noodles with its sturdy rollers and cutters. Make your dough, then cut and roll pieces through the flat rollers. A convenient numbered regulating dial determines the thickness of the sheet of dough being rolled. Repeat the process several times to achieve the desired consistency and thickness. Then insert the sheet of dough into the cutter for the desired type of pasta. An extra-large clamp secures the machine to your worktable for hassle-free operation. Atlas accessories include an angel hair, trenette, ⅛-inch spaghetti, ½-inch and 2-inch curly lasagna, ravioli, and canelloni attachments.
Warranty: parts and labor, one year.

Approx. retail price	Approx. low price
$50	$50

Prices are accurate at time of printing; subject to manufacturer's change.

SIMAC PASTAMATIC MX700

 ✓BEST BUY

The Simac PastaMatic MX700 is a fully automatic pasta machine. Just place ingredients into the bowl and push the start button. The machine does the rest. In only 15 minutes, this unit mixes and kneads the dough for you, then cuts it into any of eight different shapes using the supplied discs. Make cappellini, spaghetti, linguini, small fettucini, rigatoni, lasagna, and more. Other discs are sold separately for a variety of noodles from ziti to small shells to ravioli and gnocchi. The PastaMatic MX700 produces up to 1½ pounds of fresh pasta in a single batch.
Warranty: parts and labor, one year.

> **Approx. retail price**
> $300

> **Approx. low price**
> $270

Bread Makers

MAXIM ACCU-BAKERY BB1

 ✓BEST BUY

The Maxim Accu-Bakery BB1 is a fully automatic multigrain breadmaker. With micro-computer programming, this unit can bake regular white bread as well as French, whole grain, and rye breads. Simply add ingredients for the desired bread type, close the lid, set timer and selector switches, and let the machine go to work. In 2 hours and 20 minutes, you'll have a delicious loaf of fresh baked bread. The heavy baking pan has a nonstick coating for easy cleanup. Other features include a color selector that lets you choose standard or dark bread, indicator lights that signal at each stage of breadmaking, timesaver bread and dough-only programs, and ready beeper.
Warranty: one year.

> **Approx. retail price**
> $200

> **Approx. low price**
> not available

REGAL DELUXE AUTOMATIC BREADMAKER K6771

RECOMMENDED

The Regal Deluxe Automatic Breadmaker K6771 is a simple, easy way to have fresh, homemade bread any time. Simply

Prices are accurate at time of printing; subject to manufacturer's change.

CONSUMER GUIDE®

measure your ingredients directly into the removable nonstick bread pan, close the lid, and push the start button. Hot, crusty bread is ready in 3 hours and 40 minutes. For added convenience, the automatic timer can be set up to 13 hours in advance so that you can have fresh, hot bread waiting for you when you awaken in the morning, return home after work, or any time. This machine bakes three loaf sizes—small, medium, and large. It also offers a choice of light, medium, or dark crust. Other features include a digital timer that displays the time remaining in the cycle, a see-thru window, a rapid-bake cycle, and heat sensor controls to assure perfect bread every time. It also has convenient cord storage.

Warranty: one year, limited.

Approx. retail price	Approx. low price
$350	$250

Cappucino/Espresso Machines

MR. COFFEE CAFFEE RISTORANTE ECM2   ✓ BEST BUY

The Mr. Coffee Caffee Ristorante ECM2 heats enough water to make four two-ounce cups of espresso and 15 to 30 seconds on continuous steam froths milk for cappucino. This attractive, contemporary, high-gloss black machine is compact and features a ready light to let you know when the water is hot.

Warranty: one year.

Approx. retail price	Approx. low price
$70	$62

KRUPS "IL PRIMO" 972   ✓ BEST BUY

The Krups "Il Primo" 972 does not make you wait for the water to heat up; it's ready to brew up to four cups of espresso or froth milk for cappucino instantly. This model comes with a glass carafe, or you can brew directly into demitasse cups.

Warranty: one year, limited.

Approx. retail price	Approx. low price
$100	not available

Prices are accurate at time of printing; subject to manufacturer's change.

Barbecue Grills

Grilling popularity has surpassed the traditional summer weekend barbecue. The health benefits and national preference for grilled foods keep the coals burning nearly year-round in most households. Whether you have a large family that loves the classic simplicity of hamburgers and hot dogs, or a small group that prefers the taste of smoked salmon—there's a grill design that's perfect for you and your budget.

Cooking Fast with Gas

This is the best category for fast start-ups and even heat. Other advantages include cleanup convenience (no messy ashes to handle), fancy features (such as temperature gauges, side racks, and food-view windows), and permanent ceramic briquettes (or "lava rocks") that remain in the grill so you don't have to add new coals every time you cook. The downside is that these grills are generally more expensive than charcoal versions, and most gas fuel tanks must be refilled. Also, gas grills will never give you true charbroiled taste, but mesquite and other wood chips formulated for use with gas grills offer a great-tasting alternative.

Traditional Taste with Charcoal

There's no artificial replacement for charcoal taste, so it's no wonder that this grill style is still the favorite of most consumers.

Charcoal cookers are also the least expensive alternative. The new generation of outdoor chefs is not forgotten in this category. They can get a variety of gourmet tastes by using mesquite and other woods in combination with the charcoal and/or grills that double as water tray smokers. These smoker styles are designed to cook food at low heat for a long time (a couple of hours or longer). The results produce a juicy, flavorful entree. Best of all, these grills will usually function as a straightforward charcoal brazier as well. Charcoal versions are not without flaws. There's the mess of ash clean-up, the long wait for briquette heat-up, the inability to accurately control cooking temperature, and the expense and hassle of briquettes.

Grilling Ease with Electricity

These grills are gaining acceptance because they offer the convenience of the gas grill (with quick heating and easy cleanups), without the hassle of the gas tank refill. The drawback is that you're limited to cooking near an outdoor outlet. (Safety note: always use an outdoor extension cord if you need to grill further from the electrical source.)

Features and Terminology

Braziers are open-air grills that cook foods uncovered.

Btuhs are a measure of the amount of heat produced by a gas grill. Select the appropriate power level for your cooking needs.

Cooking surfaces are usually measured in square inches. Some manufacturers add the dimensions of the warming racks to the cooking surface, so when you compare dimensions, make sure you are considering only the area over the coals.

Kettles are grills that offer a cover for slower roasting, or in some cases smoking (brazier and kettle functions are often offered in the same grill model).

Preassembled is a term that might be important to you if you're less than handy with a screwdriver (before any grill purchase, it's wise to check out the assembly instructions in advance).

Best Buys '92

Our Best Buy barbecue grills follow. They are arranged in these categories: large charcoal, tabletop charcoal, fixed gas, portable gas, tabletop gas, and electric. All these grills have been selected on the basis of their features, performance, and overall value. Within each category, the item we consider the best of the Best Buys is listed first, followed by our second choice, and so on. Remember that the Best Buy designation applies only to the model listed; it does not necessarily apply to other models made by the same manufacturer.

LARGE CHARCOAL GRILLS

WEBER ONE-TOUCH KETTLE 71001 ✔ BEST BUY

The Weber One-Touch Kettle 71001 offers an ample 397 square inches of cooking surface in a no-nonsense grill. It's large enough to cook a whole turkey and vegetables. You will not have trouble finding this model in local stores, since it has been a top-seller because of its simplicity of design and sturdiness. It gets its name from a patented single-lever feature that sweeps ashes into a lower bowl for easy disposal. The bowl and lid are constructed of heavy-gauge sealed steel with rust-resistant jet-black porcelain enamel.
Specifications: weight, 34 pounds. **Warranty:** five years, limited.

Approx. retail price	**Approx. low price**
$90	$71

MECO SMOKER 5022 ✔ BEST BUY

The Meco Smoker 5022 is a full-featured, two-tiered model that's perfect for grilling and smoking various quantities of food. It boasts 380 square inches of cooking surface and is available in classic matte black or flashy red. Heat resistant wooded side and hood handles make this model comfortable and easily portable. Sliding doors allow easy access to charcoal and/or smoker water trays. A temperature gauge adds to this unit's desirability.
Specifications: weight, 24 pounds. **Warranty:** 90 days.

Approx. retail price	**Approx. low price**
$77	$53

Prices are accurate at time of printing; subject to manufacturer's change.

TABLETOP CHARCOAL GRILL

BRINKMANN COOK 'N' CARRY ✔**BEST BUY**

The Brinkmann Cook 'N' Carry is a black portable grill that handles smoking and grilling and has a 15½-inch cooking surface. A cool-to-touch wooden handle on the double-latched lid allows the grill to be toted around.

Specifications: weight, 15 pounds. **Warranty:** one year.

Approx. retail price	Approx. low price
$40	$36

FIXED GAS GRILL

NORDICWARE NATURAL GAS GRILL 73161 ✔**BEST BUY**

The Nordicware Natural Gas Grill 73161 is a full-featured post-style grill. The cooking surface measures 365 inches with an additional 142 square inches of warming space. The grill is rated at 34,000 Btuhs. Luxuries include a full-view window, temperature indicator, dual controls, automatic ignition, and two mahogany side shelves. It is available in black, red, or almond. An optional kit converts the grill for permanent installation in your yard, where it attaches to a gas line to eliminate the need to refill the gas tank.

Specifications: weight, 95 pounds. **Warranty:** one year.

Approx. retail price	Approx. low price
$349	not available

PORTABLE GAS GRILL

SUNBEAM 23622 ✔**BEST BUY**

The Sunbeam 23622 is a full-featured cart-style grill with 261 square inches of cooking surface and an extra 161 square inches for warming. It comes in driftwood gray and has 30,000 Btuhs of power.

Prices are accurate at time of printing; subject to manufacturer's change.

BARBECUE GRILLS

Specifications: weight, 80 pounds. **Warranty: casting/grill housing,** ten years; **burner,** three years; **remaining parts,** one year.

Approx. retail price	Approx. low price
$159	not available

TABLETOP GAS GRILL

SUNBEAM 8205

The Sunbeam 8205 is a great low-cost carry-and-go grill that is perfect for a small picnic or camping trip. It weighs only 16 pounds and is carried by stay-cool wood handles. Chrome-plated legs fold up to secure the lid to the grill for easy transport. The cooking surface measures 187 square inches and the grill is powered with 12,000 Btuhs. A 14 1/10- or 16 2/3-ounce propane cylinder (not included) provides the gas fuel.

Specifications: weight, 16 pounds. **Warranty:** one year.

Approx. retail price	Approx. low price
$30	$27

ELECTRIC GRILLS

SUNBEAM GRILL/CART 1661

The Sunbeam Grill/Cart 1661 is a full-size cart-style grill that functions efficiently with 1,800 watts of power. It comes in black, has redwood shelves, and 200 square inches of cooking surface.

Specifications: weight, 48 pounds. **Warranty:** one year; **casting,** ten years.

Approx. retail price	Approx. low price
$129	not available

MECO 9200-8

The Meco 9200-8 is a super-looking electric tabletop grill with a full-size cooking surface (176 square inches). It's powered with

---

Prices are accurate at time of printing; subject to manufacturer's change.

1,670 watts and sports a permanently hinged hood. It has a textured black-satin finish.

Specifications: weight, 15 pounds. **Warranty:** one year, limited.

Approx. retail price	Approx. low price
$99	$68

Microwave Ovens

Although the most popular use for a microwave oven is to heat frozen convenience foods, many cooks use it as an auxiliary oven to prepare or heat vegetables, baked goods, meats, and poultry.

The microwave oven cooks faster than conventional ovens and it produces less heat in the kitchen. Because the interior surfaces don't get hot, spills won't bake on, and they can be easily cleaned with a damp sponge.

Many models still come in simulated woodgrain cabinets, which were popular in the 1980s. The most popular styles of the 1990s promise to be all-white, black, charcoal pinstripe, and faux stone.

Due to a new method of rating the oven's cooking wattage, the ovens on the market this year are rated at about 100 watts higher than they used to be. Microwave recipes are formulated for units with 700 to 800 watts of cooking power; using a less powerful model will jeopardize your results. We recommend an oven with a capacity of at least $\frac{7}{10}$ cubic foot, 700 watts of cooking power, and no fewer than three power levels.

Microwave ovens are covered by a radiation safety standard enforced by the Food and Drug Administration. This standard requires ovens to be equipped with two independent interlock systems to stop the operation of microwaves the moment the door latch is released. A monitoring system stops the oven if one of the interlock systems fails.

Features and Terminology

Automatic cook and defrost lets you automatically set a time and power level simply by pressing touchpads to indicate the type of food you are cooking or defrosting and/or its weight.

Automatic start lets you put food in the oven and program it to begin cooking up to 12 hours later.

Convection cooking uses super-heated, circulating air to brown, bake, broil, and crisp foods.

Rotisserie, available on some convection models, slow turns boneless roasts, poultry, or kebabs to seal in juices and brown uniformly.

Cooking power is the percentage of total cooking power a microwave oven uses to defrost food or to cook different foods properly. Better ovens let you select 10 levels ranging from 10 percent to 100 percent of total power.

Crisp systems are special trays that bottom-brown and crisp foods such as pizza, French fries, and fish sticks.

Humidity sensors let you automatically set a cooking stage for certain types of food. When the sensor detects the food is done, it turns the oven off.

Invertor power works like a dimmer control on a light switch and allows you to more precisely control lower power levels needed for egg dishes, sauces, and seafood.

Memory allows you to program the oven for a sequence of two to five cooking stages. For example, you can set the oven to bring food to a boil, reduce to simmer, and then hold at the proper serving temperature.

One-touch keys let you properly heat foods such as popcorn, pizza, and a cup of tea with a single stroke.

Preprogrammed probes automatically vary the power level, and some probes have a hold function to keep food at a specified temperature.

Slow-cook features permit timed cooking up to four hours.

Temperature probes work like a continuous-reading meat thermometer, measuring the interior temperature of the food during cooking.

Turntables are slowly revolving platforms on which food is placed for uniform penetration of microwaves. Without a turntable or microwave rotor, you have to rotate the food manually for best results.

Most models on the market have electronic controls, which can be set for timed defrosting and cooking for up to 100 minutes.

Best Buys '92

Our Best Buy and Recommended microwave ovens follow. They have been selected on the basis of overall value and efficient performance. The microwave ovens are presented in the following categories: full-size ovens with a capacity of more than 1 cubic foot; medium-size ovens with a ⅘- to 1-cubic-foot capacity; compact ovens with a ½- to ⅘-cubic-foot capacity; subcompact ovens with a ⅜-cubic-foot capacity; over-the-range microwave ovens; and microwave/convection ovens. Within each category, ovens are listed in order of quality. The items we consider to be the best of the Best Buys is listed first, followed by our second choice, and so on. Remember that a Best Buy or Recommended designation applies only to the model listed, and not necessarily to other models made by the same manufacturer or to an entire product line. Microwave ovens that are built into gas or electric ranges are reviewed in the next chapter.

FULL-SIZE MICROWAVE OVENS

SHARP R-4A83

The Sharp R-4A83 is a full-size countertop or optional built-in microwave oven with electronic controls, a turntable, and several convenient one-touch automatic functions. This year it has a stone-gray finish. Model R-4A93 is identical, except it comes in an all-white cabinet with an optional kit for installation above an all-white wall oven. Features include one-touch keys for popcorn, a hot beverage, and a dinner of leftovers. It also has automatic defrost, automatic cooking by food type, ten power levels, and four-stage memory. Kits are available for built-in installation.

Prices are accurate at time of printing; subject to manufacturer's change.

Specifications: height, 12¼"; **width,** 21⅝"; **depth,** 17"; **capacity,** 1⅛ cubic feet. **Cavity dimensions: height,** 8¼"; **width,** 15"; **depth,** 16⅛". **Cooking power:** 900 watts. **Controls:** electronic. **Warranty: parts and labor,** one year; **magnetron tube,** five years.

Approx. retail price $300	Approx. low price not available

PANASONIC NN-6500 ✓BEST BUY

The Panasonic NN-6500 is a full-size countertop microwave oven with electronic controls, a turntable, and several one-touch automatic functions for popcorn, potatoes, and three types of frozen convenience foods: entrees, dinners, and vegetables. It also has automatic defrost, automatic start, power levels from 90 to 800 watts, and three-stage memory. Model NN-6500 comes in a simulated woodgrain cabinet with a black door. Model NN-6550 is identical, except it comes in white. Trim kits are available for built-in installation.
Specifications: height, 12¹⁄₁₆"; **width,** 21⅞"; **depth,** 16¹¹⁄₁₆"; **capacity,** 1¹⁄₁₀ cubic feet. **Cavity dimensions: height,** 7⅞"; **width,** 14¹³⁄₁₆"; **depth,** 15⁹⁄₁₆". **Cooking power:** 800 watts. **Controls:** electronic. **Warranty: parts and labor,** one year; **magnetron tube,** five years.

Approx. retail price $250	Approx. low price $195

SHARP R-5A83 ✓BEST BUY

The Sharp R-5A83 has features much like the top-rated Sharp R-4A83, except it is bigger. In fact, the R-5A83 is the largest-capacity model we found on the market. Its new stone-gray finished cabinet also sets it apart from other models. A kit is available for built-in installation.
Specifications: height, 13¼"; **width,** 24"; **depth,** 18⅛"; **capacity,** 1⅗ cubic feet. **Cavity dimensions: height,** 9¼"; **width,** 16⅞"; **depth,** 17⅜". **Cooking power:** 900 watts. **Controls:** electronic. **Warranty: parts and labor,** one year; **magnetron tube,** five years.

Approx. retail price $350	Approx. low price not available

Prices are accurate at time of printing; subject to manufacturer's change.

GENERAL ELECTRIC JE1423H

The General Electric JE1423H is a basic full-size countertop microwave oven with simple electronic controls. It has ten power levels and three-stage memory. The cabinet comes in a simulated woodgrain finish. A kit for built-in installation is optional.

Specifications: height, 14½"; **width,** 23⅝"; **depth,** 15¹⁵⁄₁₆"; **capacity,** 1⅖ cubic feet. **Cavity dimensions: height,** 10⅝"; **width,** 16"; **depth,** 13⅝". **Cooking power:** 800 watts. **Controls:** electronic. **Warranty: parts and labor,** one year (in-home service); **magnetron tube,** ten years.

Approx. retail price	Approx. low price
$240	$219

MEDIUM-SIZE MICROWAVE OVENS

PANASONIC NN-5500A

The Panasonic NN-5500A is a medium-size better-quality microwave oven with some popular automatic functions and a turntable. It has automatic defrost, automatic start, three-stage memory, and single-touch control keys for popcorn, potatoes, and three types of frozen convenience foods: dinners, entrees, and vegetables. Model NN-5500A comes in a simulated woodgrain cabinet with a black door.

Specifications: height, 12¹⁄₁₆"; **width,** 20¹⁄₁₆"; **depth,** 14³⁄₁₆"; **capacity,** ⅘ cubic foot. **Cavity dimensions: height,** 7⅞"; **width,** 13"; **depth,** 13". **Cooking power:** 700 watts. **Controls:** electronic. **Warranty: parts and labor,** one year; **magnetron tube,** five years.

Approx. retail price	Approx. low price
$210	$189

SHARP R-3A83

The Sharp R-3A83 is a medium-size microwave oven that comes with a stone-gray finish. It has several automatic functions and a turntable. Model R-3A93 is identical, except it comes in an all-white cabinet. A CompuCook key automatically selects the time and power level when you punch in your choice of potatoes, rolls, or vegetables. Other features include automatic defrost, automatic start, four-stage memory, and single-touch functions for heating a beverage, cooking popcorn, and heating a plateful of leftovers.

Specifications: height, 11⅝″; **width,** 20½″; **depth,** 15¼″; **capacity,** ⁹⁄₁₀ cubic foot. **Cavity dimensions: height,** 7¾″; **width,** 13¾″; **depth,** 14½″. **Cooking power:** 800 watts. **Controls:** electronic. **Warranty: parts and labor,** one year (carry-in service); **magnetron tube,** five years.

Approx. retail price	Approx. low price
$270	not available

SAMSUNG MW5510T

The Samsung MW5510T is a medium-size microwave oven with several automatic functions and a turntable. Features include automatic start, automatic defrost, four-stage memory, and popcorn key. It comes in a simulated woodgrain cabinet with a black door.

Specifications: height, 12½″; **width,** 20½″; **depth,** 14¾″; **capacity,** one cubic foot. **Cavity dimensions: height,** 9⁷⁄₁₀″; **width,** 13″; **depth,** 13⅛″. **Cooking power:** 800 watts. **Controls:** electronic. **Warranty: parts and labor,** one year; **magnetron tube,** eight years.

Approx. retail price	Approx. low price
$230	not available

QUASAR MQS0806W

The Quasar MQS0806W is a medium-size microwave oven with several automatic functions, including a humidity sensor. We found the sensor was helpful for reheating leftovers because, unlike frozen convenience foods, they do not come with microwave cooking instructions on the package. Features include popcorn key, automatic defrost, three-stage memory, and five power levels. Model MQS0806W comes in a simulated woodgrain cabinet with a black door. An under-the-cabinet mount is available. A new model, MQS0806H, is identical, except it is all-white.

Prices are accurate at time of printing; subject to manufacturer's change.

Specifications: height, 12″; **width,** 20⅛″; **depth,** 14½″; **capacity,** ⅘ cubic foot. **Cavity dimensions: height,** 8¹⁄₁₆″; **width,** 13″; **depth,** 13″. **Cooking power:** 800 watts. **Controls:** electronic. **Warranty: parts,** 90 days; **labor,** one year; **magnetron tube,** five years.

Approx. retail price	Approx. low price
$200	$190

COMPACT MICROWAVE OVENS

SHARP R-2A82/B

✓BEST BUY

The Sharp R-2A82/B is a compact microwave oven with a turntable. Features include ten power levels, two-stage memory, automatic cook, and popcorn and beverage keys. It comes in a white cabinet with a black door and control panel.
Specifications: height, 11¼″; **width,** 17¾″; **depth,** 13⅜″; **capacity,** ⅗ cubic foot. **Cavity dimensions: height,** 7¼″; **width,** 11¼″; **depth,** 12⅜″. **Cooking power:** 600 watts. **Controls:** electronic. **Warranty: parts and labor,** one year (carry-in service); **magnetron tube,** five years.

Approx. retail price	Approx. low price
$240	not available

WHIRLPOOL MS1650XW

✓BEST BUY

The Whirlpool MS1650XW is a compact microwave oven with a removable glass tray. It has ten power levels, temperature probe, and four-stage memory. An under-the-cabinet mount is available. Model MS1650XW comes in a simulated woodgrain cabinet with a black door and control panel. Model MS1651XW is identical, except it comes in all-white.
Specifications: height, 10″; **width,** 18³⁄₁₆″; **depth,** 12¹³⁄₁₆″; **capacity,** ⅗ cubic foot. **Cavity dimensions: height,** 7½″; **width,** 11½″; **depth,** 12½″. **Cooking power:** 600 watts. **Controls:** electronic. **Warranty: parts and labor,** one year; **magnetron tube,** five years.

Approx. retail price	Approx. low price
$179	$172

Prices are accurate at time of printing; subject to manufacturer's change.

SUBCOMPACT MICROWAVE OVEN

GENERAL ELECTRIC JE48A [RECOMMENDED]

The General Electric JE48A is a subcompact microwave oven handy for heating leftovers and single-portion frozen convenience foods. Word prompts tell you what keys to touch to operate this oven. It has ten power levels. We feel this model falls short of designation as a Best Buy because of its low cooking power and small size. It comes in a simulated woodgrain finish with a black door and control panel. A hanging kit is available.

Specifications: height, 9″; **width,** 18″; **depth,** 12⅜″; **capacity,** ⅗ cubic foot. **Cavity dimensions: height,** 5½″; **width,** 11″; **depth,** 11″. **Cooking power:** 575 watts. **Controls:** electronic. **Warranty: parts and labor,** one year (carry-in service); **magnetron tube,** five years.

Approx. retail price	Approx. low price
$139	$132

OVER-THE-RANGE MICROWAVE OVENS

GENERAL ELECTRIC JVM150J

The General Electric JVM150J is an over-the-range microwave oven with lots of automatic features. It has a concealed rotor, which is supposed to distribute microwaves evenly without the need for a turntable. Features include automatic cook and defrost, automatic start, ten power levels, temperature probe, five-stage memory, and a removable shelf. Word prompting guides you through the programming process. Like most better-quality over-the-range models, it is made for vented installation and has a two-speed exhaust fan, a cooktop light, and a night light.

Specifications: height, 16½″; **width,** 29⅞″; **depth,** 13″; **capacity,** one cubic foot. **Cavity dimensions: height,** 8⅜″; **width,** 18″; **depth,** 11¼″. **Cooking power:** 750 watts. **Controls:** electronic. **Warranty: parts and labor,** one year (in-home service); **magnetron tube,** ten years.

Prices are accurate at time of printing; subject to manufacturer's change.

Approx. retail price	Approx. low price
$509	$444

SHARP R-1831

✓ **BEST BUY**

The Sharp R-1831 is a full-featured over-the-range microwave/convection oven with a turntable. Features include a humidity sensor, automatic cook and defrost, automatic start, slow cook, a temperature probe, a rack and broiling trivet, ten power levels, four-stage memory, and one-touch keys for popcorn, pizza, and beverages. Model R-1831 can be installed for ducted or non-ducted use with a charcoal filter. It has a dual-speed exhaust system, a cooktop light, and an impressive, lighted stainless-steel interior. It comes in an all-white cabinet. Model R-1830 is identical, except it is black.
Specifications: height, 16½"; **width,** 29⅞"; **depth,** 15"; **capacity,** ⁹⁄₁₀ cubic foot. **Cavity dimensions: height,** 8⅜"; **width,** 13⅝"; **depth,** 13½". **Cooking power:** 800 watts. **Controls:** electronic. **Warranty: parts and labor,** two years (in-home service); **magnetron tube,** seven years.

Approx. retail price	Approx. low price
$820	not available

MICROWAVE/CONVECTION OVENS

SHARP R-9H83

RECOMMENDED

The Sharp R-9H83 is a full-size microwave/convection oven with many automatic features and a turntable. Features include a humidity sensor, automatic cook and defrost, automatic start, slow cook, a temperature probe, a rack and broiling trivet, ten power levels, four-stage memory, and one-touch keys for popcorn, pizza, and beverages. It has an impressive, stainless-steel interior. This model comes in charcoal pinstripe. Model R-9H93 is identical, except it comes in white pinstripe. Built-in kits are available.
Specifications: height, 14¾"; **width,** 24⅝"; **depth,** 18⅜"; **capacity,** 1½ cubic feet. **Cavity dimensions: height,** 9⅝"; **width,** 16⅛"; **depth,** 16⅛". **Cooking power:** 900 watts. **Controls:** electronic. **Warranty: parts and labor,** one year (carry-in service); **magnetron tube,** five years.

Prices are accurate at time of printing; subject to manufacturer's change.

Approx. retail price	Approx. low price
$600	not available

KENMORE 89969   `RECOMMENDED`

The Kenmore 89969 is a full-size microwave/convection oven with several automatic functions and a turntable. Features include automatic cook and defrost, and three-stage memory. **Specifications: height,** 15³⁄₁₆″; **width,** 23½″; **depth,** 18⅛″; **capacity,** 1³⁄₁₀ cubic feet. **Cavity dimensions: height,** 9⁷⁄₁₆″; **width,** 15¾″; **depth,** 15⅛″. **Cooking power:** 700 watts. **Controls:** electronic. **Warranty: parts and labor,** one year; **magnetron tube,** five years.

Approx. retail price	Approx.low price
$400	not available

Ranges

The heart of any kitchen is the cooking appliance, whether it's a full range or separate built-in oven and cooktop. If you're shopping for a new range or built-in, you'll find many choices. New technology has made it easier to match the product's capabilities to your own cooking preferences and your family's lifestyle. If you spend a lot of time in your kitchen and you love to cook, your choice of a range is much more important than it is for the person who only occassionally broils a steak.

Because the latest ranges offer so many styles and feature options, some advance planning will help you shop. Take time to think about how you cook, what types of meals you prepare, and how much time you can spend on meal preparation. Also, think about where the new appliance will go in your kitchen and how much space is available.

Today, ranges, ovens, and cooktops may look very different from the cooking appliances you grew up with; in fact, many *are* different. The traditional electric-coil heating elements and gas burners are still around, but today you also have other choices. You can choose from a broad variety of cooktop options— including sealed gas burners, solid-disc electric elements, and smoothtop cooking surfaces—and choose how you want to clean your oven, as well. And if you want a true custom cooking center, you can buy a convertible range or cooktop with plug-in modules to mix and match according to your needs.

336

Gas or Electric

Your kitchen may dictate your choice of gas or electric, unless you plan to undertake a costly remodeling job. Electric ranges require a 208- or 240-volt line. Gas ranges need a gas line, as well as a 115-volt outlet for the lights, clock, and burner-ignition system.

Range Designs

Freestanding ranges have a cooktop and an oven (or two), and they stand on the floor between two base cabinets or at the end of a line of cabinets. Freestanding ranges are usually 30 inches wide, but they are also made in other widths ranging from 21 to 40 inches.

Over-and-under ranges are also called double-decker, eye-level, or high-low ranges. This range has two ovens: one above and one below the cooktop. Both ovens may be gas or electric, or one oven may be a microwave, convection, or a combination microwave/convection unit.

Slide-in and drop-in ranges fit between two cabinets or into a space in a cooking island. The sides of these ranges are usually unfinished. A slide-in range sits on the floor; a drop-in range may hang from the countertop or sit on a low base.

Built-in ovens and cooktops are ranges divided into separate units for flexibility in kitchen design. A built-in oven may have one or two oven cavities.

Cooktops

Traditional cooktops have four cooking elements. On most gas models, the burners are all the same size. Some gas cooktops offer higher power on one burner for faster heating. Most electric cooktops have two six-inch and two eight-inch coil elements. On both gas and electric cooktops, heating elements may be grouped together in a cluster, with no work space in the center. Others may have a divided configuration with burners grouped on either side of the cooktop, with a work space, griddle, or fifth burner in the middle. Some built-in cooktops have burners arranged in an inverted U.

A modular, or convertible, cooktop has plug-in, interchangeable optional accessories that may include extra burners, a grill, griddle, rotisserie, wok, deep-fat fryer, or smooth glass-ceramic cooking surface. The electric heating elements under a smoothtop may be radiant or halogen. A solid-element electric cooktop has smooth discs, or hobs, rather than coil elements. These raised or flush-mounted discs take longer to heat up than coils, but they offer more uniform heating and more precise temperature control, especially at low settings.

Ovens

In addition to a conventional electric or gas oven, you may want a microwave or convection oven in your range. Convection ovens cook faster and cooler than regular ovens, because hot air is forced into the oven by a high-speed fan. The heated air goes to the food to start the cooking process immediately and makes preheating unnecessary. The drawbacks of a convection oven are the noise of the fan and the care you must take when you place food in the oven to prevent overcooking and drying. Microwave ovens cook with electromagnetic waves produced by a magnetron tube. For more information, see the chapter on microwave ovens.

Cleaning Your Oven

A self-cleaning oven uses intense heat (up to 800°F) to burn spills to powdery ash that is easily wiped off after the cleaning cycle has finished. This feature can add $100 or more to the cost of a range, but it is relatively inexpensive to operate.

A continuous-cleaning oven has a special catalytic coating on the oven walls that partially absorbs and spreads the soil during normal baking. Major spills must be wiped up promptly, or they remain on the oven floor and burn. Racks and door parts must be cleaned by hand, but you cannot scrub the interior of a continuous-cleaning oven with abrasives or use conventional oven cleaners because they ruin the special finish.

Many ranges or cooktops also have other features to make them easier to clean. On some models, the cooktop surface lifts up and locks in place so you can clean the burner box underneath, where crumbs collect. Some ranges have an upswept cooktop design that eliminates crevices at the back and sides where dirt and grime can build up. Some built-in cooktops have raised edges so spills will not run over to the countertop. And some ovens, even self-cleaning models, have removable oven doors to make it easier to spot-clean spills between cleaning cycles.

Best Buys '92

Our Best Buy and Recommended ranges follow. They were selected on the basis of quality, efficiency, energy use, and value. The ranges are divided into gas and electric categories, each with several subcategories. Within each subcategory, models are arranged by quality. The best of the Best Buys is listed first, followed by our second choice, and so on. Remember that a Best Buy or Recommended designation refers only to the model listed and not necessarily to other models made by the same manufacturer. Approximate prices apply to models in basic white or the finish mentioned in the description.

GAS RANGES

Freestanding Gas Ranges

TAPPAN 30-3991 ✓ BEST BUY

The Tappan 30-3991 is a 30-inch gas range that is particularly easy to clean. Its upswept cooktop eliminates hard-to-clean cracks and crevices, the oven is self-cleaning, and the burners are sealed so there is no need to clean them underneath; they prevent spills from dripping below the cooktop. Square burner grates let pots slide easily from back to front. The 30-3991 has a waist-high broiler and a storage drawer below the oven that is removable for cleaning. A digital clock timer programs the oven. This range has electronic pilotless ignition. The 30-3991 comes in white or almond.
Specifications: overall dimensions: height, 45⁵⁄₃₂″; **width,** 29⁷⁄₈″; **depth,** 25⅜″; **oven dimensions: height,** 15⅞″; **width,** 23″; **depth,** 19³⁄₁₆″. **Warranty: parts and labor,** one year.

>   **Approx. retail price**   **Approx. low price**
>   **$699**   **$693**

GENERAL ELECTRIC JGBC12GEN

The General Electric JGBC12GEN is a gas range with an unusually large oven. The oven is continuous-cleaning with a spacious roll-out broiler underneath. The JGBC12GEN has a

---

Prices are accurate at time of printing; subject to manufacturer's change.

digital clock with ten-hour timer and a black-glass oven door. The upswept cooktop has no cracks or crevices to collect dirt. The cooktop lifts up to make cleaning the burner box easier. This range has pilotless electric ignition. It comes in white.
Specifications: overall dimensions: height, 46½″; **width,** 30″; **depth,** 28¼″; **oven dimensions: height,** 17″; **width,** 24″; **depth,** 19″. **Warranty: parts and labor,** one year.

Approx. retail price	Approx. low price
not available	$445

Over-and-Under Gas Range

CALORIC RST399

The Caloric RST399 is a double-oven gas range with a self-cleaning lower oven and a manual-clean upper oven. The lower oven is programmable, offering delay/start cooking convenience. An efficient broiler in the lower oven concentrates infrared heat directly on the food for faster, juicier broiling. The well-lit cooktop has sealed gas burners, including one designed for simmering. The cooktop, burner grates, and control knobs are all removable for cleaning, as is the windowed black-glass door on the lower oven. A removable storage drawer is below the lower oven. This range comes in almond or white.
Specifications: overall dimensions: height, 65¾″; **width,** 30″; **depth,** 25¼″; **upper oven dimensions: height,** 11¼″; **width,** 20″; **depth,** 12½″; **lower oven interior dimensions: height,** 16″; **width,** 23″; **depth,** 17½″. **Warranty: parts,** three years.

Approx. retail price	Approx. low price
not available	$1,165

Combination Gas/Microwave Over-and-Under Ranges

MAGIC CHEF 24N-7CKVWV8-EV

The Magic Chef 24N-7CKVWV8-EV combines gas and microwave cooking in one convenient model. Its lower gas oven is self-cleaning, with a waist-high broiler; a storage drawer is underneath. Both ovens are programmable; the gas oven has electronic pilotless ignition. The lower oven door is removable for cleaning. The cooktop is illuminated by a bright work light and has sealed burners to contain spills. The one-cubic-foot upper microwave oven has touch controls for ten cooking levels. This range comes in white.

Specifications: overall dimensions: height, 65¾"; **width,** 30"; **depth,** 25½"; **lower oven dimensions: height,** 8"; **width,** 18"; **depth,** 12½". **Warranty: parts and labor,** one year.

Approx. retail price	Approx. low price
$1,550	$1,388

WHIRLPOOL SM988PES

The Whirlpool SM988PES is a streamlined cooking center with a self-cleaning lower gas oven and a spacious, 1⅗-cubic-foot microwave oven above. Its well-illuminated, lift-off cooktop has removable square burner grates and removable chrome burner bowls. Both ovens have black-glass doors with windows; the lower door comes off for spot cleaning. The lower oven has a waist-high broiler; a storage drawer is underneath. An automatic digital clock/timer offers programmed cooking in both ovens. The microwave oven has electronic touch controls for ten power levels and a probe. This range has automatic pilotless ignition. The SM988PES comes in white or almond.

Specifications: overall dimensions: height, 72"; **width,** 30⅛"; **depth,** 27⅞"; **upper oven dimensions: height,** 9⅞"; **width,** 16⁷⁄₁₆"; **depth,** 17½". **Warranty: parts and labor,** one year; **magnetron tube,** five years.

Approx. retail price	Approx. low price
$1,529	$1,259

Drop-in/Slide-in Gas Range

CALORIC RST307 ✓BEST BUY

The Caloric RST307 is a full-featured slide-in model with a self-cleaning oven and an automatic clock/timer that programs the oven for delay/start. The cooktop has raised edges to contain

Prices are accurate at time of printing; subject to manufacturer's change.

spills, and the oven door comes off for spot cleaning. The burners are sealed so spills can't drip through. The RST307 has an efficient waist-high infrared broiler and pilotless ignition. A storage drawer is below the oven. This range comes with a brushed chrome cooktop as RST307-UK, an almond cooktop as RST307-UL, or a white cooktop as RST307-UW.

Specifications: overall dimensions: height, 36"; **width,** 30"; **depth,** 25¼"; **oven dimensions: height,** 16"; **width,** 23"; **depth,** 17½". **Warranty: parts,** three years, limited; **labor,** one year.

Approx. retail price	Approx. low price
not available	$869

Built-in Gas Oven

ROPER BGS470WB

The Roper BGS470WB is a good choice for the cook who wants the convenience of a self-cleaning gas wall oven. It has automatic pilotless ignition, and the removable black-glass oven door has a window. An electronic clock with ten-hour timer programs this oven to turn on and off. The broiler is inside the oven. The BSG470WB is one of the few built-in gas ovens with a separate storage drawer.

Specifications: overall dimensions: height, 38⁷⁄₁₆"; **width,** 23⅜"; **depth,** 25⅜"; **oven dimensions: height,** 16"; **width,** 17"; **depth,** 18½". **Warranty: parts and labor,** one year.

Approx. retail price	Approx. low price
$729	$726

Gas Cooktops

CALORIC RTG350-UD

The Caloric RTG350-UD cooktop is a 30-inch model with four sealed gas burners to contain spills. Two of the burners, at 10,000 Btuh, are more powerful than those on many other gas cooktops. Two smaller burners, at 6,000 Btuh, do a good job of

simmering delicate sauces or melting chocolate. This cooktop
has pilotless ignition. The RTG350-UD comes in black glass.
Model RTG350-UWW, which comes in white glass with white
controls, is $40 more.
Specifications: height, 2⁷⁄₁₆″; **width,** 30″; **depth,** 21″.
Warranty: parts, three years, limited; **labor,** one year.

Approx. retail price	Approx. low price
not available	$446

GENERAL ELECTRIC JGP600EH ✓ BEST BUY

The General Electric JGP600EH is a well-made basic 36-inch
cooktop that lifts up for cleaning. Its chrome burner bowls are
removable for convenient cleaning as well. This model has
electronic pilotless ignition. The burners are arranged in an
inverted U shape, with the controls up front. The JGP600EH
comes in brushed chrome; model JGP600AEH comes in
almond.
Specifications: height, not available; **width,** 36″; **depth,** 18⅝″.
Warranty: parts and labor, one year.

Approx. retail price	Approx. low price
not available	$268

Modular Gas Cooktops

WHIRLPOOL SC8900EXW ✓ BEST BUY

The Whirlpool SC8900EXW is a gas cooktop that comes with
modules for a grill and two gas burners. It can accept optional
plug-in modules for additional burners, a griddle, or a rotisserie.
This cooktop has raised edges to contain spills and offers energy-saving pilotless ignition. A downdraft vent at the center of
the cooktop removes smoke and cooking odors from the
kitchen. The SC8900EXW comes in white; model SC8900EXB
comes in black.
Specifications: height, 16½″; **width,** 36″; **depth,** 21″.
Warranty: parts and labor, one year.

Approx. retail price	Approx. low price
$739	not available

Prices are accurate at time of printing; subject to manufacturer's change.

MODERN MAID PGT-193UWW

The Modern Maid PGT-193UWW is a 36-inch gas cooktop with downdraft ventilation and pilotless ignition. The venting system draws cooking smoke over the food as it cooks, adding char-broiled flavor, then pulls the smoke down and out of the kitchen. The cooktop has raised edges to contain spills. The entire unit, including the control panel, can go into the dish-washer. The PGT-193UWW comes with modules for two gas burners and a grill. You can also buy three interchangeable car-tridges: two additional burners, a nonstick griddle, and a rotis-serie. This cooktop comes in brushed chrome. Model PGT-193UB, in black, is $30 more; model PGT-193UW, in white, is $50 more.

Specifications: height, not available; **width,** 34¾"; **depth,** 20⅜". **Warranty: parts,** one year.

Approx. retail price	Approx. low price
not available	$673

ELECTRIC RANGES

Freestanding Electric Ranges

FRIGIDAIRE REG34N

The Frigidaire REG34N is a well-constructed 30-inch range that offers good value and is particularly easy to clean. It has a self-cleaning oven and an oven control that programs the oven to turn on and off, plus a clock/timer. The REG34N has an upswept cooktop with no crevices to collect grime, and the cooktop lifts up for easy cleaning underneath. The oven door is removable for spot cleaning as well. This range has a wide, waist-high broiler that comes on at partial power during baking to help food brown evenly. A storage drawer is below the oven. The REG34N comes in white or almond.

Specifications: overall dimensions: height, 46⁹⁄₁₆"; **width,** 30"; **depth,** 27¼"; **oven dimensions: height,** 16"; **width,** 23"; **depth,** 18¾". **Warranty:** one year.

Prices are accurate at time of printing; subject to manufacturer's change.

Approx. retail price	Approx. low price
$529	$503

HOTPOINT RB536N

The Hotpoint RB536N is a good basic electric range with several convenient features but few frills. The oven must be cleaned manually. It has an upswept cooktop that lifts for easy cleaning. This model has an automatic clock/timer that can preset the oven to start and stop. The broiler is waist-high, and a storage drawer is below the oven. This range comes in almond, with a window in the oven door.

Specifications: overall dimensions: height, 44⅝"; **width,** 29⅞"; **depth,** 27"; **oven dimensions: height,** 16"; **width,** 23"; **depth,** 17¼". **Warranty: parts and labor,** one year.

Approx. retail price	Approx. low price
$390	$364

ROPER FES340V

The Roper FES340V is a well-made 30-inch range with a self-cleaning oven and an electronic clock with a ten-hour timer that programs the oven for delay/start cooking. The cooker lifts up for cleaning and the oven door is removable. The broiler is waist-high. A storage drawer is below the oven. The FES340V comes in white or almond. Both models come with a black-glass oven door.

Specifications: overall dimensions: height, 45⁷⁄₁₆"; **width,** 30"; **depth,** 27⅞"; **oven dimensions: height,** 16"; **width,** 23"; **depth,** 17½". **Warranty: parts and labor,** one year.

Approx. retail price	Approx. low price
$489	$430

MAYTAG CRE655

The Maytag CRE655 is a deluxe 30-inch range that is very reliable. The oven is self-cleaning, and the cooktop lifts up so you can clean underneath. This range has a dual-bake function that uses both upper and lower heating elements for more even baking. The oven cavity is not as tall as many other electric ranges, which could be a problem when cooking a turkey or a large casserole. The CRE655 has a programmable delay/start

Prices are accurate at time of printing; subject to manufacturer's change.

function, plus a clock with a 60-minute timer. The broiler is waist-high, and a storage drawer is underneath the oven. This range comes in white or almond and has a black-glass oven door with a window.
Specifications: overall dimensions: height, 44½″; **width,** 30″; **depth,** 27″ (with handle); **oven dimensions: height,** 14″; **width,** 22″; **depth,** 18″. **Warranty: parts,** two years; **labor,** one year; **replacement of solid disc or ceramic cooktop elements,** five years.

Approx. retail price	Approx. low price
$589	$574

Over-and-Under Electric Ranges

WHIRLPOOL RE960PXV

The Whirlpool RE960PXV offers the convenience of a continuous-cleaning upper oven and a self-cleaning lower oven, with broilers at the top of both ovens. The brightly lit, crevice-free cooktop lifts so you can clean underneath it. Controls for both ovens are at eye level and include a digital automatic clock that programs the lower oven and a timer. Both ovens have black-glass doors with windows. A storage drawer is below the lower oven. This range comes in almond and white.
Specifications: overall dimensions: height, 66⅛″; **width,** 30″; **depth,** 27⁵⁄₁₆″; **upper oven dimensions: height,** 14″; **width,** 20¼″; **depth,** 13″; **lower oven dimensions: height,** 16¾″; **width,** 22″; **depth,** 18¼″. **Warranty: parts and labor,** one year.

Approx. retail price	Approx. low price
$1,199	$1,110

FRIGIDAIRE REG638BN ✔BEST BUY

The Frigidaire REG638BN has a self-cleaning lower oven; the upper oven must be cleaned manually. A single, eye-level panel holds controls for both ovens. The panel includes a digital clock and an automatic timer to program the lower oven. The lift-up cooktop is well lighted. The lower oven has a wide broiler at waist level that comes on at partial power during baking for even browning. Both ovens have black-glass oven doors with

Prices are accurate at time of printing; subject to manufacturer's change.

windows; the lower door is removable. A storage drawer is below the lower oven. The REG638BN comes in almond or white.

Specifications: overall dimensions: height, 66⅜₆″; **width,** 30″; **depth,** 25⅝″; **upper oven interior dimensions: height,** 12″; **width,** 20⅜″; **depth,** 13″; **lower oven interior dimensions: height,** 16″; **width,** 23″; **depth,** 18¾″. **Warranty:** one year.

Approx. retail price	Approx. low price
$849	$761

Combination Electric/Microwave Over-and-Under Ranges

CALORIC EKT396

The Caloric EKT396 is a sleek cooking center with a self-cleaning lower oven and a spacious, 1⅗₀-cubic-foot upper microwave oven. Easy-clean features include a removable door on the lower oven and a lift-up cooktop. The EKT396 has a digital electronic clock/timer that can program both ovens for delay/start cooking. The powerful, 800-watt microwave oven has electronic touch controls for ten power levels and a probe. A very efficient infrared broiler is waist-high in the lower oven; a storage drawer is underneath. This range comes in white or almond, and both ovens have black-glass doors with windows.

Specifications: overall dimensions: height, 65¾″; **width,** 30″; **depth,** 27″; **upper oven dimensions: height,** 9⅞″; **width,** 16⅜″; **depth,** 13⅞″; **lower oven dimensions: height,** 16″; **width,** 23″; **depth,** 17½″. **Warranty: parts,** three years, limited.

Approx. retail price	Approx. low price
not available	$1,102

GENERAL ELECTRIC JHP69GN

The General Electric JHP69GN combines the speed and convenience of microwave cooking with a self-cleaning electric oven. An eye-level control panel has touch controls to program both ovens for delay/start cooking. The cooktop is well lighted. The extra-large, 1⅗-cubic-foot upper microwave oven has an automatic sensor to tell when food is properly cooked and offers 10 power levels. A storage drawer is below the lower oven. Both oven doors have windows; the lower door is removable. The JHP69GN comes in almond with black-glass oven doors.

Specifications: overall dimensions: height, 65$\frac{13}{16}$″; **width,** 30″; **depth,** 28$\frac{5}{8}$″; **upper oven dimensions: height,** 11$\frac{1}{8}$″; **width,** 16″; **depth,** 13$\frac{3}{8}$″; **lower oven dimensions: height,** 15$\frac{3}{4}$″; **width,** 22$\frac{3}{4}$″; **depth,** 17″. **Warranty: parts and labor,** one year; **magnetron tube,** five years.

Approx. retail price	Approx. low price
not available	$1,416

Drop-in/Slide-in Electric Ranges

FRIGIDAIRE REG533N

The Frigidaire REG533N is a high-quality electric drop-in range that sits in a cutout in the counter. It has a self-cleaning oven. An automatic clock/timer programs the oven for delay/start cooking. The cooktop is well designed, with raised edges to contain spills. The REG533N has a waist-high broiler, but no storage drawer because of its drop-in design. The oven door has a window. This range comes in brushed chrome.

Specifications: overall dimensions; height, 29$\frac{3}{8}$″; **width,** 30″; **depth,** 23″; **oven dimensions: height,** 16″; **width,** 23″; **depth,** 18$\frac{3}{4}$″. **Warranty:** one year.

Approx. retail price	Approx. low price
$669	$597

WHIRLPOOL RS373PXW

The Whirlpool RS373PXW is a deluxe slide-in range with a convertible cooktop, providing cooking flexibility at a premium price. It comes with a grill module; optional additional modules include coil elements, solid-disc elements, and a smoothtop cooking surface. The RS373PXW has a built-in downdraft venting system to remove smoke and odors from the kitchen. The oven is self-cleaning, and an electronic clock/timer programs the oven for delay/start cooking. The removable black-glass

Prices are accurate at time of printing; subject to manufacturer's change.

oven door has a window. A storage drawer is below the oven.
Specifications: overall dimensions: height, 36″; **width,**
29¹⁵⁄₁₆″; **depth,** 26¾″; **oven dimensions: height,** 16″; **width,**
23″; **depth,** 17½″. **Warranty: parts and labor,** one year.

Approx. retail price	Approx. low price
$1,169	**$1,063**

Built-in Electric Oven

GENERAL ELECTRIC JKP26GP

The General Electric JKP26GP is an efficient built-in oven with
two cooking cavities. The upper oven is self-cleaning, but the
lower oven must be cleaned manually. A digital clock with automatic timer programs both ovens for delay/start cooking.
Broilers are at the top of both ovens, and both black-glass oven
doors have windows. Both upper and lower oven doors are
removable for cleaning.
Specifications: overall dimensions: height, 50⅝″; **width,**
26⅝″; **depth,** 23½″; **upper oven dimensions: height,** 15″;
width, 19″; **depth,** 18″; **lower oven dimensions: height,** 15″;
width, 19″; **depth,** 18″. **Warranty: parts and labor,** one year.

Approx. retail price	Approx. low price
not available	**$831**

Built-in Electric/Microwave Ovens

TAPPAN 57-2709

The Tappan 57-2709 combines a spacious 1³⁄₁₀-cubic-foot
microwave oven with a self-cleaning electric oven for cooking
versatility. Separate touch controls provide programmed cooking for each oven. The broiler is at the top of the lower oven.
The upper microwave oven has ten power levels, a turntable,
and a built-in browning element. Both ovens have black-glass
oven doors with windows; the lower door is removable.
Specifications: overall dimensions: height, 46⅞″; **width,**
26⅞″; **depth,** 25⅜″; **upper oven dimensions: height,** 9⅜″;

RANGES

width, 15½"; depth, 14½"; **lower oven dimensions: height,** 16"; **width,** 18½"; **depth,** 18½". **Warranty: parts and labor,** one year.

Approx. retail price
$1,159

Approx. low price
$1,034

KITCHENAID KEMI371T

The KitchenAid KEMI371T is a deluxe double wall oven with a roomy, 1⅗-cubic-foot microwave above and a self-cleaning electric oven below. The lower oven is programmed by a digital clock/timer and has a variable-temperature broiler at the top of the cavity. The upper microwave oven has touch controls for 10 power levels, plus a temperature probe and a 99-minute and 99-second clock/timer for programmed cooking. It includes a rack so several items can be cooked at once.
Specifications: overall dimensions: height, 50⅛"; **width,** 26"; **depth,** 26½"; **upper oven dimensions: height,** 10⅛"; **width,** 14¾"; **depth,** 16¼"; **lower oven dimensions: height,** 15"; **width,** 19½"; **depth,** 17¾". **Warranty: parts and labor,** one year; **magnetron tube and electric elements,** five years; **oven cavity and inner door,** ten years.

Approx. retail price
$1,399

Approx. low price
$1,391

Electric Cooktops

WHIRLPOOL RC8536XT ✔BEST BUY

The Whirlpool RC8536XT is a 36-inch built-in electric cooktop with four coil heating elements arranged around a central griddle. The griddle has a cover that can be used as additional work space. The cooktop's edges are raised to contain spills, and the control knobs come off for cleaning. The RC8536XT comes in brushed chrome.
Specifications: height, 3"; **width,** 36"; **depth,** 21¾". **Warranty: parts and labor,** one year.

Approx. retail price
$359

Approx. low price
$337

Prices are accurate at time of printing; subject to manufacturer's change.
CONSUMER GUIDE®

WHITE-WESTINGHOUSE KP332L

The White-Westinghouse KP332L is a well-constructed basic 30-inch built-in cooktop. Its four coil heating elements are arranged in a square pattern, and they lift off for cleaning. The cooktop's edges are raised to prevent spills from running onto the counter.

Specifications: height, 3″; **width,** 30″; **depth,** 21½″. **Warranty: parts and labor,** one year.

Approx. retail price	Approx. low price
$250	$250

Modular Electric Cooktops

JENN-AIR C2200B

The Jenn-Air C2200B is a convertible cooktop that lets you choose from among four different control styles, as well as optional cooking modules. One type of control panel mounts on the front of the cabinet, so the cooktop is completely flush with the countertop. The C2200B includes an efficient downdraft ventilation system that activates automatically when the grill turns on. The C2200B comes with an energy-saving grill cartridge; you must buy one additional module with the cooktop to plug into the other side. Optional modules are a radiant heating element, a halogen element, a wok, an additional grill, or a canning element.

Specifications: height, 17½″; **width,** 30¹⁵⁄₁₆″; **depth,** 21⅛″. **Warranty: parts and labor,** one year; **parts,** two years, limited; **electric control modules, labor,** two years.

Approx. retail price	Approx. low price
$799	$605

Smoothtop Electric Cooktops

AMANA AK2H30HR

The Amana AK2H30HR is a high-tech glass-ceramic cooktop with heating elements that glow red beneath a smooth black

surface. One 8-inch and one 6-inch circular quartz-halogen element beneath the smooth surface heat up almost instantly when turned on. The AK2H30HR also has two radiant heating elements below the surface. One element is 7 inches in diameter the other is a dual element that can change from 6 to 9 inches in diameter, depending on the size of the pot you want to use. This cooktop can be installed with the controls on either the right or the left side. The AK2H30HR is scratch- and stain-resistant, and the smooth surface can be used as extra counter-space when the cooktop is not in use. It comes in black.
Specifications: height, 3⅝″; **width,** 29⁹⁄₁₆″; **depth,** 21½″.
Warranty: parts and labor, one year; **heating elements,** four years; **glass ceramic top, parts and labor,** four years.

Approx. retail price	Approx. low price
not available	$571

WHIRLPOOL RC8600XV   ✔BEST BUY

The Whirlpool RC8600XV is a glass-ceramic cooktop with 4 high-speed heating elements—one 8-inch, one 7-inch, and two 5½-inch—installed beneath a smooth black-glass surface. Controls mounted on the right side provide infinite levels of heat and they lift off for cleaning. An indicator light shows when the cooking surface is hot. This cooktop is scratch- and stain-resistant. The RC8600XV comes in black.
Specifications: height, 4″; **width,** 30⅜″; **depth,** 21″. **Warranty: parts and labor,** one year; **cooktop system,** five years.

Approx. retail price	Approx. low price
$499	$463

Refrigerators

Of all the appliances in your home, just one operates continuously—your refrigerator. Since energy costs over the refrigerator's 13-year-plus life expectancy will exceed its purchase price, you should shop for an energy-efficient model big enough to meet your needs for the next 13 years.

Compare the energy efficiency of each model by examining the bright yellow "EnergyGuide" label. You should also get a current *Consumer Selection Guide,* which lists the estimated energy cost of each model, by sending a check for $2.00 to the Association of Home Appliance Manufacturers (AHAM), 20 North Wacker Drive, Chicago, Illinois 60606.

In addition to the manufacturer's warranty, there's a bit more consumer protection available to you. Most of the models listed in this section come under the protection of the Major Appliance Consumer Action Panel (MACAP). You can appeal to this independent complaint resolution group if you take steps recommended by the manufacturer to resolve any problems and still feel the manufacturer has not backed the refrigerator you bought to your satisfaction. You can get more information about MACAP by contacting AHAM.

Matching Refrigerator Size to Your Needs

Buying a larger refrigerator than you need wastes money. Bigger units tend to be less energy efficient than smaller refrigerators, and you may end up cooling unused space inside your refrigerator. As a rule of thumb, plan for eight to ten cubic feet of cavity space for a family of two; add one cubic foot for each additional family member. The freezer section should provide three cubic feet for two people, with another cubic foot for each additional person.

Refrigerator Configurations

Single-door refrigerators range in storage capacity from 1½ to 19 cubic feet. Models under six cubic feet are compacts. Single-door refrigerators are less expensive to buy and operate than other styles. Most models have a small interior freezer that may have to be defrosted manually.

Two-door bottom-mount refrigerators have a freezer compartment below the refrigerator section. This configuration is not widely available, but some people prefer to have the refrigerator compartment at eye level. Bottom-mounted freezers tend to be larger than top-mounted freezers.

Two-door side-by-side refrigerators are large capacity, freestanding units that have doors running their full length. Some models have a small door built into the refrigerator door to get at frequently used beverages without opening the entire door. Others dispense ice and chilled water through the freezer door.

Built-in refrigerators are often camouflaged with custom cabinet work. This type of refrigerator is larger, more expensive, and more costly to operate than freestanding models.

Features and Terminology

Energy labels are mandated by federal law and state the expected annual operating cost of the appliance based on a power cost of 8.04 cents per kilowatt-hour. The actual cost of your power may be higher or lower, but this figure is useful when you compare different models.

Frostless, or **frost-free,** refrigerators automatically eliminate frost with heaters that melt the frost and evaporate the water. This is not an energy-efficient system, but it saves you time and effort by eliminating the need to defrost the refrigerator.

Energy-saving features are included in the design of many refrigerators. A **power-saver switch** saves energy by turning off the door heater (a loop or coil that carries hot refrigerant gas around the inside of the door to remove condensation during periods of high humidity). **Separate temperature controls** for the freezer and refrigerator also save energy.

Food shelves are adjustable in most refrigerators, so you can place the shelves to suit your needs. Glass shelves contain food spills and wipe clean easily. Extra-deep door shelves, which hold items such as gallon jugs, give you more room on the interior shelves for larger items.

Built-in ice makers and dispensers are either standard or optional, depending on the model. This convenience adds upwards of $100 to the cost of the appliance. Installation may require a plumber.

Best Buys '92

Our Best Buy and Recommended refrigerators follow. They are divided into these categories: single-door, two-door bottom-mount, two-door top-mount, side-by-side, and built-in refrigerators. Within each category, the refrigerators are listed in ascending order of size. Remember that a Best Buy or Recommended designation applies only to the model listed.

SINGLE-DOOR REFRIGERATORS

WELBILT W-1011 ✔ BEST BUY

The Welbilt W-1011 is a value-priced 11¹⁄₁₀-cubic-foot single-door refrigerator. It requires less energy to operate than larger refrigerators, so it is less expensive to own in the long run. It does not have automatic defrosting, which also saves energy. The W-1011 comes in white and has three adjustable wire shelves, one fixed glass shelf, a crisper, a meat-keeper compartment, an egg/dairy compartment, three door shelves, and four leveling legs. Like other single-door models, the freezer compartment is recommended only for short-term storage of frozen foods, and it will not keep ice cream solidly frozen.

Specifications: height, 55⁵⁄₁₆″; **width,** 24⅜″; **depth,** 27½″; **shelf capacity,** not available. **Energy cost:** not available. **Warranty: parts and labor,** one year; **compressor,** five years.

Approx. retail price	Approx. low price
$349	$338

Prices are accurate at time of printing; subject to manufacturer's change.

HOTPOINT TA14SP

RECOMMENDED

The Hotpoint TA14SP is an energy saver. It only has 13%0 cubic feet so it requires less energy to operate than larger models. It does not have automatic defrosting, which also saves energy. Model TA14SP has 11% cubic feet of refrigerator capacity and a 2⅒-cubic-foot freezer compartment. This compartment is recommended only for short-term storage of frozen food, and will not keep ice cream frozen solid. Available in white or almond, it has two white epoxy-coated wire shelves, including one adjustable shelf, and a fixed plastic shelf above the crisper. It also has egg pockets, a spreads bin, and three molded door shelves.

Specifications: height, 61″; width, 28″; depth, 27″; shelf capacity, 15⅜ square feet. Energy cost: $58 per year. Warranty: parts and labor, one year; sealed system, parts, five years.

Approx. retail price not available	Approx. low price $342

TWO-DOOR BOTTOM-MOUNT REFRIGERATOR

AMANA BZ20Q

✓ BEST BUY

The Amana BZ20Q provides access to its 13⅜-cubic-foot refrigerator at eye level. The freezer has 6⅝ cubic feet. The BZ20Q has three adjustable, half-width glass shelves; a fixed half-width shelf; and a fixed full-width shelf. There are two large, humidity-controlled crispers; a sealed, adjustable-temperature meat keeper; a removable egg bucket; a dairy bin; and two microwave-safe leftover containers that fit in the door. Separate thermostats for the refrigerator and freezer maintain constant storage temperatures. The freezer's shelf and glide-out storage basket provide easy access to frozen foods. Shelf huggers, a bottle rack, and rollers are also included. It comes in white or almond. An ice maker is available.

Specifications: height, 68″; width, 32″; depth, 32½″; shelf capacity, 27⅛ square feet. Energy cost: $88 per year. Warranty: parts and labor, one year; sealed system, parts, five years.

Prices are accurate at time of printing; subject to manufacturer's change.

Approx. retail price	Approx. low price
$899	$835

TWO-DOOR TOP-MOUNT REFRIGERATORS

HOTPOINT CTX14CP

The Hotpoint CTX14CP is a small no-frost refrigerator with a freezer that maintains a near-zero temperature. The 10½-cubic-foot refrigerator section has 2 adjustable, white-epoxy-coated wire shelves; a fixed shelf above the crisper; 2 molded door shelves; and 2 dairy bins. The 3⅝-cubic-foot freezer has a door shelf and a juice-can rack. The CTX14CP comes in white or almond. An ice maker is optional.

Specifications: height, 61″; **width,** 28″; **depth,** 29⁹⁄₁₆″; **shelf capacity,** 17⁷⁄₁₀ square feet. **Energy cost:** $58 per year. **Warranty: parts and labor,** one year; **sealed system, parts,** five years.

Approx. retail price	Approx. low price
$550	$443

FRIGIDAIRE FPD17TP

The Frigidaire FPD17TP is a medium-size no-frost refrigerator with top-mounted freezer. Its 12⅝-cubic-foot fresh-foods section has three slide-out wire shelves, one fixed shelf, 2½ molded door shelves, two crispers, and a spreads bin. The 3⅝-cubic-foot freezer has two molded door shelves. The FPD17TP has high-density insulation, an energy-efficient compressor, and power-saving loop and switch work to make it one of the most energy-efficient models of its size. It comes in white and almond. An ice maker is available.

Specifications: height, 64³⁄₁₆″; **width,** 28″; **depth,** 30²³⁄₃₂″; **shelf capacity,** 20⅖ square feet. **Energy cost:** $60 per year. **Warranty: parts and labor,** one year; **refrigeration system,** five years.

Approx. retail price	Approx. low price
$599	$523

GIBSON RT17F3WX

✓BEST BUY

The Gibson RT17F3WX is a medium-size no-frost refrigerator with a top-mounted freezer. For a unit this size, it is value-priced. Its 13-cubic-foot refrigerator section has two slide-out, white epoxy-coated wire shelves; one fixed shelf; and a crisper. The door has two molded shelves, an egg compartment, and a spreads bin. The 3⅘-cubic-foot freezer has two molded door shelves. Model RT17F3WX also has an energy-saver switch and optional ice maker. It comes in white or almond.
Specifications: height, 64 3/16″; **width,** 28″; **depth,** 31⅛″; **shelf capacity,** 20⅕ square feet. **Energy cost:** $64 per year. **Warranty: parts and labor,** one year; **sealed system,** five years; **compressor,** ten years.

Approx. retail price **$529** | **Approx. low price** **$489**

WHIRLPOOL ET18ZKXX

✓BEST BUY

The Whirlpool ET18ZKXX is a medium-size no-frost top-mounted refrigerator/freezer. This model has one adjustable, half-width, white epoxy-coated wire shelf; one adjustable full-width wire shelf; and a fixed shelf atop its two crispers. Its 13⅕ cubic feet of refrigerated space includes three molded door shelves, including one extra-deep shelf to hold gallon jugs, a utility bin, a butter bin, and a meat bin. It has separate, up-front temperature controls for the refrigerator and the freezer. The 4⅘-cubic-foot freezer has one interior shelf, and two molded door shelves. It comes in white or almond.
Specifications: height, 66¼″; **width,** 29½″; **depth,** 29½″; **shelf capacity,** 23⅗ square feet. **Energy cost:** $65 per year. **Warranty: parts and labor,** one year; **sealed system,** five years.

Approx. retail price **$639** | **Approx. low price** **$612**

GENERAL ELECTRIC TBX21JP

✓BEST BUY

The General Electric TBX21JP is a large no-frost top-mounted refrigerator/freezer with glass shelves. It has three adjustable,

Prices are accurate at time of printing; subject to manufacturer's change.

half-width shelves and one fixed shelf atop its two crispers. The 14⅓-cubic-foot fresh-food section also has a sealed meat pan, an egg bin, two utility bins, and two molded door shelves. The 6⅓-cubic-foot freezer has a wire shelf, two molded door shelves, an ice bin, and an optional ice maker. It comes in white or almond.

Specifications: height, 66¼″; **width,** 31¼″; **depth,** 31½″; **shelf capacity,** 25⅜ square feet. **Energy cost:** $74 per year. **Warranty: parts and labor,** one year; **sealed system,** five years.

Approx. retail price	Approx. low price
$729	$649

GIBSON RT21F7WX

The Gibson RT21F7WX is a large no-frost top-mounted refrigerator/freezer. The 15-cubic-foot refrigerator section has three adjustable glass shelves, one fixed shelf, two crispers, an egg shelf, a spreads bin, and two molded door shelves. The 5⅜-cubic-foot freezer has a full-width shelf, two molded door shelves, a juice-can dispenser, and an optional ice maker. It comes in white or almond.

Specifications: height, 66¹⁄₁₆″; **width,** 31″; **depth,** 30¹⁵⁄₁₆″; **shelf capacity,** 27⅛ square feet. **Energy cost:** $72 per year. **Warranty: parts and labor,** one year; **sealed system,** five years; **compressor,** ten years.

Approx. retail price	Approx. low price
$669	$539

SEARS KENMORE 70581

The Sears Kenmore 70581 is a large no-frost top-mounted refrigerator/freezer. It has three half-width adjustable glass shelves, one fixed shelf, an adjustable-temperature meat drawer, two crispers (one with adjustable humidity control), a butter bin, and an egg bin. The door is very spacious with one full-width and two half-width extra-deep adjustable bins. The 7⅜-cubic-foot freezer has 2 adjustable wire shelves, 3 half-width door bins, and an ice maker. It comes in white. Model 70588 is identical, except it comes in almond.

Specifications: height, 67″; **width,** 34½″; **depth,** 32¾″; **shelf**

capacity, 33$\frac{3}{5}$ square feet. **Energy cost:** $94 per year. **Warranty: parts and labor,** one year; **sealed system,** five years.

Approx. retail price	Approx. low price
$1,100	$1,035

SIDE-BY-SIDE REFRIGERATORS

HOTPOINT CSX20EM

✓BEST BUY

The Hotpoint CSX20EM is a value-priced small no-frost side-by-side refrigerator. The 12$\frac{9}{10}$-cubic-foot refrigerator section has 4 adjustable wire shelves, 1 fixed shelf, a sealed crisper, an adjustable-temperature meat pan, a utility bin, an egg bin, and five molded door shelves. The 6$\frac{4}{5}$-cubic-foot freezer has 4 wire shelves, 6 molded door shelves, a sliding storage bin, an ice bin, and room for an optional ice maker. This model comes in white or almond.
Specifications: height, 66$\frac{5}{8}$"; **width,** 30$\frac{1}{2}$"; **depth,** 31$\frac{1}{2}$"; **shelf capacity,** 22$\frac{1}{2}$ square feet. **Energy cost:** $90 per year. **Warranty: parts and labor,** one year; **sealed system,** five years.

Approx. retail price	Approx. low price
$800	$721

WHIRLPOOL ED22PWXX

✓BEST BUY

The Whirlpool ED22PWXX is a deluxe-featured medium-size no-frost side-by-side refrigerator. Its 14$\frac{4}{5}$-cubic-foot refrigerator section has 3 adjustable glass shelves, a fixed shelf, a crisper, an adjustable-temperature meat pan, a spreads bin, and 4 molded door shelves, including one extra-deep shelf that holds two gallon jugs. The 7$\frac{1}{5}$-cubic-foot freezer has 3 wire shelves, a slide-out storage bin, 5 molded door shelves, and an ice maker with through-the-door cube and water dispenser. It comes in white or almond.
Specifications: height, 66$\frac{1}{2}$"; **width,** 32$\frac{3}{4}$"; **depth,** 32$\frac{3}{8}$"; **shelf capacity,** 21$\frac{7}{10}$ square feet. **Energy cost:** $95 per year. **Warranty: parts and labor,** one year; **sealed system,** five years.

Prices are accurate at time of printing; subject to manufacturer's change.

Approx. retail price
$1,199

Approx. low price
$1,102

FRIGIDAIRE FPCE24VWP ✓**BEST BUY**

The Frigidaire FPCE24VWP is a large deluxe-featured frost-free side-by-side refrigerator with a through-the-door ice cube and water dispenser. The 14⁷⁄₁₀-cubic-foot refrigerator section has three glass shelves, which are adjustable. It also has one humidity-controlled and one sealed hydrator, an adjustable-temperature meat pan, and a wine rack. The door has three adjustable shelves, a beverage dispenser, spreads and egg bins, and three microwave-safe leftover storage containers. The 9³⁄₁₀-cubic-foot freezer has four wire shelves and five door shelves. It comes in white or almond. A black panel kit and custom-frame kit are optional.

Specifications: height, 66"; **width,** 36"; **depth,** 31⁷⁄₈"; **shelf capacity,** 26³⁄₁₀ square feet. **Energy cost:** $103 per year. **Warranty: parts and labor,** one year; **refrigeration system,** five years.

Approx. retail price
$1,259

Approx. low price
$1,134

SEARS KENMORE 50551 ✓**BEST BUY**

The Sears Kenmore 50551 is a large deluxe-featured frost-free side-by-side refrigerator with a through-the-door ice dispenser. The 15⅕-cubic-foot refrigerator section has 3 adjustable glass shelves, a fixed shelf, a crisper, a meat drawer, a double butter bin, and 3 adjustable door shelves that are deep enough to hold gallon jugs. The 9⅖-cubic-foot freezer has 3 wire shelves, a slide-out storage basket, and an ice bin. This model comes in white; model 50558 comes in almond.

Specifications: height, 68⅞"; **width,** 35½"; **depth,** 32¾"; **shelf capacity,** 24½ square feet. **Energy cost:** $103 per year. **Warranty: parts and labor,** one year; **sealed system,** five years.

Approx. retail price
$1,150

Approx. low price
$1,150

Prices are accurate at time of printing; subject to manufacturer's change.

HOTPOINT CSX27DM

The Hotpoint CSX27DM is a 26⅛-cubic-foot deluxe-featured frost-free side-by-side refrigerator with an ice maker and through-the-door ice cubes, crushed ice, and water dispenser. The 16⅛-cubic-foot refrigerator section has three adjustable glass shelves, a sealed snack pan, an adjustable-temperature meat pan, an egg bin, and two crispers (one sealed). The door has a dairy compartment and five shelves, four of which are adjustable and deep enough to hold gallon jugs. The freezer has three interior shelves, a storage bin, and five door shelves. This unit also has an enamel-on-steel cabinet liner and adjustable rollers. It comes in white or almond. A custom trim kit and a black Lexan or a black acrylic panel kit are optional.
Specifications: height, 68¾"; **width,** 35¾"; **depth,** 32½"; **shelf capacity,** 28⅛ square feet. **Energy cost:** $109 per year. **Warranty: parts and labor,** one year; **sealed system,** five years.

Approx. retail price	Approx. low price
not available	$1,721

BUILT-IN REFRIGERATOR

SUB-ZERO 561

The Sub-Zero 561 is a true built-in refrigerator in a 36-inch-wide side-by-side design. Like most built-in models, it is available from custom kitchen dealers rather than appliance stores. It has separate compressors for the 12½-cubic-foot refrigerator and the 8⁹⁄₁₀-cubic-foot freezer, both of which have an all-white interior. The fresh-foods section has five glass shelves, four of which are adjustable; two sealed, humidity-adjustable crispers; a utility drawer; an egg rack; a spreads bin; and three adjustable door shelves. The freezer has an ice maker and ice drawer, four pull-out baskets, three shelves, and five adjustable door shelves. In addition to custom trim, it is available in white, almond, stainless steel, coffee, avocado, or harvest gold.
Specifications: height, 84"; **width,** 36"; **depth,** 24"; **shelf capacity,** not available. **Energy cost:** $95 per year. **Warranty:**

parts and labor, one year; **mechanical parts, parts and labor,** two years; **sealed system,** five years; **sealed system, parts,** 12 years.

Approx. retail price
not available

Approx. low price
$2,697

Freezers

What costs even more than the price of a freezer is the cost of electricity it will use over its lifespan, and an average freezer lasts about 13 years. Therefore, it's wise to shop for the most energy-efficient model that is big enough to meet your needs.

Compare the energy efficiency of each model by examining the bright yellow "EnergyGuide" label. Or send for a copy of the latest *Consumer Selection Guide for Refrigerators and Freezers* by writing the Association of Home Appliance Manufacturers (AHAM), 20 North Wacker Drive, Chicago, Illinois 60606. Enclose a check for $2.00.

In addition to the manufacturer's warranty, the association gives you a bit more consumer protection, if you should ever need it, for most name brands. If you take steps recommended by the manufacturer to resolve any problems and still feel the manufacturer has not backed the product to your satisfaction, you can appeal to the Major Appliance Consumer Action Panel. For details about this independent complaint resolution group, contact AHAM.

Upright or Chest

There are two styles of freezers: upright and chest.

Convenience: An upright offers the convenience of front-door loading. It also has shelves for easy access to foods. In a chest freezer, goods have to be stacked rather than shelved, and they are less accessible. Many chest freezers have pull-out baskets to make it easier to store and remove frozen food.

Expense: Compared to an upright model of comparable size, a chest freezer is less expensive to buy and operate.

Size: Upright freezers range in capacity from under 1½ cubic feet to about 30 cubic feet. Chest freezers have capacities from roughly 4⁷⁄₁₀ cubic feet to 28 cubic feet.

Space: An upright takes up less space than a chest unit. An upright is a good choice if you want the convenience of a freezer in the kitchen. A chest freezer is often preferred for a basement where floor space is not a problem.

How Large a Freezer Do You Need?

A freezer that is too large will be inefficient and costly to operate. But a freezer that is too small defeats its purpose and causes a lot of frustration. Allow about three cubic feet of freezer space for each family member. Add another two cubic feet for special purposes, and two to three cubic feet if you plan to freeze game or produce, or if you prepare meals in advance.

Features and Terminology

Baskets: For storing bulk items, baskets are useful. Chest freezers usually have one or more sliding baskets, combined with step dividers, which provide direct access to the total freezer space. Upright models usually have one basket or bin.

Controls: A freezer works best at 0°F or slightly below. Some models have a temperature control.

Defrost systems: Chest freezers and some upright models must be defrosted manually. A few upright models come with automatic defrosting, which will add about $100 to the purchase price and 15 to 20 percent per year to the operating cost.

Energy efficiency: Since 1972, freezers have become over 65 percent more energy-efficient because of improved condensers, evaporators, fan motors, door seals, and insulating techniques. The energy labels on freezers let you compare the energy use of comparable models. They show the estimated annual operating cost, based on an energy cost of $0.0675 per kilowatt-hour. (In 1989, the federal government calculated a nationwide average rate of $0.077 per kilowatt-hour, which would more accurately reflect a freezer's expected annual operating cost.)

Fast-freezing shelves: Some shelves have an extra cooling coil running through them to facilitate faster freezing. These may be called fast-freeze or refrigerated shelves.

Interior light: This can help you find what you're looking for, especially in a chest freezer located in a dark basement.

Lock: A lock on your freezer is very important if there are young children who might climb inside a freezer and get trapped. It is also useful if your freezer is in a garage or where the contents may not be secure without a lock.

Best Buys '92

Our Best Buys and Recommended upright and chest freezers follow. We have listed models in descending order of total capacity. Remember that a Best Buy or Recommended designation applies only to the model listed; it does not necessarily apply to other models made by the same manufacturer.

UPRIGHT FREEZERS

GIBSON FV19F5WX

✔**BEST BUY**

The Gibson FV19F5WX is an 18⁷⁄₁₀-cubic-foot upright no-frost freezer. It has five wire shelves, a slide-out storage basket, four deep-door package racks, and two juice-can racks. This model also has a key-eject lock, leveling legs, a power-cord retainer, and a temperature guard that emits an audible alarm if the cavity temperature rises above 20°F. It comes with a very good food-loss protection plan. This model comes in white only.
Specifications: height, 64½"; **width,** 32"; **depth,** 26⅜"; **shelf capacity,** 22⁷⁄₁₀ square feet. **Energy cost:** $81 per year. **Warranty: parts and labor,** one year; **refrigeration system and liner,** five years; **compressor, parts,** ten years.

Approx. retail price
$459

Approx. low price
not available

GIBSON FV16M2WX

✔**BEST BUY**

The Gibson FV16M2WX is a 16-cubic-foot, manually defrosted upright freezer. It has three refrigerated shelves, three deep-door package racks, two juice-can racks, a key-eject lock, a

---

Prices are accurate at time of printing; subject to manufacturer's change.

CONSUMER GUIDE®

power-cord retainer, and leveling legs. This model has good energy efficiency. It comes in white. Gibson freezers also come with a very good food-protection warranty.

Specifications: height, 59"; **width,** 28"; **depth,** 28⅜"; **shelf capacity,** 16⅔ square feet. **Energy cost:** $56 per year. **Warranty: parts and labor,** one year; **refrigeration system and liner,** five years; **compressor, parts,** ten years.

Approx. retail price	Approx. low price
$419	$410

FRIGIDAIRE UFP16N

The Frigidaire UFP16N is a 15⅞-cubic-foot frost-proof upright freezer. While most freezers need to be emptied and defrosted every few months, this one is frost-free. This feature means it requires more electricity to operate, however. Model UFP16N has four shelves, a slide-out basket, four door shelves, a juice-can door shelf, an adjustable temperature control, leveling legs, a key-eject light, and a power-cord retainer. It comes in almond. Frigidaire freezers have a good food-spoilage warranty.

Specifications: height, 61½"; **width,** 32"; **depth,** 26⅜"; **shelf capacity,** 18⅛ square feet. **Energy cost:** $70 per year. **Warranty: parts and labor,** one year; **sealed system,** five years.

Approx. retail price	Approx. low price
$549	$463

GENERAL ELECTRIC CA13SM

The General Electric CA13SM is a 13⅜-cubic-foot, manually defrosted upright that has good energy efficiency for its size. It has three fast-freezing shelves, a top cold plate, four door shelves, a key-eject lock, an adjustable temperature control, and a quality, baked enamel-on-steel cabinet liner. It comes with a very good food-protection warranty. It is only available in white.

Specifications: height, 54½"; **width,** 28"; **depth,** 26⅜"; **shelf capacity,** 14⅛ square feet. **Energy cost:** $48 per year. **Warranty: parts and labor,** one year; **sealed system,** five years.

Prices are accurate at time of printing; subject to manufacturer's change.

Approx. retail price
$369

Approx. low price
$369

WHIRLPOOL EV120FXXN ✔**BEST BUY**

The Whirlpool EV120FXXN is a 12¹⁄₁₀-cubic-foot manually defrosted upright. It has three interior shelves, a bulk storage gate, five door shelves, an adjustable temperature control, leveling legs, and a power-cord lock. Whirlpool freezers come with a very good food-protection warranty. It comes in almond.
Specifications: height, 60"; **width,** 24"; **depth,** 30⅛"; **shelf capacity,** 12⅛ square feet. **Energy cost:** not available. **Warranty: parts and labor,** one year; **sealed system,** ten years.

Approx. retail price
$429

Approx. low price
$399

CHEST FREEZERS

SEARS KENMORE 21871 ✔**BEST BUY**

The Sears Kenmore 21871 is a 23-cubic-foot chest freezer with very good energy efficiency. It has three white-powder-coated baskets, an adjustable temperature control, an interior light, and a security lock. This model comes in almond only.
Specifications: height, 35"; **width,** 65¼"; **depth,** 29½". **Energy cost:** $58 per year. **Warranty: parts and labor,** one year; **sealed system,** five years.

Approx. retail price
$650

Approx. low price
$420

FRIGIDAIRE CF16D ✔**BEST BUY**

The Frigidaire CF16D is a 15⅗-cubic-foot chest freezer with very good energy efficiency. A large, epoxy-coated sliding basket provides convenient storage for frequently used foods. This model also has an interior light, an adjustable temperature control, a key-eject lock, and a combination divider/drainer pan. All Frigidaire freezers come with a good food-spoilage warranty. This model comes in almond only.

Prices are accurate at time of printing; subject to manufacturer's change.

Specifications: height, 35″; width, 47¼″; depth, 29½″. Energy cost: $46 per year. Warranty: parts and labor, one year; sealed system, five years.

Approx. retail price	Approx. low price
$419	$339

GENERAL ELECTRIC CB10DM ✓BEST BUY

The General Electric CB10DM is a 10-cubic-foot chest freezer with deluxe features and excellent energy efficiency. It is defrosted manually, which means it consumes relatively little energy. It has an adjustable temperature control, a removable sliding storage basket, an interior light, a key-eject lock, and an up-front drain. An audible alarm is sounded if the cavity temperature rises above 20°F. General Electric freezers have a very good warranty against food spoilage. This model comes in white only.

Specifications: height, 35″; width, 42⅛″; depth, 24¼″. Energy cost: $32 per year. Warranty: parts and labor, one year; sealed system, five years.

Approx. retail price	Approx. low price
$329	$299

GIBSON FHO8M5DX ✓BEST BUY

The Gibson FHO8M5DX is an 8³⁄₁₀-cubic-foot, manually defrosted chest freezer. It offers an adjustable temperature control, key-eject lock, a lift-out storage basket, and a power-cord retainer. This model has a very good warranty against food loss. It comes in an almond cabinet with a brown lid.

Specifications: height, 34¹⁄₁₆″; width, 35″; depth, 23″. Energy cost: $32 per year. Warranty: parts and labor, one year; refrigeration system and liner, five years; compressor, parts, ten years.

Approx. retail price	Approx. low price
$289	$279

Dishwashers

A dishwasher not only saves time, it actually gets dishes cleaner and more germ-free than you could by hand. It's been estimated that a dishwasher will save the average homemaker four hours a week.

Built-in dishwashers are permanently attached to water pipes, drains, and electrical lines. The main disadvantage of a built-in dishwasher is that it deprives you of kitchen cabinet space. There are a few compact built-in models, which are slimmer than the standard 24 inches.

Portable dishwashers roll on casters, connect to the sink faucet, and drain with hoses. Most portables have a flow-through valve that lets you draw water from the faucet while the appliance is in operation. Some models can be converted to built-in units. If you are a renter who hopes someday to own a house or condominium where you will permanently install a dishwasher, a convertible model is a good choice.

Some dishwashers offer increased cleaning vigor, quiet operation, and many energy-saving features. All dishwashers have an air-dry feature that saves energy by turning off the heating element used in the regular heat-dry cycle. Some models have shorter, energy-efficient cycles for fine china and lightly soiled dishes. Other features include shorter rinse and dry cycles, built-in water softeners, and heating elements that quickly heat the wash and rinse water to 140°F. Except for cookware with burned-on food, dishes do not need to be rinsed before you put them in the dishwasher.

For most brand-name models and all of our selections, the Association of Home Appliance Manufacturers (AHAM) offers a bit of consumer protection in addition to the manufacturer's warranty. If you take steps recommended by the manufacturer to resolve any problems and still feel the manufacturer has not backed the product to your satisfaction, you can appeal to the Major Appliance Consumer Action Panel. For details about this independent complaint resolution group, write to AHAM, 20 North Wacker Drive, Chicago, Illinois 60606.

Features and Terminology

Construction: The dishwasher tub must withstand continual contact with hot water and detergents. Stainless steel, used in fewer and fewer high-quality models, is the most durable and the most expensive tub material. Porcelain enamel on steel is also durable, especially if it has two or three coats. Polypropylene is an inexpensive alternative. Different models have up to three layers of sound insulation to muffle operating noise.

Controls: Push-button or dial controls are the most economical and reliable. Electronic touch controls add a bit more to the cost of the machine and give it a high-tech look.

Cycles: A dishwasher can have from 2 to 9-or-more cycles. Three basic cycles handle most chores: a light wash (called energy-saving wash by some manufacturers), a normal wash, and a heavy-duty cycle for pots and pans.

Spray-washing action: The best washing action comes from a three-level spray assembly that has arms at the top and bottom and a turret to help spray the upper rack. The problem with the three-level assembly is that the center turret takes up some of the washer's capacity. Units with two-level spray arms also do a good job, and sometimes the increased capacity of the unit is more important than three-level washing. One-level washing may not provide satisfactory cleaning.

Time delay: Many models now have a time-delay setting, which starts your dishwasher automatically at a preset time.

Water heating: A growing number of models feature an internal water-temperature booster system that ensures consistently hot water of about 140°F for the wash and rinse cycles.

You can reduce the cost of operating your hot water heater by setting the thermostat as low as 120°F.

Best Buys '92

Our Best Buy dishwashers follow, divided into the categories of built-in dishwashers and portable models. Within each category, the best of the Best Buys is listed first, followed by our second choice, and so on. Remember that a Best Buy designation applies only to the model listed; it does not necessarily apply to other models by the same manufacturer or to an entire product line.

BUILT-IN DISHWASHERS

IN-SINK-ERATOR CLASSIC SUPREME ✔ BEST BUY

The In-Sink-Erator Classic Supreme is an underrated built-in dishwasher of impressive quality. Its value is evident in the triple-coated porcelain-on-steel tank and inner door, the powerful ½-horsepower motor, and the multiposition upper rack. It has four cycles: pots and pans, normal, light, and rinse/hold. The Classic Supreme has easy-to-use push-button operation; sound insulation on the top, sides, and back of the tank; a self-cleaning, three-stage filtration system; an automatic intake water temperature booster; and a fan-driven, heated-air drying system.
Specifications: height, adjustable from 33¹¹⁄₁₆″ to 35″; **width,** 24″; **depth,** 26″; **heating element wattage,** 750 watts; **volts,** 115; **water use,** regular wash, 9¾ gallons. **Warranty: parts and labor,** one year; **motor,** five years; **tank and inner door,** ten years.

    Approx. retail price   **Approx. low price**
    $549   **$531**

MAYTAG WU404 ✔ BEST BUY

The Maytag WU404 is a value-priced, better-quality built-in dishwasher. It has a powerful ⅓-horsepower motor, a three-stage filtration system (hard- and soft-food disposers and a mesh filter), and three kinds of sound insulation. This model

---

Prices are accurate at time of printing; subject to manufacturer's change.

has five cycles: regular, light, pots and pans, rinse and hold, and sani-wash, which is said to be more effective in killing germs. It is available in a choice of four panel colors: white, black, almond, or Harvest Wheat.

Specifications: height, adjustable from 34″ to 35½″; **width,** 24″; **depth,** 24⅛″; **heating element wattage,** not available; **volts,** 115; **water use,** regular wash, 11 gallons. **Warranty: parts and labor,** one year; **cabinet against rust, parts,** five years; **wash system, parts,** five years; **tub and liner, parts,** ten years.

Approx. retail price	Approx. low price
$509	$490

HOTPOINT HDA969P

The Hotpoint HDA969P is a value-priced built-in dishwasher with push-button controls and several quality features, including a plate warmer, three-level washing action, and a water-temperature booster, which raises intake water from as low as 120°F to 140°F. This model has a deep upper rack and a soft-food disposer. It has five cycles: pots and pans, normal, light, rinse and hold, and plate warmer. It comes with a reversible door panel in black and almond and a certificate for a free, factory-supplied panel if you prefer another color. A trim kit for custom panels up to ¼ inch thick is available.

Specifications: height, adjustable from 34″ to 35″; **width,** 24″; **depth,** 26¼″; **heating element wattage,** 700 watts; **volts,** 120; **water use,** regular wash, 11 gallons. **Warranty: parts and labor,** one year; **tub and door liner,** ten years.

Approx. retail price	Approx. low price
$379	$349

KITCHENAID KUDC22OT

The KitchenAid KUDC22OT is an exceptional high-quality dishwasher with push-button controls. It has a powerful ½-horsepower motor, two-level washing action, and a water temperature booster that heats intake water from 120°F up to 140°F. Its fiberglass sound insulation is not as effective as the insulation on some of KitchenAid's higher-priced models, if quiet operation is important to you. The KUDC22OT has four cycles: pots and pans, normal, light/china, and rinse and hold. It comes with a reversible door panel in black and almond and a coupon for a free, factory-supplied panel in white and Harvest Wheat if you prefer. Quarter-inch custom panels may also be installed.

Specifications: height, adjustable from 33¹¹⁄₁₆″ to 35″; **width,** 24″; **depth,** 26″; **heating element wattage,** 1360 watts; **volts,** 115; **water use,** regular wash, 9¾ gallons. **Warranty: parts and labor,** one year; **motor, parts,** five years; **tank and inner door,** ten years.

Approx. retail price	Approx. low price
$489	$488

MAGIC CHEF DU85

✔**BEST BUY**

The Magic Chef DU85 is a good-quality built-in dishwasher with easy-to-use push-button controls. Features include a soft-food disposer, a three-level wash system, an extra utensil rack, and a hot wash option. It has four cycles: super scrub, normal, light, and rinse and hold. It comes with reversible panels in almond, Snow White, black, and Harvest Wheat. It will also accept ¼-inch custom trim panels.

Specifications: height, adjustable from 34″ to 35″; **width,** 23¾″; **depth,** 26¼″; **heating element wattage,** not available; **volts,** not available; **water use,** not available. **Warranty: parts and labor,** one year; **tub and door liner,** ten years.

Approx. retail price	Approx. low price
$439	$385

WHIRLPOOL DU8000XX

✔**BEST BUY**

The Whirlpool DU8000XX is a very good built-in dishwasher with two-level spray-wash action. It has mechanical controls, a removable utensils basket, and comes in three front-panel colors: black, white, or almond. Its washing cycles are normal, light, and rinse and hold.

Specifications: height, 33⅞″; **width,** 23⅞″; **depth,** 24″; **heating element wattage,** 500 watts; **volts,** 120; **water use,** not available. **Warranty: parts and labor,** one year; **tub and liner, parts,** ten years.

Approx. retail price	Approx. low price
$299	$273

Prices are accurate at time of printing; subject to manufacturer's change.

PORTABLE DISHWASHERS

WHITE-WESTINGHOUSE SP550N

The White-Westinghouse SP550N is a value-priced full-size portable dishwasher with mechanical controls. It has very good three-way spray action, a ⅛-horsepower motor, deluxe racks, a soft-food disposer, and a removable utensils basket. This model has four cycles: scrub, normal, light, and rinse and hold. It has sound-dampening insulation on two sides. Model SP550N comes in an almond cabinet and top with white, almond, and black panel inserts. A kit is available for ¼-inch custom trim.

Specifications: height, 34″; **width,** 24″; **depth,** 23¾″; **heating element wattage,** not available; **volts,** not available; **water use,** not available. **Warranty: parts and labor,** one year; **water distribution system, parts,** two years; **tub and liner,** ten years.

Approx. retail price	Approx. low price
$419	$386

MAYTAG WC204

The Maytag WC204 is a better-quality full-size portable/convertible dishwasher with mechanical controls. It has a porcelain-enamel tub, a powerful ⅛-horsepower motor, a 3-stage filtration system (hard- and soft-food disposers and a mesh filter), 3 kinds of sound insulation and 2-level spray action. It has three cycles: pots and pans, regular, and light wash. It comes in white or almond with a simulated butcher block top.

Specifications: height, 36½″; **width,** 24″; **depth,** 27″; **heating element wattage,** not available; **volts,** 115; **water use,** regular wash, 11 gallons. **Warranty: parts and labor,** one year; **parts,** two years; **cabinet against rust, parts,** five years; **wash system, parts,** five years; **tub and liner, parts,** ten years.

Approx. retail price	Approx. low price
$519	$482

GENERAL ELECTRIC GSC770M

The General Electric GSC770M is a full-size, full-featured portable/convertible dishwasher with mechanical controls and a durable, porcelain-enamel tub. It has five cycles: Potscrubber, normal, light wash, rinse and hold, and plate warmer. This model has three-way washing action, a soft-food disposer, a deluxe upper rack, and a built-in water temperature booster. It is available in white or almond with a wood-veneer top.

Specifications: height, 36¾"; **width,** 25"; **depth,** 26"; **heating element wattage,** not available; **volts,** 120; **water use,** regular wash, 11 gallons. **Warranty: parts and labor,** one year; **tub and liner,** ten years.

Approx. retail price	Approx. low price
$469	$415

Food-Waste Disposers and Trash Compactors

Taking out the garbage is often a dreaded household chore. The food waste, scrap paper, discarded containers, and other debris that a typical family generates every day can make garbage duty a grubby, often smelly job. But two specialized appliances—the food-waste disposer and the trash compactor—can take much of the mess and work out of kitchen cleanup.

A food-waste disposer, installed under the kitchen sink, takes care of everything from eggshells to chicken bones to orange peels by grinding it up and flushing it down the drain, using water from the faucet to carry it away quickly and easily. A trash compactor, which may be built in under a counter or freestanding, tackles the non-food wastes—such as cans, paper, plastic, or glass—by compressing them into a neat, manageable bundle that can easily be carried out to the curb for pickup.

Food-Waste Disposers

You can pay as little as $50 for a food-waste disposer or as much as $300. The lowest-price models, however, have smaller motors (less than ½ horsepower) that are not as sturdy and are more likely to jam. CONSUMER GUIDE® recommends buying a disposer with at least a ½-horsepower motor for maximum efficiency and reliability. These more powerful (and more expensive) models also have better sound insulation (although no disposer is truly quiet during operation), and are more likely to resist corrosion.

You can probably install a disposer under the kitchen sink and hook it up yourself, especially if you are replacing an existing model. Before buying a unit, check your local building codes to make sure they allow installation of a disposer. Some urban areas do not allow food-waste disposers.

Continuous or Batch Feed?

Disposers are available in continuous-feed or batch-feed configurations. Both mount under the sink and grind up food wastes in the same way. The difference between the two is the way they operate.

A continuous-feed disposer is activated by a remote switch (usually on the wall behind or next to the sink). With the disposer turned on and cold water running, waste can be fed into it continuously. Most continuous-feed disposers come with a safety cover or lid to keep waste from flying out.

A batch-feed disposer is activated only when its cover, or the stopper, is in place. The cover is the switch that turns on the motor. You load the unit with about a quart of food waste, turn on the water, and insert the cover. You cannot add more waste without stopping the disposer.

Although continuous-feed units handle more waste more quickly, a batch-feed disposer may be a safer choice for households with small children. From a price standpoint, both types are about equal. Continuous-feed models usually cost less to buy but are more expensive to install because you need a wall switch. A batch-feed model costs more to buy but less to install. If you are replacing an existing disposer and installing the new one yourself, stick to the type you are replacing because the proper connections are already in place.

Disposer Features

Anti-jam systems: Better disposers have anti-jamming cycles that reverse the motor's direction to clear jams. Others clear jams by applying jolts of power to the machine. We prefer the reversing feature because the jolt-of-power system may stress the motor and grinding blades.

Corrosion resistance: CONSUMER GUIDE® recommends disposers made of stainless steel or corrosion-resistant metal alloys.

Dishwasher-drain access: If you have a dishwasher or plan to install one, make sure the disposer you select has a side opening to connect to a dishwasher-drain hose.

Mounting system: If you are planning to install the disposer, look for a quick-mount system that requires no special tools.

Sound insulation: Good sound insulation, usually rubber or plastic foam, helps reduce noise and vibration while the disposer is in use.

Trash Compactors

A trash compactor, which is about half the size of a standard dishwasher, compresses dry trash—such as bottles, cans, and paper—into dense bundles. Since it only handles dry trash, a compactor will not replace your kitchen garbage can or food-waste disposer, but it will greatly reduce the volume of trash you have to deal with. All compactors have some kind of deodorizing system, but they are not equipped to deal with the strong odors that would result from storing compressed food wastes for several days. Also, certain other kinds of trash, such as aerosol cans, should not be compacted for safety and environmental reasons.

Trash Compactor Features

Operating Convenience: Several models have bars at the base so you can open the loading drawer with a touch of your toe if your hands are full. Others have special loading chutes so trash can be dropped inside without opening the drawer. Some compactors have indicator lights to let you know that they are operating or that they have jammed.

Price: Trash compactors cost from about $300 to $600, or more. Operating expenses, in addition to the purchase price, include the bags used for trash storage. Some models use ordinary plastic garbage bags or generic compactor bags that may be purchased at a supermarket or discount store, while others require special bags that must be bought from a dealer. You will also periodically need to replace the charcoal filters or the liquid or solid deodorant used in the deodorizing system to keep your kitchen smelling fresh.

Safety features: Safety features, such as key locks, prevent curious children from opening the trash drawer or operating the compactor accidentally. If you have children in the house, make sure the model you buy has a safety lock.

Sound insulation: Improved motor designs and increased insulation have reduced the operating noise of today's trash compactors. Also, faster operation and larger capacity mean the noise is emitted for shorter periods of time and less frequently.

Best Buys '92

Our Best Buy food-waste disposers (divided into continuous-feed and batch-feed models) and trash compactors are listed below. The best of the Best Buys are listed first, followed by our second choice, and so on. Remember that a Best Buy rating applies only to the model listed, not necessarily to other models built by the same manufacturer or to an entire product line.

CONTINUOUS-FEED DISPOSERS

FRIGIDAIRE ELIMINATOR D7501

The Frigidaire Eliminator D7501 is a strong, durable continuous-feed disposer at a moderate price. It has a sturdy ¾-horsepower motor and a fully insulated sound shell that effectively muffles operating noise. This disposer is extremely resistant to rust and corrosion, with a stainless-steel grinding ring and turntable and a nylon grinding chamber. The motor has automatic reversing action to eliminate jams. The Eliminator D7501 has a dishwasher-drain connection.

Specifications: drain diameter, standard (1½"); **volts,** 115.
Mounting: E-Z Mount. **Warranty:** five years replacement.

Approx. retail price	Approx. low price
$129	**$113**

KITCHENAID SUPERBA KCDS250S

The KitchenAid Superba KCDS250S has a powerful one-horse-power motor and an excellent warranty. Although more expensive than some other models, it is extremely reliable and well constructed. This disposer has two 360-degree swivel impellers that can tackle all but the toughest bones without jamming. If a jam does occur, the impellers reverse automatically to clear it. A full polystyrene sound shield keeps this disposer quiet during operation. The KCDS250S has a corrosion-resistant stainless-steel grinding chamber, a polypropylene drain chamber, and a chrome shredder ring. This disposer includes a dishwasher-drain connection.

Specifications: drain diameter, standard (1½"); **volts,** 120.
Warranty: parts and labor, seven years.

Approx. retail price	Approx. low price
$249	**$235**

IN-SINK-ERATOR BADGER 5 ✓BEST BUY

The In-Sink-Erator Badger 5 is an efficient continuous-feed disposer for the budget-conscious shopper. It has a ½-horsepower motor and two 360-degree swivel impellers that resist jamming during the grinding operation. If a jam occurs, it can be cleared manually with a wrench that is included. The impellers are rust-resistant stainless steel, and the polyvinylchloride grinding chamber and galvanized-steel shredder ring also resist corrosion. The Badger 5 lacks the full sound insulation found in higher-priced disposers, so it may be noisier than some other models. A manual reset button restarts the disposer in case of an overload. The Badger 5 includes a dishwasher-drain connection.

Specifications: drain diameter, standard (1½"); **volts,** 115.
Mounting: Quick-Lock. **Warranty: parts and labor,** one year.

Approx. retail price	Approx. low price
$65	**not available**

Prices are accurate at time of printing; subject to manufacturer's change.

BATCH-FEED DISPOSERS

SEARS KENMORE 6072 ✔BEST BUY

The Sears Kenmore 6072 is a batch-feed disposer offering jam-resistant, stainless-steel, 360-degree swivel impellers, a strong one-horsepower motor, and an excellent warranty. Its impellers, grinding chamber, and stopper are all corrosion resistant stainless steel. A thick upper shell of insulation effectively muffles operation noise. The 6072 has automatic reversing action to eliminate jams. If a jam does occur, a small wrench is included to clear it. A manual reset button protects the motor. The 6072 has a dishwasher-drain connection.
Specifications: drain diameter, standard (1½″); **volts,** 120. **Mounting:** quick mount. **Warranty: parts and labor,** seven years.

Approx. retail price	Approx. low price
$200	$200

IN-SINK-ERATOR CLASSIC L/C ✔BEST BUY

The In-Sink-Erator Classic L/C is a heavy-duty batch-feed disposer with a powerful one-horsepower motor and an excellent warranty. The Classic L/C also has a very effective polystyrene sound barrier, making it extremely quiet during operation. This disposer's 360-degree swivel impellers automatically reverse to prevent jams. If a jam does occur, you can clear it with the small wrench that is included with the Classic L/C. A manual reset button restarts the motor in case of overload. This disposer has a stainless-steel grinding chamber and impellers, plus a dishwasher-drain connection.
Specifications: drain diameter, standard (1½″); **volts,** 115. **Mounting:** Quick-Lock. **Warranty: parts and labor,** seven years.

Approx. retail price	Approx. low price
$250	not available

HOTPOINT GFB1050G

The Hotpoint GFB1050G is a batch-feed disposer with a sturdy ¾-horsepower motor. Its stainless-steel swivel impellers reverse automatically to avoid jamming during the grinding operation. The drain housing is made of corrosion-resistant glass-filled polyester, and the hopper is nylon. This model is fully insulated to reduce operating noise, and has a manual reset button in case the motor overloads. The GFB1050G has a dishwasher-drain connection. An identical model is sold as the General Electric GFB1050G.

Specifications: drain diameter, standard (1½"); **volts,** 115. **Mounting:** quick mount. **Warranty: parts and labor,** one year.

Approx. retail price	Approx. low price
$229	$188

TRASH COMPACTORS

GENERAL ELECTRIC GCG950

The General Electric GCG950 is a slim, convertible compactor that can be used as a freestanding unit or installed under the counter. It is extremely efficient and convenient to operate; it is also powerful. A step-on floor drawer opener lets you open the compactor easily when your hands are full. This unit uses a solid air freshener to reduce odors. The GCG950 operates with a removable key-lock, and includes a storage compartment for extra bags. It comes with both a reversible front panel in black/almond and a white panel.

Specifications: height, 34½"; **width,** 12"; **depth,** 20¼"; **volts,** 120. **Compaction force,** 5,000 pounds. **Warranty: parts and labor,** one year.

Approx. retail price	Approx. low price
$429	$388

IN-SINK-ERATOR CLASSIC 3304

The In-Sink-Erator Classic 3304 installs under the counter. This model is extremely reliable and well built. The drawer has drop-down sides so a full bag can be slid out easily. An automatic drawer-tilt switch prevents the compactor from operating if it is improperly loaded. The Classic 3304 starts with a removable key-lock, and has a cut-off switch to prevent it from starting if the drawer is open. This compactor uses a solid air freshener,

Prices are accurate at time of printing; subject to manufacturer's change.

but does not have a bag storage area. The Classic 3304 comes with a black front panel. It is also available in white as model 3304-WH.

Specifications: height, 34¼"; **width,** 15"; **depth,** 24"; **volts,** 120. **Compaction force:** 2,300 pounds. **Warranty: parts and labor,** one year.

Approx. retail price	Approx. low price
$419	not available

WHIRLPOOL TU8700XX ✔BEST BUY

The Whirlpool TU8700XX is an undercounter trash compactor. It is very well insulated, making it quieter to operate than many other compactors. One side panel drops down, forming a ramp to make removing a loaded bag easier. The TU8700XX also comes with a reusable bag caddy that has handles to facilitate carrying a full bag. This compactor has a toe bar for hands-free opening. Its removable key-lock is located inside the trash drawer, for greater security. It uses special plastic bags that are scented to combat trash odors. Its reversible front panel is black and almond.

Specifications: height, 34"; **width,** 15"; **depth,** 24³⁄₁₆"; **volts,** 120. **Compaction force:** 2,300 pounds. **Warranty: parts and labor,** one year.

Approx. retail price	Approx. low price
$459	$428

Vacuum Cleaners

It seems that shopping for a vacuum should be easy: the stronger the suction, the better the product. But it turns out to be much more complex since vacuum cleaners come in all shapes and sizes, with a full range of accessories and features. A smart shopping strategy is necessary to beat the sales pitch and to go home with the right product.

Before you hit the stores, you need to answer some questions.

What size is your home? There's no need for a huge model if you have limited closet space and bare floors throughout your house, but even a small home with thick carpeting will not be easy to tackle with a mini machine.

What types of flooring do you have? If you have a sea of wall-to-wall carpeting, a powerful upright will probably be most effective. Lots of tile and wood will be maintained well with a straight suction canister or even a mini-broom vacuum. A mixture of surfaces might be cleaned best with a power-head canister or possibly an upright and handheld combination.

What type of vacuum cleaner are you most comfortable using? Logic may lead you to a certain type of cleaner. Your home may be crying out for canister, but if you are most at ease operating an upright, it may be best to go with what you know. Vacuuming is unpleasant enough without making it more awkward with a machine that goes against your grain. The most effective way to test your adaptability to something new is to test a unit in the store. In fact, you shouldn't buy a cleaner without plugging it in and really trying it. Many dealers are willing to send you home with a loaner.

The best shopping tip of all is to be educated about the advantages and disadvantages of every category of cleaner. Here is a breakdown to give you a hand.

Upright, Canister, or Power-Head Vacuum Cleaner?

An upright is best for rug and carpet cleaning. Its beater bar brush digs up embedded dirt and grit from even high pile carpeting. Currently available uprights are more lightweight than other models, making them easier to handle on stairs, but they still cannot boast the maneuverability of a canister. The upright generally loses to the canister in above-the-floor cleaning (such as upholstery, window sills, draperies, etc.) since attachments to tackle these jobs are not as accessible and because the upright does not roll along with the job as easily.

A new generation of uprights store above-floor tools on the unit, and some even have attached hoses. Their convenience is greatly increased by these innovations, but keep in mind that anything that adds to ease above the floor generally takes some power away from the motor's ability to clean carpets with full upright strength.

Canister vacuum cleaners are designed to make up for the shortcomings of uprights. The canister is usually quieter than the upright and does a fine job of cleaning bare floors and low-pile carpets. The nozzle's low-profile permits better access under furniture, in tight spaces, and on stair treads. The canister's easy-to-change attachments allow it to effectively remove dust from walls, curtains, and lamp shades. Because it lacks the upright's beater barbrush, the canister does not remove dirt that has sifted down into carpet pile as well as the upright. Most new canister models are extremely lightweight and maneuverable.

A strong canister vacuum cleaner with a power-head combines the best of both the upright and the standard canister. It has a rolling tank (usually with a tool caddy), a hose, and a nozzle just like the canister, but it also has a power-head, which is the beater barbrush similar to that on an upright. When you shop for a power-head, examine the brush roll carefully. Some have an independent motor that allows them to dig deeper into thick pile carpet. Others have a turbo or suction-driven brush roll that has less strength but still may be adequate.

Mini Vacuum Cleaners

Compact vacuum cleaners come in many shapes and sizes. They are designed for quick spot clean-ups of dry spills. These scaled-down units can be a great convenience, as long as you remember that they are intended for small jobs. The motors on minis have limited power, and the dust bag or cup must be emptied often. Cordless minis are portable and ideal for room-to-room touch-ups as well as car care. Corded models have greater strength and do not run out of juice, but you will have to work with the same outlet area limitations of a regular vacuum cleaner though minis made specifically for cars have adapters for plugging into your car lighter.

Wet/Dry Vacuum Cleaners

Wet/dry vacuum cleaners handle messes indoors and out. Full-size models quickly clean up a muddy garage or soapy washing machine overflow. Some feature a blower for added versatility. Cordless handheld versions offer the ultimate convenience in quick clean-ups of spilled drinks or other small wet/dry spills. Families with small children often find these handy and convenient for clean up after mealtimes.

Safety

As with any electrically powered product, you want to be sure that your vacuum cleaner will be safe to use. Look for the Underwriters Laboratories (UL) seal, which means the product meets their safety standards. Most vacuum cleaner manufacturers will not introduce a vacuum cleaner to the public without this seal. The product selections in this chapter are UL listed.

Features and Terminology

Bag-full indicator: Some models have a signal light that lets you know when to change the bag. This is a great feature since cleaning performance drops considerably when the bag is full and the motor may overheat.

Cord reel: This feature provides for cord storage hidden within the vacuum body. The cord automatically rewinds in a flash. Most other vacuum cleaners require cording to be hand wound around storage hooks on the outside of the cleaner.

Dust bag/cup: The dust bag should be large enough to avoid frequent changes but easy to change when necessary. Be sure the particular disposable bag size and style that your vacuum cleaner uses is readily available. Most new uprights have top-loading vacuum bags; this means the dust and dirt enter the bag from the top rather than being pushed up from the bottom. This takes stress off the motor and provides better and stronger vacuum cleaner performance.

Overall efficiency: You can get a good idea of a vacuum cleaner's efficiency by testing it on gritty, granular materials, such as sand or salt, which are difficult to pick up. (Cotton fiber or fine powder may look bad on a carpet, but they actually require very little suction to remove.) After running the machine, examine the carpet pile to see if the substance was picked up or just pushed into the carpet.

Self propulsion: Self-propelled machines glide easily over thick carpets with only gentle guidance from the user.

Suction selector: This control allows you to determine the amount of suction needed for cleaning jobs and is especially useful for cleaning draperies, upholstery, and delicate fibers. A concentration of suction can be used on areas with stubborn lint or pet hair.

Wattage, horsepower (HP), or amps: Vacuum cleaner manufacturers rate the power of their products in different ways. To make it possible to compare the Best Buy models, we've converted all power measurements into watts. You can also make comparisons by judging two units on their HP or amps (if this figure is available for both). Remember, when discussing the strength of a cordless vacuum, the wattage rating will only apply to recharging. The vacuum cleaner itself is driven by a power cell battery that runs at a higher rate of power than the wattage indicates. Also keep in mind that elements other than watts and HP determine the performance of the model. Use power ratings as a guide, and always test several models yourself to verify your choices.

Best Buys '92

Our Best Buy vacuum cleaners follow. They are arranged in the following categories: upright, canister, power-head, mini, and wet/dry vacuum cleaners. These appliances have been selected on the basis of convenience, performance, and overall value. Within each category, the item we consider the best on the Best Buys is listed first, followed by our second choice, and so on. Remember that the Best Buy designation applies only to the model listed; it does not necessarily apply to other models made by the same manufacturer.

UPRIGHT VACUUM CLEANERS

EUREKA BOSS E.S.P. UPRIGHT 2034 ✔ BEST BUY

The Eureka Boss E.S.P Upright 2034 has remained one of the best-selling models in the country and for good reason. It's powerful, at 1000 watts, and reliable. The no-nonsense Boss is an attractive black model that features a generous 11-quart top-loading disposable bag. It's an easy-to-carry 15 pounds. The standard 12-inch agitator bar is made of extra-strong chrome-plated steel for longevity. The 20-foot cord wraps around hooks on the vacuum for storage. Attachments are not the draw for this model; however, there is an optional 6-piece attachment set offered for $12.

Warranty: five years.

Approx. retail price	Approx. low price
$180	$103

SHARP EC3320

The Sharp EC3320's price and maneuverability make this sleek gray vacuum a true value. It has an ample 10-quart top-loading dust bag and an 18-foot cord. The EC3320 weighs a manageable 12 pounds. It operates with 650 watts of power and has a 10-inch acrylic agitator bar. An optional accessory package ($19.99) includes eight pieces.

Warranty: parts and labor, one year.

Approx. retail price	Approx. low price
$170	$146

Prices are accurate at time of printing; subject to manufacturer's change.

PANASONIC MC-6317

The Panasonic MC-6317 is an impressive and good-looking deep wine-colored model that is powerful (800 watts) and boasts an oversize 14-inch strong metal agitator bar. The cord length is also generous, measuring 25 feet. The MC-6317 weighs 15 pounds and features a full 10-quart top-loading bag. A bag-full indicator and headlight add to the appeal. An eight-piece attachment kit also comes with the cleaner.

Warranty: parts and labor, one year.

Approx. retail price	Approx. low price
$240	$227

HOOVER U4617-910

The Hoover U4617-910 is a reliable crimson-colored vacuum that offers a lot for the price. Features include an 11½-quart top-loading dust bag, a 12-inch plastic agitator bar, a headlight, a 20-foot wraparound cord, and 590 watts of power. Best of all, this upright has easy-to-change tools (5 pieces in all) stored on-board. The 13½-pound weight makes it easy to manipulate.

Warranty: parts and labor, one year.

Approx. retail price	Approx. low price
$145	$110

REGINA HOUSEKEEPER HO6331

The Regina Housekeeper HO6331 is light gray and is an ergonomic masterpiece. The Housekeeper has many advantages: It weighs only 11 pounds and probably has the easiest on-board tool changing capabilities of any upright on the market. A permanently attached 36-inch hose facilitates quick changes. The 20-foot cord, 684 watts of power, and 3¹⁄₁₀ quart-bag capacity are acceptable. The maple-wood agitator bar measures an adequate 11 inches.

Warranty: parts and labor, one year.

Approx. retail price	Approx. low price
$100	$89

Prices are accurate at time of printing; subject to manufacturer's change.

CANISTER VACUUM CLEANERS

SEARS 20035

The Sears 20035 has 3½ horsepower and a low price tag. The light gray 20035 is quite a buy. This effective appliance has a 20-foot wraparound cord and a 7-foot hose. It uses a 4⅚-quart disposable bag, and a reusable cloth bag is available.
Warranty: parts and labor, one year.

Approx. retail price	Approx. low price
not available	$115

EUREKA RALLY 3850

The Eureka Rally 3850 sports an apricot color and tobacco trim. It delivers 1,000 watts of power. Eight tools are stored on the cleaner for easy access. The canister weighs 15 pounds and has a generous 7-foot hose.
Warranty: parts and labor, one year.

Approx. retail price	Approx. low price
$190	$161

SANYO SC27 R/BK

The Sanyo SC27 R/BK is a real find for the bargain hunter. It is lightweight at only 6⅚ pounds. Still, at 850 watts, this canister is no wimp. The SC27 R/BK is offered in two color combinations: in red with black trim or black with red trim. The features include a retractable cord, a reusable dust cup, and a six-piece on-board tool kit.
Warranty: parts and labor, one year.

Approx. retail price	Approx. low price
$90	not available

POWER-HEAD VACUUM CLEANERS

EUREKA RALLY 3930 POWER-TEAM ✔BEST BUY

The Eureka Rally 3930 Power-Team is an attractive teal-colored cleaner that packs 900 watts of power. It weighs only 13¾

pounds and features a 12-inch chrome-steel agitator bar, a 20-foot wraparound cord, a 7-foot hose, a headlight, an 8-piece attachment set (stored on the canister), and a bag-full indicator.
Warranty: parts and labor, one year.

Approx. retail price	Approx. low price
$270	$176

SANYO SCP90

The Sanyo SCP90 has a full 1,400 watts of power, making it an exceptional vacuum cleaner. It weighs 15 pounds and boasts a bag-full indicator. Other features include a 7½-quart dust bag, a retractable 20-foot cord, and a swivel hose. Three other attachments are standard and stored on-board: a crevice tool, a dusting brush, and an upholstery brush. The SCP90 also has a slow suction switch to regulate power for lightweight jobs, such as draperies and rugs.
Warranty: parts and labor, one year.

Approx. retail price	Approx. low price
$300	$300

PANASONIC MC-9520

The Panasonic MC-9520 may be higher priced, but the 1,350 watts of power and the features behind it make it worth the money. This is a quality appliance, and sturdiness takes precedence over weight—it weighs 23 pounds. The off-white and taupe MC-9520 boasts a bag-full indicator, a 9⅝-quart bag, and an extra-wide 14-inch strong metal agitator bar. There are eight attachments that are stored neatly away on the canister body.
Warranty: parts and labor, one year.

Approx. retail price	Approx. low price
$400	$276

MINI VACUUM CLEANERS

PANASONIC MC-1060

The Panasonic MC-1060 is a corded mini that has exceptional power for the mini category and a large dust cup (⅗₀ quart). The

MC-1060 doesn't skimp on the cord either; you get a full 25 feet. The rotating brush agitator is quite effective for deep cleaning—a dream for carpeted stair treads.
Warranty: parts and labor, one year.

Approx. retail price	Approx. low price
$76	$68

BLACK & DECKER POWERPRO DB6000

The Black & Decker Powerpro DB6000 is a truly effective cordless mini that holds a charge and maintains strength for a long time. It's a good-looking black vacuum that doesn't offer any extra attachments. You pay for the simplicity of a strong, high-performance product. Reliability is so sure that the vacuum carries a full two-year warranty. If attachments are necessary, they can be purchased separately.
Warranty: parts and labor, two years.

Approx. retail price	Approx. low price
$72	$54

EUREKA SUPERBROOM 175

The Eureka Superbroom 175 is proof that the days of the weak powerbroom are gone. This stand-up mini vacuum is packed with 420 watts of power and incorporates a full 11-inch floor nozzle, a retractable bristle strip, and a 20-foot cord. There's no bag-full indicator light, but the six-quart dust cup is transparent, so you can see when it is time to empty it. The blue topaz/pewter stick vacuum weighs only 5¾ pounds.
Warranty: parts and labor, one year.

Approx. retail price	Approx. low price
$60	$49

WET/DRY VACUUM CLEANERS

EUREKA 8-GALLON 2808A

The Eureka 8-Gallon 2808A is a full-size wet/dry vacuum cleaner for a super-low price. It weighs only ten pounds and has an

Prices are accurate at time of printing; subject to manufacturer's change.

internal shut-off switch to prevent overflows. The 2808A is 2-tone gray with red accents, and has a 12-foot cord and 4 attachments (2 wands, a 6-foot hose, and a floor nozzle with removable squeegee strip).

Warranty: parts and labor, one year.

Approx. retail price	Approx. low price
$90	$70

HOOVER DUBL-DUTY 300 S1103 ✔BEST BUY

The Hoover Dubl-Duty 300 S1103 offers a convenient, cordless way to tackle small wet and dry spills around the house at a surprising price. It's lightweight, only 1⁹⁄₁₀ pounds, and has an 8-ounce transparent dust cup. The S1103 comes in oyster white with smoked gray accents.

Warranty: one year.

Approx. retail price	Approx. low price
$50	$32

SHOP VAC WET/DRY VACUUM WITH POWER BLOWER 333-40 ✔BEST BUY

The Shop Vac Wet/Dry Vacuum with Power Blower 333-40 is a full-size vacuum cleaner that's sturdy and simply designed. It cleans up messes indoors and out, and has an ample ten-gallon dry capacity (eight gallons wet). This vacuum is made of dent- and rust-resistant plastic, and is styled in orange and black. The unit can be converted into a handheld electric blower. It features automatic shut-off to prevent overflow. Many accessories are available, from car cleaning tools to upholstery cleaning attachments. This company pioneered wet/dry vacuums, and this model is a good example of how experience pays.

Warranty: parts and labor, two years.

Approx. retail price	Approx. low price
$99	$78

Clothes Washers

In the fifties, clothes washers belonged only in the basement or laundry room. Today, more and more machines are being found in or near the kitchen, the bedroom, and the bathroom. It makes sense to put them where the dirty clothes are. Some of today's innovative styles will fit in tight spaces in your home.

Modular Parts and Microelectronics

The use of modular internal parts is making washing machine repairs easier and less expensive. Modular snap-in and snap-out parts facilitate in-home maintenance. Be sure your washer has front access to its mechanical parts.

Energy-Saving Features

Clothes washers can have many energy-saving features. Some machines automatically rinse with cold water. Rinsing a typical load of wash with cold instead of warm water reduces energy consumption by up to eight percent. Some machines use less water for a standard load. Mini baskets and small-load features also save on water consumption.

Federal law requires clothes washers to carry an energy label stating the expected annual operating cost of the appliance based on a power cost of 7 cents per kilowatt-hour. The actual cost of your power is likely to differ, but this figure is a standard that you can use when comparing the energy efficiency of different models.

Safety Factors

A washer is a potentially lethal combination of 220 volts of electricity and a tub of water. As with all electrical devices, look for the Underwriters Laboratories (UL) seal, which indicates the machine meets their stringent safety requirements.

If you have young children, look for a lid switch that stops the agitator or spin action when the lid is raised. Some washers have an automatic lock that prevents the lid from being opened during the spin cycle.

For most brand-name models, the Association of Home Appliance Manufacturers (AHAM) offers you a bit of consumer protection in addition to the manufacturer's warranty. If you take steps recommended by the manufacturer to resolve any problems and still feel the manufacturer has not backed the product to your satisfaction, you can appeal to the Major Appliance Consumer Action Panel. For details about this independent complaint resolution group, write to AHAM, 20 North Wacker Drive, Chicago, IL 60606.

Features and Terminology

Capacity: Tub sizes range from 1½ cubic feet to 3 cubic feet, but there is no standardized terminology for machine capacity. Some standard-capacity machines are labeled large capacity, which can be confusing. Large items, such as queen and king-size bedding, require the largest-capacity machines.

Controls: Almost every manufacturer offers one or two models with electronic controls. While you may wish to give all of your appliances the most modern appearance, we believe the dials and push buttons found on most machines are more reliable than electronic controls.

Cycles: Three wash cycles (regular, permanent press, and delicate) and a soak setting can handle most household laundry chores. Cycles can be preset prior to each load (semiprogrammed) or entirely automatic (fully programmed).

Lint filter: This mechanism filters lint out of the rinse water and keeps lint from being deposited on your clothes. A lint filter should be easy to remove and clean, if necessary. Many machines have self-cleaning filters.

Load-balance stabilizer: When a load becomes unbalanced, some washers buzz a warning, some shut off, and others slow down and compensate automatically for the imbalance. The buzzer system is generally the most effective, assuming you are in earshot and can redistribute the load.

Speed: Most machines offer two speeds, but there are other combinations. Normal agitate/normal spin and slow agitate/slow spin are the most common.

Water temperature: Several combinations of hot, warm, and cold water temperatures are available for wash and rinse cycles. A warm rather than hot rinse is kinder to clothes and more energy efficient. A warm-rinse cycle may add $40 to the cost of the machine. A cold-rinse cycle is often as effective as a warm one, and is more energy efficient.

Best Buys '92

Our Best Buy clothes washers follow, arranged in the following categories: large-capacity, standard-capacity, compact washers, and over-and-under combination washers and dryers. The machines within a category are listed in order of quality. The best of the Best Buys is listed first, followed by our second choice, and so on. A Best Buy designation applies only to the model listed. It does not necessarily apply to other models made by the same manufacturer.

LARGE-CAPACITY WASHERS

MAYTAG A9700

The Maytag A9700 is a quality-crafted, extra-large-capacity clothes washer. This dual-speed machine has a ⅓-horsepower motor. It has four cycles: regular, permanent press, knits/delicates, and automatic presoak. It also has four water temperature selections for washing and rinsing: warm/cold, hot/cold, cold/cold, and hot/warm. Other features include an infinitely adjustable water-level control, bleach and fabric softener dispensers, and a self-cleaning lint filter. Model A9700 comes in white, almond, and Harvest Wheat.

Specifications: height, 43⅝"; **width,** 25½"; **depth,** 27"; **volts/amps,** 120/15. **Warranty: labor,** one year; **parts,** two years; **cabinet, computer controls, and dryer drum against rust (parts only),** five years; **transmission (parts only),** ten years.

Approx. retail price	Approx. low price
$619	$575

GIBSON WA27F2WX ✔ BEST BUY

The Gibson WA27F2WX is a value-priced, extra-large-capacity clothes washer. This single-speed model has a ½-horsepower motor. It has three water-level settings and three wash/rinse settings: warm/cold, hot/cold, and cold/cold. The WA27F2WX has four cycles: regular, sanitize/custom soak, permanent press, and knits/delicates. Other features include a self-cleaning lint filter and a tough polypropylene tub.

Specifications: height, 43⅝"; **width,** 27"; **depth,** 27"; **volts/amps,** 120/15. **Warranty: labor,** one year, limited; **parts,** two years, limited; **transmission (parts only),** five years; **tub (parts and labor),** 25 years.

Approx. retail price	Approx. low price
$399	$383

SEARS KENMORE 29841 ✔ BEST BUY

The Sears Kenmore 29841 is a reliable, better-quality, extra-large-capacity clothes washer. This dual-speed, ½-horsepower machine has five cycles at each speed: presoak, prewash, cotton/sturdy, permanent press, and knits. It has five water-temperature combinations for wash and rinse and an infinitely adjustable water-level control.

Specifications: height, 43"; **width,** 27"; **depth,** 25½"; **volts/amps:** 120/not available. **Warranty:** one year.

Approx. retail price	Approx. low price
$485	$480

HOTPOINT WLW3700B ✔ BEST BUY

The Hotpoint WLW3700B is a reliable, extra-large-capacity clothes washer with a feature that does hand-washables. This

Prices are accurate at time of printing; subject to manufacturer's change.

dual-speed machine has seven cycles: regular heavy, regular normal, regular light, permanent press, knits/delicates, soak, and handwash. Its wash-and-rinse combinations are warm/cold, hot/cold, and cold/cold. The WLW3700B has an infinitely variable water-level control. Other features include bleach and fabric softener dispensers and a self-cleaning lint filter. It comes in white and almond.
Specifications: height, 42½"; **width,** 27"; **depth,** 25"; **volts/amps,** 115/15 or 20. **Warranty: parts and labor,** one year; **transmission (parts only),** five years.

Approx. retail price	Approx. low price
$429	$393

STANDARD-CAPACITY WASHERS

MAYTAG A7800 ✓BEST BUY

The Maytag A7800 is a better-quality, standard-capacity clothes washer. This dual-speed machine has a ⅓-horsepower motor. Its four cycles are regular, permanent press, knits/delicates, and automatic presoak. Model A7800 has four wash/rinse water temperature settings: warm/cold, hot/cold, hot/warm, and cold/cold. Other features include an infinitely variable water-level control, self-cleaning lint filter, and bleach and fabric softener dispensers. It comes in white and almond.
Specifications: height, 43⅝"; **width,** 25½"; **depth,** 27"; **volts/amps,** 120/15. **Warranty: labor,** one year; **parts,** two years; **cabinet, computer controls, and dryer drum against rust (parts only),** five years; **transmission (parts only),** ten years.

Approx. retail price	Approx. low price
$579	$556

WHIRLPOOL LA5500XT ✓BEST BUY

The Whirlpool LA5500XT is a good value in a standard-capacity clothes washer. It has two speeds and a hefty ½-horsepower motor. The LA5500XT has eight cycles: super wash, regular normal, regular heavy, permanent press normal, permanent press light, knits/gentle normal, knits/gentle light, and soak. It

Prices are accurate at time of printing; subject to manufacturer's change.

CLOTHES WASHERS

has three water-level settings and three wash/rinse temperature combinations: warm/cold, hot/cold, and cold/cold. The tub
on this model is made of tough polypropylene. It also has a
self-cleaning lint filter. Colors are white and almond.
Specifications: height, 42⅜"; **width,** 26⅞"; **depth,** 25½";
volts/amps, not available. **Warranty: parts and labor,** one
year; **gear assembly and top against rust (parts only),** five
years; **outer tub (parts only),** ten years.

Approx. retail price	Approx. low price
$439	$399

GENERAL ELECTRIC WWA5800M ✓BEST BUY

The General Electric WWA5800M is a standard-capacity, single-speed clothes washer that has the features most users
need, including a mini-tub for delicates and small items. It has
four water-level selections, three wash temperature settings (all
with cold rinse), and six cycles (regular heavy, regular normal,
regular light, regular soak, permanent press normal, and permanent press light). It has a lint filter but no bleach or fabric
softener dispensers. It comes in white or almond.
Specifications: height, 42"; **width,** 27"; **depth,** 25"; **volts/
amps,** 115/15 or 20. **Warranty: parts and labor,** one year;
transmission (parts only), five years.

Approx. retail price	Approx. low price
$399	$369

HOTPOINT WLW1500B ✓BEST BUY

The Hotpoint WLW1500B is a no-frills, standard-capacity, single-speed clothes washer. It has three water-level settings,
three wash temperature settings (all with cold rinse), and six
cycles (regular heavy, regular normal, regular light, permanent
press, knits/delicates, and soak). This model has a self-cleaning lint filter but no bleach or fabric softener dispensers. It
comes in white or almond.
Specifications: height, 42"; **width,** 27"; **depth,** 25";
volts/amps, 115/15 or 20. **Warranty: parts and labor,** one
year; **transmission (parts only),** five years.

Approx. retail price	Approx. low price
$379	$343

Prices are accurate at time of printing; subject to manufacturer's change.

COMPACT WASHERS

WHIRLPOOL LC4900XT

The Whirlpool LC4900XT is a compact portable/convertible two-speed clothes washer that has many of the features found on full-size models, including a powerful ½-horsepower motor. Paired with its matching clothes dryer, you can fit an entire laundry center into a tight space. This is a great advantage if space is a crucial problem, but the capacity of this machine is 1½ cubic feet compared to 2⅗ cubic feet in a standard-size machine. This model has six cycles: super wash, regular/heavy, permanent press, knits/gentle, soak, and prewash. It has four water-level settings and four wash/rinse combinations: hot/warm, hot/cold, warm/cold, and cold/cold. The LC4900XT comes with casters and a faucet attachment, or it can be permanently installed with an optional conversion kit. It comes in white or almond.

Specifications: height, 32½"; **width,** 23⅞"; **depth,** 23⅝"; **volts/amps,** not available. **Warranty: parts and labor,** one year; **gear assembly and top against rust (parts only),** five years; **outer tub,** ten years.

Approx. retail price	Approx. low price
$519	$469

HOTPOINT WWP1180G

The Hotpoint WWP1180G is a compact, single-speed washer designed for tight spaces. There is also a companion wall-mounted dryer. It has three wash temperature selections, all with cold rinse. A bi-fold lid provides easy access in under-the-dryer installation. The WWP1180G has three cycles: regular, delicate, and permanent press. Other features include a self-cleaning lint filter and a polypropylene basket.

Specifications: height, 34"; **width,** 23½"; **depth,** 24¾"; **volts/amps,** 120/15 or 20. **Warranty: parts and labor,** one year; **transmission (parts only),** five years.

Approx. retail price	Approx. low price
$499	$439

Prices are accurate at time of printing; subject to manufacturer's change.

OVER-AND-UNDER COMBINATIONS

MAYTAG S7800 ✓BEST BUY

The Maytag S7800 is a better-quality, full-size, stacked washer and dryer with mechanical controls. The single-speed washer has three water-level settings, three water temperature settings, and three cycles: regular, permanent press, and delicate/knits. It has a capable, 1/3-horsepower motor; a self-cleaning lint filter; and bleach and fabric softener dispensers. The top-mounted dryer offers three temperature selections, automatic drying cycles, and an end-of-cycle signal.

Washer specifications: height, 35″; **width,** 27½″; **depth,** 27½″; **volts/amps,** 115/15. **Warranty: labor,** one year; **parts,** two years; **cabinet against rust (parts only),** five years; **transmission (parts only),** ten years. **Dryer specifications: height,** 38″; **width,** 27½″; **depth,** 21″; **volts/amps,** 115/240/30 (electric), 115/15 (gas); **venting,** one-way; **lint trap location,** front. **Warranty: labor,** one year; **parts,** two years; **drum and cabinet against rust (parts only),** five years.

Approx. retail price	Approx. low price
$1,029	$957
(electric dryer)	(electric dryer)
$1,069	$1,002
(gas dryer)	(gas dryer)

GIBSON EL27M6WX/GL27M6WX ✓BEST BUY

The Gibson EL27M6WX (electric dryer) and the GL27M6WX (gas dryer) are value-priced, full-size stacked washers and dryers with mechanical controls and powerful, ½-horsepower motors. The dual-speed washer has four wash/rinse water temperature settings: warm/warm, warm/cold, hot/cold, and cold/cold. It has three water-level selections and six cycles: regular, permanent press, knit/delicate, prewash, timed soak, and heavy wash. Its polypropylene tub is covered by an incredible 25 year warranty. The dryer has five timed and automatic cycles, four temperature settings, a drying rack, and a lighted drum.

Washer specifications: height, 36¹⁄₁₆″; **width,** 27″; **depth,** 30¹³⁄₁₆″; **volts/amps,** 120/30. **Warranty: labor,** one year; **parts,**

Prices are accurate at time of printing; subject to manufacturer's change.

two years; **transmission (parts only),** five years; **tub,** 25 years. **Dryer specifications: height,** 39⅝"; **width,** 27"; **depth,** 25¼"; **volts/amps,** 120/208/30 or 120/240/30 (electric), 120/20 (gas). **Warranty: labor,** one year; **parts,** two years.

Approx. retail price	Approx. low price
$900	$900
(electric dryer)	(electric dryer)
$999	$855
(gas dryer)	(gas dryer)

Clothes Dryers

It's preferable—but not essential—for your new clothes dryer to match your clothes washer in color and capacity. It's best, however, to select a dryer that closely matches your drying needs. Permanent press sportswear, for example, requires low-temperature drying with a cool-down cycle. If many of your clothes are permanent press, be sure to choose a dryer with a permanent press cycle. King- and queen-size sheets and comforters require a large-capacity machine.

Gas or Electric

Natural gas clothes dryers generally cost $20 to $40 more than electric ones, but in most parts of the country, they cost about two-thirds as much to operate. Both gas and electric dryers come in full-size and compact models; you can also get small-capacity portable electric units. Gas dryers must be installed permanently because they are attached to the gas line and vented to the outside. Most gas models include an energy-saving electronic-ignition system—the burner ignites after the power has been turned on.

Features and Terminology

Air fluff: On this setting, the machine tumbles the load without heat; it is used for drying or freshening pillows, down jackets, and blankets.

Controls: Three kinds of controls are available. A timed control permits you to run the machine for a period of one hour or longer. An automatic control can be set for the desired degree of dryness. An electronic control senses when the load is dry and shuts off the dryer.

Drying cycles: Three basic cycles handle most kinds of fabric: regular, permanent press, and air fluff. A permanent press cycle has a cool-down period of about five minutes, during which the drum rotates with the heat off. This cycle minimizes heat-set wrinkles and should bring the load to room temperature. A delicate or gentle cycle runs on low heat.

Dryness sensor: This is a safeguard against over-drying. It detects the moisture content of the clothes or of the dryer's exhaust, and automatically shuts off the unit when the humidity reaches a certain level.

Lint filter: An effective lint filter is essential to the performance of a dryer. It should be accessible and easy to remove for cleaning. Some lint filters have audible alerts that signal when they are full.

Drying rack: If you frequently wash sneakers or other items that you would prefer to dry without tumbling, get a model that comes with a drying rack.

Wrinkle prevention: This fabric-care system is convenient if you are unable to unload your dryer as soon as it stops. The unit continues to tumble the load intermittently without heat for as long as 2½ hours. On some models a buzzer sounds at intervals during this period.

Consumer Protection

All our selections are backed with an extra bit of consumer protection if you should ever need it. If you have problems with any brand-name dryer and follow all of the manufacturer's recommendations to resolve them, and you still are not satisfied, you can appeal to the Major Appliance Consumer Action Panel. For details about this complaint resolution group, contact the Association of Home Appliance Manufacturers, 20 N. Wacker Drive, Chicago, Illinois 60606.

Best Buys '92

Our Best Buy clothes dryers follow. Dryer types are divided into the following categories: large-capacity dryers, standard-capacity dryers, and compact dryers. Because gas and electric conversions of the same dryer are most often identical except for their model numbers and the power source they use, we give the two model numbers at the beginning of the product review and discuss the product features as they apply to both. If there are distinctions between the gas and electric versions of a model, these differences are itemized. If a particular model is unavailable in a gas or electric version, this is also stated.

Remember that a Best Buy designation applies only to the model listed. It does not necessarily apply to other models made by the same manufacturer.

LARGE-CAPACITY DRYERS

MAYTAG D7500 ✓BEST BUY

The Maytag D7500 (electric or gas) is a large-capacity, better-quality clothes dryer with a dryness sensor for two drying cycles: regular and permanent press with cool-down. It also has a timed cycle for up to one hour of air-fluff only. Its temperature selections are regular and delicate. A diagonal airflow pattern during operation is said to provide improved performance.

Specifications: height, 43⅝"; **width,** 28½"; **depth,** 27"; **volts/amps,** 240/30 (electric), 120/15 (gas); **venting,** three-way; **lint trap location,** front, in opening. **Warranty: labor,** one year; **parts,** two years; **cabinet against rust and drum, parts,** five years.

Approx. retail price	Approx. low price
$429 (electric)	$416 (electric)
$479 (gas)	$456 (gas)

SEARS KENMORE 69831/79831 ✓BEST BUY

The Sears Kenmore 69831 (electric) or 79831 (gas) is a better-quality, large-capacity clothes dryer with a variety of timed and automatic cycles and a hefty ⅓-horsepower motor. Its six drying cycles are cotton/sturdy, permanent press, knits, delicate, touch-up, and air-fluff. Each cycle can be set either by the built-in timer or by the dryness sensor. Select from five temperature settings. An end-of-cycle alarm with variable volume control alerts you when the cycle is done. An audible alarm goes off when the lint filter needs to be cleaned.

Specifications: height, 43"; **width,** 27"; **depth,** 27½"; **volts/amps,** 120 or 240/30 (electric), not available (gas); **venting,** four-way; **lint trap location,** front. **Warranty: parts and labor,** one year.

Approx. retail price	Approx. low price
$410	$400
(69831)	(69831)
$450	$455
(79831)	(79831)

GENERAL ELECTRIC DDE8000M/DDG8080M ✓BEST BUY

The General Electric DDE8000M (electric) or DDG8080M (gas) is a better-quality, extra-large-capacity dryer with timed and automatic cycles. Its automatic cycles are regular, permanent press, and damp dry. This model has timed drying up to 70 minutes and 4 temperature settings, including air-fluff.

Specifications: height, 42½"; **width,** 27"; **depth,** 27⅜"; **volts/amps,** 120 or 240/30 (electric), 120/15 (gas); **venting,** three-way (gas) or four-way (electric); **lint trap location,** front, bottom of access. **Warranty: parts and labor,** one year.

Approx. retail price	Approx. low price
$349	$318
(DDE8000M)	(DDE8000M)
$429	$346
(DDG8080M)	(DDG8080M)

STANDARD-CAPACITY DRYERS

HOTPOINT DLB2650B/DLL2650B ✓BEST BUY

The Hotpoint DLB2650B (electric) or DLL2650B (gas) is a full-featured, reliable, standard-capacity clothes dryer. It has a

Prices are accurate at time of printing; subject to manufacturer's change.
CONSUMER GUIDE®   407

timed cycle of up to 50 minutes and 4 automatic cycles for heavy fabric, normal fabric, permanent press, and knits. Other features are an adjustable-volume end-of-cycle signal, porcelain-enamel drum, wrinkle prevention, and a drum light. **Specifications: height,** 42½"; **width,** 27"; **depth,** 25"; **volts/amps,** 120 or 240/30 (electric), 120/15 (gas); **venting,** four-way (electric), three-way (gas); **lint trap location,** front, bottom of access. **Warranty: parts and labor,** one year.

Approx. retail price	Approx. low price
$349	$318
(DLB2650B)	(DLB2650B)
$389	$346
(DLL2650B)	(DLL2650B)

WHIRLPOOL LE5800XS/LG5801XS ✔BEST BUY

The Whirlpool LE5800XS (electric) or LG5801XS (gas) is a durable, energy-saving clothes dryer with multiple fabric-care selections. It has a hefty ⅓-horsepower motor. With the infinitely variable temperature control, you can choose the right amount of heat for each load. The six drying cycles are automatic regular, automatic permanent press (with cool-down cycle), timed drying up to 70 minutes, damp dry, air-fluff, and tumble press. There is an audible signal at the end of each cycle and when the lint trap needs cleaning. Colors are white and almond. **Specifications: height,** 42⅜"; **width,** 29"; **depth,** 25¹³⁄₁₆" (electric), 26³⁄₁₆" (gas); **volts/amps,** not available; **venting,** one-way; **lint trap location,** top rear, right. **Warranty: parts and labor,** one year.

Approx. retail price	Approx. low price
$379	$379
(LE5800XS)	(LE5800XS)
$419	$407
(LG5801XS)	(LG5801XS)

GENERAL ELECTRIC DDE7208M/DDG7288M ✔BEST BUY

The General Electric DDE7208M (electric) or DDG7288M (gas) is a reliable, standard-capacity clothes dryer. It has sensor-con-

---

trolled and timed drying of up to 70 minutes for each of two cycles: regular and permanent press plus cool-down. Temperature selections are high, medium, low, and air-fluff. It comes in white or almond.

Specifications: height, 42½"; **width,** 27"; **depth,** 25"; **volts/amps,** 120 or 240/30 (electric), 120/15 or 20 (gas); **venting,** four-way (electric), three-way (gas); **lint trap location,** front, bottom of access. **Warranty: parts and labor,** one year.

Approx. retail price	Approx. low price
$329	not available
(DDE7208M)	(DDE7208M)
$369	not available
(DDG7288M)	(DDG7288M)

COMPACT DRYERS

WHITE-WESTINGHOUSE DE250K/DG250K

✔ **BEST BUY**

The White-Westinghouse DE250K (electric) or DG250K (gas) is an economical clothes dryer that can be stacked above the brand's Space Mates front-loading washer. It has three automatic cycles—regular, permanent press, delicates—plus timed drying. This model has four temperature settings, wrinkle prevention, and an end-of-cycle alert with adjustable volume control.

Specifications: height, 34⅝"; **width,** 27"; **depth,** 25½"; **volts/amps,** 120/208 or 120/240/30 (electric), 120/15 (gas); **venting,** four-way (electric), two-way (gas); **lint trap location,** front, bottom of access. **Warranty: parts and labor,** one year.

Approx. retail price	Approx. low price
$429	$425
(DE250K)	(DE250K)
not available	$472
(DG250K)	(DG250K)

HOTPOINT DDP1380G
✔ **BEST BUY**

The Hotpoint DDP1380G is a compact electric dryer that can be wall- or rack-mounted above the matching Hotpoint

CLOTHES DRYERS

WWP1180G clothes washer. In addition to timed drying of up to 80 minutes, this model has 4 automatic cycles: normal, permanent press, knits, and delicate. There are four temperature choices, including air-fluff. It comes in white or almond.
Specifications: height, 33¼"; **width,** 23½"; **depth,** 24½"; **volts/amps,** 240/208/30; **venting,** four-way; **lint trap location,** front, in access. **Warranty: parts and labor,** one year.

Approx. retail price	Approx. low price
$389	not available

WHIRLPOOL LE4930XT/LG4931XT ✓BEST BUY

The Whirlpool LE4930XT (electric) or the LG4931XT (gas) is an economical compact clothes dryer. It stacks neatly above a companion clothes washer and fits in tight spaces. This model has timed drying for regular/heavy, permanent press, and air-fluff cycles, as well as an end-of-cycle signal. While its best feature is that it fits in tight spaces, its drawback is that it dries a load half the size handled by large-capacity dryers. It comes in white or almond.
Specifications: height, 32"; **width,** 23⅞"; **depth,** 21¹⁵⁄₁₆"; **volts/amps,** 240/30 (electric), 120/15 (gas); **venting,** one-way; **lint trap location,** inside, back of drum. **Warranty: parts and labor,** one year.

Approx. retail price	Approx. low price
$359	not available
(LE4930XT)	(LE4930XT)
$399	not available
(LG4931XT)	(LG4931XT)

Air Conditioners

On a hot, muggy summer day, stepping into the cool comfort of an air-conditioned room can improve anyone's mood. Although central air conditioning systems are growing in popularity, a room air conditioner can provide cooling relief at a considerable cost savings. Not only are room air conditioners much less expensive to purchase, their energy bills amount to only a fraction of the cost of operating a central system. By closing off and cooling only specific rooms or areas of your home during different times of the day or night, you avoid wasting money to cool the entire house unnecessarily.

Don't wait for the dog days of summer to shop for a room air conditioner—if you delay until the heat has arrived, prices are likely to be higher and product selection slim. To find the lowest price, shop in the fall, when the season is winding down and stores want to clear out their air conditioner inventories. To get the best selection, shop in the early spring, when dealers are bringing in new models to get ready for the coming hot weather.

Energy Efficiency

Today's room air conditioners are more energy efficient than ever before. Under provisions of a federal law that took effect

AIR CONDITIONERS

January 1, 1990, energy-efficiency standards for air conditioners have been made stricter. All room air conditioners manufactured after that date must now have an Energy Efficiency Rating (EER) of at least 8.0 (the EER is computed by dividing cooling capacity, measured in British thermal units per hour, or Btuh, by the watts of power used). All the models listed here have high ratings, making them particularly energy efficient.

The federal government requires all air conditioners to carry a bright-yellow energy label giving cost-of-operation information, including the EER. The higher the EER, the more efficient the air conditioner and the lower its operating cost. Even though a model with a high EER may carry a higher price tag, you will save money in the long run with lower electricity bills.

Your Cooling Needs

You want to buy a room air conditioner with enough cooling capacity for your needs. If a unit is too small, your room will never be sufficiently cool. If a unit is too large, it will not dehumidify properly, and the room will be uncomfortable and clammy. Also, large units tend to be noisier than smaller ones. Sometimes it is better to buy two or three smaller units than one large one. This allows you to cool the rooms you use most.

Area to be Cooled (in square feet)	Cooling Capacity (in Btuh)
Up to 150	4,000-5,000
150-250	5,000-6,000
250-450	6,000-8,500
450-600	8,500-11,000
600-900	11,000-14,000
900-1,200	15,000-19,000

Features and Terminology

Efficiency in both performance and energy should be your primary concern when you buy an air conditioner. But you should also consider moisture-removal rates. If the air is cool but humid, you will not feel comfortable. All the models listed here have good moisture-removal rates for their size.

Air movement: Look for fully adjustable louvers and vents that let you adjust air movement in different directions. Avoid units with motor-driven louvers.

Electrical requirements: Room air conditioners operate on 115-volt or 230-volt circuits. Most household outlets are 115 volts, 15 amps. The National Electrical Code allows a room air conditioner rated at 115 volts and 7½ amps or less to use this circuit. An appliance branch circuit (115 volts and 15 amps) is a special circuit provided only for the connection of a major appliance. The code allows a room air conditioner rated at 115 volts and 12 amps or less to use this circuit. Appliances requiring greater power are generally operated on a 230-volt circuit installed by an electrician.

Energy savers: Energy-efficient models usually have fans that turn on and off with the compressor. This action can be automatic, or you may have to start it yourself.

Filters: The filter should be cleaned or replaced at the start of the cooling season and then cleaned once a month during the season. Make sure that the air conditioner you choose has an easily accessible filter.

Thermostatic controls: This numbered dial or series of buttons alters the frequency with which the compressor turns on and off. Some thermostatic controls have one or more fan-only settings that run without the compressor.

Best Buys '92

Our Best Buy air conditioners follow. They are arranged in three categories, according to their cooling capacity. The categories are 5,000 to 8,000 Btuh, 8,000 to 10,000 Btuh, and over 10,000 Btuh. Within each category, the units are listed in order of quality. The best of the Best Buys is listed first, followed by our second choice, and so on. A Best Buy designation applies only to the model listed; it does not necessarily apply to other models made by the same manufacturer.

AIR CONDITIONERS FROM 5,000 TO 8,000 BTUH

EMERSON QUIET KOOL 7DC73 ✔BEST BUY

The Emerson Quiet Kool 7DC73 (EER, 10.0) is a highly efficient compact model with a cooling capacity of 7,200 Btuh—a good choice to cool a bedroom or a den. It offers three fan speeds and an adjustable thermostat that offers a choice of cooling temperatures from 65 to 85 degrees. This unit has a powerful exhaust system to remove stale room air. Its adjustable front also has an automatic energy-saver feature, so the fan runs only when the unit is cooling. This air conditioner is extremely well made and reliable. It has a washable filter that slides out for cleaning without removing the front grille, and it mounts flush to the window.

Specifications: height, 13½″; **width,** 20¼″; **depth,** 17¼″; **weight,** 64 pounds; **maximum window width,** 36″; **watts,** 720; **volts,** 115; **amps,** 6⁷⁄₁₀; **moisture removal rate,** two pints per hour; **air delivery,** 220 maximum cubic feet per minute. **Warranty: parts and labor,** one year.

    Approx. retail price   **Approx. low price**
    $530   **$420**

AMANA 7P2MB

The Amana 7P2MB (EER, 10.0) is a well-constructed 6,550-Btuh air conditioner that is very energy-efficient for its size. It has corrosion-resistant components and a quiet, sturdy compressor. This unit has push-button controls to adjust its three fan speeds and an eight-position thermostat. Its fan operates only when the unit is cooling, to save energy. The 7P2MB also has an effective exhaust/vent system and three-way adjustable air louvers. The front grille is removable for easy access to the filter.

Specifications: height, 13⅜″; **width,** 19″; **depth,** 20¹⁄₁₆″; **weight,** 75 pounds; **maximum window width,** 36″; **watts,** 655; **volts,** 115; **amps,** 6½; **moisture removal rate,** two pints per hour; **air delivery,** 185 maximum cubic feet per minute. **Warranty: parts and labor,** one year; **sealed system,** five years.

    Approx. retail price   **Approx. low price**
    $399   **$366**

WHIRLPOOL ACQ052XW ✔**BEST BUY**

The Whirlpool ACQ052XW (EER, 9.0) is a compact, 5,000-Btuh unit that offers several important features. It has three fan speeds and an adjustable thermostat. The ACQ052XW has a highly efficient compressor that uses less air flow for cooling than comparable models, making it considerably quieter when operating. It has an exhaust function to remove stale air, but no energy-saver switch.

Specifications: height, 12¼"; **width,** 18⅞"; **depth,** 14½"; **weight,** 56 pounds; **maximum window width,** 38"; **watts,** 555; **volts,** 115; **amps,** 5; **moisture removal rate,** 1⅗ pints per hour; **air delivery,** 120 maximum cubic feet per minute. **Warranty: parts and labor,** one year; **sealed system,** five years.

Approx. retail price	Approx. low price
$319	$297

GENERAL ELECTRIC AJ806LF

The General Electric AJ806LF (EER, 8.7) is a slim, 6,200-Btuh unit that offers good cooling flexibility, although it is heavier than some other models its size. It has a ten-level thermostat and two fan speeds. The AJ806LF also has an air exchanger and an energy-saver switch. Its louvers are adjustable in four directions, and the filter pops out easily for washing.

Specifications: height, 15⅝"; **width,** 26"; **depth,** 16⅞"; **weight,** 95 pounds; **maximum window width,** not available; **watts,** 710; **volts,** 115; **amps,** 6⅗; **moisture removal rate,** 1⅗ pints per hour; **air delivery,** 270 maximum cubic feet per minute. **Warranty: parts and labor,** one year; **sealed refrigeration system,** five years.

Approx. retail price	Approx. low price
not available	$413

AIR CONDITIONERS FROM 8,000 TO 10,000 BTUH

FEDDERS A1R10F2B

The Fedders A1R10F2B (EER, 9.0) is a 9,500-Btuh model that offers three fan speeds and a thermostat control concealed behind a panel. Its air exchanger function is particularly powerful, and its air flow is adjustable from side to side. The filter is made of washable, germicidal treated foam. This is a sturdily constructed air conditioner that does a good job.

Specifications: height, 12½"; **width,** 20"; **depth,** 19%₂"; **weight,** 79 pounds; **maximum window width,** 39"; **watts,** 1060; **volts,** 115; **amps,** 12; **moisture removal rate,** 3%₀ pints per hour; **air delivery,** 160 maximum cubic feet per minute. **Warranty: parts and labor,** one year; **sealed system,** five years; **fan motor,** two years.

Approx. retail price	Approx. low price
$547	**$485**

CARRIER CMB1091 ✔BEST BUY

The Carrier CMB1091 (EER, 9.5) is an efficient 8,800-Btuh air conditioner with a motorized air circulator that effectively distributes cool air evenly throughout the room. It has separate exhaust and vent systems, plus three fan speeds and an adjustable thermostat. The CMB1091 includes a 24-hour timer that can be set to turn the air conditioner on and off automatically. The filter is removable for cleaning.

Specifications: height, 15%₆"; **width,** 24⅞₆"; **depth,** 27⅝₆"; **weight,** 104 pounds; **maximum window width,** 44"; **watts,** 925; **volts,** 115; **amps,** 8⅜; **moisture removal rate,** 2⅝ pints per hour; **air delivery,** 300 maximum cubic feet per minute. **Warranty: parts,** five years, limited; **labor,** one year with allowance in second through fifth years.

Approx. retail price	Approx. low price
$499	**$497**

PANASONIC CW-801HU ✔BEST BUY

The Panasonic CW-801HU (EER, 9.1) is a uniquely designed 8,000-Btuh air conditioner. Its compressor hangs outside the window, so it is especially quiet. The front panel is only 13¹³⁄₃₂ inches high—blocking a smaller portion of the window than other models. This well-constructed unit has two fan speeds, a ten-position adjustable thermostat, and four-way air louvers. It does not have an exhaust or energy-saver switch, however. The easily accessible filter slides out with the front grille in place.

Prices are accurate at time of printing; subject to manufacturer's change.

Specifications: height, 13¹³⁄₃₂″; **width,** 22″; **depth,** 23⅝″; **weight,** 77 pounds; **maximum window width,** 40¹³⁄₁₆″; **watts,** 875; **volts,** 115; **amps,** 7½; **moisture removal rate,** 2⁷⁄₁₀ pints per hour; **air delivery,** 190 maximum cubic feet per minute. **Warranty: parts and labor,** one year; **sealed system,** five years.

Approx. retail price	Approx. low price
$600	$489

GENERAL ELECTRIC AMD10AA

The General Electric AMD10AA (EER, 9.5) is a 10,000-Btuh model that offers three fan speeds and a ten-position adjustable thermostat. It has a capable exhaust/vent function that does a good job of keeping room air fresh. Four-way adjustable louvers control air direction. The filter slides out for easy cleaning.

Specifications: height, 14¼″; **width,** 22″; **depth,** 23⅜″; **weight,** 95 pounds; **maximum window width,** not available; **watts,** 1,050; **volts,** 115; **amps,** 9⅝; **moisture removal rate,** 3⅛ pints per hour; **air delivery,** 310 maximum cubic feet per minute. **Warranty: parts and labor,** one year; **sealed system,** five years.

Approx. retail price	Approx. low price
not available	$427

AIR CONDITIONERS OVER 10,000 BTUH

FEDDERS A1M12E2A ✔BEST BUY

The Fedders A1M12E2A (EER, 9.2) is a quiet, efficient 12,500-Btuh unit with three fan speeds and an infinitely adjustable thermostat for cooling flexibility. It has an energy-saver setting and an efficient air exhaust/vent system to provide fresh air. Air-circulation louvers can be adjusted in four directions. The washable filter is easily accessible for cleaning.

Specifications: height, 16⅜″; **width,** 24¹⁹⁄₃₂″; **depth,** 27″; **weight,** 116 pounds; **maximum window width,** 39″; **watts,**

1360; **volts,** 115; **amps,** 12; **moisture removal rate,** 2⅝ pints per hour; **air delivery,** 310 maximum cubic feet per minute. **Warranty: parts and labor,** one year; **sealed system,** five years; **fan motor,** two years.

Approx. retail price	**Approx. low price**
$720	$505

✔**BEST BUY**

FRIEDRICH SM14H10A

The Friedrich SM14H10A (EER, 10.5) is a large, very energy-efficient room air conditioner with a cooling capacity of 14,000-Btuh, enough to cool several rooms. This air conditioner is particularly well-insulated and it provides quiet operation. It has an energy-saver button, a five-speed fan, and nine cooling levels. The SM14H10A has louvers that adjust to send air in six directions. Its heat-anticipating thermostat maintains the preset temperature at an even level. This model has an air intake/exhaust control, and its filter is treated with a germicide to screen out mosquitos and impurities in the air.

Specifications: height, 17¹¹⁄₁₆″; **width,** 25¹⁵⁄₁₆″; **depth,** 27¼″; **weight,** 128 pounds; **maximum window width,** 42″; **watts,** 1330; **volts,** 115; **amps,** 12; **moisture removal rate,** 3³⁄₁₀ pints per hour; **air delivery,** 375 maximum cubic feet per minute. **Warranty: parts and labor,** one year; **sealed refrigeration system,** five years, limited.

Approx. retail price	**Approx. low price**
$909	$770

Ceiling Fans

In the hot summer months, ceiling fans can go a long way to provide cooling circulation of air throughout almost any room in the house. In all but the hottest climates, ceiling fans can nearly eliminate the need for air conditioning and greatly reduce energy bills as a result. There's a wide price range to contend with when it comes to purchasing a fan. Generally, a more expensive fan will feature quieter operation and more attractive design, but unless you're looking for a fan that becomes a design element in itself, good low- to mid-price range fans will offer excellent air circulation and last for years.

Aside from finding a fan that complements your decor, the most important consideration, especially for a bedroom fan, is the noise level. As a rule, since larger fans can move more air at lower fan speeds, they tend to be quieter. Except where size would restrict blade movement, it's best to choose 52-inch fan blades.

Excessive noise is usually caused by poorly balanced motors and blades, poor bearing tolerance, or loose motor windings. Background noise in most stores limits your ability to judge just how quietly a fan runs or to detect other problems. Always insist on a return or exchange privilege in case the fan proves to be too noisy.

Most ceiling fans offer three forward speeds and at least one reversible speed. (The reverse speed is designed to circulate heat better in the winter by pulling air up from the center of the room and circulating warm air that rises to the ceiling. Actually, we've found the need for and the effectiveness of this feature to be questionable.) Most fans either come with a light fixture or offer optional lighting packages. The big difference among the many fans available is usually quality, not features. There are a number of fans in lower price ranges that are very good buys and there are some recognizable companies that only produce good, dependable fans. We've tried to choose representative fans from each group.

One recent ceiling fan innovation is infrared remote control. Essential for very high ceiling installations and spots where wall-mounted controls are impossible, these fans are a luxury item elsewhere in the home, allowing you to adjust your fan from your easy chair.

Installation

If you are using a ceiling fan to replace an existing ceiling light fixture, you can probably install it yourself without any difficulty by following the manufacturer's instructions. Check this out in advance; because of its greater weight and the "torque rebound" when the motor is started, a ceiling fan requires more support than a conventional ceiling light. If the room has no ceiling light in the area where you would like to mount the fan, you may have to call in an electrician or use a surface wiring material, such as Wiremold, to install a fixture box in the area where you want to place the fan. If it is necessary to call in an electrician, be sure to take this cost into consideration in your planning. Since installation costs vary widely, get an estimate before you finalize your purchase. Often stores that carry ceiling fans offer installation for some added cost—compare that price with an electrician's rate in your area. If you plan to use a multiposition, wall-mounted speed control, choose the one recommended by the manufacturer for easiest installation and best results, especially in terms of noise level. If you use an independent control, be sure that it is the type of control that prevents motor hum.

Best Buys '92

Our Best Buys were chosen on performance and estimated overall value. Within each category, products are listed in order of estimated overall quality. The best of the Best Buys is listed first, and so on. Remember that a Best Buy or Recommended designation applies only to the model specified; it does not necessarily apply to other products by the same manufacturer or, except where specified, to an entire product line.

HUNTER ORIGINAL 25780

The Hunter Original 25780 fan comes with a variety of finishes and features, such as Hunter's Switch Blades (fan paddles that are reversible to give the owner different color options). The durable motor is warranted for a lifetime. It's a smooth, quiet, three-speed fan with reverse speeds.
Warranty: lifetime.

Approx. retail price	Approx. low price
$270	$270

HUNTER OUTDOOR ORIGINAL 25596

The Hunter Outdoor Original 25596 is basically the same fan as the Original 25780–it has the same durable motor and features. The finish, available in white or sand, is treated to withstand dampness, making this the ideal fan for outdoor use. The sail-cloth blades come in a variety of colors and are easily removed for cleaning.
Warranty: lifetime.

Approx. retail price	Approx. low price
$270	$257

NUTONE CENTURY PFFR-52 RECOMMENDED

The NuTone Century PFFR-52 comes with a computerized, wall-mounted control. It offers five speeds and a choice of lighting styles. The fan itself is an elegant Victorian-styled model with five blade finishes to choose from. It's well balanced, reversible, and quiet.
Warranty: As long as you own your home.

Approx. retail price	Approx. low price
$337	$229

Prices are accurate at time of printing; subject to manufacturer's change.

CREST CANISTER FAN

`RECOMMENDED`

The Crest Canister Fan, a low-priced option, is sturdy and dependable. It is traditionally styled with several metal finish choices. It features lighting options and three speeds. There are separate pull chains for the lighting and fan operations.
Warranty: five years.

Approx. retail price	**Approx. low price**
$70	**not available**

BROAN DESIGNER SERIES (521-524D)

`RECOMMENDED`

The Broan Designer Series (521-524D) are extremely streamlined with lacquer-look metal trim. These fans offer the styling of very expensive fans at a mid-range price. The motor and operation are very quiet. There are three reversible speeds and lighting options.
Warranty: five years.

Approx. retail price	**Approx. low price**
$250	**$200**

Space Heaters

Today's portable space heaters, unlike their turn-of-the-century forerunners, are seldom used as a primary heat source in any room. Instead, they're often used to save money by "zoning" heat in certain parts of the house, to warm up unheated workshops, to augment the effects of central heating systems that fail to reach certain parts of the home, or to produce more heat for people who need or like a warmer atmosphere than others.

Stringent Underwriters Laboratories (UL) requirements make today's heaters far more safe and dependable than ever before. An important consideration in buying any portable heater is to be sure it is UL listed. Both kerosene and electric heaters are equipped now with elaborate guards to prevent contact with flammable materials and body parts. Tip-over switches turn off heaters if they are accidentally overturned.

Electric space heaters have no emissions, but the cost of operation is significantly higher than that of kerosene heaters (up to three times as much depending on the relative cost of electrical power and high-grade kerosene where you live). They are not portable, since an outlet is required in the vicinity, and so they are not useful for emergency heat during a power outage. However, they don't produce any odors and there is no need to replenish the fuel. With a kerosene heater, this can be a messy chore. The heater (or removable tank) must be carried outdoors, and you must use extreme care to avoid spilling kerosene when refilling the tank. Otherwise, you may be faced with a safety hazard or you could transport the odor back into the house.

Both electric and kerosene heaters come in two basic types—convection and radiant. Convection-type heaters warm the air in the room and are omnidirectional. Radiant heaters are usually identified by their reflective shield and brightly glowing heat sources. Radiant energy travels through the air and does not generate heat until it strikes an object, which may be a person, a wall, or furnishings in the room. (Radiant heat also travels through glass, so don't waste heat by directing it toward a patio door or window.) The big advantage of radiant heaters is that they allow you to enter a cold room, turn them on, and feel a pleasant warmth almost immediately. Convection heaters require some time to warm all the air within the room. The radiant heater's coverage is usually limited to about a 30-degree angle from the face of the heater.

Ceramic-element electric heaters are a new type of heater. A ceramic thermistor (or electrical resistor) carries resistance according to temperature. This thermistor is housed in a small box, usually about the size of an eight-inch cube, complete with a fan and an element. This type of heater is self-limiting in that the resistance increases in proportion to temperature so that it provides a constantly modulating heat surface. This allows it to discharge a relatively large volume of heated air over a large surface area of element surface, making it particularly safe. Be aware that some inexpensive heaters are packaged to look like ceramic heaters, but in reality, they contain the conventional nichrome element that does not possess the safety characteristics of a true ceramic element.

Kerosene heaters have relatively high efficiency ratings. Our recommendation has a double-clean system that costs a bit more, but the high efficiency and low emissions make for the best value. All electric heaters have the same 100 percent efficiency rating because they deliver 3,412 Btuhs of heat for every watt of power consumed—there's no such thing as one electric heater being more efficient than another. The differences among electric heaters are in the way they distribute heat, the sturdiness of construction, and the safety features.

Best Buys '92

Our Best Buys and Recommended heaters were chosen on performance, estimated overall value, and safety. Within each category, products are listed in order of estimated overall quality. The best of the Best Buys is listed first, followed by our second choice, and so on. Remember that a Best Buy or Recommended designation applies only to that model. It does not necessarily apply to other models or products by the same manufacturer.

ELECTRIC SPACE HEATERS

HOLMES AIR INSTAFURNACE HPH-3070

The Holmes Air Instafurnace HPH-3070 heater features a ceramic safety control. It boasts two heat settings (750/1,500 watts). There is a fan-only option and an automatic thermostat with anti-freeze setting. The two automatic overheat shutoffs make it particularly safe. A light indicates when the power is on. **Specifications: height,** 7"; **width,** 5⅝"; **depth,** 5⅝"; **weight,** 2½ pounds. **Warranty:** one year.

Approx. retail price	Approx. low price
$45	$35

RIVAL TITAN UTILITY HEATER T771

The Rival Titan Utility Heater T771 is a hardworking heater that is great for shop or garage use. The heater features steel construction, and two fan-forced heat settings (1,300/1,500 watts). It has an automatic thermostat, and it automatically shuts off when the unit is overturned. The plug is grounded, and a light indicates when the power is on.
Specifications: height, 17½"; **width,** 10¾"; **depth,** 10¾"; **weight,** one pound. **Warranty: parts and labor,** one year.

Approx. retail price	Approx. low price
$57	$47

Prices are accurate at time of printing; subject to manufacturer's change.

TATUNG PERSONAL FAN HEATER EH-1502

The Tatung Personal Fan Heater EH-1502 is great for people who always seem to need a little extra heat in whatever room they are in. This compact model is very light and easy to tote around. It offers a 1,500-watt heat setting and comes complete with tip-over safety switch and a top-mounted control panel. The charcoal-colored plastic casing remains cool to the touch.
Specifications: height, 10½"; **width,** 10"; **depth,** 5½"; **weight,** 3⅓ pounds. **Warranty:** one year.

Approx. retail price	Approx. low price
$25	not available

PORTABLE KEROSENE HEATER

TOYOSTOVE DC100

The Toyostove DC100 double-clean model is the only top-ranked kerosene heater. This is due to the double-clean burner that keeps emissions at levels far below those of conventional kerosene heaters. It is excellent quality and incorporates the usual safety devices, plus a wick-stop that prevents overextending of the wick.
Specifications: height, 24⅜"; **width,** 18⅝"; **depth,** 18⅝"; **weight,** 26‰ pounds. **Warranty: parts,** one year.

Approx. retail price	Approx. low price
$300	not available

Prices are accurate at time of printing; subject to manufacturer's change.
426   CONSUMER GUIDE®

Baby Equipment

Today, thoughtful engineering, new materials, and sleek design make the latest baby equipment better than ever, and often it's quite affordable, too. From among the many products on the current market, we have selected five items that every baby will need to keep him or her comfortable and *safe*.

Safety has to be your first consideration when you purchase baby equipment. Despite strict federal safety regulations regarding manufacture, accidents still occur. No matter how safe a product is, it can be hazardous if it is used incorrectly. So, make sure to read all of the manufacturer's directions for use and closely follow all recommendations for safe assembly.

Safety Tips

After making sure that the product has passed all federal safety regulations, perform the following tests:

Run your fingers over the equipment. Touch every spot your baby is likely to explore or come in contact with. Are the surfaces rough or soft to the touch?

Inspect all hinges, springs, or moving parts, and note whether there are any places where your baby's hands, feet, fingers, or toes could get caught or pinched.

Meticulously examine all small parts. Are they fastened securely? Make sure nothing can come loose that your baby could swallow.

If a product is designed to hold a child, determine if it is easy to use. For example, will the seat belt prove difficult to latch? Is it easy to adjust for the baby's comfort? Any kind of belt or harness must hold the baby securely and comfortably. Make sure there is no way your baby can climb or wiggle out. Examine carriers and seats. Is there any chance that an active child could tip the seat over?

Product Design

In addition to keeping in mind a product's saftey, remember that if a product is not designed and engineered to work easily, the temptation to use it improperly, or not to use it at all, becomes great. So, consider the ways in which you plan to use a particular item and whether its design will help or hinder you. For example, if you are looking at a stroller, try folding it a few times. Lift it in the folded position to see whether or not it will fit easily into your car trunk. Remember, a crying baby does not have very much patience.

Also, remember that extras can add to the price without necessarily adding quality. Do you really need a stroller that comes with a blanket? Examine the materials. Are they easy to clean? Are pads removable?

Look for equipment that conforms to standards established by the Juvenile Products Manufacturers Association. These standards are voluntary, but some items, such as car seats, must meet federal regulations.

Best Buys '92

Our Best Buy baby equipment follows. We reviewed products in the following categories: portable cribs, strollers, car seats, baby carriers, and nursery monitors. Within each category, products are listed in order of quality, workmanship, and safety. The item we consider the best of the Best Buys is listed first, followed by our second choice, and so on. Remember that a Best Buy rating applies only to the model listed; it does not necessarily apply to other models made by the same manufacturer or to an entire product line.

PORTABLE CRIBS

Since today's families are always on the go, functional, well-designed portable cribs are becoming more available and at moderate prices. You will want to make sure the crib is sturdy and safe, as you would with their permanent counterparts. Also, since you will be toting it along with you on your travels, you will want to make sure it folds and stores easily. Avoid any portable crib that lacks proper support or one that collapses too easily. When it's open, give it a shake to test its sturdiness. Examine all surfaces that come in contact with the baby to make sure they are all smooth and do not have exposed hardware. Check beneath the mattress for a strong support bar. And don't forget to pick it up when it's folded to make sure you can lift it without too much effort.

EVENFLO HAPPY CAMPER 342101 ✔ BEST BUY

The Evenflo Happy Camper 342101 portable crib has an attractive designer print. The crib also has blue legs and corner caps. It is lightweight (about 25 pounds) despite its sturdy frame construction. It sets up in minutes and folds easily to compact size for traveling and storage. The durable nylon fabric wipes clean. The crib features a mattress with fitted sheets and it has see-through mesh on two sides and on one end panel. The other end panel, made of nylon, acts as a draft guard and contains a handy, good-size storage pocket. Mosquito netting makes the crib perfect for camping trips. It comes fully assembled; when standing, there are no loose parts. It stores in a zippered carrying bag.
Warranty: one year.

Approx. retail price	Approx. low price
$129	$119

KOLCRAFT SLEEP-A-WAY 18101 ✔ BEST BUY

The Kolcraft Sleep-A-Way 18101 portable travel crib and playpen weighs about 27 pounds and boasts a sturdy frame and floor to provide the baby with adequate support and safety. It is easy to set up and take apart. A thick foam mattress over a center support bar provides sturdy comfort. Padded railings

Prices are accurate at time of printing; subject to manufacturer's change.

protect the baby, and all-vinyl end panels block out drafts; durable mesh sides let you view the sleeping infant. The compact crib totes easily in its own zippered, vinyl carry case.
Warranty: one year.

Approx. retail price $79	Approx. low price $70

STROLLERS

There are several types of strollers on today's market: standard strollers; umbrella strollers, which are lightweight, collapsible, and handy for travel or occasional use; tandem strollers, which can seat more than one child; and strollers/carriages. We have reviewed strollers that perform several functions well. They are all heavy enough to withstand everyday use, but lightweight enough for lifting into the trunk of a car. They offer upright, semi-upright, and prone seat positions, and they feature canopies that can be removed or pushed back.

The best strollers are designed with safety in mind. They maneuver easily and have solid wheels, which, at least in the rear, come equipped with shock absorbers. Seats are comfortable and covered with soft, absorbent fabric. Belts are attached securely. Though these strollers collapse easily, they employ safety features that lock them into the open position.

GRACO BROUGHAM 7500N

The Graco Brougham 7500N is a sturdy, easy-to-use stroller. Made of molded plastic and steel, it comes with a navy blue washable, quilted, wide padded seat. The reversible handle and the guard rail are both padded. The plastic and vinyl parts can be wiped clean. The double front wheels swivel for handling ease. Other features include three-position reclining, a collapsible canopy, and a one-second folding mechanism.
Warranty: one year.

Approx. retail price $109	Approx. low price $103

Prices are accurate at time of printing; subject to manufacturer's change.

CENTURY REATTA 11-660

The Century Reatta 11-660 features color-coordinated reflectors on all wheels and a wide body frame for the baby's comfort. The deluxe rounded canopy has a coordinating line and a peek-a-boo window with a cover. A rear storage pouch holds bottles and toys. The handle on this full-reclining stroller is reversible and adjusts to fit most heights and strides. The leatherette outer fabric wipes clean; the thick quilted comfort pad removes for washing. A snap-on windshield protects the baby from the rain. New two-step fold prevents unintentional stroller folding. An extra-large, under-stroller mesh basket holds extra diapers and more.
Warranty: one year.

Approx. retail price	**Approx. low price**
$135	**$125**

KOLCRAFT TIARA 16138

The Kolcraft Tiara 16138 stroller features a padded multiposition reversible handle, quattro balloon wheels for easy swiveling, and an adjustable canopy with a see-through window. In addition to the seat, the wipe-down plastic sides and the footrest are fully quilted for baby's comfort; the quilting is machine washable. This stroller folds in seconds.
Warranty: one year.

Approx. retail price	**Approx. low price**
$130	**$130**

CAR SEATS

Car seats for infants and young children are mandatory in most states. All car seats are required to conform to Federal Motor Vehicle Safety Standards. Infants under 20 pounds must be belted in the seat, facing the rear of the car, and in a reclining position. Older children may sit upright facing forward. Except for infant seats, most car seats convert from a reclining position to upright and can be used for children up to 40 pounds.

Incorrect use of car seats can be dangerous, as well as against the law. If a car seat is difficult or confusing to operate, it may be used in an incorrect or improper manner. In evaluating car seats, our primary consideration was their ease of use. We also looked for comfort and special features. All three of our selections may be used from infancy to approximately 40 pounds.

PLAYSKOOL CONVERTIBLE CAR SEAT WITH COMFORT PUMP ✓**BEST BUY**

The Playskool Convertible Car Seat with Comfort Pump features a new, exclusive inflatable head support system to keep the baby's head upright. Just squeeze the pump and the cushion inflates on both sides to keep an infant comfortable. The seat also has an easy harness adjustment from either side and a removable, washable cloth pad. An easy-to-use push-button release buckle makes fastening and unfastening the baby a simpler task and holds the child securely when locked. The molded plastic shell is smooth and free of jagged edges.
Warranty: one year.

Approx. retail price	**Approx. low price**
$90	$83

CENTURY 3000 STE SERIES ✓**BEST BUY**

The Century 3000 STE Series of car seats is adjustable, having six unique growth combinations through three shoulder and two crotch positions, which come in handy in the winter when children wear heavy snowsuits. Made of molded plastic, this model has a wrapover, machine-washable fabric pad. Other features include quick-change harness positions with a simple pull-front strap; an overhead shield that doubles as a handy play surface; and three seating positions.
Warranty: one year.

Approx. retail price	**Approx. low price**
$80	$77

FISHER-PRICE 9101 ✓**BEST BUY**

The Fisher-Price 9101 car seat is easy to handle, making it a popular model. The exclusive auto-restraint safety system locks and unlocks with the press of a thumb. When locked, the belt

Prices are accurate at time of printing; subject to manufacturer's change.

automatically adjusts to the right fit; when unlocked, restraint belts move freely. The machine-washable pad is easily removed for cleaning. The seat installs quickly with standard automotive belt systems, and it offers three comfortable reclining positions. This model meets all federal safety regulations. In the rear-facing position it accommodates infants up to 20 pounds; in the front-facing position it holds children up to 40 pounds.
Warranty: three years.

Approx. retail price	Approx. low price
$75	$69

BABY CARRIERS

By now, we hope, everyone knows that baby carriers are not car seats, but are great for traveling because they provide a convenient seat for your baby while she or he is being fed. Designed for babies up to about 18 pounds, baby carriers are constructed of molded plastic. They provide gentle, sturdy support for your baby when you are not holding the baby or when you and the baby are in a room that does not have a crib or a playpen. Many baby carriers fit into a shopping cart. Also, some are rockers, so your baby can nap, too—but do not leave the baby unattended. Although our selections are lightweight, they will not tip over if the baby is within the recommended weight limits.

Before purchasing a carrier, make sure the surface is smooth all over and that the safety strap is easy to use and secure.

FISHER-PRICE SUPER SOFT CARRIER 9111

 ✓ BEST BUY

The Fisher-Price Super Soft Carrier 9111 is a lightweight carrier for a newborn baby up to 18 pounds. Its reclining seat-back adjusts to two comfortable positions. Padded handles make portability easy and convenient. The carrier also has an adjustable canopy to provide shade. Designed to fit into most carriages and strollers, it has a front zipper for easy access and security. The back is reinforced for support.
Warranty: one year.

Prices are accurate at time of printing; subject to manufacturer's change.

Approx. retail price $40	**Approx. low price** not available

CENTURY KANGA-ROCKA-ROO 1560 ✔️ BEST BUY

The Century Kanga-Rocka-Roo 1560 baby carrier is made of white molded plastic with a wipe-clean vinyl pad featuring pattern choices of Bear Parade, Gum Balls, Teddi Confetti, or Fun for All. A handy lidded storage compartment in back will hold a bottle, an extra diaper, and a toy; it's removable for cleaning. A four-position carrying handle adjusts for rocking, feeding, napping, and carrying. A quick-lock buckle on a three-point waist strap makes entry and exit easy. It is designed for infants up to 18 pounds.
Warranty: one year.

Approx. retail price $25	**Approx. low price** $22

KOLCRAFT CARRI-CRADLE 12000 ✔️ BEST BUY

The Kolcraft Carri-Cradle 12000 infant carrier is constructed of smooth, sturdy, but lightweight white molded plastic. The vinyl padding comes in three patterns: ABC Primary, Autumn Mist, and Baby Blocks. The Carri-Cradle combines three functions: carrier, infant seat, and rocker. It has an adjustable handle and is crafted extra wide and deep to accommodate a growing baby. A tapered headrest lends upperbody support. It is easy to keep clean with a damp sponge. The Kolcraft Carri-Cradle 12000 is recommended for infants up to 20 pounds.
Warranty: one year.

Approx. retail price $20	**Approx. low price** $20

NURSERY MONITORS

Thanks to technology, you *can* be in the same room with your baby at all times. Well, almost. With a nursery monitor you can keep in touch via sound. A nursery monitor uses a transmitter in the baby's room to relay noises—even soft cooing sounds—to a receiver, which remains with you in another part of the house or even outdoors. Most transmitters pick up sounds with-

Prices are accurate at time of printing; subject to manufacturer's change.

in a 10-foot radius. Receivers are battery powered, and most have belt clips, so you are free to move around.

FISHER-PRICE 1510

The Fisher-Price 1510 nursery monitor will light up to alert you of a baby's tiniest sounds. A light indicator lets you know if your baby is cooing or crying even when you are outdoors or in a noisy room. The louder your baby's sound, the more lights. A portable transmitter permits the monitor to go wherever the baby goes. Use the handy receiver belt clip to allow you freedom of movement. Two AC adapters are included. The transmitter also will operate with four C-size batteries; the receiver takes one 9-volt battery. Features also include a low-battery indicator, a channel selector, and a rotary on/off volume control. This model is listed with Underwriters Laboratories.
Warranty: one year.

Approx. retail price	**Approx. low price**
$50	**$45**

COSCO TEDDY CARE DUAL LAMP AND NURSERY MONITOR 300

The Cosco Teddy Care Dual Lamp and Nursery Monitor 300 is a nursery monitor and lamp in one. A transmitter in the lamp's base permits parents in another room to listen while their baby sleeps. The lamp features a plush bear and fabric lamp shade. The monitor operates separately from the lamp. The portable clip-on receiver with antenna and adjustable volume control keeps you in touch up to 150 feet away. The receiver operates on an AC adapter or on a nine-volt battery. Two channels let you switch off interference. The indicator light shows power charge. The lamp/monitor comes in white.
Warranty: one year.

Approx. retail price	**Approx. low price**
$70	**$62**

SONY NTM-1

The Sony NTM-1 is an attractively styled electronic monitoring system that lets parents pursue other activities while monitoring

Prices are accurate at time of printing; subject to manufacturer's change.

their baby. The transmitter, which plugs into a wall outlet, audibly and clearly picks up and transmits a baby's sounds from as far away as 10 feet. A receiver, which operates on a single 9-volt battery or with an electrical wall-plug adapter, features a handy belt clip. The monitor light blinks when picking up loud sounds; the volume is adjustable. Its rounded antenna has no sharp points and can be wall mounted or set on a table. The receiver has a two-channel selector and a power light that indicates a low battery.

Warranty: one year.

Approx. retail price	**Approx. low price**
$60	**$53**

Home Safety

If there are two home products that should be termed "worth their weight in gold," it would be smoke detectors and fire extinguishers. Their modest prices (the most expensive product listed here is less than $35.00) are far outweighed by their potential savings in damage to property—or lives.

If your home is not properly equipped with these products, put them on your priority list. If your home *is* equipped, take a moment to be sure all are still operating properly: Both smoke detectors and fire extinguishers have simple built-in test features (which vary by brand and model) to indicate whether the unit is functional.

Best Buys '92

Our Best Buy and Recommended home safety products follow. In each category, the consumer market is dominated by only a few companies—ones we consider reliable. We have therefore condensed individual product descriptions just to special features of that unit. For basic information on the category as a whole, please read the introductory paragraphs.

SMOKE DETECTORS

Little over a decade ago, smoke detectors were somewhat of a novelty and considerably more expensive than they are today. By 1989, according to the National Fire Protection Association, some 85 percent of U.S. homes had at least one smoke detector.

While there are two basic types of smoke detectors (operating on ionization or photoelectric sensing systems), nearly all the ones you'll find now are the ionization type, primarily because they're cheaper to produce. Ionization detectors respond more quickly to blazing fires; photoelectric units to smoldering fires. But simply *having* a home properly equipped with functional smoke detectors is more important than the type.

Because basic design and performance of smoke detectors are similar, we're incorporating that information in this introduction, and shortening the reviews to specific features. And, while smoke detectors can be wired in to the house electrical system, most sales (except for new home construction) are the battery-operated type, which is what we have concentrated on.

Placement and use. All but small homes or apartments probably should have more than one smoke detector. The primary area that needs protection is the bedroom wing. Most residential fire fatalities occur at night. Even though the fire might originate in another part of the house, a smoke detector on or near the ceiling outside bedroom doors would alert sleepers before smoke or toxic fumes waft into their rooms. Other locations include near the kitchen (where many fires start) and on each floor of a house.

FIRST ALERT DUAL SENSOR SA301

The First Alert Dual Sensor SA301 combines an ionization sensor (for detection of fast, flaming fires) and a photoelectric sensor (for smoldering fires) in one unit. Because of this dual protection, its price is higher and many stores may not stock it—but it's worth asking for. Both systems are powered by the same nine-volt battery. The unit has two test buttons. A bug screen reduces nuisance alarms.

Warranty: five years, limited.

Approx. retail price	Approx. low price
$33	$27

Prices are accurate at time of printing; subject to manufacturer's change.

JAMESON CODE ONE 2000 SMOKE & FIRE ALARM AUTO TEST

✓ **BEST BUY**

The Jameson Code One 2000 Smoke & Fire Alarm Auto Test is only four inches in diameter (smaller than other smoke detectors), but equally effective and deliberately designed to be unobtrusive. This unit automatically tests itself weekly and will beep six times if it's working properly. Since the self-testing feature coincides with the time of installation, do this at a time when you'll be home—such as brunch on Saturday or a regular weekday evening.

Warranty: five years, limited.

Approx. retail price	Approx. low price
$20	not available

FIRST ALERT KITCHEN SA88

✓ **BEST BUY**

The First Alert Kitchen SA88 is the perfect alarm for your kitchen, where two out of three residential fires start. But there's a problem with many ionization smoke detectors: They react too quickly to humidity and fumes that are a *normal* part of cooking operations. "False alarms" from smoke alarms placed in the cooking area have caused many people to remove the battery from their kitchen smoke detectors. First Alert's solution is a silencing button that you simply push to quiet a nuisance alarm. Three minutes later, the unit returns to optimum sensitivity. At all other times, shining a flashlight on the unit verifies whether the unit is functioning properly.

Warranty: five years, limited.

Approx. retail price	Approx. low price
$18	$15

FAMILY GARD FG 888D

RECOMMENDED

The Family Gard FG 888D is a basic, battery-operated ionization smoke detector. It includes a 30-day, low-battery beeping signal.

Warranty: three years, limited.

Approx. retail price	Approx. low price
$9	not available

Prices are accurate at time of printing; subject to manufacturer's change.

FIRST ALERT PROFESSIONAL SA67D

RECOMMENDED

The First Alert Professional SA67D is a basic unit from the major manufacturer of smoke detectors. It uses a nine-volt battery and has a dual chamber ionization sensor. A flashing light indicates that the detector is receiving power. This unit has a 30-day low battery signal.
Warranty: five years, limited.

Approx. retail price	Approx. low price
$14	$10

FIRE EXTINGUISHERS

A fire extinguisher should be considered the *second* line of defense in coping with a house fire (the first line of defense is calling the fire department and getting everyone out of the house). Small contained fires, however, often can be controlled and put out by quick, efficient use of the proper fire extinguisher.

When choosing a fire extinguisher, don't be tempted to think that "bigger is better." The larger the unit (which translates almost directly to the size of fire it can handle), the bulkier it is. That makes it the more difficult to carry and use effectively. The units we recommend are sized (fire-fighting capacity and weight) to handle the most common types of home fires. They're also designated for the types of fires most likely to occur in a home.

Choosing and Using. Fires—and therefore fire extinguishers—are classified by Underwriters Laboratories (UL) into three types:

Class A fires are from ordinary combustible materials, such as paper, wood, fabric, rubber, and plastic.

Class B fires are those caused by flammable liquids—oil, grease, gasoline, paints, or cleaning solvents.

Class C fires involve an electrical component—an appliance, television, computer, or wiring.

Extinguishers also are rated (again by UL standards, although other laboratories are qualified to conduct tests based on these standards) for the relative size of each type of fire they

Prices are accurate at time of printing; subject to manufacturer's change.

can handle. A "2A" or "2B" listing, for example, means the unit has twice the fire fighting capability of a "1" rating. (C is not rated numerically. That designation simply means that the extinguishing agent is not electrically conductive.)

We recommend having at least one multipurpose (ABC) fire extinguisher at a central point in the home, plus a BC unit near the kitchen. It's also a good idea to have a multipurpose fire extinguisher in the garage or workshop, and one on each level of a multilevel house.

While operation instructions will be on each unit, all family members should memorize the acronym PASS: Pull the pin; Aim the nozzle; Squeeze or press the handle; Sweep from side to side at the *base* of the fire.

KIDDE FIRE AWAY 1102

The Kidde Fire Away 1102 is a multipurpose, monammonium phosphate dry chemical unit, which is rated 1A:10B:C. This is the best-selling brand and model in the consumer market. It offers protection for all areas of the home, and also meets U.S. Coast Guard approval (for use on boats) with included bracket. A dial-type pressure gauge shows at a glance whether or not the unit is fully charged.
Warranty: six years, limited.

Approx. retail price	**Approx. low price**
$20	$17

FIRST ALERT MULTI-PURPOSE FE1A10

The First Alert Multi-Purpose FE1A10 is another popular model for general household use. It is a monammonium phosphate dry chemical unit, which is rated 1A:10B:C. It features an easy-push trigger, easy-hold handle, and it meets DOT (Department of Transportation) requirements. It also includes a U.S. Coast Guard-approved bracket. A push-to-test button indicates whether or not the unit is fully charged.
Warranty: one year, limited.

Approx. retail price	**Approx. low price**
$20	$14

Prices are accurate at time of printing; subject to manufacturer's change.

FIRST ALERT KITCHEN KFE2

The First Alert Kitchen KFE2 was designed for kitchen use, where two out of three home fires start. Compact and easy to use, it is a sodium bicarbonate dry chemical unit, which is rated 2BC, to fight grease, oil, and electrical fires. White decorator styling (unlike the bright red of most other fire extinguishers) makes it unobtrusive. A wall-mount bracket and quick release, easy access cap put it within arm's reach for immediate use. A push-to-test button allows for easy pressure checks.

Warranty: one year, limited.

Approx. retail price	Approx. low price
$15	$12

Index

CONSUMER GUIDE®